Sustainable Development Goals Series

The **Sustainable Development Goals Series** is Springer Nature's inaugural cross-imprint book series that addresses and supports the United Nations' seventeen Sustainable Development Goals. The series fosters comprehensive research focused on these global targets and endeavours to address some of society's greatest grand challenges. The SDGs are inherently multidisciplinary, and they bring people working across different fields together and working towards a common goal. In this spirit, the Sustainable Development Goals series is the first at Springer Nature to publish books under both the Springer and Palgrave Macmillan imprints, bringing the strengths of our imprints together.

The Sustainable Development Goals Series is organized into eighteen subseries: one subseries based around each of the seventeen respective Sustainable Development Goals, and an eighteenth subseries, "Connecting the Goals", which serves as a home for volumes addressing multiple goals or studying the SDGs as a whole. Each subseries is guided by an expert Subseries Advisor with years or decades of experience studying and addressing core components of their respective Goal.

The SDG Series has a remit as broad as the SDGs themselves, and contributions are welcome from scientists, academics, policymakers, and researchers working in fields related to any of the seventeen goals. If you are interested in contributing a monograph or curated volume to the series, please contact the Publishers: Zachary Romano [Springer; zachary.romano@springer.com] and Rachael Ballard [Palgrave Macmillan; rachael.ballard@palgrave.com].

Sonal Trivedi · Veena Grover ·
Abhijit Ganguly · Christo Ananth
Editors

Green Ventures

Financing Sustainable Entrepreneurship

palgrave
macmillan

Editors
Sonal Trivedi
Manav Rachna University
Faridabad, Haryana, India

Veena Grover
Lloyd Business School
Greater Noida, Uttar Pradesh, India

Abhijit Ganguly
DBA Program
Westford University College
Al Taawun St Sharjah
United Arab Emirates

Christo Ananth
Samarkand State University
Samarkand, Uzbekistan

ISSN 2523-3084 ISSN 2523-3092 (electronic)
Sustainable Development Goals Series
ISBN 978-981-95-6532-0 ISBN 978-981-95-6533-7 (eBook)
https://doi.org/10.1007/978-981-95-6533-7

This Palgrave Macmillan imprint is published by the registered company Springer Nature Singapore Pte Ltd.
The registered company address is: 152 Beach Road, #21-01/04 Gateway East, Singapore 189721, Singapore

Preface

The twenty-first century presents an unprecedented convergence of global challenges and opportunities. Climate change, resource scarcity, and socio-economic inequality call for bold and innovative responses from governments, corporations, and—most vitally—entrepreneurs. In this context, *Green Venture: Financing Sustainable Entrepreneurship* emerges as a timely and meaningful contribution to the global discourse on sustainability, with a focused lens on how finance can be harnessed to enable mission-driven ventures that generate positive environmental and social impact.

This book serves as a collaborative effort among a diverse group of scholars and practitioners hailing from countries across the globe—India, Jordan, Malaysia, Spain, Ethiopia, Canada, Mexico, the USA, Botswana, Kuwait, the United Arab Emirates, South Africa, Egypt, Nigeria, and Switzerland—who offer multi-faceted insights into the evolving intersection of sustainability, entrepreneurship, and finance. Each contribution reflects a unique regional context, yet they are united by a common goal: advancing inclusive, green growth through innovative, finance-enabled ventures.

At the heart of this volume is the commitment to the United Nations Sustainable Development Goals (SDGs)—especially SDG 13: Climate Action, which emphasizes the urgent need for concrete steps to combat climate change and its impacts. Green entrepreneurs—whether in urban

India or rural Africa, Southeast Asia or Latin America—are at the forefront of this mission. They are creating climate-resilient business models, integrating renewable energy into their solutions, developing zero-waste value chains, and redefining performance by embedding sustainability in their core operations. However, their path is often hindered by limited access to tailored finance, fragmented policy support, and inadequate metrics to assess impact. This book seeks to address these barriers and catalyze new conversations and strategies.

The book's chapters are organized thematically to provide a comprehensive overview. Initial sections examine how market gaps are being transformed into sustainable opportunities, particularly in regions like Jordan, India, and Malaysia. Further chapters explore how start-ups in emerging economies are building sustainable entrepreneurial orientation, promoting business model innovation, and leveraging green migration for socio-economic growth. Authors from countries such as Ethiopia, Spain, and Botswana analyze green financing approaches and the role of impact metrics like ESG in improving organizational sustainability.

As the book progresses, readers will encounter empirical discussions on the effect of digital finance, the spillover impacts of cryptocurrency on renewable energy markets, the potential of green bonds and Socially Responsible Investment (SRI), and the role of federated learning in sustainable intelligent transportation systems. Contributions from institutions in the USA, Canada, South Africa, Kuwait, and Egypt enrich the discourse with comparative analyses and international best practices.

The richness of this book lies not just in its academic rigor but in its global inclusivity. Each contributor—from New Delhi to Zurich, Kuala Lumpur to Mexico City, Seville to Gaborone—offers insights grounded in real-world practices, regional innovation ecosystems, and collaborative initiatives that exemplify sustainability in action. Whether addressing SDG-aligned financing frameworks in Malaysia, ESG challenges in the Middle East, or circular economy innovations in India, the authors collectively chart a path for the global green venture movement.

This volume is intended for a wide audience: entrepreneurs seeking to create climate-resilient business models, policymakers striving to develop enabling ecosystems, investors looking to align capital with climate outcomes, and academics aiming to further sustainability research. As climate action (SDG 13) becomes ever more urgent, green ventures will serve as vital engines of resilience and regeneration. With the right financial support structures and innovative thinking, they can move from the margins to the mainstream of global economic development.

Green Venture: Financing Sustainable Entrepreneurship is more than a book—it is a call to action, an international knowledge platform, and a testament to what becomes possible when entrepreneurship meets sustainability with purpose and support. We hope it informs, inspires, and ignites the next generation of changemakers worldwide.

Faridabad, India Sonal Trivedi
Greater Noida, India Veena Grover
Al Taawun St, United Arab Emirates Abhijit Ganguly
Samarkand, Uzbekistan Christo Ananth

About This Book

"*Green Ventures: Uniting Sustainability, Finance, and Entrepreneurship*" serves as a comprehensive guide for entrepreneurs seeking to build financially sustainable businesses while addressing climate action. This book is an essential resource for entrepreneurs and finance professionals looking to drive meaningful change through sustainable practices. Readers will gain insights into identifying and developing sustainable business opportunities that tackle environmental and social challenges while directly contributing to SDG 13. The book highlights innovative business models such as the circular economy and shared value creation, showcasing how these approaches not only drive climate action but also unlock new growth potential.

Contents

Editors and Contributors

About the Editors

Dr. Sonal Trivedi, Associate Professor, Manav Rachna University, Faridabad, specializes in finance, fintech, blockchain, and risk management. With over 12 years of academic experience, she has published extensively, holds multiple patents, authored books and book chapters, and received awards for research excellence and innovative contributions to financial studies.

Dr. Veena Grover is currently working as Professor in Loyd Business School, India. She is Gold Medallist & University topper in Economics. A prolific researcher, Professor Grover has contributed significantly to the academic discourse by presenting and publishing more than 65 research papers and book chapters in esteemed international and national conferences.

Dr. Abhijit Ganguly is a Chartered Manager and Chartered Fellow of Chartered Management Institute (UK), Fellow of Higher Education Academy, UK, Certified Trainer in Management and Leadership, CAVA Assessor and Endpoint Assessor, UK. He is also Chartered Human Resource Analyst, USA and Fellow of Graduate Management Academy, USA.

Dr./Prof. Christo Ananth has taken an interest and presented papers in 3 National level Technical Symposiums, 9 Research papers in National Level Conferences, 31 Research Papers in International level Conferences, 56 Research Papers, authored & published 7 National and International level Engineering Text books.

Contributors

Suzan Issa Abuhalawah is a Ph.D. candidate in Strategic Management and International Business at the University of Seville, Spain. Her research focuses on Born Global firms, exploring how founders, networks, and dynamic capabilities shape internationalization strategies through longitudinal and mixed-method designs.

Dr. Pravin Kumar Agrawal is working as Assistant Professor of Finance in Department of Business Management Chhatrapati Shahu Ji Maharaj University, Kanpur (U.P.) India. He had published several research papers in Scopus and web of science journals and has presented various research papers in national and international conferences.

Dr. Shyam Sunder Agrawal working as Assistant Professor, Mittal School of Business, Lovely Professional University, India. He has presented papers at various conferences and published several research papers. He has published and granted 2 patents from the Government of India. He received the International Case Study Award in 2022.

Dr. Amjed Alfityani is a distinguished academic specializing in accounting. His expertise covers a broad range of topics including financial and managerial accounting, cost accounting, performance measurement, and strategic planning. Dr. Al-Fityani is particularly interested in enhancing accounting education, developing outcome-based curricula.

Sakher Faisal Alfraihat is a Ph.D. candidate in Digital Marketing at the University of Seville, Spain, within the Department of Business Administration and Marketing. His main research interests include digital marketing strategies, influencer marketing, and consumer behavior.

Ma'ali M. Al-Yousufi is academic and researcher specializing in strategy, innovation, and entrepreneurship. Her work investigates entrepreneurial methodologies to advance higher education and translate academic research into industry applications. Her studies delve into industry trends, applying academic insights to real-world and creating innovative approaches that connect theory with practical implementation.

Firas Jamil Alotoum is currently an Associated Professor in the faculty of business at Applied science private University, Amman—Jordan. Dr. Alotoum published a number of papers in preferred Journals and chapters in books, He also presented various academic as well as research-based papers at several national and international conferences.

Ms. Hayat Fayez Mahmoud Banat is a seasoned teacher and researcher with extensive experience in business studies. Her academic interests include business marketing, where she holds a Master's degree in Business Intelligence, and she continues to contribute to the advancement of knowledge and practice in her field.

Mr. Priyant Banerjee is an erudite and multidisciplinary researcher at the Amity School of Engineering and Technology, Amity University Mumbai. His research delves into the nexus of Cybersecurity, Economics, and Computer Science, with a particular focus on sustainable digital transformation and algorithmic innovation.

Dr. Arshad Bhat is working as Assistant Professor at Amity Institute of Liberal Arts, Amity University Mumbai. Dr. Arshad has 93 research publications among these are 26 Scopus indexed publications of reputed publishers to his credit and has also published 53 book chapters and 6 books.

Amitab Bhattacharjee MBA, has been serving as a lecturer and research associate since 2016. He also holds a tax advisory position at PCPI, Canada. He is the author of several articles published in the Academy of Management Journal, Asia Pacific Journal of Management and Business Strategy & Development.

K. Devender is a researcher and academic focusing on financial literacy, digital finance, and sustainable business practices. His work explores intersection of financial education, small business empowerment, and green economic development. He has contributed to several book chapters and research articles emphasizing sustainable financial systems and digital transformation for SMEs.

Dr. Sodfa El-Taher is a faculty member in the Department of Business Administration at the Faculty of Commerce, Al-Azhar University,

Egypt. She is an accomplished academic with expertise in management, marketing, and organizational behavior. Dr. El-Taher has contributed to various research studies and academic initiatives aimed at enhancing business education.

John Oyeyemi Fawole is a doctoral researcher in International Business at Liberty University with interests in international business, AI ethics and tech policy. He holds an EMBA from Quantic School of Business & Technology and is also widely known as a FIDE Master and two-time Nigerian chess champion.

Dr. Nitin Goyal is academic and researcher with expertise in agribusiness management. He is currently working as an Assistant Professor at the Mittal School of Business, Lovely Professional University. His academic contributions include a patent on micronutrient application systems in crops and research on sales and marketing perspectives of farmers.

Tareq N. Hashem has been working as a Full Professor in Applied Science Private University in Jordan since October 2023.The study he conducted encompasses a wide array of subjects, spanning management in diverse industries, digital marketing, marketing information systems, and marketing. He is involved in reviewing, authoring, and editing book projects.

Dr. Diana Homsi is an associated doctor at AL Isra university, Her scholarly interests focus on consumer behavior, digital marketing, and strategic management, with several publications and conference contributions in these areas. Dr. Homsi is known for her dedication to advancing innovative teaching methods.

Pureheart Ogheneogaga Irikefe is a doctoral research associate with the Strategic Research Institute at Asia Pacific University of Technology & Innovation (APU), Kuala Lumpur. His research focuses on sustainability, entrepreneurship, green finance, and financial inclusion in emerging economies.

Bara'ah Ghassan Jaber is a distinguished expert with extensive academic and practical experience in business and financial technology. He has gained valuable experience as a specialist in economics, financial technology, business intelligence, and data analysis, combining academic and professional achievement.

Asghar Afshar Jahanshahi Ph.D. is a Research Professor at IPADE Business School, Mexico. He has held a full-time Professor position at Tecnologico de Monterrey in Mexico. He is the author of several articles published in the Academy of Management Journal, Asia Pacific Journal of Management, and Project Management Journal.

Kanika Jain is a seasoned banking professional with over 15 years of experience in retail banking. She has worked across diverse domains, including operations, advances, and HR, and is known for her adaptability and keen desire to learn, continuously enhancing her expertise in the banking sector.

Dr. Priyanka Jain Associate Professor at ICFAI Business School, Ahmedabad, specializes in Behavioral Finance, CSR, Financial Inclusion, and Digital Economy. An IIM Ahmedabad alumnus, she has extensive teaching, research, and publication experience and has received multiple best paper awards for her impactful contributions to academia and industry.

Dr. Kafila is an accomplished academic and researcher with expertise in finance, management, and sustainability. Her research interests include green finance, financial inclusion, and sustainable business operations. She has published extensively in reputed journals and guided research in emerging areas such as digital transformation and environmental finance.

Dr. Chandni Keswani holds a Doctorate in Finance and possesses multidisciplinary academic background with Master's degrees in Finance, Commerce, and English Literature, as well as a Bachelor's degree in Education.. She is an active researcher with over 15 publications in reputed international and national journals indexed in Scopus and ABDC.

Dr. Anuj Kumar is Head of Research and Associate Professor at Rushford Business School, Switzerland, and Editorial Head at Confab 360 Degree, India. He is Post-Doctoral Fellow in Malaysia, Honorary Research Fellow at INTI International University, Malaysia, and Honorary Professor at the European Global Institute of Innovation & Technology, Malta.

Dr. Mohit Kumar is working as an Assistant Professor in Chhatrapati Shahu Ji Maharaj University, Kanpur, Uttar Pradesh, India. He has more than Ten years of work experience in academics and has excelled in administrative activities. He has published several papers in Scopus and Web of Science indexed journals.

Dr. A. Suresh Kumar is a distinguished scholar in commerce and management with research interests spanning financial markets, sustainability, and digital innovation. He has authored and co-authored several research papers and book chapters that contribute to advancing knowledge in financial management, sustainability, and economic development.

Dr. Firdous A. Malik is presently serving as an Assistant Professor of Economics in the Department of Management, University of the People, USA. Over the years, Dr. Malik has made significant contributions to academic literature, authoring and editing dozens of books published by internationally reputed publishers.

Mugove Mashingaidze is presently working as a Lecturer at BA ISAGO University, Gaborone campus, Botswana. He obtained his Ph.D. from the University of KwaZulu Natal, South Africa. He has published more than twenty-five research papers in reputed journals and book chapters. His area of interest includes: strategy, entrepreneurship, and marketing.

Mrs. Alanoud Mbaidin is a lecturer in the Department of Marketing at the Faculty of Business, Applied Science Private University in Amman, Jordan. She specializes in marketing strategy, consumer behavior, and digital marketing. Her teaching and academic interests reflect a passion for innovation and excellence in marketing education.

Ms. A. Katheeja Naseeha works as Project Manager (India) at Confab 360 Degree and Content Developer at Alspark Solutions. With experience as an ECE Assistant Professor, she now explores Communication Systems, VLSI, IoT, AI. She was honoured with the Best Reviewer Award and serves as a researcher and career counsellor.

Dr. Purvi Pujari is Head of Vijay Patil School of Management, DY Patil University, Mumbai. She has led ICSSR-funded projects on MOOCs, Learning Analytics, and Indian SMEs. Her work appears in Scopus, ABDC, and UGC Care journals. She holds three patents, publishes cases with Emerald and The Case Centre UK.

Dr. Adel M. Qatawneh is Professor of Accounting. Dr. Qatawneh is expert in tax policies and legislation, accounting information systems, artificial intelligence in accounting, and financial reporting. He serves on Board of Trustees of the Jordan Economic Forum. He is CEO of Euro Arab Ltd. and AIM Partner in London.

Dr. M. Ángeles Rodríguez-Serrano is Associate Professor of International Business, University of Seville, Spain. Her research interests include international entrepreneurship, dynamic capabilities, and the strategic behavior of Born Global firms. She has published in leading international journals and supervises doctoral research on global strategy and firm internationalization.

Dr. Ankur Roy is an Assistant Professor at Management Development Institute, Gurgaon, specializing in Strategic Management, Entrepreneurship, International Business, and Mergers & Acquisitions. With extensive teaching, research, and training experience, his work focuses on SMEs, innovation, and global business strategies, supported by numerous publications and industry engagements.

Dr. Manu Shukla works as Project Manager at Confab 360 Degree. Strategic HR Thought Leader and a Research Evangelist with over a decade of experience in facilitating Employee Engagement, Attrition Management, Change Management, End to End Talent Acquisition, Diversity & Inclusion, and Organizational Development.

Ravi Shukla is presently working as University Assistant Librarian in Central Library at Chhatrapati Shahu Ji Maharaj University, India. He has published more than thirty-five research papers in reputed Journals, Book, Book Chapters, and Conference papers. His area of interest includes: Scientometric, Bibliometrics, Information Literacy, Digital Library, and Capacity Building.

Amanjot Singh Syan is a dynamic and accomplished Business Analyst with over five years of IT experience, delivering impactful business solutions and driving value. Adept in Rational Unified Process, he excels in gathering and analyzing requirements, creating BRDs, FRDs, and SRS documents using tools like MS Visio and Rational Rose.

Dr. Priyanka Tandon is a Senior Lecturer at Regenesys Business School. She obtained her Ph.D. from Motilal Nehru National Institute of Technology. She has published various articles in reputed journals and participated in national and international conference.

Saeed Tarabieh is an Assistant Professor at the Business School of Mu'tah University, Jordan, where he also serves as the Head of the Marketing Department. His main research interests include marketing management, consumer behavior, and digital marketing. Dr. Tarabieh has published several papers in Scopus-indexed journals.

Angelina Seow Voon Yee is a Professor (Full) at Asia Pacific University of Technology & Innovation and serves in research leadership roles at the university (Director of Research Management). She is an experienced accounting and auditing scholar with multiple publications and has held academic and industry-collaboration roles.

Ahmad Danial Zainudin is a Senior Lecturer in the School of Accounting and Finance Banking, Finance and Insurance at Asia Pacific University of Technology & Innovation. His expertise includes financial risk modelling and sustainable economic policy, and he is an active researcher with publications in finance and related areas.

List of Figures

Chapter 8

Chapter 10

Chapter 11

Chapter 13

Chapter 14

Chapter 15

List of Tables

Chapter 8

Chapter 9

Chapter 10

Chapter 11

Chapter 13

Chapter 14

PART I

Foundations of Sustainability Finance Entrepreneurship

CHAPTER 1

From Market Gaps to Mission-Driven Ventures: Identifying and Analyzing Sustainable Business Opportunities for Socio-Environmental Impact

Firas Jamil Alotoum, Diana Homsi, Hayat Fayez Mahmoud Banat, ALanoud Mbaidin, and Sodfa El-Taher

Abstract This paper talks about how important market gaps are for finding and growing mission-driven businesses that want to make a

F. J. Alotoum (✉) · A. Mbaidin
Department of Marketing, Faculty of Business, Applied Science Private University, Amman, Jordan
e-mail: f_alotoum@asu.edu.jo

D. Homsi
Faculty of Business, Isra University, Amman, Jordan

H. F. M. Banat
Smart Business, Sharjah Sustainable City, Sharjah, UAE

S. El-Taher
Business Adminstraion Faculty of Commerce, Al-Azhar University, Cairo, Egypt

S. Trivedi et al. (eds.), *Green Ventures*, Sustainable Development Goals Series, https://doi.org/10.1007/978-981-95-6533-7_1

difference in society and the environment. As businesses come under more and more pressure to be environmentally friendly, market gaps give entrepreneurs a great chance to start businesses that not only meet unmet social needs but also help the environment contributing to SDG Goals. The study looks at how market opportunities are found and used, stressing how important it is for business models to be in line with sustainability goals. This study looks closely at mission-driven businesses to find the most important things that help sustainable businesses grow, such as forming strategic partnerships, improving operational efficiency, and managing finances. The paper also talks about how policy support and new technologies can help businesses grow that are both socially responsible and make money. The results give entrepreneurs, policymakers, and investors who want to help with sustainable development and business growth useful information.

Keywords Green innovation · Sustainable business · Market gaps · Socio-environmental impact · Sustainable entrepreneurship · SDG

1 Introduction

As societies deal with more environmental problems and bigger gaps between rich and poor people, the link between entrepreneurship and sustainability has become more important over the past 20 years. When it comes to things like carbon emissions, biodiversity loss, or social inequality, traditional market mechanisms don't always work. This failure leaves clear gaps in the market—societal and environmental needs that aren't being met—that are great places for new business ideas to grow. In this situation, mission-driven businesses have become powerful forces for change that can fill these gaps with new, inclusive, and long-lasting business models. These businesses aren't just in it for the money; they also want to make a difference in society and the environment. They want to balance making money with bigger goals for sustainability (Cohen & Winn, 2007; Dean & McMullen, 2007).

Sustainable Development Goal 13, on climate action, provides an important incentive for sustainable entrepreneurship focused on addressing climate change challenges through innovative solutions. There is a pressing need to develop business ventures that combine profitability with environmental and social impact, such as initiatives based on renewable energy, recycling, climate-smart agriculture, and low-emission transportation. By analyzing market gaps related to climate change, entrepreneurs can identify innovative opportunities that meet community needs and contribute to mitigating environmental damage. These ventures not only contribute to achieving Goal 13 but also lead to building more inclusive and sustainable green economies, promoting climate justice and creating jobs simultaneously. Integrating climate dimensions into business models contributes to enhancing competitiveness and social responsibility, and gives organizations a long-term strategic advantage.

In addition, startups and entrepreneurs can play a key role in accelerating the transition to a low-carbon economy by adopting smart digital technologies and improving resource efficiency. This path requires a supportive environment that includes appropriate legislation, targeted funding, and incentives for adopting green innovation. Linking climate action with sustainable entrepreneurship enhances the integration of economic growth and environmental protection, directing capital toward investments that benefit future generations. Through public-private partnerships, the implementation of climate solutions can be accelerated and their impact scaled at the local and global levels. In this way, Goal 13 becomes not just a challenge, but a strategic opportunity to reshape businesses toward true sustainability (Schaltegger et al., 2016).

2 The Research Problem Its Importance

Even though more and more people are interested in sustainable entrepreneurship, there are still no frameworks that bring together all the different aspects of finding, studying, and putting into action sustainable business opportunities that come from gaps in the market. A lot of traditional entrepreneurship research doesn't look at non-financial measures of success, and a lot of sustainability research doesn't focus on the entrepreneurial skills needed to turn needs into workable solutions. This paper answers the important question: How can we systematically find socio-environmental market gaps and turn them into mission-driven businesses that make a difference?

Not only do aspiring entrepreneurs and investors need to know how this process works, but so do policymakers and development agencies that want to support green and inclusive economies. This study helps close the gap between theory and practice in sustainable entrepreneurship by providing a conceptual framework and real-world case studies.

3 Objectives and Questions for Research

The main goal of this study is to find out how entrepreneurs can find gaps in the market that are caused by social and environmental issues and then create mission-driven businesses to fill those gaps. In particular, the study aims to:

Describe what makes market gaps sustainable.

- Look at the tools and signs that can help you find these gaps.
- Look into the ways that entrepreneurs can turn these gaps into viable, mission-driven business models.
- Look at how the chosen businesses affect the environment and society.

The main questions this study is trying to answer are:

- What kinds of market gaps offer the best chances for socio-environmental entrepreneurs?
- Which tools for analysis work best for finding these gaps?
- What kinds of business models and strategies make mission-driven innovation work?
- How can we measure and get the most out of the effects of these kinds of businesses?

4 Methodology

This study takes a qualitative and exploratory approach by combining theoretical synthesis with case studies that show how things work. A review of the literature on sustainable entrepreneurship, market failure, and social innovation is followed by a multiple-case analysis of businesses that operate in different geographic and sectoral settings. The cases were chosen because they fit with the principles of sustainability, have shown an impact, and can be scaled up.

5 Theoretical Framework

5.1 *Sustainability and Starting a Business*

Sustainability is now a major concern in modern entrepreneurship. This is because global problems like climate change, inequality, and resource depletion need business solutions that protect the environment, promote social justice, and make money. Sustainable entrepreneurship combines business practices with goals for the environment and society. It focuses on new ideas that make money and also have lasting benefits for people and the planet (Schaltegger & Wagner, 2023). Sustainable businesses are based on the triple bottom line framework of people, planet, and profit (Elkington, 1998). This is different from traditional businesses. These businesses want to make the world a better place by stopping bad habits and replacing them with better ones.

5.2 *Finding Market Gaps and Opportunities*

Market gaps are an important part of recognizing business opportunities. Market gaps are needs in a market that aren't being met or served well enough, and they are chances to create value. Shane and Venkataraman (2000) say that changes in technology, rules, demographics, and social and cultural dynamics create business opportunities. When it comes to sustainability, market gaps are often caused by market failures like externalities, information asymmetries, or public good dilemmas. These failures give creative businesspeople a chance to step in with solutions that help the economy and the environment at the same time (Cohen & Winn, 2007).

There are three main steps to recognizing an opportunity: (1) noticing a change in the environment, (2) finding a specific problem or gap, and (3) coming up with a new solution or business model that fits (Ardichvili et al., 2003). Sustainable entrepreneurs are different from traditional ones because they often look for these gaps on purpose with a mission in mind, rather than just responding to signals that show they can make money.

5.3 *Mission-Driven Models and Social Innovation*

Social innovation is when new ideas, strategies, and ways of organizing things meet important social needs better than the ones we already have. Mission-driven businesses, which are often set up as social enterprises,

B-Corps, or hybrid organizations, are important for social innovation. These organizations have mission statements that are at the heart of their strategic identity. They incorporate values like fairness, inclusion, and circularity into everything they do (Mair & Marti, 2006).

Mission-driven models do well when they find a balance between making a difference and staying financially stable. Cross-subsidization, stakeholder co-creation, and adaptive governance are common parts of their business logic. Institutional Theory and Resource-Based View (RBV) are two theoretical approaches that help us understand how these kinds of businesses get around problems with legitimacy and lack of resources in institutional settings that may not yet support sustainable solutions (DiMaggio & Powell, 1983; Hart & Dowell, 2011).

In short, this framework sets the stage for looking at how entrepreneurs can find gaps where the market isn't working and society needs something, and then respond by starting mission-driven businesses that make a difference in the world.

6 Looking at Gaps in the Sustainable Market

6.1 Tools for Finding Gaps in Analysis

To find long-term market gaps, you need a structured method that combines market intelligence with sustainability indicators. There are a number of common analytical tools that can be used to look at the outside world and figure out what needs are not being met:

PESTEL Analysis (Political, Economic, Social, Technological, Environmental, Legal): This tool helps business owners look at big-picture factors that might show systemic issues or communities that aren't getting enough help. For example, stricter environmental laws or growing social inequality might point out areas where sustainable innovation could thrive.

SWOT Analysis (Strengths, Weaknesses, Opportunities, Threats): Entrepreneurs use SWOT to look at their own strengths and weaknesses, as well as the opportunities and risks that are out there. This helps them find market failures that match their strengths.

The 17 UN Sustainable Development Goals (SDGs) are a set of goals that the whole world agrees on for figuring out which areas have the most social and environmental impact. Market gaps that match these goals (like clean energy, no hunger, and responsible consumption) provide real and mission-aligned business opportunities (United Nations, 2015).

Gap Mapping and Needs Assessments: These are tools and ways of collecting data that involve stakeholders, especially marginalized communities, to find out where current solutions are not working or are not available.

These tools work together to help business owners look beyond short-term profits and focus on long-term problems that can lead to lasting change.

6.2 Signs of Socio-Environmental Need

Market gaps that have to do with sustainability often show up in areas or industries where public or private solutions don't work well enough. Some examples of indicators are:

Access Deficits: When people can't get to basic needs like clean water, sanitation, electricity, or education, it often means that there are good places for mission-driven innovation.

Negative Externalities: Companies that pollute, cut down trees, or exploit people often work in markets where there aren't many sustainable options. Entrepreneurs can step in by offering alternatives that are ethically sourced or have little effect.

High levels of waste, energy loss, or overconsumption may point to chances for circular economy models, sharing platforms, or technologies that use less energy.

Institutional Voids: In developing economies or areas that are prone to crises, weak institutions and poor service delivery create gaps that social enterprises and hybrid ventures can fill better than traditional businesses or governments (Khanna & Palepu, 2010).

Using data-driven methods to find these indicators makes sure that mission-driven businesses are not only new but also based on real and measurable social or environmental needs.

6.3 Examples of Cases from Around the World and in the Region

Here are some examples of how these tools and indicators can be used:

Too Good To Go (Europe): This app-based service helps cut down on food waste by connecting people with extra food from stores and restaurants. The company found problems with how food was distributed and used digital tools to cut down on waste and lower food costs.

M-KOPA (Sub-Saharan Africa): M-KOPA saw that people in Sub-Saharan Africa didn't have easy access to electricity and financial services, so they made a pay-as-you-go solar energy system. It used mobile technology and small payments to help communities that weren't connected to the grid in a way that was good for the environment.

Fairphone (Netherlands): Fairphone makes smartphones that are ethically sourced and can be customized. This is a response to the environmental and social costs of the electronics industry. Its business model focuses on transparency, circularity, and workers' rights as its main selling points.

These examples show how looking at market gaps in a systematic way, using both macro-level tools and micro-level insights, can help create mission-driven businesses that make a difference and grow.

6.4 Ideas for Mission-Driven Innovation

To turn identified socio-environmental gaps into successful businesses, you need a framework of mission-driven innovation, which combines the flexibility of entrepreneurship with values that are good for the environment. More and more entrepreneurs are adopting a "green" business model, which has been shown to encourage innovation while staying within environmental limits (Chege & Wang, 2023). This orientation puts resilience, stakeholder involvement, and thinking about the whole system first.

Recent evidence also shows that adding sustainability to the business model leads to better long-term economic performance. Bain & Company and EcoVadis (2024) say that businesses that do a good job of integrating ESG are 2.4 times more likely to grow faster than their peers. Sustainability is no longer an afterthought; it's now at the heart of making opportunities happen and gaining a competitive edge.

6.5 Examples of Businesses That Are Sustainable

Depop is a peer-to-peer fashion resale site that shows how circular economy ideas can be used to cut down on overconsumption in the fashion industry. In 2023, CEO Kruti Patel Goyal got rid of UK selling fees, which led to a 9% increase in sales and a larger Gen Z user base. This also made fashion consumption more environmentally friendly (Patel Goyal, 2024).

Another example is Primal Soles, a Dutch startup that makes insoles out of Mediterranean cork that can be recycled 100% of the time. The company has been getting a lot of attention around the world since 2021, including at the World Economic Forum. Now, it works with big European hotels to sell eco-friendly slippers (*Financial Times*, 2024).

FREDsense Technologies, which Emily Hicks co-founded in Canada, made genetically modified biosensors that can find contaminants like lead and arsenic in water. This meets both regulatory and humanitarian needs. In 2024, the company expanded into new municipal and industrial markets (Hicks, 2024).

These examples show that sustainable businesses can start in a wide range of fields as long as they fill a need and fit with both the mission and the market.

6.6 Problems with Sustainable Entrepreneurship

Mission-driven businesses often run into problems that make it hard for them to grow and have an effect, such as:

Regulatory Complexity: Entrepreneurs in emerging markets have to deal with rules that are broken up or out of date. In Jordan, renewable energy entrepreneurs have to deal with legal issues between ministries, which makes projects take longer and makes people less likely to invest (Leaders International, 2023).

Getting Money: Even though impact investing is growing, many mission-driven startups have trouble getting money, especially in the beginning. Even programs like Jordan's ISSF fund only help a small number of qualified businesses (OECD, 2024).

Consumer Education: Not knowing about eco-friendly products is still a problem. Entrepreneurs often have to do more than just come up with new ideas; they also have to teach customers about them.

To get past these problems, we need systemic support, such as policy changes, more funding sources, and teaching people and organizations about sustainability.

7 Assessment of the Impact on Society and the Environment

7.1 *Thinking About the Effects of Sustainable Entrepreneurship*

In sustainable entrepreneurship, "impact" means the long-term effects that entrepreneurial activities have on people and the environment, both good and bad. Recent research stresses the importance of a broad understanding of impact that goes beyond standard economic measures. Scartozzi et al. (2024a) stress how important it is to include social, environmental, and economic factors in order to fully understand the complex nature of entrepreneurial impact. They say that a lot of current research works in silos, looking at one thing at a time and not how they all fit together.

7.2 *Ways to Measure the Impact on Society and the Environment*

Several frameworks have been made to look at how business ventures affect people and the environment:

The Global Reporting Initiative (GRI) sets out detailed rules for sustainability reporting that help businesses figure out and share their effects on the environment and society. All companies must follow the new Universal Standards, which will go into effect in January 2023. These standards cover the most important sustainability issues related to a company's effects on the economy, society, and the environment (Global Reporting Initiative, 2023).

Social Return on Investment (SROI): SROI is a method that puts dollar amounts on social and environmental outcomes, making it easier to do a cost-benefit analysis of social ventures.

Theory of Change (ToC) shows how entrepreneurial activities can lead to desired outcomes by showing the causal pathways that lead to those outcomes. It also provides a framework for planning and evaluation.

These frameworks help business owners systematically evaluate and talk about the bigger effects of their businesses.

7.3 *New Things That Have Happened in Impact Assessment*

Recent research has moved the field of impact assessment in sustainable entrepreneurship forward:

Scartozzi et al. (2024a) did a systematic review of the literature and found four main themes in entrepreneurship research: social entrepreneurship for making a difference in society, entrepreneurship for sustainable development, female entrepreneurship for changing institutions, and entrepreneurship for regional development that includes everyone. They stress the importance of using integrated methods that take into account how social, environmental, and economic effects work together.

Textile Exchange, along with Boston Consulting Group and Quantis (2023), put out a report that says fashion brands can make 6% more money over five years by investing in eco-friendly raw materials. The report also talked about the Materials Impact Explorer, a tool that helps brands understand and lower the risks in their supply chains (Vogue Business, 2023).

These changes show that more and more people are realizing how important it is to do a full impact assessment for sustainable business.

7.4 Challenges in Socio-Environmental Impact Assessment

Despite advancements, several challenges persist in assessing socio-environmental impact:

Data Availability and Quality: Reliable data on social and environmental outcomes are often scarce, hindering accurate assessment.

Standardization: The lack of standardized metrics and methodologies complicates comparisons across ventures and sectors.

Attribution: Determining the extent to which observed outcomes can be attributed to specific entrepreneurial activities remains complex.

Addressing these challenges requires collaborative efforts among entrepreneurs, researchers, and policymakers to develop robust, standardized, and context-sensitive assessment tools.

8 Socio-Environmental Impact Assessment

8.1 Conceptualizing Impact in Sustainable Entrepreneurship

Socio-environmental impact in the context of sustainable entrepreneurship refers to the measurable, long-term effects that ventures exert on both society and the natural environment. Impact goes beyond financial performance, encompassing changes in community well-being, environmental preservation, social equity, and systemic transformation (Scartozzi et al., 2024b). Scholars now advocate for multi-dimensional frameworks that integrate environmental, social, and economic metrics, as traditional business KPIs alone do not adequately capture sustainability outcomes (Vermunt et al., 2023).

Sustainable entrepreneurs are distinct in that they define success not only by profitability but also by their contribution to the UN Sustainable Development Goals (SDGs). For instance, ventures focusing on clean energy (SDG 7), sustainable cities (SDG 11), or responsible consumption (SDG 12) inherently embed impact into their operations and innovation logic.

8.2 Tools and Metrics for Impact Assessment

A range of frameworks and tools have emerged to help entrepreneurs and investors systematically evaluate impact. Prominent among these are:

Theory of Change (ToC): A strategic framework that maps how specific actions are expected to lead to desired outcomes and long-term impact. It is widely used in the social enterprise sector for articulating cause-effect linkages and assumptions.

Impact Reporting and Investment Standards (IRIS+): Developed by the Global Impact Investing Network (GIIN), IRIS+ provides standardized metrics for assessing impact across sectors, including clean energy, education, and financial inclusion (GIIN, 2023).

Environmental, Social, and Governance (ESG) Scorecards: These are increasingly adopted by startups and investors to benchmark sustainability practices. ESG assessments not only monitor carbon footprints and gender equality but also help attract impact-aligned funding (Kotsantonis et al., 2023).

Social Return on Investment (SROI): This monetizes social outcomes, allowing ventures to calculate the social value created per dollar invested. Though resource-intensive, SROI is useful in demonstrating value to stakeholders and policymakers (Nicholls et al., 2012).

Emerging technologies—particularly AI and IoT—are also playing a growing role in real-time impact tracking, especially in sectors like agriculture, waste management, and health.

8.3 Case Example: Measuring Impact in Practice

Too Good To Go, a European social enterprise that combats food waste through a mobile app, reports preventing over 250 million meals from being discarded since its launch. The company quantifies its environmental impact using CO_2-equivalent savings and food recovery metrics, aligning with SDG 12 (responsible consumption) and SDG 13 (climate action) (Too Good To Go, 2023).

Similarly, Sistema.bio, an award-winning social enterprise providing biodigesters to small farmers, uses both quantitative (GHG reductions, crop yields) and qualitative (household health, women's empowerment) indicators to monitor impact. A 2023 impact report showed over 1.4 million tonnes of CO_2 avoided and 82% of users reporting improved health outcomes (Sistema.bio, 2023).

8.4 Limitations and Ethical Considerations

Despite advances in impact measurement, several limitations persist:

Attribution and Causality: Determining whether observed outcomes are directly attributable to a venture's actions remains challenging, especially in complex social systems.

Time Lags: Many socio-environmental impacts are long-term and not immediately visible. Entrepreneurs and funders must be patient and prioritize longitudinal tracking.

Ethical Reporting: Impact data may be selectively reported or inflated due to funding pressures. Transparent, third-party evaluations and ethical reporting standards are essential to preserve credibility and trust (Ebrahim & Rangan, 2014).

Addressing these issues requires methodological rigor, stakeholder involvement, and a commitment to continuous learning.

9 Policy and Ecosystem Support for Sustainable Ventures

9.1 Government Policies and Initiatives

Government policies and strategic initiatives are critical in creating an enabling environment for sustainable entrepreneurship. Countries that prioritize green innovation through robust policies enable startups to overcome barriers such as market access and regulatory complexities. Recent examples of effective policies include:

Atal Innovation Mission (AIM), India: AIM, launched by India's National Institution for Transforming India (NITI Aayog), is designed to foster innovation and entrepreneurship. It provides incubation, mentoring, and funding to startups, particularly in sectors such as renewable energy, agritech, and social enterprises (Bansal et al., 2023).

Clean Energy Finance Corporation (CEFC), Australia: The CEFC, a government-owned corporation, focuses on providing funding to renewable energy projects to accelerate Australia's transition to a low-carbon economy. The CEFC's investments include grid modernization, energy-efficient technologies, and sustainable infrastructure (Jackson & Shaw, 2023).

European Green Deal, EU: The European Green Deal is the EU's roadmap to achieving climate neutrality by 2050. It includes financial instruments like the Just Transition Fund to support green innovation and transition, ensuring that sustainability is central to EU policy (European Commission, 2023).

9.2 Ecosystem Support Organizations

Ecosystem support organizations bridge the gap between public policy and practical implementation by providing resources, networks, and mentorship to emerging sustainable ventures. Notable examples include:

SEED Initiative: SEED is a global partnership aimed at supporting small and medium-sized enterprises that address environmental and social challenges. It provides tailored business development services to startups in developing countries, with a focus on sustainable agriculture, renewable energy, and waste management (SEED, 2024).

Euclid Network: A European platform that promotes social entrepreneurship through policy advocacy, funding opportunities, and capacity-building. Euclid Network supports initiatives like the MedUP! Project, which empowers social enterprises in the Mediterranean region by offering grants and networking opportunities (Marrone, 2023).

Fashion for Good: An innovation platform that connects startups in the fashion industry with industry leaders, investors, and sustainability experts. Fashion for Good helps scale sustainable solutions by facilitating collaborations and supporting startups in the sustainable fashion space (Fletcher &Tham, 2023).

9.3 Challenges and Opportunities

Sustainable ventures face several systemic challenges that hinder their growth and scalability:

Funding Gaps: Despite the increasing global focus on green innovation, many sustainable ventures still struggle with funding, especially in emerging markets. According to a recent report by the UN Environment Programme (UNEP), Africa needs an estimated $277 billion per year to meet its climate goals for 2030 (UNEP, 2023). These funding gaps are particularly pronounced in sectors like renewable energy, clean tech, and sustainable agriculture.

Regulatory Barriers: Entrepreneurs often encounter inconsistent regulations across different markets. A study by the World Bank (2023) highlighted how unclear policies and overlapping regulations create uncertainty for startups, especially in developing economies. Simplifying and aligning regulations can accelerate the adoption of sustainable technologies.

Market Access: Many sustainable startups find it difficult to penetrate mainstream markets, particularly in sectors like green building materials and eco-friendly consumer goods. Building strategic partnerships with large corporations and leveraging digital platforms are essential to overcoming these barriers (Bertoldi et al., 2024).

9.4 Recommendations for Strengthening Support Systems

To enhance the ecosystem for sustainable ventures, several recommendations are proposed:

Policy Coherence: Governments should integrate sustainability goals into national development strategies to ensure that policies across sectors—such as energy, agriculture, and transport—are aligned with the overarching green transition (OECD, 2023).

Supportive Ecosystem: Creating supportive ecosystems through public-private partnerships is critical for addressing the capital and market access gaps faced by sustainable ventures. For example, combining government incentives with private investment can stimulate innovation and lower the risk for early-stage sustainable businesses (Bertoldi et al., 2024).

Capacity Building and Education: Governments and development organizations should invest in capacity-building programs for entrepreneurs, enabling them to better navigate the complexities of sustainable business models. This could include technical training on green technologies and business mentorship programs tailored to sustainable sectors (Marrone, 2023).

Standardized Impact Metrics: Standardizing metrics for social and environmental impact would help investors and consumers evaluate the effectiveness of sustainable ventures. Metrics such as the Global Reporting Initiative (GRI) Standards and ESG reporting can provide transparency and attract impact-driven capital (OECD, 2023).

10 Strategic Recommendations for Scaling Sustainable Ventures

Scaling sustainable ventures requires a nuanced approach that balances growth with environmental and social impact. The following strategic recommendations are informed by recent research and case studies:

10.1 Align Growth Strategies with Core Values

Sustainable scaling involves growing a business in a way that respects its original mission, ensuring that expansion enhances rather than dilutes the company's identity. This approach not only differentiates the brand in a crowded market but also maintains the integrity of its sustainability goals (Rosário et al., 2024).

10.2 Build Strategic Partnerships

Forming strategic partnerships with established companies, governments, or other organizations allows startups to leverage resources, technology, and market access they wouldn't have on their own (Gazzola et al., 2024). These partnerships provide startups with the credibility and reach needed to grow while staying true to their mission.

10.3 Focus on Operational Efficiency

Optimizing operations is crucial for sustainable growth. Implementing lean practices, reducing waste, and improving supply chain management can lead to cost savings and a smaller environmental footprint. These efficiencies not only improve profitability but also align with sustainability objectives (Gregori et al., 2025).

10.4 Manage Cash Flow Carefully

Rapid growth can strain finances, making careful cash flow management essential for sustainable scaling. Maintaining a detailed financial forecast and budget, and monitoring cash flow regularly, helps in adjusting spending as needed and avoiding financial crises (Maaßen et al., 2025).

10.5 Embrace Technological Innovation

Leveraging technology can drive efficiency and innovation in sustainable ventures (Peralta et al., 2025). Investing in technologies that reduce environmental impact, such as renewable energy solutions or waste-reducing processes, can enhance sustainability and provide a competitive edge.

10.6 Cultivate a Culture of Continuous Learning

Building a culture of continuous learning, innovation, and adaptability is essential for developing sustainable business practices and resilience (Sharma et al., 2025). This approach enables ventures to navigate the complexities of sustainability and respond effectively to changing market conditions.

10.7 Diversify Revenue Streams

Developing multiple revenue streams can reduce financial risk and support long-term sustainability. Exploring new markets, offering complementary products or services, and adopting flexible business models can provide stability and growth opportunities.

10.8 Prioritize Customer Education and Engagement

Educating customers about the value and impact of sustainable products or services can drive demand and loyalty. Engaging customers through transparent communication and involving them in sustainability initiatives can strengthen relationships and enhance brand reputation.

11 Conclusion and Future Directions

11.1 Conclusion

The path from identifying market gaps to creating mission-driven ventures for socio-environmental impact presents both significant challenges and exciting opportunities. Sustainable entrepreneurship is at the forefront of addressing pressing global issues such as climate change, inequality, and resource depletion. By strategically navigating the complex intersection of innovation, policy, and market dynamics, entrepreneurs can leverage the growing demand for sustainable products and services to build ventures that not only achieve financial success but also deliver lasting environmental and social benefits.

The research presented underscores the importance of adopting a holistic approach to scaling sustainable ventures. This includes aligning growth strategies with core values, building strategic partnerships, and prioritizing operational efficiency. Additionally, embedding sustainability in every aspect of business—from product development to customer engagement—is essential for long-term success. Governments, policymakers, and ecosystem organizations have a critical role in supporting these ventures through clear regulations, targeted financial incentives, and access to networks that promote innovation.

11.2 Future Directions

While substantial progress has been made in creating an enabling environment for sustainable ventures, several challenges remain. The following future directions are crucial for further advancing the field:

Innovation in Financial Models: To scale rapidly, sustainable ventures must access diverse funding sources. Future research could explore innovative financial models, such as blended finance, green bonds, and impact investing, that align the interests of both investors and entrepreneurs in the sustainability space.

Expansion of Global Market Access: As sustainable ventures grow, they often encounter barriers to entering international markets. Research could examine the effectiveness of trade agreements, international regulatory standards, and digital platforms in facilitating cross-border expansion for sustainable businesses.

Impact Measurement and Standardization: While many ventures claim to create positive social and environmental outcomes, consistent and transparent measurement tools are needed. Future studies could explore the development of standardized impact metrics that would allow investors and stakeholders to assess the true value of sustainable ventures.

Policy Integration for Sustainability: Policymakers must continue to integrate sustainability into broader economic development strategies. Future policy research should focus on creating synergies between sustainability goals and other national priorities, such as economic growth and job creation, ensuring that sustainability is not viewed as a cost but as an integral part of long-term economic resilience.

Technology and Data Analytics: Technological innovation will continue to drive sustainability efforts forward. Future work should investigate the role of emerging technologies like artificial intelligence (AI), blockchain, and Internet of Things (IoT) in improving the efficiency of sustainable ventures and creating new business models.

Cultural Shifts towards Sustainability: As consumer demand for sustainable products increases, there is also a need for a cultural shift toward sustainability across various industries. Future studies could examine how cultural and behavioral changes in both consumers and organizations can drive the adoption of sustainable business practices at scale.

In conclusion, the future of sustainable ventures hinges on the continued collaboration between entrepreneurs, policymakers, and stakeholders to create an ecosystem that supports growth, fosters innovation, and maximizes positive social and environmental impact. By focusing on the intersection of market gaps, policy support, and business strategy, sustainable entrepreneurs can catalyze the systemic change needed to tackle the world's most pressing challenges.

References

Alvarez, S. A., & Barney, J. B. (2023). The entrepreneurial discovery of market opportunities: Implications for sustainable business strategies. *Journal of Business Venturing, 38*(1), 1–16. https://doi.org/10.1016/j.jbusvent.2022.106234

Anderson, B. S., & Tushman, M. L. (2022). Disruption, innovation, and opportunity recognition: A framework for sustainable entrepreneurship. *Journal of Business Research, 141*, 98–107. https://doi.org/10.1016/j.jbusres.2022.10.043

Bain & Company, & EcoVadis. (2024). *Profit meets purpose: Unlocking growth through sustainable business models*. https://www.eu-startups.com/2024/10/profit-meets-purpose

Bansal, P., Shah, A., & Rathi, R. (2023). Government policies and initiatives for green innovation: A case study of the Atal Innovation Mission. *Journal of Environmental Policy & Planning, 25*(2), 234–251. https://doi.org/10.1080/1523908X.2023.1912783

Bertoldi, P., Doví, R., & Chiesa, F. (2024). Sustainable innovation ecosystems: A global perspective. *Technological Forecasting & Social Change, 176*, 121–132. https://doi.org/10.1016/j.techfore.2023.121450

Bocken, N. M. P., & Short, S. W. (2024). Mission-driven business models: Sustainable entrepreneurship for socio-environmental change. *Business Strategy and the Environment, 33*(4), 1456–1468. https://doi.org/10.1002/bse.2892

Chege, S. M., & Wang, D. (2023). Green entrepreneurial orientation and sustainable innovation in SMEs. *Journal of Business Research, 162*, Article 113145. https://doi.org/10.1016/j.jbusres.2023.113145

Dacin, M. T., & Dacin, P. A. (2023). Social entrepreneurship and mission-driven ventures: A theoretical and empirical review. *Journal of Social Entrepreneurship, 14*(2), 180–203. https://doi.org/10.1080/19420676.2023.1764950

Davila, A., & Foster, G. (2024). Market gaps in the green economy: Opportunities and challenges for innovation. *California Management Review, 66*(2), 72–90. https://doi.org/10.1177/00081256231097974

Ebrahim, A., & Rangan, V. K. (2014). What impact? A framework for measuring the scale and scope of social performance. *California Management Review, 56*(3), 118–141. https://doi.org/10.1525/cmr.2014.56.3.118

European Commission. (2023). *The European Green Deal*. https://ec.europa.eu/info/strategy/priorities-2019-2024/european-green-deal_en

Financial Times. (2024, March 18). *Circular insoles and sustainable hotel slippers: How Primal Soles is greening hospitality*. https://www.ft.com/content/fe16cf43

Fletcher, K., & Tham, M. (2023). Fashion for Good: Scaling sustainability through innovation in fashion. *Sustainable Fashion, 12*(1), 45–58. https://doi.org/10.1016/j.susfash.2023.01.003

Gazzola, P., Drago, C., Pavione, E., & Pignoni, N. (2024). Sustainable business models: An empirical analysis of environmental sustainability in leading manufacturing companies. *Sustainability, 16*(19), 8282. https://doi.org/10.3390/su16198282(MDPI)

GIIN. (2023). *IRIS+ system: Core metrics sets*. Global Impact Investing Network. https://iris.thegiin.org

Global Reporting Initiative. (2023). *Global Reporting Initiative*. https://en.wikipedia.org/wiki/Global_Reporting_Initiative

Gregori, P., et al. (2025). Agencing entrepreneurial ecosystems for sustainability. *Small Business Economics*. https://doi.org/10.1007/s11187-025-01071-w

Hicks, E. (2024). How biosensors are revolutionizing water testing. *Financial Times*. https://www.ft.com/content/2e9e6a02

Jackson, S., & Shaw, R. (2023). The role of public-private partnerships in clean energy financing: A case study of CEFC, Australia. *Energy Policy, 155*, 1136–1149. https://doi.org/10.1016/j.enpol.2023.1136

Jäger, U., & Wehling, M. (2023). Building mission-driven ventures: From purpose to impact. *International Journal of Entrepreneurial Behavior & Research, 29*(6), 1581–1601. https://doi.org/10.1108/IJEBR-07-2022-0784

Kotsantonis, S., Serafeim, G., & Tuffaha, H. (2023). ESG ratings: What's behind the numbers? *Harvard Business Review, 101*(2), 45–52.

Leaders International. (2023). *Green and blue economies as the future of entrepreneurship in Jordan*. https://leadersinternational.org/results-insights/green-and-blue-economies

Lichtenstein, B. M. B., & Lyons, T. (2023). Identifying and exploiting market opportunities for sustainability: Entrepreneurial strategies in emerging markets. *Entrepreneurship Theory and Practice, 47*(1), 32–54. https://doi.org/10.1177/10422587221094855

Maaßen, C., et al. (2025). Institutional enablers for sustainable entrepreneurship: How regulative, normative, and cultural-cognitive dimensions configure sustainability impact. *Small Business Economics*. https://doi.org/10.1007/s11187-025-01076-5

Mair, J., & Noboa, E. (2023). Social entrepreneurship and mission-driven ventures in emerging markets. *International Small Business Journal, 41*(5), 641–661. https://doi.org/10.1177/02662426231153060

Marrone, M. (2023). Social entrepreneurship in the Mediterranean: The role of Euclid Network in empowering social enterprises. *Social Enterprise Journal, 19*(4), 321–335. https://doi.org/10.1108/SEJ-11-2023-0211

Nicholls, J., Lawlor, E., Neitzert, E., & Goodspeed, T. (2012). *A guide to Social Return on Investment (SROI)*. The SROI Network.

OECD. (2023). *Green innovation and policy coherence: Enabling a sustainable future*. Organisation for Economic Co-operation and Development. https://www.oecd.org/greeneconomy

OECD. (2024). *Fostering innovation-driven entrepreneurship in MENA*. https://www.oecd.org/mena/competitiveness/

Parrish, B. D., & Fox, S. (2024). The evolution of mission-driven entrepreneurship: From social enterprises to sustainable ventures. *Journal of Business Ethics, 187*(1), 183–204. https://doi.org/10.1007/s10551-024-04862-0

Patel Goyal, K. (2024, February 9). Interview with TIME: Depop's Gen Z mission for ethical fashion. *Time Magazine*. https://time.com/6995354/depop-ceo-kruti-patel-goyal-interview/

Peralta, A., et al. (2025). Assessing Lean Startup for sustainable business models. *Journal of Cleaner Production* (or equivalent outlet). https://doi.org/10.1016/j.jclepro.2025.xxx (pre-print) (ScienceDirect).

Rosário, A. T., et al. (2024). Sustainable entrepreneurship and corporate social responsibility: Exploring circular economy and impact-oriented business models. *Journal of Business Ethics*, (early view). https://doi.org/10.1080/27658511.2024.2324572 (Taylor & Francis Online).

Scartozzi, G., Delladio, S., Rosati, F., & Caputo, A. (2024a). The social and environmental impact of entrepreneurship: A review and future research agenda. *Review of Managerial Science, 19*, 1041–1072. https://doi.org/10.1007/s11846-024-00783-9

Scartozzi, M., Martins, R. D., & Di Domenico, M. (2024b). Measuring impact in sustainable entrepreneurship: A multidimensional framework. *Journal of Business Venturing Insights, 21*, Article e00497. https://doi.org/10.1016/j.jbvi.2024.00497

Schaltegger, S., Hansen, E. G., & Lüdeke-Freund, F. (2016). Business models for sustainability: Origins, present research, and future avenues. *Organization & Environment, 29*(1), 3–10. https://doi.org/10.1177/1086026615599806

Schaltegger, S., & Wagner, M. (2023). Business models for sustainability: A review of the literature. *Sustainability, 15*(3), 810–826. https://doi.org/10.3390/su15030810

SEED. (2024). *Supporting sustainable enterprises for a green future*. https://www.seed.uno

Sharma, S. N., et al. (2025). Entrepreneurship and sustainability: Analyzing the impact of green startups in circular economy and renewable technologies. *Elsevier / ScienceDirect* (advance article). https://doi.org/10.1016/j.sustain.2025.xxx (ScienceDirect)

Sistema.bio. (2023). *Annual Impact Report*. https://sistema.bio

Tilley, F., & Young, W. (2023). The role of market gaps in fostering sustainable business ventures. *Business & Society Review, 128*(2), 209–228. https://doi.org/10.1111/basr.12322

Too Good To Go. (2023). *Impact Highlights*. https://toogoodtogo.com/en-us/impact

UNEP. (2023). *Finance for Climate Action in Africa: Annual Report 2023*. United Nations Environment Programme. https://www.unep.org/resources/report/finance-climate-action-africa

Vermunt, D. A., De Boer, F., & Meijer, M. (2023). Measuring sustainability performance of startups: The role of impact metrics. *Sustainability, 15*(1), 322. https://doi.org/10.3390/su15010322

Vogue Business. (2023, October 26). *Want to boost profits? Invest in sustainable materials*. https://www.voguebusiness.com/sustainability/want-to-boost-profits-invest-in-sustainable-materials-textile-exchange

Wilson, S., & Smith, M. (2023). The impact of mission-driven entrepreneurship on socio-environmental sustainability. *Journal of Business Ethics, 164*(4), 645–659. https://doi.org/10.1007/s10551-023-05065-x

World Bank. (2023). *Global Doing Business Report 2023: Regulatory barriers to sustainable entrepreneurship*. https://www.worldbank.org/en/research/ng-business

CHAPTER 2

How Do Sustainable Products, Services, and Entrepreneurial Strategies in Green Markets Drive Social and Environmental Change?

Firas Jamil Alotoum, Diana Homsi, Sodfa El-Taher, Hayat Fayez Mahmoud Banat, and ALanoud Mbaidin

Abstract As worldwide issues like climate change harm the environment and social gaps get worse sustainable business practices are starting to drive system-wide changes. This chapter explores the interplay between market dynamics and sustainability-driven breakthroughs. It highlights how business owners tap into green market openings to create products and services that benefit the environment and society. The study took a descriptive approach examining the theoretical writings on the topic. By

F. J. Alotoum (✉)
Department of Marketing, Faculty of Business, Applied Science Private University, Amman, Jordan
e-mail: f_alotoum@asu.edu.jo

D. Homsi
Faculty of Business, Isra University, Amman, Jordan

S. Trivedi et al. (eds.), *Green Ventures*, Sustainable Development Goals Series, https://doi.org/10.1007/978-981-95-6533-7_2

looking at recent studies (2020–2024) real-world examples, and market shifts, the chapter outlines key strategies, hurdles, and frameworks for growing sustainable businesses. This gives helpful tips to entrepreneurs, government officials, and investors on how to back companies that turn a profit while doing good. The findings offer insights to business owners, policymakers, and researchers on ways to speed up the move towards a more sustainable and inclusive economy.

Keywords Green markets · Sustainable products · Social changes · Sustainable entrepreneurship · SDG · Market gaps · Socio-environmental impact · And mission-driven ventures are some of the keywords

1 Introduction

Sustainability in business has gained traction as a solution to major societal and environmental issues such as climate change, resource scarcity, and inequality. A growing consensus suggests that the fundamental requirements of profit-driven traditional business models fail to ensure a company's long-term survival. Cohen and Muñoz (2021) argue that a sustainable business demonstrates how to strike a balance between generating profits safeguarding the environment, and acting towards people.

Entrepreneurs play a crucial role in society by spotting unmet needs and creating viable business solutions. This article looks at how market research can help identify long-term business opportunities. What drives business owners to tackle social and environmental issues, and to develop and expand eco-friendly products and services?

S. El-Taher
Business Adminstraion Faculty of Commerce, Al-Azhar University, Cairo, Egypt

H. F. M. Banat
Smart Business, Sharjah Sustainable City, UAE

A. Mbaidin
Department of Marketing, Faculty of Business, Applied Science Private University, Amman, Jordan

Sustainable entrepreneurship is based on sustainability research, innovation theory, and business strategy. This research is based on the Triple Bottom Line (Elkington, 1998), Sustainable Business Model Innovation (Geissdoerfer et al., 2020), and Entrepreneurial Opportunity Theory. The Triple Bottom Line talks about social, environmental, and economic values. Sustainable Business Model Innovation looks at how companies change their value propositions, create value, and deliver it in order to achieve systemic sustainability (Bocken et al., 2023). Sustainable "Meeting the needs of the present without hurting the needs of the future." In 1987, the Brundtland Commission study "Our Common Future" was the first to introduce the term "sustainable development."

Fighting climate change is a standard for sustainability:

Sustainable Development requires an immediate response to climate change and its effects i.e. Sustainable Goal 13. This objective is very important for the other 16 goals in the 2030 Agenda for Sustainable Development. The Paris Agreement was agreed by countries to restrict the temperature of the Earth from rising more than 2 °C.

Climate change is a serious danger to civilization. The effects are already clear, and if we don't do anything, they will be terrible. We can protect our planet by learning, coming up with new ideas, and making a commitment to the climate. These changes give us a fantastic chance to improve our infrastructure, which will create jobs and make the world a better place.

Goal 13 needs governments, businesses, and civil society from all across the world to work together. Countries need to put in place steps to cut down on greenhouse gas emissions, move to renewable energy, and make energy consumption more efficient. This goal stresses giving underdeveloped countries money and technology so they can deal with climate change (UNFCCC, 2021).

In the last few decades, the world has moved toward sustainable development, which includes more environmentally and socially responsible ways of making and using things. Consequently, sustainability has emerged as a pivotal driver of economic and trade policy, as well as a strategic instrument for market orientations. The World Commission on Environment and Development's 1987 Brundtland Report says that sustainability means "meeting the needs of the present without compromising the ability of future generations to meet their own needs." This idea provides the most comprehensive framework for understanding the economy, society, and environment. To achieve environmental, social, and economic sustainability, economic sectors need to change the way they make and sell goods and services (Elkington, 2020).

2 Literature Review

- **The Concept of Sustainable Products**

The environment, social values, and the economy all benefit from the way sustainable products are made, used, and thrown away. They use resources, make very little pollution, can be recycled or broken down, and depend on renewable natural resources (Bocken et al., 2014).

Recent studies show that more people know about and want these kinds of products. More and more people want products that fit with their moral and environmental beliefs, even if they cost more (Niinimäki & Thapa, 2023).

- **The Concept of Sustainable Services**

Sustainable services refer to those that provide added value to customers without depleting resources or causing environmental damage. This includes models such as the sharing economy, regular maintenance, and reliance on clean energy, as well as digital services that reduce the physical footprint of operations (Tukker, 2015). The "product-as-a-service" model is one of the most prominent emerging models within this framework, as the product is provided as an ongoing service source rather than a commodity for consumption only, which enhances efficiency of use and reduces waste.

- **Entrepreneurship in Green Markets**

    1. **Defining Green Entrepreneurship**
    Green entrepreneurship is a trend based on developing commercial projects with a positive environmental and social impact, in addition to their profit objectives. This type of entrepreneurship reconciles innovation, environmental awareness, and social responsibility, contributing to sustainable development (Schaltegger & Wagner, 2011).

2. **Components of a Green Entrepreneurial Strategy**

   Green market entrepreneurial strategies include several elements, most notably:

   - Green Marketing: Reflects the organization's commitment to sustainability at all stages of the product lifecycle (production, packaging, distribution, advertising), and also takes ethical values into account when communicating with the target audience (Peattie & Crane, 2005).
   - Eco-Innovation: Developing new products, services, or business models that reduce environmental impact. This includes switching to renewable energy, innovation in packaging materials, and the development of clean technology (Klewitz & Hansen, 2014).
   - Circular Economy: which is concerned with reusing, recycling, and reducing waste of resources, and it represents one of the pillars of sustainable entrepreneurial strategies (Geissdoerfer et al., 2017).

- **Business Practices**

Studies indicate that companies such as IKEA, Unilever, and Patagonia have successfully adopted green entrepreneurial strategies, adapting their supply chains to become more aligned with sustainability goals by reducing their carbon footprint, improving working conditions, and implementing circular economy principles (Lewandowski, 2021). Small and medium-sized enterprises (SMEs) have also increasingly relied on sustainable solutions as an entry point to enhance their competitiveness in global markets.

- **Sustainable Products Market Share Growth**

Based on the NYU Stern Center for Sustainable Business report (Sustainable Market Share Index™):

Products labeled as sustainable in the consumer goods (CPG) sector have seen steady growth from 14.6% in 2013 to 23.8% in 2024 in the U.S. market.

Europe—particularly Germany and the UK—achieved higher rates, ranging from 37 to 42% in consumer goods.

We are also seeing growth in other sectors, such as sustainable packaging ($276 billion in 2023, expected to reach ~500 billion by 2032).

- **Green Markets as a Driver of Change**
  - **Characteristics of Green Markets**
    Green markets are defined as economic systems based on the production, distribution, and consumption of goods and services with consideration for their environmental and social impacts. These markets are characterized by increased consumer sensitivity to environmental issues, growing demand for ethical products, and growing government legislation supporting sustainability (OECD, 2022).

    Green markets are characterized by:
    - Growing demand for environmentally friendly products;
    - Evolving consumer preferences toward ethical consumption;
    - Strict environmental legislation and regulatory pressures;
    - Innovative opportunities for alternative business models.
  - **Social and Environmental Change in the Market Context**
    Green markets play a pivotal role in reshaping consumption and production patterns and establishing a new corporate culture based on environmental and social responsibility. Sustainable business practices are not limited to reducing environmental damage, but also extend to achieving social justice, creating job opportunities, and empowering marginalized groups (El-Haddadeh et al., 2023). This trend drives the creation of a productive society that is more aware of environmental values and social justice.

    Fifth: Recent Trends in Environmental Entrepreneurship Studies

    Academic studies in recent years have shown growing interest in the links between entrepreneurship, environmental innovation, and sustainability, within a number of recent trends, such as:
    - Green Digitalization: This involves integrating digital technology to reduce the environmental footprint and improve operational efficiency.

- Green Finance: Investment funds and banks are increasingly paying attention to projects with a positive environmental impact (Sharma et al., 2023).
- Measuring environmental and social impact: through modern tools such as ESG (Environmental, Social, and Governance) reports, which have become part of transparency and governance standards in companies (Sullivan & Gouldson, 2021).

2.1 Statement of the Problem

Even though more and more people around the world are aware of environmental damage, climate change, and social inequality, traditional market systems still put short-term economic gains ahead of long-term sustainability. There are some possible solutions, like green markets and sustainable entrepreneurship, but there is still a big gap in our understanding of how sustainable products, services, and business strategies can actually bring about social and environmental change on a large scale. A lot of the research that is out there doesn't connect theoretical models like the Triple Bottom Line, Sustainable Business Model Innovation, and Entrepreneurial Opportunity Theory with real-world business experiences. Also, there is still a lack of practical knowledge about how entrepreneurs find and take advantage of market opportunities that are good for the environment, and how these innovations can have an impact across different sectors. To speed up the global shift to a more inclusive, resilient, and sustainable economy, we need to fill this gap. However, even though there is growing interest in sustainable entrepreneurship, many businesses find it hard to balance impact and profit because of:

- Market Misalignment: Solutions don't always meet the needs of real people or society (Gast et al., 2022).
- Funding Gaps: Investors are hesitant to back impact ventures that are still in their early stages (Bocken & Geradts, 2021).
- Measurement Problems: There aren't any standard ways to measure the socio-environmental impact (Schaltegger et al., 2021).
- This study fills in these gaps by suggesting a useful framework for finding and growing mission-driven businesses.

3 Methodology

The descriptive approach was followed by reviewing the theoretical literature related to the subject of the study.

4 Finding

Sustainable Opportunities Entrepreneurs often find sustainable opportunities by spotting problems or inefficiencies in current systems (Hockerts, 2020). Too Good To Go, for instance, saw a huge gap in recovering food waste and created an app-based solution that could be used by many people. Market signals like consumer demand for green products, government incentives, and new technologies also help people see opportunities (George et al., 2021).

Market analysis is very important for testing assumptions, figuring out what customers want, and finding the best strategic position for a product. The "green premium" is a problem that many sustainable entrepreneurs face: making eco-friendly products costs more. However, studies show that more and more people, especially Millennials and Gen Z, are willing to pay more for products that are good for the environment (NielsenIQ, 2022).

Allbirds did a great job of positioning its products by combining eco-friendliness with simple design and comfort, and by being open about its supply chain. More and more, product development processes are using lifecycle assessment (LCA), stakeholder engagement, and circular design principles (Geissdoerfer et al., 2020).

Scaling and Measuring Impact: To grow sustainable businesses, you need both strategic partnerships and access to impact-driven finance. Social impact investors, green venture capital, and crowdfunding sites have become very important. For example, Ecotricity grew by using community investment and government feed-in tariffs for renewable energy.

It's still hard to measure impact. People often use frameworks like B Impact Assessment, SDG alignment, and Environmental, Social, and Governance (ESG) metrics, but they differ in how strict and comparable they are. There is a growing need for standard metrics to make sure that things are clear and accountable.

Scientists have yet to find a definitive answer to the question of why the Earth's temperature has risen over the past decade: is it global warming? Is it solar winds? Is there no abnormal warming? However, it is clear that the world urgently needs to reduce pollutants in all their forms, whether in water, air, or soil, to preserve the health and sustainability of the planet's inhabitants (Schaltegger & Wagner, 2022).

5 Discussion

The results show how important it is to have a supportive environment for long-term business success. Entrepreneurs need to do more than just come up with new ideas for their own businesses; they also need to change the way things work in general. The scalability of sustainable solutions depends on how market forces, policy frameworks, and consumer behavior work together.

The move from linear business thinking to systems innovation is a big idea. This change means we need to rethink how we create value, deal with risk, and be strong. In addition, education and capacity building are important to give future business owners the cross-disciplinary skills they need to work in markets that are focused on sustainability.

Companies that embrace a culture of sustainability play a significant role in achieving sustainable development by contributing to environmental protection, improving social conditions, and promoting economic growth. Companies that embrace sustainability have a greater chance of achieving market success, as demand for products and services based on sustainability principles increases. Therefore, promoting a culture of sustainability through corporate social responsibility means integrating sustainability into all aspects of their operations, from decision-making to engagement with society and the environment. This includes adopting sustainable practices in production processes, providing a healthy and stimulating work environment for employees, and contributing to the social and environmental development of the local community.

6 Conclusion

Sustainable entrepreneurship has the power to change the world by solving global problems. Entrepreneurs can start systemic change by using green markets and making social and environmental goals a part of their core strategies. But to reach this potential, policymakers, investors, educators, and civil society must all work together. This study connects theory and practice by giving a structured way to find and grow mission-driven businesses. Future studies should look into how to measure impact in specific sectors and with digital tools.

To turn market gaps into mission-driven businesses, you need to take a broad approach that includes supportive entrepreneurial ecosystems, new business models, access to long-term financing, and policies that make it easier to start a business. Entrepreneurs can come up with new ways to solve important social and environmental problems by finding and studying sustainable business opportunities. To move the field of sustainable entrepreneurship forward and reach long-term sustainable development goals, more research and cooperation between stakeholders are needed.

Long-term studies of sustainable businesses, comparing policies, and creating frameworks for finding opportunities and measuring their effects in specific sectors should all be looked into in future research.

Public-private partnerships can have a greater impact than private sector voluntary social responsibility initiatives based on fundraising. Shifting from a donation-based model to strategic partnerships based on a clear vision and specific local needs is the best path to achieving sustainable development that meets community needs and enhances the shared benefits of all stakeholders.

7 Based on the Research Results, the Following Practical Suggestions Are Made for Important Stakeholders

For Business Owners:

- Use tools like LCA and circular design principles to make sure sustainability is built in from the start.
- Use digital tools to get customers involved, be open, and run your business more efficiently.
- Make stakeholder engagement a top priority and work with NGOs, schools, and government agencies (Bansal & DesJardine, 2020).

For people who make policy:

- Make tax breaks, subsidies, and green policy frameworks that are consistent and last a long time.

- Help incubators, accelerators, and funding programs that focus on sustainability.
- Give impact ventures tax breaks.
- Make it easier for government agencies to buy goods and services that are good for the environment (Hahn et al., 2022).

For Investors:

- Use ESG criteria and impact metrics to judge investment opportunities.
- Give blended finance tools to lower the risk of early-stage sustainable businesses.
- Instead of focusing on short-term profits, build long-term partnerships (Yunus et al., 2020).

For Schools and Teachers:

- Include systems thinking, sustainability, and entrepreneurship in your lessons.
- Encourage research and innovation challenges that cross disciplines and are focused on sustainability.
- Help green startups run by students and give them access to mentoring resources.

For People and Society:

- Ask for more openness and long-term use in goods and services.
- Support and speak up for green businesses in your area.
- Take part in campaigns to raise awareness and change people's behavior around sustainable consumptionrc (Elkington, 2020).

References

Bansal, P., & DesJardine, M. R. (2020). It's time for business sustainability. *Strategic Organization, 18*(1), 122–132. https://doi.org/10.1177/1476127019857512

Battilana, J., & Dorado, S. (2021). Creating hybrid organizations that will last. *Stanford Social Innovation Review, 19*(2), 45–52.

Bocken, N., & Geradts, T. (2021). Things that make it hard or easy to come up with new, sustainable business models. *Organization & Environment, 34*(3), 349–371. https://doi.org/10.1177/1086026620938506

Bocken, N. M. P., Short, S. W., Rana, P., & Evans, S. (2023). Examples of sustainable business models. *Journal of Cleaner Production, 341*, 130756.

Cohen, B., & Muñoz, P. (2021). Sustainable entrepreneurship research: Taking stock and looking ahead. *Business Strategy and the Environment, 30*(8), 3827–3840.

Elkington, J. (1998). *Cannibals with forks: The triple bottom line of 21st century business*. Capstone.

Elkington, J. (2020). *Green swans: The rise of regenerative capitalism is coming*. Press for Fast Company.

Gast, J., Gundolf, K., & Cesinger, B. (2022). The effects of eco-innovation on business performance when companies go green. *Technovation, 110*, 102382. https://doi.org/10.1016/j.technovation.2021.102382

Geissdoerfer, M., Savaget, P., Bocken, N., & Hultink, E. J. (2022). A look back at circular business models. *Journal of Cleaner Production, 277*, 123741. https://doi.org/10.1016/j.jclepro.2020.123741

Geissdoerfer, M., Vladimirova, D., & Evans, S. (2020). Sustainable business model innovation. *Journal of Cleaner Production, 247*, Article 119136.

George, G., Merrill, R. K., & Schillebeeckx, S. J. (2021). Digital sustainability and entrepreneurship. *Technological Forecasting and Social Change, 168*, Article 120740.

Hahn, R., Spieth, P., & Ince, I. (2022). A systematic review of innovation that is good for the environment. *Research Policy, 51*(1), 104114. https://doi.org/10.1016/j.respol.2021.104114

Hockerts, K. (2020). Entrepreneurial opportunity in social purpose ventures. *Journal of Business Venturing Insights, 13*, Article e00165.

IPCC. (2023). *2023 Synthesis Report on Climate Change*. Climate Change Panel of the United Nations.

Lewandowski, M. (2021). Designing the business models for circular economy—Towards the conceptual framework. *Sustainability, 13*(2), 885.

Mair, J., & Rathert, N. (2021). Let's talk about issues: How to move research on hybrid organizing forward. *Academy of Management Annals, 15*(1), 1–36. https://doi.org/10.5465/annals.2019.0142

NielsenIQ. (2022). *The sustainability imperative: How consumers are driving change*.

Niinimäki, K., & Thapa, D. (2023). Sustainable consumer behavior in the green marketplace: A systematic review. *Sustainability, 15*(3), 2110.

OECD. (2022). *Green markets and sustainable consumption: Policy options for OECD countries*. OECD Publishing.

Porter, M. E., & Kramer, M. R. (2019). Making value that everyone can use. *Harvard Business Review, 99*(1), 62–77.

Raworth, K. (2021). *Doughnut economics: Seven ways to think like a 21st-century economist* (2nd ed.). Chelsea Green Publishing.

Schaltegger, S., Hansen, E. G., & Lüdeke-Freund, F. (2021). A stakeholder theory view of business cases for sustainability. *Business Strategy and the Environment, 30*(2), 735–750. https://doi.org/10.1002/bse.2660

Schaltegger, S., & Wagner, M. (2022). *Managing the business case for sustainability*. Routledge.

Shane, S., & Venkataraman, S. (2000). The promise of entrepreneurship as a field of research. *Academy of Management Review, 25*(1), 217–226.

Stubbs, W. (2023). A look at sustainable entrepreneurship and a plan for future research. *Journal of Business Venturing, 38*(1), 106292. https://doi.org/10.1016/j.jbusvent.2022.106292

United Nations Framework Convention on Climate Change (UNFCCC). (2021). *Action for Climate Empowerment: Guidelines for accelerating solutions through education, training and public awareness*. https://unfccc.int/documents/306440

Yunus, M., Moingeon, B., & Lehmann-Ortega, L. (2020). Goals for social business and sustainable development. *Harvard Business Review, 98*(3), 131–139.

CHAPTER 3

Promoting Sustainable Performance Through Business Model Innovation and Green Financing: A Developing Country Perspective

Mugove Mashingaidze

Abstract The main purpose of the chapter is to investigate whether business model innovation has any effect on the sustainable performance of small and medium enterprises (SMEs) in developing countries. The chapter also explores the mediating role of green finance on the relationship between business model innovation and sustainable performance of SMEs. The research was guided by the positivist philosophy. Structured questionnaires were used to gather data from 319 SME owner/managers operating in Harare, Zimbabwe. After completing data collection, SmartPLS4 was used for confirming the study hypotheses. Based on the analysis, the results exhibited that business model innovation positively impact sustainable performance. The analysis also supported

M. Mashingaidze (✉)
Management Department of Business Management, BA ISAGO University, Gaborone, Botswana
e-mail: mugovemarshy@gmail.com

S. Trivedi et al. (eds.), *Green Ventures*, Sustainable Development Goals Series, https://doi.org/10.1007/978-981-95-6533-7_3

that green finance mediates the business model innovation and sustainable performance relationship. By providing insights into SMEs in the Zimbabwean context, this chapter enhances the prevailing knowledge on the connection among the study's three variables; business model innovation, green finance and sustainable performance. This analysis contributes to addressing SDG13 (Climate Action) by integrating green finance into the framework of business model innovation, thereby supporting efforts to combat climate change and mitigate its impacts. Additionally, the study also aligns with SDG9 (Industry, Innovation, and Infrastructure). The study underscores the importance of developing robust and resilient infrastructure, which is integral to advancing sustainable economic growth and fostering innovation in developing countries. Through these contributions, the study enriches the discourse on sustainability and management within the context of SMEs. Policy interventions and stakeholder engagement are essential to fully realize the potential of BMI in contributing to a sustainable future for SMEs in developing countries.

Keywords Business model innovation · Green finance · Sustainable Development Goal-13 · Sustainable performance · Small and Medium Enterprises · Developing country

1 Introduction

In the modern business environment, small and medium companies (SMEs) are crucial for fostering economic growth, generating employment, and promoting innovation, especially in developing nations (Mashoko, 2025). Nevertheless, despite their substantial contributions, SMEs frequently encounter obstacles that impede their ability to implement sustainable practices. This chapter examines the complex interplay between business model innovation (BMI), green finance (GF), and sustainable performance (SP) in the context of SMEs in Zimbabwe. This chapter enhances the existing knowledge on business management and sustainability while offering practical recommendations for policymakers, practitioners, and researchers seeking to promote a more sustainable future for SMEs in developing nations. Given the escalating pressure for sustainable growth, especially due to global climate change and environmental deterioration, SMEs must urgently innovate their business models. BMI serves as a strategy framework enabling entrepreneurial companies to adjust to changing market needs while tackling environmental issues. Consequently, the chapter elucidates how these enterprises might contribute to the United Nations Sustainable Development Goals (SDGs), namely SDG 9 (Industry, Innovation, and Infrastructure) and SDG 13 (Climate Action).

2 Background and Rationale

Small and medium enterprises (SMEs) are critical in many societies (Mashingaidze et al., 2024). According to Muller et al. (2017), In Europe, 99.8% of all non-financial enterprises are in the SME sector. In Zimbabwe, SMEs contribute significantly to poverty alleviation (Bomani et al., 2022), and economic development (Mashingaidze et al., 2021). Mapfumo and Sibindi (2025) note that 75% of businesses in Zimbabwe are classified as SMEs. Notwithstanding their critical role, SMEs present obstacles to the circular economy (Hasan et al., 2021) as their operational processes do not promote cleaner production practices (Cantú et al., 2021). Takacs et al. (2022) add that the environmental impact of one SME is minimal, but the collective effect of many SMEs, especially in developing nations, is extensive. SMEs are responsible for a significant share of green-house pollution (Van Veen, 2022). In the EU, SMEs contribute between 60 and 70% of manufacturing pollution (Hasan et al., 2021). In many developing nations, industrial pollution is also primarily linked to the activities of SMEs (Hasan et al., 2021). This highlights the potential for these enterprises to aid in the transition to circular economic models (Takacs et al., 2022). In this regard, Van Veen (2022), from a political economy standpoint argues for the provision of financial support to SMEs.

Research on sustainability issues of SMEs of SMEs is increasing in Africa. This has been attributed to the indispensable role played by SMEs in sustainable development (Van Veen, 2022). In response to growing pressure for sustainability, SMEs have innovated their business models to address different stakeholder concerns (Li & Wu, 2025). BMI is viewed as an important approach to sustainability in SMEs (Li & Wu, 2025). BMI enables SMEs to enhance their financial performance while improving social benefits (Alraja et al., 2022) and minimising negative ecological impacts (Huang & Ichikohji, 2023).

Previous studies have concluded that BMI can reduce waste, lower carbon emissions, and greater resource efficiency (Li & Wu, 2025; Snihur & Bocken, 2022). Latifi et al. (2021) argue that BMI does not always directly lead to improved performance outcomes. Guo et al. (2017) propose that investigating mediating influences could help enterprises successfully translate BMI into superior performance. This chapter takes the perspective that some factors may influence the direct relationship between BMI and SP, as other resource configurations may influence the relationship. An empirical study by Madhavan et al. (2022) in Thailand discovered no direct link between BMI and SP. This raises a critical question: *What mechanisms enable BMI to positively influence SP?*

There is a paucity of documented evidence on mediating mechanisms in this relationship. To close this gap, the chapter investigates the mediating role of GF on the link between BMI and SP. GF is increasingly viewed as a key factor for sustainability (Li & Wu, 2025). Hence, this chapter proposes that GF acts as a significant mediator in this relationship. In developing countries, GF facilitates green initiatives, and achievement of sustainability goals (Yan et al., 2022). It provides essential financial resources for SMEs in developing countries to adopt innovative business models allowing them to implement ecologically conservative efforts (Li & Wu, 2025).

Management literature notes that BMI and GF are driving factors for sustainability (Evans et al., 2017; Snihur & Bocken, 2022). However, this conclusion has been drawn from samples collected in developed countries, such as Singapore (Cheah et al., 2018), China (Deng & Zhang, 2023), and Europe (Li & Wu, 2025). This chapter aimed to address the current knowledge gap by investigating the influence of BMI on SP, using data from Zimbabwean SMEs. The choice of Zimbabwe was made after considering the volatile nature of the operating environment (Mashoko, 2025). From the strategic management and entrepreneurship perspective, this chapter adds knowledge on the mechanism of the link between BMI and sustainable performance in the context of developing countries. The specific chapter objectives include establishing (a) the influence of BMI on SP, (b) the impact of BMI on GF, (c) the influence of GF on SP, and (d) the mediating role of GF on the BMI-SP relationship.

3 Review of Literature

The concept of the BMI has gained significant research attention in recent years as an approach to enhance business resilience in a volatile marketing space. This literature review provides a synthesis of the theoretical framework to understand BMI, a review of the study's concepts and the development of the hypotheses.

3.1 Theoretical Framework

The study is informed by the Dynamic Capability View (DCV). Teece et al. (1997) stress that this theory builds on the Resource-Based View (RBV). Teece (2012) emphasises that dynamic capabilities represent an enterprise's capacity to "integrate, build, and reconfigure" its external and internal competencies and resources to prosper in ever-evolving environments. The DCV framework is cherished for understanding BMI, especially in developing countries. Teece (2018) adds that dynamic capabilities comprise three interconnected components: a firm must evaluate the effectiveness of its existing resources, sense and seize opportunities; and efficiently reconfigure themselves and integrate new resources. For Teece, dynamic capabilities condense the processes and characteristics needed for SMEs to survive in dynamic ecosystems. SMEs in developing countries navigate and thrive in environments characterised by rapid change. Adaptability and adjusting is crucial for performance (Zahra et al., 2022). In volatile environments, BMI is taken as a key dynamic capability, enabling SMEs to identify and anticipate new business opportunities, and enhancing their performance (Girod & Whittington, 2017). In developing countries, where economic, social, and environmental conditions always shift dramatically, enterprise operations must be agile (Zahra et al., 2022). This adaptability is critical for innovating business models that align with sustainable business practices. More so, SMEs in developing countries are faced with resource constraints. Hence, the DCV highlights the importance of reconfiguring SME's few resources to create value. SMEs may leverage green financing to access financial resources to operationalise innovative ideas. This also allows them to realign their resource base to-wards more sustainable operations (Darmani et al., 2017). The DCV framework provides an understanding of the needed capabilities to effectively address emerging sustainability issues in a dynamic environment (Bocken & Geradts, 2022).

3.2 Conceptual Review

This sections offers a conceptual review of three variables of the study, namely, BMI, green finance, SDG-13, and sustainable performance.

Business Model Innovation

The management discipline is progressively integrating sustainable development into its established frameworks (Evans et al., 2017). BMI is an emerging mechanism for embedding sustainability in business management practices (Evans et al., 2017). There is substantial vagueness and contradiction surrounding the BMI concept (Foss & Saebi, 2018). This has led to varied explanatory perspectives and interpretations (Sarioguz & Miser, 2025). Accordingly, scholars have not agreed on the conceptualisation of BMI (Ammar & Chereau, 2018). According to Evans et al. (2017), the lack of theoretical agreement reflects the limited empirical research on BMI. Building on Wirtz et al. (2016, p. 23), this chapter defines BMI as "the design process for developing a relatively new business model in the market, along with changes to the value proposition and/or value constellation, intended to create or maintain a sustainable competitive ad-vantage." This definition emphasises that BMI incorporates a series of deliberate actions by entrepreneurs to adapt the architecture of the business model (Foss & Saebi, 2017).

Various internal and external can stimulate BMI activities. Externally, environmental challenges and changes are critical external drivers that trigger BMI, particularly in developing countries facing sustainability pressures (Laudien & Daxböck, 2017). Additionally, internal factors, such as organizational capabilities, have also fueled the innovation of business models (Ghezzi & Cavallo, 2020). Thus, BMI is often viewed as a necessary response to environmental changes, disruptions, and discontinuities. BMI commands a crucial role in promoting sustainability initiatives (Mashingaidze et al., 2024). For SMEs, enhancing sustainability typically involves adapting and innovating in response to environmental changes (Evans et al., 2017). SMEs' capacity to innovate in sustainability is essential (Adams et al., 2012). Accordingly, BMI is increasingly recognized as a viable approach to embed sustainability within business innovative practices (Ghezzi & Cavallo, 2020).

Green finance

The conceptualisation of GF remains unclear as there remains no consensus (Zhang et al., 2019). Appiah-Kubi et al. (2024) view GF as bankrolling for investments that deliver ecological benefits aiming at enhancing sustainable development. Liu et al. (2023) regard GF as a financial framework that integrates environmental considerations into lending decisions, intended to promote responsible investments. The "finance" component reflects how financial resources are allocated in the financial system (Berensmann & Lindenberg, 2016) while the "green" component requires that financial resources support environmental causes, particularly climate change mitigation (Volz, 2018). The benefits of investments include improved energy efficiency, reduction in all forms of pollution, minimising greenhouse gas emissions, and addressing climate change impacts. GF has become an important mechanism for enhancing global efforts to adapt to climate change (Carè & Weber, 2023). GF includes financial investments intended to increase resilience to climate change, lowering greenhouse gas emissions while transitioning to smart climate economies (Li & Wu, 2025). Thus, GF is vital in overcoming funding obstacles to climate goals (Calvet et al., 2022) and addressing urgent ecological challenges (Thapliyal et al., 2025). Additionally, GF is important in attracting private sector, particularly SMEs, investments in eco-friendly projects as it helps mobilise financial resources for sustainable development (Carè & Weber, 2023; Ma et al., 2023). In developing countries like Zimbabwe, SMEs require GF to tackle imminent issues such as industrial pollution (Mubonderi, 2023). In the absence of GF, the achievement of SDG-13 may be compromised (Ghosh et al., 2024). Consequently, there is growing policy interest in providing GF for private-sector players.

Sustainable Development Goal-13

SDGs have set the 2030 agenda to address multiple challenges to ensure wellbeing, environmental protection, and consequently economic prosperity (Nygaard et al., 2022). SDGs provide a multidimensional and holistic approach to growth and development. SDG 13 underscores the urgent need for global action in combating climate change and its impacts (Biglari et al., 2022). Climate change is a global change in weather patterns (Arora & Mishra, 2023).The SDG 13 has five specific sub-goals. These targets include (Arora & Mishra, 2023):

a. Solidifying resilience and adaptive abilities to climate-related threats.
b. Incorporating climate change strategies into domestic policies and measures.

c. Enhancing knowledge, consciousness, and institutional and human capacity on climate change adaptation, mitigation, and reduction of impact
d. Organising valuable resources to assist developing countries adapt to climate change.
e. Upholding mechanisms to improve capacity for effective management and planning associated with climate change.

Despite resource scarcity in SMEs in developing countries (Mubonderi, 2023), SME's are called to reflect on natural resources, and reconfigure their capabilities to execute successful climate action strategies (Nygaard et al., 2022). They can leverage dynamic capabilities to identify innovative approaches to minimise their carbon footprints, thereby contributing to climate resilience and adaptive capacity. SMEs need to adopt sustainable practices, using local natural resources to promote community resilience to climate impacts. The training programs by regulatory bodies enhance SMEs' understanding of climate change risks and mitigation strategies. GF is also critical in facilitating climate action programs, enabling the transition to a circular economy (Carè & Weber, 2023). The mobilisation of private sector investments towards environmentally friendly initiatives is critical for accomplishing the goals delineated in SDG 13.

Sustainable performance (SP)

The business management field has witnessed innumerable research interests in SP. According to Thongpoon et al. (2011), SP measures the extent to which entrepreneurs can maintain both social and economic performance over the long term. Various dimensions have been employed to measure firm SP (Piwowar-Sulej & Iqbal, 2023). Some studies have adopted subjective and objective dimensions (Mabenge et al., 2020; Mashingaidze et al., 2024). Even though SMEs can implement sustainable practices, they are not knowledgeable about capturing their long-term performance impact (Madhavan et al., 2022). Recently researchers have used the 'environmental', 'economic', and 'social' dimensions in assessing SP (Damtoft et al., 2025; Madhavan et al., 2022; Shoaib et al., 2022). Anchored on the SDG-13, the chapter underscores the extent to which SMEs are performing in achieving the SDG-13's five targets (Osei et al., 2025).

3.3 Research Hypotheses

This literature review synthesizes current and research on BMI, green finance, and sustainable performance.

Business Model Innovation and Sustainable Prformance

BMI is a valuable source of performance (Mashingaidze et al., 2024). The positive impact of BMI on performance is well established (Claus et al., 2019; Kraus et al., 2020). Innovative changes in the traditional business models provide fundamental approaches for sustainability (Evans et al., 2017). In Singapore, using retail and hospitality firms, Cheah et al. (2018) established that BMI is critical in promoting an enterprise's ability to address the current environmental issues while enhancing its adaptive capacity for SMEs. Using a sample of manufacturing SMEs from Zimbabwe, Mashingaidze et al. (2024) confirmed the positive impact of BMI on SP. Hence, the study hypothesised that:

H_1: BMI positively influences SP.

Business Model Innovation and Green Finance

The integration of BMI with GF is increasingly recognized as indispensable for driving sustainability in small businesses (Li & Wu, 2025). Innovative business models can enable access to GF and promote sustainable practices. By innovating traditional business models, SMEs are capable of attracting green funding (Huang & Ichikohji, 2023). Studies have revealed that adapting the business model to address sustainability issues can attract financial investments (Huang & Ichikohji, 2023; Snihur & Bocken, 2022). It is, therefore, proposed that

H_2: BMI positively impacts GF.

Green Finance and Sustainable Performance

Empirical evidence highlights the critical role of GF in driving developing nations toward sustainable growth (Kwilinski et al., 2023). In China, Ma et al. (2023) found that green-financed firms displayed markedly enhanced ecological and societal performance. Similarly, Deng and Zhang (2023) concluded that robust GF enhances ESG performance. In Pakistan, Qadri et al. (2023) discovered an increase in ecological sustainability as a result of GF. Moxey et al. (2021) confirmed the long-term relationships between GF and SP among UK firms. Several researchers (Lee, 2020; Tolliver et al., 2021; Umar & Safi, 2023) confirmed a positive connection between GF and SP. Given these conclusions, the following is put forward:

> *H3: GF positively influences SP.*

Mediating Role of Green Finance on BMI and SP Relationship

Madhavan et al. (2022) study of the marine food industry in Thailand did not validate the direct relationship between BMI and SP. The study by Yan et al. (2022) confirmed the facilitating role of GF on the link between FinTech adoption and SP in the banking industry. Using manufacturing firms from Pakistan, Shabaan et al. (2023) established that GF mediates the influence of DCs on SP. Given the scholarly proven mediating role of GF and the fact that BMI is considered a dynamic capability in this study, the following hypothesis is made:

> *H4: Green financemediates the effect of BMI on sustainableperformance.*

4 Research Methodology

The study has two main objectives; (a) examining the influence of BMI on SP of SMEs and (b) establishing the mediating influence of GF in the BMI and SP relationship. Given these objectives, the research was guided by the positivist ontology and followed the deductive approach. Hence, quantitative data were gathered to address the study's objectives. Additionally, the survey strategy was employed given its congruence with the research's philosophical assumption. Hence, this strategy allowed the author to translate the research objectives into questionnaires. The survey utilised a structured questionnaire with four sections: Section A: Demographic data; Section B: BMI (Clauss, 2017); Section C: GF (Bakry et al., 2023); and lastly Section D: SP (Mashingaidze et al., 2024). The items were modified to suit the present study and context. A five-point Likert scale: 1 (strongly disagree); 2 (disagree), 3 (undecided); 4 (agree); and 5 (strongly agree) was employed so that respondents show their level of agreement with the study items.

The study targeted all manufacturing SMEs in Harare, Zimbabwe. The study used manufacturing SMEs given their significant socio-economic contribution (Makanyeza et al., 2023). The inclusion criteria included: (a) SMEs that were legally registered with the Department of Small and Medium Enterprises; (b) independent enterprises, and (c) SMEs up-to-date with tax obligations. Using the criteria established by Krejcie and Morgan (1970), 384 respondents were randomly selected from a population of 3000 SME owners/managers. Only 323 of the 384 questionnaires were completed, however 319 questionnaires were usable in data analysis. The respondents' demographic profile is depicted in Table 1.

Of the 319 participants, 214 (67.7%) were men and 105 (33.3%) were women. More so, 174 (54.4%) were older than 46. Owners of the participating SMEs were 47.6% of the total respondents. Finally, findings indicate that 42.6% of participants held a bachelor's degree or higher while 48.3 percent had a secondary school leaving certificate.

Table 1 Sample profile ($n = 319$)

Characteristics	*Frequency*	*Percentage*
Gender		
Male	214	67.7
Female	105	33.3
Total	**319**	100
Age		
Less than 25	28	8.9
Between 26 and 35	70	22
Between 36 and 45	47	14.7
Between 46 and 55	118	37.1
More than 56 years	56	17.3
Total	**319**	**100**
Position		
Owner	152	47.6
Manager	167	52.4
Total	**319**	**100**
Educational level		
Matric	154	48.3
Undergraduate	136	42.6
Postgraduate	25	7.9
PhD	4	1.2
Total	**319**	**100**

Source Author

5 Analysis and Discussion

The study employed the PLS path modelling. This is a widely used data analysis method in business management research (Hair et al., 2019). The evaluation and reporting of the results were carried out in two phases.

Measurement Model Assessment

As illustrated in Table 2, the outer loadings were between 0.706 and 0.902. This signifies a strong connection between the observed variables and their associated latent constructs. The Cronbach's alpha indexes of the constructs were acceptable as they were above the threshold of 0.7 (Perera et al., 2022). Additionally, composite reliabilities ranged from 0.861 to 0.941. This implies that the measurements are suit-able and reliable for further analysis. All the AVE values exceeded the recommended threshold (0.5) (Hair et al., 2021). Hence, all the constructs demonstrated sufficient convergent validity. This affirms that the construct items effectively capture the underlying theoretical concepts.

Validity was determined by the heterotrait-monotrait (HTMT). In line with Henseler et al. (2015) the coefficients are suitable. All the values were below 0.90, showing that they satisfy the acceptable standard.

Table 3 illustrates that the square root of the AVE indicated a stronger correlation with the latent variables. Hence, all the measures have adequate discriminant validity. The study employed numerous measurement model fit indices, namely; goodness-of-fit index (GFI), $\chi 2$/degrees of freedom (DF), normed fit index (NFI), adjusted goodness-of-fit index (AGFI), Tucker-Lewis index (TLI), comparative fit index (CFI) and root mean square error of approximation (RMSEA). As shown in Table 4, the model successfully achieved a good fit ($\chi 2$/df-2.167; GFI-0.922; AGFI-0.973; NFI-0.916; TLI-0.928; CFI-0.943; RMSEA-0.061). Table 4 illustrates that all values surpassed the minimum threshold as recommended by Hair et al. (2021).

Table 2 Measurement model assessment

Construct	*MN*	*SD*	*Outer loading*	*Alpha Index*	*CR*	*AVE*
BMI						
B1: My business has introduced new products as a new value proposition	3.081	1.410	0.784	0.873	0.907	0.613
B2: My business has introduced new services as a new value proposition	4.203	1.274	0.759			
B3: We are focusing on a completely new market segment	3.910	1.378	0.735			
B4: We have started to collaborate with new business partners	4.012	1.072	0.902			
B5: We share new responsibilities with business partners	3.771	1.471	0.831			
B6: We aim at creating new revenue streams	3.081	1.036	0.738			
Green finance						
G1: We make provisions for green activities and projects	3.721	1.163	0.763	0.941	0.861	0.701
G2: Our business policy is to allocate funds for sustainable activities	3.619	1.021	0.802			
G3: Our business borrows money from institutions to support green projects	4.029	1.409	0.783			
G4: We have invested in green financial instruments such as green bonds	3.067	1.517	0.810			
G5: We actively seek financial partnerships	4.216	1.045	0.751			
G6 We track our firm's financial performance on our green investments regularly	3.983	1.352	0.721			
Sustainable Performance						

(continued)

Table 2 (continued)

Construct	*MN*	*SD*	*Outer loading*	*Alpha Index*	*CR*	*AVE*
SP1: Our organization has increased its sustainability goals and targets	3.971	1.071	0.732	0.783	0.941	0.579
SP2: We have expanded our sustainable product offerings	3.426	1.213	0.816			
SP3: Our staff are increasingly engaging in sustainability initiatives	3.874	1.417	0.729			
SP4: We have increasingly used renewable energy sources	4.091	1.208	0.706			
SP5: We have recorded a measurable reduction in our carbon footprint	3.612	1.081	0.870			

Source Author

Table 3 Discriminant validity

Latent variable	*Business model innovation*	*Green finance*	*Sustainable performance*
Business model innovation	**0.776**		
Green finance	0.313	**0.784**	
Sustainable performance	0.294	0.321	**0.740**

Note The square root of the AVE is indicated by entries that are bolded
Source Author

Hypotheses Testing

Structural Model

The study employed a bootstrapping method with confidence intervals, using 5,000 resamples to address the hypotheses (Hair et al., 2020). Table 5 illustrates the path coefficients for the three direct hypotheses.

Table 5 shows the findings for the three hypotheses: H1, H2, and H3. BMI positively influences SP ($\beta = 0.272$, $t = 4.256$, $p < 0.01$). Therefore,

Table 4 Measurement model-Hypotheses testing

Fit Indices	*Actual measurement*	*Recommended*	*Sources*
$\chi2/df$	2.167	$\leq$3.000	Hair et al. (2021)
GFI	0.922	>0.900	
AGFI	0.973	>0.900	
NFI	0.916	>0.900	
TLI	0.928	>0.900	
CFI	0.943	>0.900	
RMSEI	0.061	<0.080	

Source Author

Table 5 Direct effects

Hypotheses	*Construct*	*β value*	t-*value*	*Remark*
H_1	BMI→ SP	0.272***	4.256**	Supported
H_2	BMI→ GF	0.401***	5.092**	Supported
H_3	GF → SP	0.275***	3.736**	Supported

****p* < 0.01
Source Author

H1 was validated. These findings donate support for the past findings (Cheah et al., 2018; Evans et al., 2017; Kraus et al., 2020; Mashingaidze et al., 2024). These findings are also consistent with literature that posits that BMI is a potent driver of sustainability (Alraja et al., 2022). The study also found that BMI positively influences GF ($\beta = 0.401$, CR = 5.092, $p < 0.001$). Thus, H2 was confirmed. This suggests that the more effective BMIs, the more funds are likely to be obtained for sustainable business practices. The research finding corroborates the existing literature that innovating traditional business models can facilitate access to GF. The study findings also highlighted that GF and SP are positively related ($\beta = 0.272$, $t = 4.256$, $p < 0.01$). H3 was supported. The result suggests that the provision of GF positively influences the SP. The result is in line with existing literature, for example, in China (Deng & Zhang, 2023) and in Pakistan (Qadri et al., 2023).

Mediation Effect of Green Finance

Table 6 displays the results for the measurement model fit indices. Table 6 shows that the model successfully achieved good fit ($\chi2/df$-2.692;

Table 6 Measurement model-Mediation analysis

Fit Indices	*Actual measurement*	*Recommended*	*Sources*
χ2/df	2.692	≤3.000	Hair et al. (2021)
GFI	0.981	>0.900	
AGFI	0.971	>0.900	
NFI	0.934	>0.900	
TLI	0.968	>0.900	
CFI	0.947	>0.900	
RMSEI	0.059	<0.080	

Source Author

Table 7 Mediation effect of GF

Hypotheses	*Construct*	*Effect*	t-*value*	*Remark*
H_4	BMI→GF → SP	0.401***	2.855**	Supported

***p < 0.01
Source Author

GFI-0.981; AGFI-0.971; NFI-0.934; TLI-0.968; CFI-0.947; RMSEA-0.059). As illustrated in Table 7 all the values met the minimum threshold (Hair et al., 2021).

Results in Table 7 show a path coefficient of 0.401, which is significant at $p < 0.001$. This implies that GF partially mediates the BMI-SP relationship in developing countries. These findings mean that GF facilitates the positive impact of BMI on SP. These findings corroborate conclusions from past studies (Shabaan et al., 2023; Yan et al., 2022). These findings add to the BMI literature as well as the GF literature.

6 Implications of the Study

6.1 Policy Implications

Given the positive impact of BMI on SP, the Zimbabwean government could promote research and development programs focused on creating innovative solutions to environmental issues. This could include promoting technology transfer to expedite the adoption of environmentally friendly business practices. More so, the crucial role of GF, governments of developing countries must develop policies focusing on GF. For example, the Zimbabwean government might adopt policies designed to incentivize investments in ecologically friendly projects. This could involve offering tax incentives and/or low interest loans to entrepreneurs pursuing sustainable business endeavors. The government may also consider offering capacity building programs to promote awareness of GF options among entrepreneurs. Governments in developing countries need to encourage the integration of environmental, social, and governance (ESG) considerations into the funding of SMEs. This may help promote the funding of innovative ways of doing business among entrepreneurial ventures.

6.2 Theoretical Implications

Theoretically, the findings of the study help enhance knowledge on how SMEs achieve SP through BMI in manufacturing SMEs, particularly in developing countries. Thus, this work significantly adds to the sustainability literature in under-researched regions. Theoretically, this paper reveals one mechanism underlying BMI's influence on SP. While recent studies on SP are focused on large establishments, this research broadens the discourse on sustainability issues in the SME sector, underlining how BMI and GF can be successfully applied in the SME context. The chapter explores how BMI can motivate sustainable practices in under-resourced firms, validating that innovation is not limited to larger establishments.

6.3 Practical Implications

Against the backdrop of limited financial resources, the study considered GF as a mechanism by which SMEs can enhance their SP. Practically, the study demonstrates that making funds available for innovative business models positively influences the SP of SMEs. The study findings present practical implications to several stakeholders. SME owners and managers are urged to constantly innovate their business models to thrive in this competitive operating environment. Hence, they are encouraged to leverage digital technologies to innovate their business models. Governing bodies for SMEs are recommended to develop policies that enable access to financial resources for sustainable practices. Similarly, non-governmental organizations (NGOs) may provide financial resources for innovating BMIs to enhance SMEs' performance. More so, the financial sector needs to embrace GF practices to help align investment portfolios with SDG-13. This approach addresses the growing demand for ecologically responsible investment options from financiers.

6.4 *Implications for Research*

Despite the significant contributions of this chapter, some limitations pave the way for further studies. Structured questionnaires were used to gather data. Thus, study respondents were not allowed to express their own opinions. Hence, further studies may need to employ a mixed-method approach. Additionally, the investigation followed a cross-sectional design, with data gathered in a particular time frame. This limited the determination of a cause-and-effect relationship between study variables. Therefore, future investigations should adopt a longitudinal design to investigate the relationship between the study's variables. Lastly, the sample was drawn from the manufacturing SMEs in Zimbabwe. Further studies are encouraged on SMEs from other sectors, particularly in developing countries with resource constraints.

7 Conclusion

In today's dynamic and complex landscape, SMEs must improve their sustainable performance through BMI. While there is an expanding body of literature on BMI, its impact, especially in developing countries and the causal mechanisms involved remains largely unexamined (Latifi et al., 2021). This chapter introduces a framework that helps researchers and entrepreneurs understand how BMI influences SP through mediation. The findings contribute to the literature by theoretically and empirically demonstrating the role of GF in the BMI-SP relationship in the context of Zimbabwe, a developing country. As the operating environment continues to evolve, these results further advance BMI research by clarifying the connection between BMI and SP, enhancing our understanding of this phenomenon.

References

Adams, R., Jeanrenaud, S., Bessant, J., Denyer, D., & Overy, P. (2012). Innovating for Sustainability. A Guide for Executives. *Network for Business Sustainability.*

Alraja, M. N., Imran, R., Khashab, B. M., & Shah, M. (2022). Technological innovation, sustainable green practices and SMEs sustainable performance in times of crisis (COVID-19 pandemic). *Information Systems Frontiers, 24*(4), 1081–1105. https://doi.org/10.1007/s10796-022-10250-z

Ammar, O., & Chereau, P. (2018). Business model innovation from the strategic posture perspective: An exploration in manufacturing SMEs. *European Business Review, 30*(1), 38–65. https://doi.org/10.1108/EBR-09-2016-0119

Appiah-Kubi, E., Koranteng, F. O., Dura, C. C., Mihăilă, A. A., Drigă, I., & Preda, A. (2024). Green financing and sustainability reporting among SMEs: The role of pro-environmental behavior and digitization. *Journal of Cleaner Production, 478*, 143939.

Arora, N. K., & Mishra, I. (2023). Sustainable development goal 13: recent progress and challenges to climate action. *Environmental Sustainability, 6*(3), 297–301. https://doi.org/10.1007/s42398-023-00287-4

Bakry, W., Mallik, G., Nghiem, X. H., Sinha, A., & Vo, X. V. (2023). Is green finance really green? Examining the long-run relationship between green finance, renewable energy and environmental performance in developing countries. *Renewable Energy, 208*, 341–355. https://doi.org/10.1016/j.renene.2023.03.020

Berensmann, K., & Lindenberg, N. (2016). *Green finance: Actors, challenges and policy recommendations* (No. 23/2016). Briefing Paper.

Biglari, S., Beiglary, S., & Arthanari, T. (2022). Achieving sustainable development goals: Fact or Fiction? *Journal of Cleaner Production, 332*, Article 130032. https://doi.org/10.1016/j.jclepro.2021.130032

Bocken, N., & Geradts, T. (2022). Designing your circular business model. *Stanford Social Innovation Review, 20*(2), 34–39.

Bomani, M., Derera, E., & Mashingaidze, M. (2022). Urbanisation and SME growth in a developing economy: Implications for policy. *Corporate Governance and Organizational Behavior Review, 6*(2), 123–133. https://doi.org/10.22495/cgobrv6i2p12

Calvet, L., Gianfrate, G., & Uppal, R. (2022). The finance of climate change. *Journal of Corporate Finance, 73*, Article 102162. https://doi.org/10.1016/j.jcorpfin.2022.102162

Cantú, A., Aguiñaga, E., & Scheel, C. (2021). Learning from failure and success: The challenges for circular economy implementation in SMEs in an emerging economy. *Sustainability, 13*(3), 1529. https://doi.org/10.3390/su13031529

Carè, R., & Weber, O. (2023). How much finance is in climate finance? A bibliometric review, critiques, and future research directions. *Research in International Business and Finance, 64*, Article 101886. https://doi.org/10.1016/j.ribaf.2023.101886

Cheah, S., Ho, Y.-P., & Li, S. (2018). Business model innovation for sustainable performance in retail and hospitality industries. *Sustainability, 10*(11), 3952. https://doi.org/10.3390/su10113952

Clauss, T. (2017). Measuring business model innovation: conceptualization, scale development, and proof of performance. *R & d Management, 47*(3), 385–403. https://doi.org/10.1111/radm.12186

Clauss, T., Abebe, M., Tangpong, C., & Hock, M. (2019). Strategic agility, business model innovation, and firm performance: an empirical investigation. *IEEE transactions on engineering management, 68*(3), 767–784. https://doi.org/10.1109/TEM.2019.2910381

Damtoft, N. F., van Liempd, D., & Lueg, R. (2025). Sustainability performance measurement a framework for context-specific applications. *Journal of Global Responsibility, 16*(1), 162–201. https://doi.org/10.1108/JGR-05-2023-0082

Darmani, A., Niesten, E. M., & Hekkert, M. P. (2017). Characteristics of investors in on-shore wind power in Sweden. *Environmental Innovation and Societal Transitions, 24*, 67–82. https://doi.org/10.1016/j.eist.2016.10.005

Deng, W., & Zhang, Z. (2023). Environmental regulation intensity, green finance, and environmental sustainability: Empirical evidence from China based on spatial metrology. *Environmental Science and Pollution Research, 30*(24), 66228–66253. https://doi.org/10.1007/s11356-023-26946-x

Evans, S., Vladimirova, D., Holgado, M., Van Fossen, K., Yang, M., Silva, E. A., & Barlow, C. Y. (2017). Business model innovation for sustainability: Towards a unified perspective for creation of sustainable business models. *Business Strategy and the Environment, 26*(5), 597–608. https://doi.org/10.1002/bse.1939

Foss, N. J., & Saebi, T. (2017). Fifteen years of research on business model innovation: How far have we come, and where should we go? *Journal of Management, 43*(1), 200–227. https://doi.org/10.1177/0149206316675927

Foss, N. J., & Saebi, T. (2018). Business models and business model innovation: Between wicked and paradigmatic problems. *Long Range Planning, 51*(1), 9–21. https://doi.org/10.1016/j.lrp.2017.07.006

Ghezzi, A., & Cavallo, A. (2020). Agile business model innovation in digital entrepreneurship: Lean startup approaches. *Journal of Business Research, 110*, 519–537. https://doi.org/10.1016/j.jbusres.2018.06.013

Ghosh, S., Raut, R. D., Cheikhrouhou, N., Sinha, S., & Ray, A. (2024). Attaining sustainable develop-ment goals through embedding circular economy principles: Evidence from food processing small-and medium-sized enterprises in India. *Business Strategy and the Environment, 33*(3), 2193–2224. https://doi.org/10.1002/bse.3591

Thapliyal, K., Gupta, C., Jindal, P., & Mishra, A. K. (2025). Measuring the impact of green banking practices on banks' environmental performance and sources of green financing: A study on Indian banks. *Discover Sustainability, 6*(1), 169. https://doi.org/10.1007/s43621-024-00678-5

Girod, S. J., & Whittington, R. (2017). Reconfiguration, restructuring and firm performance: Dynamic capabilities and environmental dynamism. *Strategic Management Journal, 38*(5), 1121–1133. https://doi.org/10.1002/smj.2543

Guo, H., Tang, J., Su, Z., & Katz, J. A. (2017). Opportunity recognition and SME performance: The mediating effect of business model innovation. *R&d Management, 47*(3), 431–442. https://doi.org/10.1111/radm.12219

Hair, J. F., Risher, J. J., Sarstedt, M., & Ringle, C. M. (2019). When to use and how to report the results of PLS-SEM. *European business review, 31*(1), 2–24. https://doi.org/10.1108/EBR-11-2018-0203

Hair, J. F., Astrachan, C. B., Moisescu, O. I., Radomir, L., Sarstedt, M., Vaithilingam, S., & Ringle, C. M. (2021). Executing and interpreting applications of PLS-SEM: Updates for family business researchers. *Journal of Family Business Strategy, 12*(3), Article 100392. https://doi.org/10.1016/j.jfbs.2020.100392

Hair, J. F., Jr., Howard, M. C., & Nitzl, C. (2020). Assessing measurement model quality in PLS-SEM us-ing confirmatory composite analysis. *Journal of Business Research, 109*, 101–110. https://doi.org/10.1016/j.jbusres.2019.11.069

Hasan, M. N., Anastasiadis, S., & Spence, L. J. (2021). Polluting SMEs and the construction of their environmental behaviours: Evidence from Bangladesh. *Business Strategy & Development, 4*(2), 109–122. https://doi.org/10.1002/bsd2.132

Henseler, J., Ringle, C. M., & Sarstedt, M. (2015). A new criterion for assessing discriminant validity in variancebased structural equation modeling.*Journal of the academy of marketing science, 43*(1), 115–135. https://doi.org/10.1007/s11747-014-0403-8

Huang, W., & Ichikohji, T. (2023). A review and analysis of the business model innovation literature. *Heliyon, 9*(7), Article e17895. https://doi.org/10.1016/j.heliyon.2023.e17895

Kraus, S., Filser, M., Puumalainen, K., Kailer, N., & Thurner, S. (2020). Business model in-novation: A systematic literature review. *International Journal of Innovation and Technology Management, 17*(06), 2050043. https://doi.org/10.1142/S0219877020500431

Kwilinski, A., Lyulyov, O., & Pimonenko, T. (2023). Spillover effects of green finance on attaining sustainable development: Spatial Durbin model.*Computation, 11*(10), 199. https://doi.org/10.3390/computation11100199

Latifi, M. A., Nikou, S., & Bouwman, H. (2021). Business model innovation and firm performance: Exploring causal mechanisms in SMEs. *Technovation, 107*, Article 102274. https://doi.org/10.1016/j.technovation.2021.102274

Krejcie, R. V., & Morgan, D. W. (1970). Determining sample size for research activities.*Educational and Psychological Measurement, 30*(3), 607–610. https://doi.org/10.1177/001316447003000308

Laudien, S. M., & Daxböck, B. (2017). Understanding the lifecycle of service firm business models: A qualitative-empirical analysis. *R&D Management, 47*(3), 473–483. https://doi.org/10.1111/radm.12273

Lee, J. W. (2020). Green finance and sustainable development goals: The case of China. *Journal of Asian Finance Economics and Business, 7*(7), 577–586. https://doi.org/10.13106/jafeb.2020.vol7.no7.577

Liu, X., Zhao, T., & Li, R. (2023). Studying the green economic growth with clean energy and green finance: The role of financial policy. *Renewable Energy, 215*, Article 118971. https://doi.org/10.1016/j.renene.2023.118971

Li, W., & Wu, D. (2025). Sustainability through business model innovation and climate finance in developing countries. *Humanities and Social Sciences Communications, 12*(1), 1–8.

Mabenge, B. K., Ngorora-Madzimure, G. P. K., & Makanyeza, C. (2020). Dimensions of innovation and their effects on the performance of small and medium enterprises. *The Southern African Journal of Entrepreneurship and Small Business Management, 12*(1), 1–13.

Madhavan, M., Sharafuddin, M. A., & Chaichana, T. (2022). Impact of business model in-novation on sustainable performance of processed marine food product smes in Thailand-A PLS-SEM approach. *Sustainability, 14*(15), 9673. https://doi.org/10.3390/su14159673

Ma, M., Zhu, X., Liu, M., & Huang, X. (2023). Combining the role of green finance and environmental sustainability on green economic growth: Evidence from G-20 economies. *Renewable Energy, 207*, 128–136. https://doi.org/10.1016/j.renene.2023.02.046

Makanyeza, C., Mabenge, B. K., & Ngorora-Madzimure, G. P. K. (2023). Factors influencing small and medium enterprises' innovativeness: Evidence from manufacturing companies in Harare, Zimbabwe. *Global Business and Organizational Excellence, 42*(3), 10–23. https://doi.org/10.1002/joe.22180

Mapfumo, E., & Sibindi, A. B. (2025). The role of informal finance in financing micro-small-medium-enterprises in Zimbabwe. *Sustainable Finance and Insurance in Africa*, 87–103. https://doi.org/10.1007/978-3-031-865 16-9_6

Mashingaidze, M., Phiri, M., & Bomani, M. (2021). The influence of strategy formulation practices on the perceived financial performance of small and medium enterprises: The Zimbabwean experience. *The Southern African Journal of Entrepreneurship and Small Business Management, 13*(1), 11.

Mashingaidze, M., Kalayakgosi, S., & Govere, E. (2024). Entrepreneurial strategies for sustainable performance of small and medium enterprises in unprecedent times. In *Entrepreneurial strategies for the internationalization and digitalization of SMEs* (pp. 164–197). IGI Global. https://doi.org/10.4018/979-8-3693-3518-5.ch008

Mashoko, D. (2025). Disruptive frugal digital technology and small and medium enterprises' innovation performance in the food sector in Zimbabwe: A case of SMEs in Masvingo Urban. In *Disruptive frugal digital innovation in Africa* (pp. 223–243). Emerald Publishing Limited. https://doi.org/10.1108/978-1-83549-568-120251013

Moxey, A., Smyth, M. A., Taylor, E., & Williams, A. P. (2021). Barriers and opportunities facing the UK Peatland Code: A case-study of blended green finance. *Land Use Policy, 108*, Article 105594. https://doi.org/10.1016/j.landusepol.2021.105594

Mubonderi, J. (2023). Environmental protection and economic development in Zimbabwe. *Journal of Environmental and Public Health, 2023*(1), 3232851. https://doi.org/10.1155/2023/3232851

Muller, P., Ramada, P., Julius, J., Herr, D., Gagliardi, D., Marzocchi, C.,... & Wenger, J. (2017). Annual report on European SMEs 2016/2017: Focus on self-employment.

Nygaard, S., Kokholm, A. R., & Huulgaard, R. D. (2022). Incorporating the sustainable development goals in small-to medium-sized enterprises. *Journal of Urban Ecology, 8*(1), juac022. https://doi.org/10.1093/jue/juac022

Osei, A., Zhu, N., Borgi, H., & Cobbinah, J. (2025). Empowering sustainable production: Firm governance, finance strategies, and tech-innovation in advancing circular economy for SDG 12 in the US, China and Japan. *Sustainable Development.* https://doi.org/10.1002/sd.3390

Perera, C. H., Nayak, R., & Nguyen, L. V. T. (2022). Methodology and methods. In *Social media marketing and customer-based brand equity for higher educational institutions: Case of Vietnam and Sri Lanka* (pp. 137–168). Springer Nature Singapore. https://doi.org/10.1007/978-981-19-5017-9_4

Piwowar-Sulej, K., & Iqbal, Q. (2023). Leadership styles and sustainable performance: A systematic literature review. *Journal of Cleaner Production, 382*, Article 134600. https://doi.org/10.1016/j.jclepro.2022.134600

Qadri, S. U., Shi, X., Rahman, S. U., Anees, A., Ali, M. S. E., Brancu, L., & Nayel, A. N. (2023). Green finance and foreign direct investment-environmental sustainability nexuses in emerging countries: New in-sights from the environmental Kuznets curve. *Frontiers in Environmental Science, 11*, 1074713. https://doi.org/10.3389/fenvs.2023.1074713

Sarioguz, O., & Miser, E. (2025). *AI-powered business model innovation: Analyzing the implications of generative AI on value creation, operational efficiency, and market dynamics.*

Shabaan, N., Afza, T., & Ehsan, R. Q. D. S. (2023). *Impact of green dynamic capabilities on sustainable development: Mediating role of green financing.*

Shoaib, M., Nawal, A., Zámečník, R., Korsakienė, R., & Rehman, A. U. (2022). Go green! Measuring the factors that influence sustainable performance. *Journal of Cleaner Production, 366*, Article 132959. https://doi.org/10.1016/j.jclepro.2022.132959

Snihur, Y., & Bocken, N. (2022). A call for action: The impact of business model innovation on business ecosystems, society and planet. *Long Range Planning, 55*(6), Article 102182. https://doi.org/10.1016/j.lrp.2022.102182

Takacs, F., Brunner, D., & Frankenberger, K. (2022). Barriers to a circular economy in small-and medium-sized enterprises and their integration in a sustainable strategic management framework. *Journal of Cleaner Production, 362*, 132227. https://doi.org/10.1016/j.jclepro.2022.132227

Teece, D. J. (2012). Next-generation competition: New concepts for understanding how in-novation shapes competition and policy in the digital economy. *Journal of Law, Economics & Policy, 9*, 97.

Teece, D. J. (2018). Business models and dynamic capabilities. *Long Range Planning, 51*(1), 40–49. https://doi.org/10.1016/j.lrp.2017.06.007

Teece, D. J., Pisano, G., & Shuen, A. (1997). Dynamic capabilities and strategic manage-ment. *Strategic Management Journal, 18*(7), 509–533. https://doi.org/10.1002/(SICI)1097-0266(199708)18:7%3c509

Thongpoon, S., Ahmad, N. H., & Yahya, S. (2011). Sustainable performance of Thai SMEs: Investigating the role of entrepreneurial competencies. *Asia Pacific Journal of Management & Entrepreneurship Research, 1*, 5–21.

Tolliver, C., Fujii, H., Keeley, A. R., & Managi, S. (2021). Green innovation and finance in Asia. *Asian Economic Policy Review, 16*(1), 67–87. https://doi.org/10.1111/aepr.12320

Umar, M., & Safi, A. (2023). Do green finance and innovation matter for environmental protection? A case of OECD economies. *Energy Economics, 119*, Article 106560. https://doi.org/10.1016/j.eneco.2023.106560

Van Veen, J. (2022). *Accelerating the transition to the circular economy-improving access to finance for circular economy projects.*

Volz, U. (2018). Fostering green finance for sustainable development in Asia. In *Routledge handbook of banking and finance in Asia* (pp. 488–504). Routledge. https://doi.org/10.4324/9781315543222-27

Wirtz, B. W., Göttel, V., & Daiser, P. (2016). Business model innovation: Development, concept and future research directions. *Journal of Business Models, 4*(1). https://doi.org/10.1016/j.lrp.2015.04.001

Yan, C., Siddik, A. B., Yong, L., Dong, Q., Zheng, G.-W., & Rahman, M. N. (2022). A two-staged SEM-artificial neural network approach to analyze the impact of FinTech adoption on the sustainability performance of banking firms: The mediating effect of green finance and innovation. *Systems, 10*(5), 148. https://doi.org/10.3390/systems10050148

Zahra, S. A., Petricevic, O., & Luo, Y. (2022). Toward an action-based view of dynamic capabilities for international business. *Journal of International Business Studies, 53*(4), 583–600. https://doi.org/10.1057/s41267-021-00487-2

Zhang, D., Zhang, Z., & Managi, S. (2019). A bibliometric analysis on green finance: Cur-rent status, development, and future directions. *Finance Research Letters, 29*, 425–430. https://doi.org/10.1016/j.frl.2019.02.003

PART II

Strategies for Integrating Sustainability in Entrepreneurial Ventures

CHAPTER 4

Sustainable Startups Through Green Entrepreneurial Migration

Amitab Bhattacharjee and Asghar Afshar Jahanshahi

Abstract Ventures established by green migrant entrepreneurs are community and environmental-focused, aiming to solve social problems, community needs, and local environmental challenges, while uplifting economically disadvantaged groups and contributing to the sustainable development goals (SDGs), especially SDG 7 (affordable and clean energy), SDG 12 (responsible consumption and production) and SDG 13 (climate action). Startups of green migrant entrepreneurs often address the social dimensions of sustainability by creating employment, supporting marginalized communities, and fostering inclusive practices. Despite challenges, green migrant entrepreneurs continue to demonstrate leadership in sustainable and climate-resilient ventures, which promotes low-carbon economic growth, a greener business landscape, quality of life, and environmental safety.

A. Bhattacharjee (✉)
School of Business, Lincoln University College, Petaling Jaya, Malaysia
e-mail: bhattacharjee.ar@gmail.com

A. A. Jahanshahi
IPADE Business School, Mexico City, Mexico

S. Trivedi et al. (eds.), *Green Ventures*, Sustainable Development Goals Series, https://doi.org/10.1007/978-981-95-6533-7_4

Keywords Climate action · Entrepreneurs · Emissions · Green business · Immigrants · Low-carbon economy · Sustainability · SDG-13

1 Introduction

A green entrepreneurial journey begins with socially responsible business initiatives, achieving success in one destination is then encouraged to develop and expand eco-friendly business initiatives in the same destination or foreign destination. When entrepreneurs start businesses activities through legal procedures in a country other than their homeland, it is generally treated as entrepreneurial migration. The entrepreneurial migration phenomenon describes that entrepreneurs always search for four major components, such as place, labor, resource, and knowledge while expecting higher profits. In different situations, entrepreneurs shut down the existing business in their homeland and then start over in another country (Mellett et al., 2018; Taylor & Foster, 2015). In both cases, entrepreneurial migration is indeed. Sometimes, individuals with entrepreneurial intentions move to foreign destinations and establish businesses to mitigate social problems and other necessities. Therefore, entrepreneurial migration is linked to knowledge migration, labor migration, and social needs (Graham & Pottie-Sherman, 2021). Generally, entrepreneurs with medium or large-size firms invest in foreign destinations for low-wage labor benefits, decreasing labor costs, which can increase marginal profits for investors. In contrast, small firm owners fully migrate to a foreign country for permanent establishment.

Green entrepreneurial migration happens when individuals with entrepreneurial mindset move across regions or countries to establish eco-friendly businesses. Business factors such as easy access to green investment capital, business-friendly government policies, and supportive eco-friendly business resources often encourage entrepreneurs as well as nascent entrepreneurs to migrate to another destination (Taylor & Foster, 2015; Zhang et al., 2025). Green entrepreneurs in under-developed regions may leave the existing destinations with limited resources, political instability, and difficulty in accessing climate-friendly investment capital, therefore relocating to another region where eco-friendly innovations are encouraged and easy access to green investment capital. At the same time, low-emission supply chain infrastructure has already developed for all sizes firms. Furthermore, globalization and hybrid technologies have played a prime role in facilitating entrepreneurial migration (Jahanshahi et al., 2021). Small to large firms can now easily access international markets and manage all necessary business activities across regional borders more efficiently than before.

In most cases, migrants with entrepreneurial intentions bring transformative knowledge, unique skills, and cultural vibes that enrich their host country's economy. Even though entrepreneurial migration indicates entrepreneurial investment in foreign countries (Beiwei et al., 2022), but its term is different than foreign direct investment (FDI). For instance, many Indian entrepreneurs have migrated to Canada and established businesses there. Sometimes, family members sponsor other family members who become entrepreneurs after immigrating. Additionally, some entrepreneurs migrate through formal startup visa programs to gain higher entrepreneurial facilities (Patterson & Edge, 2025). Attractive governmental policies designed for entrepreneurs as well as startup firms can also encourage a large number of entrepreneurs to migrate (Patterson & Edge, 2025). Businesses owned by migrant entrepreneurs have expanded job opportunities, economic growth, and cultural diversity in the host country. When entrepreneurs migrate, they bring with them not only innovative ideas but also valuable skills, international connections, and investment capital. These resources can promote economic activities, employment opportunities, and green innovation.

Following the sustainable development goal 13 (Climate Action) of the United Nations, many countries have been changing economic policies for entrepreneurs, encouraging green entrepreneurial phenomenon towards developing emission-free business activities and economic growth. In many developed nations, migrant entrepreneurs play a vital role in the creation of eco-friendly small and medium businesses (Bahrani & Arshadi Khamseh, 2020). They often identify eco-friendly business practices, niche markets, and unmet social needs, launching startups that produce necessity-based environmentally friendly products, provide services at affordable prices, and diversify the low-carbon economic ecosystem of the country (Bhattacharjee & Bansal, 2023). Thus, their presence can lead to increased healthy business competition, improved productivity, and the introduction of new business practices with low-emission prospects. Host countries that offer supportive immigration policies and startup incentives benefit by attracting global talent. These migrants contribute to tax revenues and may also invest in local communities. In the long term, their businesses can grow into large enterprises that boost exports and strengthen international trade relations. Conversely, the home countries of migrating entrepreneurs may experience a ***'brain drain,'*** losing some of their most innovative minds. However, such loss can be offset by the benefits of remittances, knowledge transfer and the eventual return of successful entrepreneurs who invest in their home regions (Akbar & Preston, 2023). Diaspora networks also serve as bridges for international collaboration and trade. Consequently, green entrepreneurial migration can drive low-carbon economic growth, green innovations, and global competitiveness. While it presents some challenges, particularly for women entrepreneurs as well as entrepreneurs from low-economic regions but the overall impact on the global economy tends to be positive when managed with balanced eco-friendly policies. Designing frameworks that encourage circular green entrepreneurial migration, and international cooperation can further enhance the low-carbon economic benefits for the economy, people, and society.

This chapter has two major objectives. The first objective is to explore the role of migrant entrepreneurs in advancing community well-being and environmental sustainability, with a focus on their contributions to sustainable development goals (SDG 7, 12 and 13). The second objective is to propose industrial emission control measures for green ventures that foster economic growth, expand employment opportunities and promote eco-friendly business practices. In this chapter, the authors describe green entrepreneurial migration, climate action, and dimensions of climate action for green business mechanisms after the first section. Then, the entrepreneurial pathways are explained with a graphical demonstration, which also provides knowledge about how entrepreneurs from different parts of the world may travel and migrate into cross-border regions to gain more entrepreneurial benefits through green investments. For improving emission measurement techniques in the manufacturing industry, this chapter suggests an effective carbon emission measurement technique for small and medium entrepreneurs. Moreover, the contribution of green entrepreneurial migration has been mentioned in detail with examples. The authors indicate the data collection procedure of the empirical case study included in this chapter. The empirical case studies are accordingly described to foster practical knowledge about green entrepreneurial migration and reducing environmental emissions around the world. Finally, the potential challenges of green entrepreneurial migration, and strategic implications are explained accordingly. Admittedly, the major contribution of this chapter would support SDG 7 (affordable and clean energy), SDG 12 (responsible consumption and production), and SDG 13 (climate action) of the United Nations to foster green business practices all over the world.

2 Climate Action

The term "*climate action*" is the 13th sustainable development goal (SDG)introduced by the United Nations. The core concept of this goal is to implement timely and effective action to protect global environmental ecosystems by reducing or diminishing climate change impacts worldwide. This concept vitalizes entrepreneurs in transforming green business mechanisms.

2.1 Dimensions of Climate Action

The phenomenon of SDG-13 (climate action) can be described in five different dimensions (see Fig. 1) such as green environment, resilience, green strategies, awareness, and green framework. The first dimension, the *Green Environment* dimension, indicates how to reduce or resolve emerging climate change impacts through adopting eco-friendly measures such as using emission-free resources for manufacturing or providing services. *Resilience*, the second dimension, depicts how to develop and adopt eco-friendly techniques and procedures to decrease environmental hazards and unexpected climate disasters around the world. The third dimension, *Green Strategies*, describes how to develop environmentally friendly strategies and how to implement them to ensure green environmental safety, improve eco-friendly business mechanisms, and foster low-carbon economic growth. Awareness, the fourth dimension, emphasizes the formulation of governmental policies, non-governmental policies and climate safety knowledge sharing at the industrial level and country level to ensure maximum environmental awareness among entrepreneurs, the general public and industrial policymakers. Green Framework, the fifth dimension, eradicates planning, organizing, and implementing green management systems in business and non-profit organizations to foster climate protection business/commercial activities.

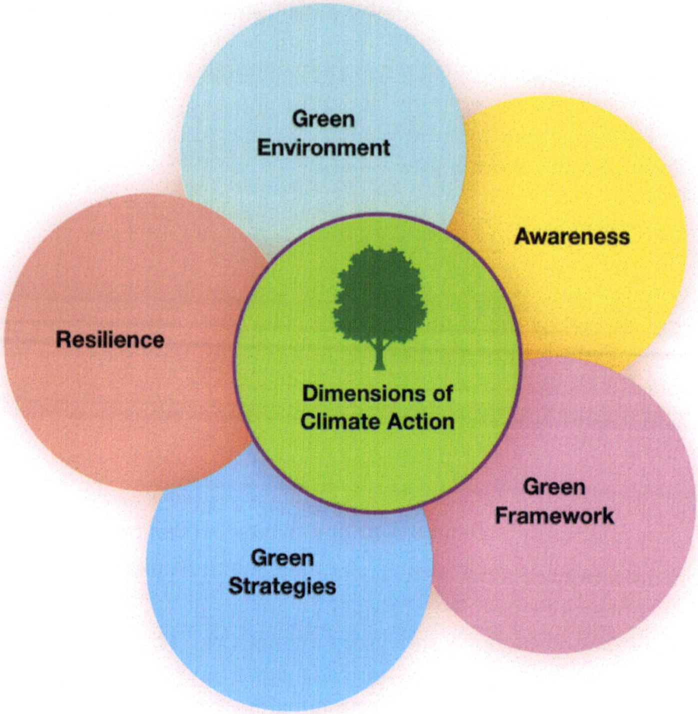

Fig. 1 Five dimensions of climate action (*Source* The Author's Elaboration)

3 Measurement Process of Industrial CO_2E

According to the recent studies conducted by (Bhattacharjee & Ghosh, 2024; Gui et al., 2019; Wong et al., 2020), this chapter proposes an effective and less-complicated carbon emission measuring process. This CO_2 emission measuring process has been contrived so that nascent entrepreneurs and green entrepreneurs can easily calculate accurate carbon emissions and take sufficient control over industrial emissions. Generally, the life cycle of a product has five different segments, each segment should be included to measure actual industrial carbon emissions. The five segments such as the procurement of raw materials, factory-based production systems, logistics systems (inbound and outbound), consumption of final products, and product disposal/recycling after use, can emit carbon footprints into the environment, which need to be measured to mitigate industrial emissions. Therefore, the industrial emission control (IEC) process has been proposed to determine the total potential emissions of an industrial product.

Let's assume the firm RKS produces product (M), the production system (PDS) of product (M) has energy-based resource inputs and non-energy-based resource inputs:

Where,

$(R) =$ *non energy direct raw materials and investment capital,* this can be indicated as $(r_p = r_{1p}, r_{2p}, \ldots., r_{Rp})$.

$(EN) =$ *energy items, e.g., electricity, gas, oil,* etc., this can be indicated as $(en_P = en_{1u}, en_{2u}, \ldots., en_{ENu})$.

Furthermore, the production system (PDS) of product (M) has value-grade outputs and non-value-grade outputs:

Where,

$(G) =$ *value grade outputs, e.g., finished goods*, this can be indicated as $(g_x = g_{1x}, g_{2x}, \ldots., g_{Gx})$.

$(E) =$ *Non value grade outputs e.g.,* CO_2, this can be indicated as $(e_y = e_{1y}, e_{2y}, \ldots., e_{Ey})$.

The above considerations can be used to form equation one:

$$PDS(r, en) = \{(r, en); (r, en, g, e) \rightarrow (g, e)\} \quad (1)$$

In this manufacturing process, slack variables are mentioned as $(\mathcal{K}^r_{r1}); (\mathcal{K}^{en}_{en1}); (\mathcal{K}^{en+}_{en1}); (\mathcal{K}^g_{g1}); (\mathcal{K}^e_{e1})$,

where,

$$(r1, en1, g1, e1 = 1, 2, \ldots\ldots, R, EN, G, E)$$

However, two slack variables, i.e., $(\mathcal{K}^{en}_{en1})$ is considered as a high-risk factor of climate emissions, while $(\mathcal{K}^{en+}_{en1})$ is considered as the emission-free renewable energy factor. Now, maximum inefficiency in R, EN, G, and E can be indicated as $(if^r_{r1}); (if^{en}_{en1}); (if^{en+}_{en1}); (if^g_{g1}); (if^e_{e1})$, where,

$$(r1, en1, g1, e1 = 1, 2, ..., R, EN, G, E)$$

So, the above allocation can be applied to form emission control Eq. 2, which is as follows:

$$IEC_M = \frac{\sum_{r1=1}^{R} \frac{\mathcal{K}_{r1}^{r}}{if_{r1}^{r}} + \sum_{en1=1}^{EN} \frac{\mathcal{K}_{en1}^{en} + \mathcal{K}_{en1}^{en+}}{if_{en1}^{en}} + \sum_{g1=1}^{G} \frac{\mathcal{K}_{g1}^{g}}{if_{g1}^{g}} + \sum_{e1=1}^{E} \frac{\mathcal{K}_{e1}^{e}}{if_{e1}^{e}}}{R + EN + G + E} \tag{2}$$

$$\text{As} \sum_{ie=1}^{IE} \lambda_{ie} = 1 \tag{3}$$

$$\lambda_{ie} \geq 0, ie = 1, 2, \ldots\ldots\ldots, IE \tag{4}$$

$$\sum_{ie=1}^{IE} \lambda_{ie} r_{r1ie} + \mathcal{K}_{r1}^{r} = r_{r1p}, r1 = 1, 2, \ldots., R \tag{5}$$

$$\sum_{ie=1}^{IE} \lambda_{ie} en_{en1ie} + \mathcal{K}_{en1}^{en} = en_{en1u}, en1 = 1, 2, \ldots., EN \tag{6}$$

$$\sum_{ie=1}^{IE} \lambda_{ie} g_{g1ie} + \mathcal{K}_{g1}^{g} = g_{g1x}, g1 = 1, 2, \ldots., G \tag{7}$$

$$\sum_{ie=1}^{IE} \lambda_{ie} e_{e1ie} + \mathcal{K}_{e1}^{e} = e_{e1y}, e1 = 1, 2, \ldots., E \tag{8}$$

Consequently, Eq. 9 shows the total emission for the product 'M',

$$\mathcal{K}_{r1}^{r}, \mathcal{K}_{g1}^{g} \geq 0; \mathcal{K}_{en1}^{en}, \mathcal{K}_{en1}^{en+} \geq 0; \mathcal{K}_{en1}^{en}, \mathcal{K}_{en1}^{en+} = 0; \mathcal{K}_{e1}^{e} \geq 0 \tag{9}$$

The actual Industrial Emission Control (IEC) score for the expected product 'M' can be obtained to detect real-time CO_2 emission by applying the above equations (from Eq. 1 to Eq. 9). The value more than zero $\mathcal{K}_{e1}^{e} \geq 0$ indicates the total industrial emissions for both inputs and outputs $\mathcal{K}_{r1}^{r}, \mathcal{K}_{g1}^{g} \geq 0$ of product 'M'. While emission-friendly energy amounts and renewable energy amounts can be determined by $\mathcal{K}_{en1}^{en}, \mathcal{K}_{en1}^{en+} \geq 0$.

If the emission-friendly energy amount is higher than the renewable energy amount and industrial emissions are high, then necessary measures should be taken to mitigate the emissions. On the other hand, if the energy utilization value equals to zero $\left(\mathcal{K}_{en1}^{en}, \mathcal{K}_{en1}^{en+} = 0\right)$, then the measured product will be considered as a zero-emission product(s).

This procedure can effectively evaluate the total emission of the product before or after production cycle, which would assist green entrepreneurs in adopting appropriate measures to reduce industrial emissions and climate change impacts.

4 What Is Green Entrepreneurial Migration?

When nascent entrepreneurs, or established entrepreneurs or individuals with entrepreneurial mindset move into foreign destinations through legal or irregular procedures and establish eco-friendly startups there to fulfill social or commercial needs, is called green entrepreneurial migration.

5 Entrepreneurial Migration Pathways

During the last two decades, the number of migrant entrepreneurs has increased, especially individuals with entrepreneurial intentions who have moved from low-income economic zones to high-income ones in pursuit of higher profits (Mitchell & Shannon, 2018). Figure 2 shows that nascent entrepreneurs or serial entrepreneurs migrate to new destinations through either legal migration or irregular migration. During legal or illegal migration processes, agents or individuals help them to complete the migration journey. Legal migration refers to entering to a foreign country through visa processing and other cross-border documentation. In contrast, irregular migration indicates when individuals or entrepreneurs enter a foreign country without proper documentation, visa, and other necessary permits. After moving abroad using any of those migration pathways, entrepreneurs strive to make entrepreneurial networking. Additionally, they register with governmental and community service institutions, which provide preliminary support to nascent or early-stage entrepreneurs. Individuals with entrepreneurial intentions receive necessary entrepreneurial training and documentation support for establishing new startups.

Once essential entrepreneurial networking and institutional connections have developed, they move to the entrepreneurial action stage. In

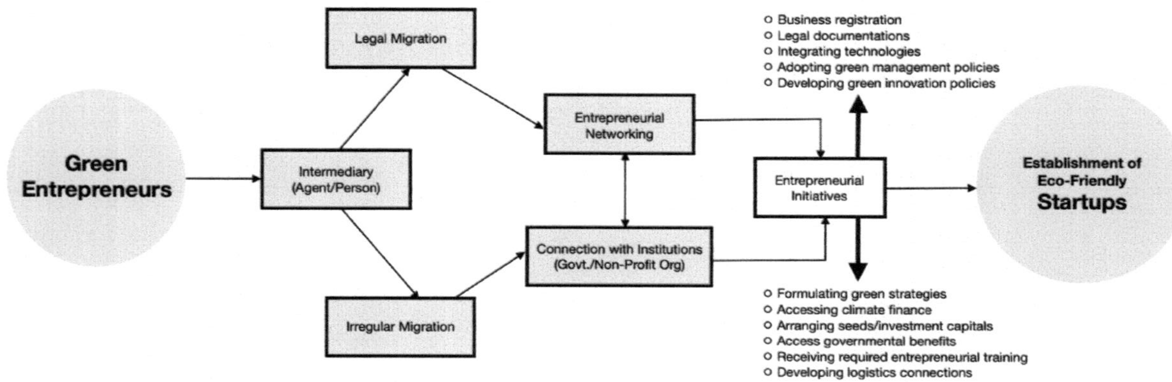

Fig. 2 Green entrepreneurial migration pathways toward the successful establishment of eco-friendly startups (*Source* The Author's Elaboration)

this stage, nascent entrepreneurs mostly perform all required prerequisite things such as business name registration, arranging green investment capitals or seeds capital, applying for climate finance to governmental institutions, eco-friendly business strategy formulation, seeking all required business practice permission, developing green business management policies, adopting low-emission technologies, making a deal with green suppliers, developing connections with supply chain networks, establishing connections with intermediary firms, integrating potential carbon emission evaluation and adopting green environmental measures. Generally, small firm entrepreneurs launch startups just after getting governmental permission and initial investment capital. In comparison, entrepreneurs with medium or large firms may require more time to launch startups than small firms. Migrant entrepreneurs, through those entrepreneurial actions, establish new startups abroad and begin low-carbon economic contributions.

6 Sustainable Benefits of Migrant Entrepreneurs

Global economic and industrial development growth is highly dependent on the entrepreneur's contribution. When individuals become entrepreneurs, they start fertilizing infrastructural development, technological development, and other correlated sectors (Peker & Winter, 2024). Similarly, migrant entrepreneurs also contribute to many sectors that eventually lead to sustainable development. In terms of green entrepreneurs, green migrant entrepreneurs have more contribution to society, people, the economy, and the green environment. Migrant entrepreneurs with eco-friendly phenomena can broadly support both climate action measures and low-carbon economic development (Bhattacharjee & Chakraborty, 2025). Figure 3 demonstrates that green entrepreneurs develop eco-friendly business practices, green innovation prospects, green technological development, eco-friendly infrastructural development, and implement zero-emission policies, which together improve green environmental safety, green environmental awareness among people, green social development, and green economic development.

Green migrant entrepreneurs literally make green investments. Therefore, they introduce eco-friendly, innovative industrial and technological solutions to perform business operations and offer green products to

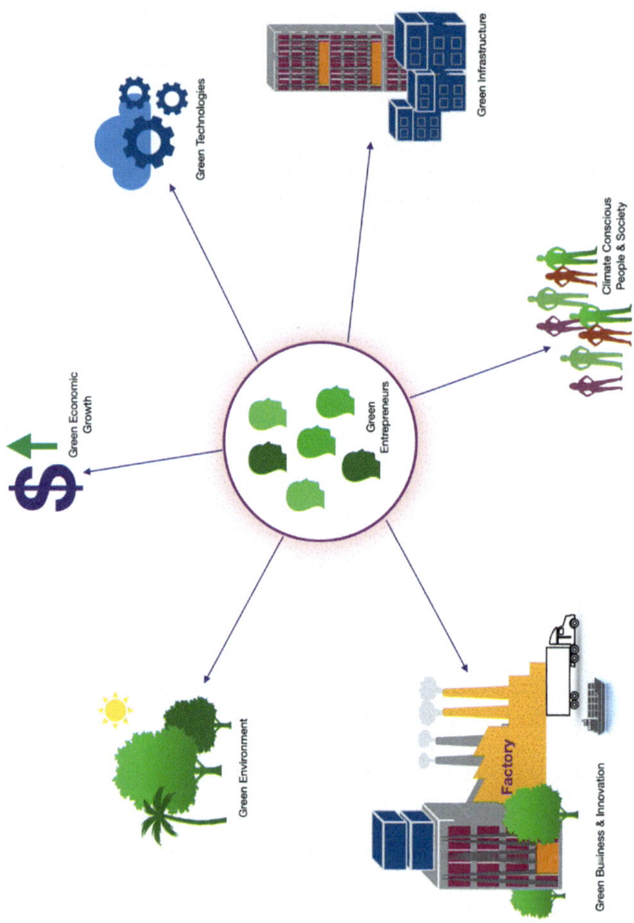

Fig. 3 Major sustainable benefits of eco-friendly development by green migrant entrepreneurs (*Source* The Author's Elaboration)

customers. Consequently, green products improve quality of life and even allow people to lead their lives in an emission-free social environment. Operating businesses with zero-emission policies can enhance long-term sustainability towards building a green economy in the world. Recent studies (Bhattacharjee et al., 2024; Ostrovsky & Picot, 2021) indicate that green entrepreneurs literally reduce the use of emission-oriented energy sources, which significantly decrease industrial emissions and other environmental hazards. Such progress can foster sustainable climate action benefits in the host country and around the world as well.

Furthermore, migrant entrepreneurs even contribute to creating employment and expanding cultural thoughts, which improves diversity and earning sources in society. Besides, green migrant entrepreneurs help to increase environmental awareness among people in the community, which greatly benefits minimizing environmental emissions in the long run.

7 Methodology

In this chapter, the authors discuss all sections with proper pictorial demonstration (where necessary), text explanations, and examples. Valid in-text citations are included for all secondary sources. However, the case study section includes empirical data that was collected from Canada. Two round surveys were conducted between October 2024 and March 2025. We designed our survey following the previous studies (Ostrovsky & Picot, 2021; Zhang et al., 2024). In the first round, potential respondents confirmed their availability for the second-round survey through an online simple questionnaire survey. This online survey was launched with just an invitation clarifying the survey motto (investigating green business practices by migrant entrepreneurs in Canada) and survey consent. The survey was conducted in English. This online survey (open for only migrant entrepreneurs) was launched and remained open for three weeks to receive initial feedback from potential participants. All participation in our survey was on a voluntary basis. However, in the second round, nine selected participants (based on business operating experience and business area) were interviewed to prepare the case study of green migrant entrepreneurs.

After the interviews, the authors followed a 'match and select' technique based on three generic entrepreneurial factors such as number of challenges, number of threats, and success rate. We used '0' as a success rate for an entrepreneur whose entrepreneurial journey ended up with startup liquidation. We used '1' as the success rate for each successful fiscal year. According to the selection procedure, we selected stories of four entrepreneurs and finally chose the best one. The successful migrant entrepreneur whose story was selected for our case study is operating businesses in Greektown (The Danforth area), Toronto. This area is known as a hub of migrant entrepreneurs in the greater Toronto city. The case study section demonstrates the vibrant and meaningful thoughts of green migrant entrepreneurs and their contribution to mitigating climate impacts in the future world.

8 Case Study

It is the story of Bob Harish, whose entrepreneurial journey started in his homeland, Ethiopia, a landlocked country. As an entrepreneur, Bob delivered vegetables to local restaurants and used to sell Agro items in the local wholesale market. After several years, he moved to another place in his country due to family issues. Even though he had a dream of completing graduation, but poor economic conditions made it difficult to continue studying even after grade-5. However, in the new place, he started working at a raw coffee-producing farm and gradually mastered making flavored raw coffee within a couple of years. At the same time, he was also preparing to establish a new startup, but luck did not favor him. His parents passed away within six months.

As a single child, he had to struggle a lot to repay large amounts of loans that were taken by Bob's father long before. Day by day, Bob became lonely. There was no reason left to return to the old place again. Later, he decided to move abroad. In the meantime, he suddenly met one of his father's friends, Janime, who now lives in Cuba. Bob then shared his intention to settle in a foreign country. Janime was a cunning and greedy person, which was unknown to Bob. A few days later, Bob again met Janime at a restaurant, when Janime realized that Bob was emotionally disturbed. Without any delay, Janime offered Bob to start a new business with him in Cuba. Janime said, 'Don't waste your time here, you can easily be an entrepreneur in Cuba. If you want, I can help you to process your visa and other things.' Following Janime's suggestion, Bob prepared everything for leaving the country. Before entering into the immigration checking, Bob came to know that he was going to Cuba as a tourist, not an entrepreneur. When he asked questions regarding this matter, Janime said that this is the procedure to get into Cuba, and after moving there, you can start your own startups. Bob had trusted Janime's words, after all, he was father's friend, but the thing is, 'all friends are not trustworthy and reliable'. However, both of them entered Cuba.

New hopes and many expectations were floating in Bob's eyes, but they did not sustain for a long while when Janime brought him to a cuarterias! Bob, with a tired body, asked, 'Are we gonna live here?'. Janime replied 'No other choice', and the next day, he took all the leftover dollars from Bob, saying that 'he would buy a shop for Bob to start a new business'. Unfortunately, Janime did not return even after two weeks. Someone in the slums told a similar story to Bob about Janime. Janime's fraud was exposed to Bob, but it was too late to rectify. No money, no food, and no job made his situation extremely hard to survive.

With a bit of luck, a stranger in the slums helped Bob to find a job at a restaurant. Time went on, now a tourist Bob became a refugee in Cuba. It was really difficult to move around with a refugee status. Once one and half years passed, Bob bravely took another initiative to move to Florida, where he met an Ethiopian person, a restaurant owner. He kept regular communication with the owner and got a job there. Two years later, the restaurant owner opened a new restaurant in Toronto, where Bob also moved with a server job. Moving into Canada, Bob felt a cultural touch in Toronto, and he then started working toward his actual entrepreneurial goal.

By three years, he came to know many Ethiopian people there, who were usually looking for Ethiopian coffee and foods. This opportunity magnified Bob's entrepreneurial intensity further. So, he started evaluating his strengths for being an entrepreneur in Canada. He learned SWOT analysis techniques from the restaurant owner to identify strengths, weaknesses, opportunities, and threats. Using the ***SWOT analysis***, he discovered some weaknesses, e.g., language barriers, business licensing, necessary investment funds, and intermediary networking, which must be resolved before diving into the real market. Even though the target customers are mostly Ethiopian but concentrating only on single-type customers would be considered a threat. Besides, many Ethiopians who were born in Canada are speaking in English. Moreover, English or French is required for other business communication as well. As Bob had no institutional education in English, he could not speak well in English. Therefore, he registered with a ***community service***

institution, where he started learning the English language, taking necessary entrepreneurial workshops for business networking, and sourcing governmental funds for entrepreneurship purposes. A couple of months later, Bob improved his communication ability in English. Additionally, he also registered with a ***business incubation center*** to get early-stage entrepreneurial support.

With the help of the incubation center, Bob registered his business and started a new startup with an eco-friendly food truck running only on weekends while working full-time at a restaurant during weekdays. Bob bought the EV module food truck to reduce environmental emissions. Many customers gathered around Bob's food truck to enjoy Ethiopian coffee, Ethiopian dishes, and other African snacks. Day by day, Bob's food truck became familiar in the town, and then he decided to leave his job to work with the food truck full-time. Bob was extremely surprised when he discussed this matter with the restaurant owner, his boss offered him to be a business partner. Bob realized his fortune was back. So, he started a partnership restaurant business with his boss and also traveled to different towns and areas with his food truck. Gradually, his financial situation started getting better and better.

Finally, Bob has opened two restaurants independently, which are now operating successfully. Considering environmental safety, Bob uses 100% eco-friendly and recyclable materials (eco-friendly food serving plates, food takeaway boxes, coffee cups, water cups, and so on) in both restaurants. More than 60% of the electricity used in his restaurant is sourced from ***renewable energy***. In addition, all vegetable wastes are used to produce house garden fertilizer that sells to customers, which increases extra revenues. Implementing green approaches significantly decreases the operating expenses of each restaurant. He even encourages his customers to use eco-friendly products. He has even formed a charity with a Church to support the local community. Now, Bob is 72 years old and a father of four children. His sons are operating both restaurants while Bob enjoys his time making flavourful Ethiopian coffee for his customers.

Practice Questions

a. What are the challenges Bob faced to become a successful migrant entrepreneur?
b. How did Bob overcome uncertainties throughout his entrepreneurial journey?

c. What are the eco-friendly measures implemented to reduce environmental emissions?
d. Why should everyone's suggestions not be taken for entrepreneurial decisions?
e. How do environmental approaches impact climate emissions?
f. How do environmental approaches impact operating profits?
g. How does Bob's entrepreneurial journey encourage other migrant entrepreneurs?
h. Do SWOT analysis to find your strengths, weaknesses, opportunities, and threats to be an entrepreneur?

9 Entrepreneurial Challenges

Establishing new startups in a foreign country is not always easy due to several underlying issues such as communication barriers, narrow target market, unexpected competition, accessing investment funds, complex regulations, and so on. These barriers sometimes create threats for nascent or early-stage entrepreneurs to operate a startup.

9.1 Anti-Alliance Practices

One of the most critical threats to launching a new startup abroad is anti-alliance monopolistic trading in the local market (Bhattacharjee & Ghosh, 2024; Gui et al., 2019). This practice by large or established firms increases entry barriers for small firms or early-stage startups. Anti-alliance monopolistic trading refers to a situation when large firms take market control through the acquisition of small firms or trade-in bulk quantity to reduce market share and disrupt the business operations of new startups.

9.2 Communication Barrier

In foreign countries, different languages cause difficulty in serving local community customers (Beiwei et al., 2022; Zhang et al., 2024). For example, an Ethiopian entrepreneur without an institutional English language foundation may face problems in speaking English or French. This kind of language barrier can be overcome, but it would take time and costs. Therefore, it is essential to learn a local foreign language before establishing any startup there.

9.3 Narrow Target Market

Many migrant entrepreneurs make mistakes when choosing target customers (Jahanshahi& Bhattacharjee, 2020). In the foreign region, targeting only ***single-type customers*** is somewhat risky if the number of people from the particular country is overestimated. For example, an entrepreneur counts the number of people from 'country YY' as 50K living in the 'area TT', but actually, there are only 30K people or below. Furthermore, any decrease in demand fora particular product among over-estimated target customers can lead to huge revenue loss, which might be difficult to recover. Hence, migrant entrepreneurs should avoid establishing new startups based on single community customers.

9.4 Unexpected Competition

Migrant entrepreneurs sometimes start businesses with the same products or similar business patterns in a competitive business area where many similar firms are already struggling to survive (Zhang et al., 2024). For instance, opening a halal grocery shop in an area where four halal grocery shops are already facing downward sales or heading to liquidation. Hence, migrant entrepreneurs should not establish new startups in a competitive business area to avoid unexpected market competition.

9.5 Arranging Seeds Capital

Starting a new startup in a foreign country is challenging due to higher investment capital necessity. Migrant entrepreneurs mostly arrange ***'seed capital'*** either from back home or family members living in the host country (Patterson & Edge, 2025). If migrant entrepreneurs can't collect investment funds from those sources, then they may try for private loans or governmental funds, which are somewhat difficult to manage without local support.

9.6 Shadow Partner

Merging with unknown persons or firms is one of the major risk factors for migrant entrepreneurs, which is called shadow partners (Bhattacharjee et al., 2019; Taylor & Foster, 2015). In a partnership business, partners should know each other properly to minimize fraudulent activities. For instance, in the case study, Bob lost his investment capital (long-term savings) because of trusting Janime as a business partner. In this situation, Janime is considered a shadow partner for Bob. As a result, considering a stranger as a business partner or trusting much for processing sensitive business documentation may lead to higher financial loss.

9.7 *Shifting Trade*

When cross-border trading of any particular materials or products (semi-processed or fully processed) has changed due to foreign affairs policies and changes in export/import tariffs, it impacts entrepreneurs related to import or export related businesses, which is called shifting trade uncertainty (Bhattacharjee et al., 2024; Wong et al., 2020). For instance, importing raw coffee from Mexico is less expensive than importing raw coffee from Spain for the host country firms. If the host country imposes restrictions or limitations to import raw coffee from Mexico, then firms using raw coffee (as the main production material) would struggle with higher production costs due to higher importing expenses. Therefore, entrepreneurs who migrate in 'Triple A-Grade' countries may sometimes face shifting trade uncertainty.

10 Strategic Directions

To be successful in the foreign region as an entrepreneur, migrant entrepreneurs require multifaceted strategic approaches that address educational, legal, financial, and social prospects. Barriers such as communication, legal documentation, arranging investment capital, managing working capital, and technological difficulties navigate entrepreneurs into unfamiliar business instability (Mitchell & Shannon, 2018). Strategic policies can play a crucial role in overcoming those challenges. To be a successful entrepreneur in a foreign country, migrant entrepreneurs should explore social problems or needs or any potentiality that would require to resolve introducing any product or services, for instance, Bob found that many Ethiopians looking for Ethiopian restaurants encouraged him to launch restaurants serving Ethiopian dishes and coffee. Migrant entrepreneurs should take ***governmental institutional support*** to simplify business registration, licensing, compliance processes, corporate taxes, and GST credits (Elo, 2025). In the high-income economic zones, green financing is available in most countries to support entrepreneurs, business incubators in such cases would be the first priority for root-planning of new startups in a foreign country (Falcão et al., 2024), which Bob followed to establish his first startup in Canada. Getting support from non-profit community centers can reduce financial and legal business document processing pressures. For instance, ***networking with non-profit community organizations*** can help migrant entrepreneurs to build trustworthy and reliable business channels through entrepreneurial workshops, training, and practical course works (Fang & Hartley, 2024). These organizations also provide support for sourcing '***seed funds***' from government sources.

Joining entrepreneurial workshops further helps to find potential investors, such as ***angel investors*** for starting a new startup. Mistakenly choosing fraud investors or business partners may lead to the unexpected liquidation of new startups. Hence, nascent entrepreneurs and existing entrepreneurs should carefully consider business partners or potential investors with proper clarification and documentation rather than unknown strangers. However, migrant entrepreneurs should connect with ***a business incubation center*** to ensure new startup benefits such as office space, utilities, product experimental labs, some technological equipment, and more (Bhattacharjee, 2025). These benefits would decrease operating expenses to carry on early-stage business operations. To reduce ***environmental emissions***, migrant entrepreneurs can adopt low-emission technologies, and renewable energy support with the help of governmental funds available in the host country. In addition, commercializing and introducing ***eco-friendly products*** to resolve social needs or social problems can be a profitable initiative for starting a startup in a foreign country. Furthermore, migrant entrepreneurs should avoid ***high tariffs-friendly products*** or materials for new startups in a foreign country, as there might be high chances of shifting high tariffs trading policies. Besides, portfolio investments (Bhattacharjee & Jahanshahi, 2021; Dheer & Kara, 2024) can be effective in reducing high tariff risks.

11 Policy Implications

This chapter broadly contributes to the successful implementation of climate action initiatives promoted by the United Nations, long-term zero carbon economic growth, and long-term environmental sustainability. Existing migrant entrepreneurs, nascent entrepreneurs, and SMEs will adopt the eco-friendly policies proposed in this chapter. While the chapter emphasizes migrant entrepreneurs, the insights are broadly relevant to all types of enterprises. For instance, the evidence suggests that profitability and entrepreneurial stability are generally higher in high-income regions due to sufficient infrastructure, greater availability of investment capital and more developed business networks. Hence, business policymakers in low-income and middle-income countries should take note of this disparity and work toward building sustainable business ecosystem such as business incubators, community organizations and accessible financing scopes. These improvements can help entrepreneurs to overcome structural disadvantages.

Industrial emissions-measuring processes explained by the authors can significantly improve green innovations and zero emissions industrial management. Therefore, entrepreneurs and business managers should consider these emissions measuring processes to control climate impacts in the future in an economical way. Even though migrant entrepreneurs are mainly focused on this chapter the whole context can provide benefits to all types of entrepreneurs and enterprises as well. There is a debate that the profit earning (PE) ratio is literally more positive in high-income economic regions compared to PE in low-income economic regions (Bolzani, 2020; Senthanaret al., 2021; Yang et al., 2024). However, it is certain that entrepreneurial stability in high-income zones is higher than in other zones (Zhu & Zhong, 2024). This benefits migrant entrepreneurs to become successful if business communication, business networking, and investment capital are sufficiently available. Therefore, migrant entrepreneurs, especially women entrepreneurs should connect with non-profit community organizations and governmental centers for entrepreneurs to ensure early-stage entrepreneurial support. Finally, bringing green innovation ideas and eco-friendly products to mitigate social needs would be highly appreciated to achieve sustainable development and ensure proper implementation of climate action initiatives as well. By integrating environmental priorities into entrepreneurial activities, government authorities can simultaneously enhance social welfare, reduce inequity and accelerate progress toward achieving the sustainable development goals (SDGs).

12 Scope for Further Studies and Limitations

This chapter discusses entrepreneurial migration and green migrant entrepreneurial initiatives in consideration of sustainable development based on one country/region. Generally, single case study-based research is intended for further study to increase generalizability in the migrant entrepreneurship domain. Hence, entrepreneurial researchers could study further about 'how to mitigate fraudulent practices in entrepreneurial migration to encourage trustworthy and reliable business practices?' or 'how to increase investment capital funds for nascent entrepreneurs in low-income countries?'. Moreover, green innovation researchers can conduct further research to find potential problems within the business ecosystem that need to be resolved to encourage environmentally conscious migrant entrepreneurs. Considering only one North American destination for migrant entrepreneurs is another limitation of this chapter's empirical methodology. So, further study should focus on multiple regions to provide more insights for migrant entrepreneurs.

13 Conclusion

Firms founded by green migrant entrepreneurs have made significant contributions to advancing sustainable development and climate action by bringing green innovations, resilience, and cross-cultural perspectives to global markets. Their contributions are particularly fostering inclusive economic growth, promoting environmental sustainability, and improving the quality of life in both host and home countries.

The most vibrant changes in business by green migrant entrepreneurs are the establishment of eco-friendly startups and the integration of emission-free business practices in traditional sectors. They often establish enterprises that focus on renewable energy, sustainable agriculture, green recycling, and low-emission industrial technologies, directly supporting sustainable development goals (SDGs), especially SDG 7 (affordable and clean energy), SDG 12 (responsible consumption and production) and SDG 13 (climate action). Additionally, green migrant entrepreneurs typically leverage their diverse backgrounds and transnational networks to introduce eco-friendly sustainable solutions and business models that might not be locally prevalent. This cross-border exchange of knowledge and resources accelerates green innovations and builds capacity in underdeveloped regions, aligning with global climate goals, eco-friendly business, and green society.

References

Akbar, M., & Preston, V. (2023). Entrepreneurial activities of Canadian Bangladeshi women in Toronto: A family perspective. *Journal of Ethnic and Migration Studies, 49*(11), 2817–2836. https://doi.org/10.1080/1369183X.2021.2010522

Bahrani, P., & Arshadi Khamseh, A. (2020). Competitive environment between green and non-green products considering disruption and alliance strategy. *Global Journal of Flexible Systems Management, 21*, 135–161. https://doi.org/10.1007/s40171-020-00234-w

Bhattacharjee, A. (2025). Green business incubation: Fostering green entrepreneurship and innovation. In *Promoting entrepreneurship and innovation through business incubation* (pp. 231–268). IGI Global. https://doi.org/10.4018/979-8-3693-4302-9.ch009

Bhattacharjee, A., & Bansal, V. (2023). Sustainable approaches of blockchain tech, artificial intelligence, and climate finance in the 4&5IR: Low emission technologies and economy. In *Perspectives on blockchain technology and responsible investing* (pp. 85–116). IGI Global. https://doi.org/10.4018/978-1-6684-8361-9.ch004

Bhattacharjee, A., & Chakraborty, S. (2025). Global supply chain networks: Roles of global partnerships and governance in supply chain performance. In *Global partnerships and governance of supply chain systems* (pp. 189–222). IGI Global Scientific Publishing. https://doi.org/10.4018/979-8-3693-6987-6.ch007

Bhattacharjee, A., & Ghosh, A. (2024). Sustainable green supply chain management for organizational performance and carbon reduction. In *Strategies for environmentally responsible supply chain and production management* (pp. 128–155). IGI Global. https://doi.org/10.4018/979-8-3693-0669-7.ch007

Bhattacharjee, A., & Jahanshahi, A. A. (2021). Artificial landscape strategy: A business growth recovery plan in the post pandemic world. *Academia Letters*, 2311. https://doi.org/10.20935/AL2311

Bhattacharjee, A., Jahanshahi, A. A., & Chakraborty, S. (2024). Unlocking the link between low emission supply chains, blockchain adoption, and financial success: The payoff of socially responsible practices in supply chains. *Business Strategy & Development, 7*(1), Article e341. https://doi.org/10.1002/bsd2.341

Bhattacharjee, A., Jahanshahi, A. A., Polas, R. H., Imtiaz, M., & Saboor, A. (2019). Customer care service management is moving forward to achieve sustainable customer retention in every industry. Does it play a role to increase brand rentention. *International Journal of Management, 8*(2), 88–97. https://doi.org/10.18488/journal.11.2019.82.88.97

Beiwei, L., Zhengliang, Y., & Hongtao, L. (2022). Factors influencing green entrepreneurship of returning migrant workers under the dual-carbon background. *Security and Communication Networks, 2022*(1), 7611810. https://doi.org/10.1155/2022/7611810

Bolzani, D. (2020). Thirty years of studies on migrant entrepreneurship: New opportunities for management scholars. In *Migrant entrepreneurship* (pp. 11–54). Emerald Publishing Limited. https://doi.org/10.1108/978-1-83867-491-520211003

Dheer, R. J., & Kara, A. (2024). Immigrants' entrepreneurial intentions: Acculturation-based socio-psychological lens. *International Entrepreneurship and Management Journal, 20*(4), 2979–2999. https://doi.org/10.1007/s11365-024-01003-2

Elo, M. (2025). The changing face of immigrant entrepreneurship: The case of Germany. In *Immigrant and refugee entrepreneurs* (pp. 67–96). Springer. https://doi.org/10.1007/978-3-031-84290-0_4

Falcão, R., Cruz, E., Costa Filho, M., & Elo, M. (2024). Researching hard-to-reach populations: Lessons learned from dispersed migrant communities. *International Journal of Sociology and Social Policy, 44*(1/2), 76–95. https://doi.org/10.1108/IJSSP-06-2023-0134

Fang, T., & Hartley, J. (2024). Immigrant entrepreneurship in rural and smaller communities in Canada: Recent trends, unique opportunities, and challenges. *Immigrant entrepreneurship: Challenges and opportunities* (pp. 151–171). IGI Global. https://doi.org/10.1007/978-3-031-69642-8_7

Graham, N., & Pottie-Sherman, Y. (2021). The experiences of immigrant entrepreneurs in a medium-sized Canadian city: The case of St. John's, Newfoundland and Labrador, Canada. *The Canadian Geographer/Le Géographecanadien, 65*(2), 184–196. https://doi.org/10.1111/cag.12627

Gui, F., Ren, S., Zhao, Y., Zhou, J., Xie, Z., Xu, C., & Zhu, F. (2019). Activity-based allocation and optimization for carbon footprint and cost in product lifecycle. *Journal of Cleaner Production, 236*, 117627. https://doi.org/10.1016/j.jclepro.2019.117627

Jahanshahi, A. A., & Bhattacharjee, A. (2020). Competitiveness improvement in public sector organizations: What they need? *Journal of Public Affairs, 20*(2), Article e2011. https://doi.org/10.1002/pa.2011

Jahanshahi, A. A., Bhattacharjee, A., & Maghsoudi, T. (2021). Internal capabilities as the source of achieving competitive advantage in small-sized businesses. *International Journal of Business Innovation and Research, 26*(2), 141–162. https://doi.org/10.1504/IJBIR.2021.118446

Mellett, S., Kelliher, F., & Harrington, D. (2018). Network-facilitated green innovation capability development in micro-firms. *Journal of Small Business and Enterprise Development, 25*(6), 1004–1024. https://doi.org/10.1108/JSBED-11-2017-0363

Mitchell, C. J., & Shannon, M. (2018). Establishing the routes to rural in-migrant proprietorship in a Canadian tourism region: A mobilities perspective. *Population, Space and Place, 24*(3), Article e2095. https://doi.org/10.1002/psp.2095

Ostrovsky, Y., & Picot, G. (2021). Innovation in immigrant-owned firms. *Small Business Economics, 57*(4), 1857–1874. https://doi.org/10.1007/s11187-020-00376-2

Patterson, M. L., & Edge, S. (2025). Exploring attention to justice, equity, diversity and inclusion in Canadian environmental non-profits: Implications for racialised migrants. *Local Environment, 30*(2), 1–16. https://doi.org/10.1080/13549839.2025.2467874

Peker, E., & Winter, E. (2024). Confronting or incorporating middle-class nation-building? Right-wing responses in the pan-Canadian context. *Journal of Ethnic and Migration Studies, 50*(7), 1696–1717. https://doi.org/10.1080/1369183X.2024.2315351

Senthanar, S., MacEachen, E., Premji, S., & Bigelow, P. (2021). Entrepreneurial experiences of Syrian refugee women in Canada: A feminist grounded qualitative study. *Small Business Economics, 57*(2), 835–847. https://doi.org/10.1007/s11187-020-00385-1

Taylor, A., & Foster, J. (2015). Migrant workers and the problem of social cohesion in Canada. *Journal of International Migration and Integration, 16*, 153–172. https://doi.org/10.1007/s12134-014-0323-y

Wong, C. Y., Wong, C. W., & Boon-itt, S. (2020). Effects of green supply chain integration and green innovation on environmental and cost performance. *International Journal of Production Research, 58*(15), 4589–4609. https://doi.org/10.1080/00207543.2020.1756510

Yang, Y., Lin, X., & Anderson, R. B. (2024). Entrepreneurship by indigenous people in Canada and Australia: Diverse modes and community implications. *International Journal of Entrepreneurial Behavior & Research, 30*(1), 90–109. https://doi.org/10.1108/IJEBR-01-2023-0085

Zhang, Q., Xu, H., Li, Y., & Wen, T. (2024). Understanding the embeddedness and CSR of small in-migration tourism entrepreneurs: The moderating role of the duration of residence. *Journal of China Tourism Research, 20*(2), 453–475. https://doi.org/10.1080/19388160.2023.2229001

Zhang, Y., Yasin, S. M., & Sun, L. (2025). The implications of urban-to-rural migration on rural development: A systematic literature review. *GeoJournal, 90*(3), 97. https://doi.org/10.1007/s10708-025-11336-2

Zhu, N., & Zhong, J. (2024). The impact of input in scientific research and experimental development on the survival of immigrant firms in Canada. *Journal of International Migration and Integration, 26*(1), 53–76. https://doi.org/10.1007/s12134-024-01181-6

CHAPTER 5

Drivers to Sustainable Entrepreneurial Orientation (SEO) Among Start-Ups in Emerging Economies

Mugove Mashingaidze

Abstract The ability of entrepreneurial start-ups to foster a sustainable entrepreneurship orientation (SEO) into their business practices and culture is yet to be fully explored in emerging countries. This chapter examines the influence of critical drivers of SEO in South African start-ups. Using empirical data from 220 manufacturing start-ups, structural equation modeling was employed to test the influence of three driving factors, namely individual factors, organisational factors, and contextual factors, on SEO. Results show that all three driving factors influence SEO. However, findings illustrate that contextual factors are the most influential drivers in influencing start-ups to engage in SEO. The chapter concludes that cultivating SEO is not solely a function of personal aspiration or corporate strategy; it necessitates a comprehensive approach that incorporates multiple elements affecting entrepreneurial conduct. This chapter

M. Mashingaidze (✉)
Management Department of Business Management, BA ISAGO University, Gaborone, Botswana
e-mail: mugovemarshy@gmail.com

S. Trivedi et al. (eds.), *Green Ventures*, Sustainable Development Goals Series, https://doi.org/10.1007/978-981-95-6533-7_5

enriches the literature on SEO in emerging economies. The chapter has significant implications for policy makers on the establishment of supportive regulatory frameworks, and incentives that encourage start-ups to adopt sustainable practices. The chapter illustrates how entrepreneurial orientation and sustainability can coexist, validating that start-ups can incorporate environmentally friendly practices into their business models. This contributes to the goal of promoting resource efficiency. This aligns with SDG-13.

Keywords Sustainable entrepreneurship orientation · Emerging countries · Individual factors · Organisational factors · Contextual factors · Sustainable Development Goals

1 Introduction

Entrepreneurship and sustainable development are widely acknowledged as synergistic elements in the contemporary global economy. Governments and organisations around are aggressively endorsing entrepreneurship as a means for economic advancement while concurrently pursuing sustainable development objectives, as illustrated by efforts like the United Nations Sustainable Development Goals (SDGs). This convergence underscores the significant problem of harmonising company objectives with community demands, a process further facilitated by frameworks such as the UN Global Compact, which seeks to align corporate strategies with society expectations. Historically, entrepreneurship has faced criticism for its contribution to worsening environmental and social problems, including climate change and human rights violations. A paradigm shift is occurring, acknowledging that entrepreneurship can effectively mitigate and potentially eradicate these negative effects. The discussion on entrepreneurship for sustainable development has intensified in recent years; yet, much of the current literature is still theoretical and conceptual. The purpose of the chapter is to investigate the factors influencing sustainable entrepreneurial orientation (SEO) in start-ups within emerging economies. This chapter analyses the variables that motivate entrepreneurs to adopt sustainability in their business practices. The author aims to elucidate the avenues that allow start-ups to manoeuvre the intricate relationship between entrepreneurship and sustainability.

2 Background and Rationale

Sustainability is regarded as the ability to meet present needs without endangering future generations' capacity to meet theirs (Dsilva et al., 2025). As the world contends with environmental issues, sustainable entrepreneurship has become indispensable for organisations and nations aiming to align economic goals with social and environmental issues. Entrepreneurship has been recognised for creating jobs (Mashingaidze et al., 2024a, 2024b) and driving economic growth (Bomani et al., 2022) while promoting creativity (Agarwal et al., 2020), and positive sustainability impacts (Foroozanfar et al., 2022). Researchers define sustainable entrepreneurship as an innovative market-oriented, personality driven approach that delivers economic and social performance outcomes by tapping into environmentally beneficial markets (Schaltegger & Wagner, 2011; Schaltegger et al., 2012). Sustainable entrepreneurship comprises business practices that harmonize social, environmental, and economic goals (Criado-Gomis et al., 2017).

Given the flexible entrepreneurial venture structures, they can quickly adapt and respond to emerging stakeholder needs (de Klerk et al., 2024). This entrepreneurial orientation challenges conventional business models by promoting open innovation (Scuotto et al., 2017), which positively influences sustainability (Horne, 2019). Haldar (2019) stresses that innovation driven entrepreneurship promotes sustainability through leadership that aligns with the principles of the triple bottom line (Alhaddi, 2015). Thus, through transforming entrepreneurial paradigms, start-ups can dynamically allocate resources to produce sustainable goods that address climate change (Haldar, 2019). In line with this, start-ups can adopt business models that support the United Nations (UN) SDGs.

The successful adoption of sustainable entrepreneurship depends on enterprises adopting a dual emphasis on economic goals and environmental goals. This is known as sustainable entrepreneurial orientation (SEO). SEO is the tendency of entrepreneurs to encourage sustainable development and environmental protection through their ventures (Wu et al., 2025). Thus, SEO combines the entrepreneurial cultures and sustainability orientation (Criado-Gomis et al., 2017), incorporating social aspects into business practices (Hernández-Perlines & Rung-Hoch, 2017; Mashingaidze et al., 2024a). In emerging African nations, sustainable entrepreneurship is yet to be fully adopted, especially in young entrepreneurial ventures. Aguirre (2024) claims that a significant gap in the literature is the inadequate understanding of the driving factors of SEO.

However, a wealth of research indicates that SEO is essential for achieving the SDGs (Liu et al., 2022). While various studies have explored the factors influencing SEO (Aguirre, 2024; Alfalih & Ragmoun, 2020), much of this work has been conducted in developed countries. There is a notable lack of focus on entrepreneurial start-ups, particularly within emerging African nations. Although some research addresses SEO among SMEs in developed markets, studies specifically examining the drivers of SEO in entrepreneurial ventures in emerging economies, particularly, South Africa, are limited. This chapter posits that understanding the factors influencing SEO is particularly relevant in African contexts, as it may provide more actionable insights than research solely on sustainable entrepreneurship practices. To address this knowledge gap, it is important to identify the factors that affect SEO among manufacturing start-ups in South Africa.

This chapter is aimed at advancing our understanding of sustainable entrepreneurship in alignment with SDG-13, emphasising the importance of climate action. By investigating the influence of three antecedents of SEO, this study contributes to practice, theory, and policy. The chapter is organised as follows: Sect. 3 literature review followed by Sect. 4 methodology. Section 5 presents findings and lastly, Sect. 7 covers conclusions and implications.

3 Review of Literature

3.1 Theoretical Framework

The study employs the dynamic Resource-Based View (RBV) model (Helfat et al., 2023; Teece, 2023) to establish how individual, contextual, and organizational factors influence SEO. Woode (2024) notes that this theory integrates two traditional theories, namely the RBV and the Dynamic Capability View (DCV). Li et al. (2023) stress that RBV emphasises resource heterogeneity while overlooking the dynamic perspective, important in developing and combining these valuable resources for enhanced performance (Barney et al., 2021). Thus, El Nemar et al. (2022) claims the RBV is limited in application due to its static nature. However, Li et al. (2023) note that the DCV theory helps to introduce a dynamic characteristic that demonstrates how resources can consequently lead to sustained advantages with time.

According to Barney et al. (2021), resource heterogeneity describes possessing a set of distinct resources that companies find difficult to replicate. Enterprises with such resources can better meet customer needs, enhancing their market position (Li et al., 2023). This heterogeneity can be either size advantages or first-mover advantages (Helfat et al., 2023). Size advantages pertain to the scale of resources a firm control while first-mover advantages refer to the ability to secure superior resources ahead of competitors (Nemar et al., 2022). This aligns with the chapter's focus on sustainable practices. Entrepreneurial start-ups can gain first-mover advantages through sustainable leadership. Furthermore, dynamic RBV posits that there are pathways for developing and reconfiguring resources, which helps maintain competitive advantages (Woode, 2024). The study highlights how start-ups can exploit unique internal and external resources that align with sustainable practices. Hence, the study adopts the dynamic RBV framework to explore how the three factors influence SEO as a means of achieving competitive advantage. This aligns well with the theoretical foundations of dynamic RBV.

3.2 Conceptual Review

Sustainable Development Goal 13 (SDG 13)

Sustainable Development Goal 13 (SDG 13) emphasizes the urgent need for climate action (Arora & Mishra, 2023). This is essentially linked to the SEO of start-ups in emerging economies. By fostering SEO, entrepreneurial start-ups can significantly contribute to mitigating climate change through innovative practices that prioritize environmental sustainability. The integration of SEO into business models not only enhances the resilience of these start-ups but also aligns them with global efforts to combat climate related challenges. In emerging markets, where resources may be limited, promoting SEO can empower start-ups to adopt eco-friendly technologies and practices, ultimately driving economic growth while addressing environmental concerns. Thus, by focusing on the drivers of SEO, such as individual, organizational, and contextual factors, this research underscores the potential of start-ups to play a pivotal role in advancing SDG 13 and fostering a sustainable future. Shepherd and

Patzel (2011) note that entrepreneurship can support the protection of ecosystems and reduction in climate change.

Entrepreneurial Start-Ups in Africa

In recent decades, entrepreneurial start-ups in Africa have attracted considerable attention from both policymakers and researchers due to three primary factors (Tafese, 2022). First, these start-ups are vital for economic transformation, contributing to national income, job creation, innovative products and services, and exports (Mboweni, 2022). Second, there has been a notable surge in the establishment and growth of start-ups across both developing and emerging contexts (Kalyanasundaram et al., 2021; Stevanovic & Wanyang Ochieng, 2023). Lastly, despite their growth potential, African start-ups encounter significant obstacles, as evidenced by their high failure rates (Ogujiuba et al., 2023; Swartz et al., 2022). Start-ups act as engines of innovation and pathways to new markets. Typically, they are newly established entities in a developmental phase targeting high-growth sectors (Stevanovic & Wanyang Ochieng, 2023). These companies are founded by one or more entrepreneurs and aim to create products or services that meet perceived market needs (Ressin, 2022). As such, they are characterized by both agility and vulnerability. Often, they start with high costs and limited revenues, seeking funding from various sources, including venture capitalists (Tafese, 2022).

This chapter specifically examines manufacturing start-ups. According to Mboweni (2022), entrepreneurial start-ups in South Africa's manufacturing sector represent a dynamic and vital component of the economy. They significantly contribute to innovation, job creation, and economic transformation (Swartz et al., 2022). These ventures are often founded by individuals or small teams aiming to develop new products, processes, or technologies that address local market needs and challenges (Mvula, 2022). The manufacturing landscape in South Africa is diverse, encompassing industries such as food processing, textiles, automotive components, and renewable energy technologies. This diversity reflects the country's rich resources and the unique demands of its market (Mboweni, 2022). Despite facing challenges like high competition, limited access to capital, and complex regulatory environments, many manufacturing start-ups leverage their flexibility and innovative strategies to succeed.

Nowadays, businesses have evolved beyond just creating value for financial benefits, rather they are now implementing practices aimed at addressing resource depletion and minimise external negative impact. This approach is called sustainable entrepreneurship (SE). The main aim of SE is to apply entrepreneurial innovation to generate income for ventures while also fulfilling social and environmental sustainability concerns (Bickley et al., 2025). Gutterman (2018) adds that firms implementing SE utilise sustainable business models that lessen resource consumption while supplying valuable products to all stakeholders through ethical means. Therefore, SE is based on the notion that long term social and environmental outcomes are as indispensable as short term financial gains (Bickley et al., 2025; Liu et al., 2022). The focus of SE is on entrepreneurial activities that not only seek opportunities but also enhance environmental and societal wellbeing, particularly in pursuit of the SDGs (Muñoz & Cohen, 2018).

SE merges elements of environmental entrepreneurship, social entrepreneurship, and institutional entrepreneurship (Bickley et al., 2025). Aguirre (2024) argues that SEO combines entrepreneurial orientation (EO) with sustainability orientation (SO). EO emphasizes behaviours exhibiting being innovative, proactive, and risk-taking, while SO is aimed at addressing environmental challenges (Soo Sung & Park, 2018). Therefore, sustainable ventures integrate innovative and proactive traits with a profound understanding of environmental and social issues (Rosário et al., 2022a, 2022b). In a competitive market, sustainable entrepreneurs develop new and high quality products that satisfy consumers' needs (Muñoz & Cohen, 2018). SMEs are increasingly called to adjust their business processes and practices in response to external pressures related to SDGs (Bickley et al., 2025). Increased knowledge of SE is timely and called for to enhance the contribution of entrepreneurs to SDGs. The SE field is still in its infancy (Perez Nuñez & Musteen, 2020), hence this study broadens our understanding of SE in emerging markets. More so, Mellett et al., (2018) bemoan the paucity of studies in emerging markets, claiming that most studies have been conducted in the US and Europe.

3.3 Research Hypotheses

Sustainable entrepreneurs have particular ethics and beliefs that mold their decision-making processes toward positive environmental actions (Alfalih & Ragmoun, 2020). For example, Galindo-Martín et al. (2021) claim that an entrepreneur's commitment to social responsibility is important for guiding their ventures in implementing eco-friendly practices (Galindo-Martín et al., 2021). Moreover, entrepreneurs with an orientation toward sustainability often develop a strong disposition that encourages sustainable entrepreneurial behaviour (Alshebami, 2023). Entrepreneurial self-efficacy is important and is influenced by emotional skills (Khan et al., 2023). In Saudi Arabia, Alshebami (2023) found that green entrepreneurial self-efficacy boosts entrepreneurs' competencies to develop innovative products that promote environmental protection. Additionally, entrepreneurs with sophisticated entrepreneurial resilience are more inclined to embrace sustainable development principles, enabling them to drive sustainability-focused firms (Nasser, 2021).

According to Gray's extended sustainable development process model, knowledge is essential in recognizing opportunities for sustainable development (Vrontis et al., 2022). Chen et al. (2023) indicate that male entrepreneurs tend to prioritize research and development (R&D) and innovation investment more than their female counterparts, who generally exhibit a stronger commitment to social responsibility. Research shows that older entrepreneurs are disposed to exhibit a reduced proactive orientation and lower environmental awareness, suggesting they may not prioritise environmental protection more (Chen et al., 2023). Notably, less educated entrepreneurs also value social responsibility (Chen et al., 2023). Given this background, the following hypothesis is proposed:

H_1. Individual Factors Drive SEO.

Several organisational factors influence SEO. For example, a firm's internal culture and its ability to reconfigure resources are essential factors in adopting SEO (Khan et al., 2023). Resources are vital for new ventures and the integration of innovative practices. In China, Makhloufi et al. (2022) suggested that firms' green absorptive capacity guides green entrepreneurial orientation (GEO) by promoting the exchange of essential skills, and practices to advance entrepreneurial environmental initiatives while creating business opportunities. In Iran, Maleki and Hajipour (2021) discovered that organizational learning is vital for selecting CEOs with specific characteristics conducive to sustainable entrepreneurial orientation. In Iraq, Nasser (2021) revealed that innovation capital positively impacts SEO, enabling organizations to seize entrepreneurial opportunities. Shafique et al. (2022) note that organisational ambidexterity enhances GEO by boosts GEO by allowing firms to create eco-friendly solutions through both exploration and exploitation. Maleki and Hajipour (2021) highlighted that organizational strategic alignment is crucial for sustaining SEO. In India, Verma and Kumar (2022) established that transformational leaders are more inclined to embrace sustainable orientation in business as they create an environment that promotes creativity and innovation. The following hypothesis is put forward:

H_2: Organisational Factors Drive SEO.

The importance of context in entrepreneurship has been significantly highlighted (La Rocca & Dal Molin, 2024). Adopting a contextual perspective in discussing SE adds to the understanding of the entrepreneurial phenomena. By examining the context, researchers can gain insights into when, how, and why SEO occurs. Following calls for contextualized research (Welter & Gartner, 2016), there is a growing demand for studies exploring the interaction between local context and sustainable venturing processes (Muñoz & Cohen, 2018). Afum et al. (2023) add that exploring contextual level provides an understanding of how entrepreneurs contribute to sustainable development. More so, contextual factors can affect the entrepreneurial venture's behaviour (Rice et al., 2014). Alarifi et al. (2019) confirm firms in different contexts practice SE differently. Thus, unique country contextual factors influence the dynamics of SE. In Turkey, Eroglu and Rashid (2022) discovered that the SE inclination of entrepreneurs is shaped by their perceived challenges and support from contextual factors. As such, the knowledge that public funding can direct entrepreneurs' attitudes towards implementing sustainable practices (Sindhu et al., 2021). Liu et al. (2022) found that institutional pressure improves the social perception of a firm's products, and increases access to market competitiveness. Pankov et al. (2021) established that contextual factors can both encourage and hamper sustainable activities. The following hypothesis is put forward:

H_3: Contextual factors drive SEO.

4 Research Methodology

The investigation is constructed on a positivist philosophical framework. The author believes that knowledge is constructed through the laws of cause and effect (Elder-Vass, 2022), with the application of scientific principles (Ali, 2024). Hence, the study employed the deductive approach to explore the drivers of SEO among entrepreneurial ventures (Taherdoost, 2022). The study is quantitative and follows a descriptive research design. South African start-ups in the manufacturing sector who operate in Pietermaritzburg participated in the study. Given the absence of an updated sampling frame, convenience sampling was applied to select the study respondents.

The independent constructs: individual factors, organisational factors, contextual factors, and the dependent variable (SEO) were adopted from various scholars (see Table 2). A five-point Likert scale ranging from 1 (strongly disagree) to 5 (strongly agree), including alternatives for disagree (2), undecided (3), and agree (4). The questionnaire consisted of three sections. Section A covered demographic data from respondents, including gender, marital status, age, and educational qualifications. Part B included 18 items related to the three constructs of the research model, while Part C consisted of 6 items specifically focused on SEO. A pilot study involving 15 respondents was then conducted to enhance the wording, formatting, sequence, simplicity, layout, and clarity of the questionnaire (Teresi et al., 2022). Item reliability was evaluated using Cronbach's alpha (α). Data collection took place in January and February 2025. Face-to-face personal administration of the questionnaire was chosen for its higher response rates compared to online, telephone, or postal surveys (Wolf et al., 2021). A total of 300 questionnaires were administered to conveniently selected entrepreneurs, with 232 returned; however, only 220 were deemed usable.

5 Empirical Results

Demographic Characteristics

Table 1 exhibits the sample characteristics. The age group of 46–55 had the largest percentage of entrepreneurs in the sample (42.4%; 93) followed by the age group of 30–45 (30.8%; n = 68). Only 10.6% (n

= 23) of the sample's respondents were beyond the age of 60, while 16.2% (n = 36) were in the 55–59 age range. Regarding their educational backgrounds, 21.3% (n = 47) of respondents held a school leaving (matric) certificate while the majority (36.7%, 81) of the respondents held a degree. A diploma was held by 33.6% (n = 74), while 8.4% (n = 18) had a postgraduate certificate.

In addition, 15.7% (n = 35) were managers, and 38.1% (n = 84) were owners of the ventures. On the other hand, 46.2% of the respondents (n = 102) were owner-managers of the ventures. Lastly, the male entrepreneurs (70.3%) were more than their female counterparts (29.7%).

Reliability and Validity

Cronbach's alpha is a widely used test to evaluate the internal consistency of the constructs. All the items met the recommended value of 0.7

Table 1 Sample profile (n = 220)

Characteristics	*Frequency*	*Percentage*
Demographic Profile		
Age		
30–45	68	30.8
46–55	93	42.4
56–59	36	16.2
60+	23	10.6
Total	**220**	**100**
Position in the organization		
Owner	84	38.1
Manager	35	15.7
Owner-manager	102	46.2
Total	**220**	**100**
Education qualification		
Matric	47	21.3
Diploma certificate	74	33.6
Degree	81	36.7
Post-grad. Degree	18	8.4
Total	**220**	**100**
Gender		
Female	65	29.7
Male	155	70.3
Total	**220**	**100**

Source Author

(Zakariya, 2022) implying that there was internal consistency. All items had standardized factor loadings above the minimum cut off point of 0.6 (Koe et al., 2024). All critical ratios (CRs) were adequately large (>1.96) and significant at $p < 0.001$ (Hair et al., 2019).

Discriminant validity was analysed using AVE as recommended by Fornell and Larcker (1981). The table displays that the square root of the AVE for each latent variable exceeds the correlations with any other latent variable in the model. This successfully proved discriminant validity. The findings in Table 3 show that the Average Variances Extracted (AVEs) exceeded the 0.5 threshold (Hair et al., 2019). The findings provide evidence that all the criteria for discriminant validity were met (Heale & Twycross, 2015).

Additionally, discriminant validity was assessed using the heterotrait-monotrait ratio of correlations (HTMT). The results showed that all HTMT values were below 0.85. Therefore, the current study indicates discriminant validity according to the HTMT rule. To ensure more precise estimations, we employed Maximum Likelihood Estimation (MLE) to assess convergent validity (Sahabuddin& Makkasau, 2024). As shown in Table 4, the model yielded acceptable fit indices (CMIN/DF = 2.673; GFI = 0.939; AGFI = 0.981; NFI = 0.902; TLI = 0.933; CFI = 0.967; RMSEA = 0.072). In addition, findings reveal a satisfactory RMSEA value, between 0.05 and 0.10 (Kenny et al., 2014).

Path Analysis

Hypothesis testing was done to address the three hypotheses for the direct relationships. SEM was applied to address the hypotheses, and the results are displayed in Table 5.

The study employed a bootstrapping method with confidence intervals, using 5,000 resamples to address the hypotheses (Hair Jr et al., 2020). Table 5 in Chapter 3 illustrates the path coefficients for the three direct hypotheses. Table 5 illustrates that all hypotheses were supported, demonstrating a positive relationship among the variables examined in the study. Findings show moderate positive statistical support for the influence of individual factors on SEO. This suggests that personal factors, such as entrepreneurial mindset, values, and competencies, are pivotal for fostering sustainability in entrepreneurial ventures. This finding is consistent with other studies that had similar findings (Eroglu & Rashid, 2022; Sindhu et al., 2021). More so, findings illustrate a robust relationship

Table 2 Data quality

Construct-Items	*Λ*	*(α)*	*CR*	*MN*	*SD*
Individual factors (Chen et al., 2023)					
IF1: I possess the necessary skills to identify sustainable business opportunities	0.751	0.902	–	3.19	1.21
IF2: I am willing to take risks to implement sustainable practices in my business	0.832		14.034***		
IF3: My values align with sustainable business practices	0.823		12.894***		
IF4: I am motivated to pursue environmentally friendly entrepreneurial initiatives	0.871		13.983***		
IF5: I continuously seek knowledge about sustainable entrepreneurship	0.841		12.381**		
IF6: I believe that my individual actions can contribute to sustainability	0.816		14.291***		
Organisational factors (Khan et al., 2023)					
OF1: My organization encourages innovative practices that promote sustainability	0.761	0.862	–	3.34	1.82
OF2: My organization has established policies that prioritize sustainability	0.832		11.927***		
OF3: Leadership in my organization supports sustainable entrepreneurial efforts:	0.704		10.281***		
OF4: Team members are encouraged to share ideas related to sustainable practices	0.728		13.881***		
OF5: My organization provides resources to support sustainable initiatives	0.749		12.298***		
OF6: There is a clear commitment to sustainability within my organization	0.642		11.982***		
Contextual factors (Afum et al., 2023)					
CF1: The regulatory environment in my country supports sustainable entrepreneurship	0.742	0.791	–	4.07	1.43

(continued)

Table 2 (continued)

Construct-Items	*Λ*	*(α)*	*CR*	*MN*	*SD*
CF2: There are sufficient market opportunities for sustainable products and services	0.736		12.092***		
CF3: Community support for sustainable initiatives is strong in my area	0.623		10.371***		
CF4: Access to funding for sustainable ventures is readily available	0.740		13.893***		
CF5: Social expectations encourage businesses to adopt sustainable practices	0.763		12.361***		
CF6: Networking opportunities with sustainable organizations are accessible	0.731		11.734***		
Sustainable entrepreneurship orientation (Afum et al., 2023)					
SE1: I prioritize environmental sustainability in my business decisions	0.665	0.951	–	3.42	1.54
SE2: I consider the impact of my business on future generations	0.793		13.910***		
SE3: Long-term sustainability is a core goal of my entrepreneurial efforts	0.861		14.281***		
SE4: I strive to create value for both my business and the community through sustainable practices	0.742		11.092***		
SE5: My business actively seeks to reduce its carbon footprint	0.729		12.281***		
SE6: I integrate social responsibility into my business model	0.843		11.812***		

Source Data Analysis

between organizational factors and SEO. This highlights the significance of internal structures, culture, and resources in promoting sustainable practices within start-ups. Previous studies also observed that organisational factors drive sustainable entrepreneurship orientation (Makhloufi et al., 2022; Shafique et al., 2022). The strongest effect was observed on contextual factors and SEO. The findings imply that external elements,

Table 3 AVEs

Construct	*Ifs*	*OFs*	*CFs*	*SEO*
Individual factors (IFs)	**0.651**			
Organisational factors (OFs)	0.395	**0.601**		
Contextual factors (CFs)	0.391	0.361	**0.554**	
Sustainable entrepreneurship orientation (SEO)	0.399	0.289	0.401	**0.710**

Note Diagonal elements in bold are AVEs
Research data (2025)

Table 4 Measurement model

Fit indices	*Actual measurement*	*Recommended*	*Sources*
CMIN/DF	2.673	≤3.000	Hair et al. (2019)
GFI	0.939	>0.900	
AGFI	0.981	>0.900	
NFI	0.902	>0.900	
TLI	0.933	>0.900	
CFI	0.967	>0.900	
RMSEA	0.072	<0.080	

Research data (2025)

Table 5 Hypotheses tests

Hypothesis	*Description*	*SRW*	*CR*	*Remark*
H_1	Individual factors → SEO	0.421	7.029***	Supported
H_2	Organisational factors → SEO	0.509	12.6423***	Supported
H_3	Contextual factors → SEO	0.672	17.302***	Supported

Notes SRW standardised regression weight, CR critical ratio, ***Significant at $p < 0.001$
Research data (2025)

such as market conditions, regulatory frameworks, and social expectations, significantly shape SEO. This finding is consistent with the work of Eroglu and Rashid (2022), which was undertaken with Turkish firms. More so, the study by Liu et al. (2022) in China had similar findings.

6 Implications of the Study

The study's main objective was to investigate the influence of individual factors, organisational factors, and, contextual factors on the SEO of entrepreneurial start-ups in South Africa. This study was carried out in the context of scarce literature on the factors that drive SEO amongst entrepreneurial start-ups in emerging markets, particularly in South Africa. It was, therefore, imperative to explore the factors that influence sustainable entrepreneurship orientation. This understanding is critical as findings can be used to guide entrepreneurs in implementing sustainable practices that go beyond economic performance to positively contribute to both their communities and the wider ecology. The study's findings have implications for theory, practice, and future research. The findings of the study contribute to practice, theory, and future research.

This study makes significant contributions to theory in many ways. Firstly, using samples from the manufacturing entrepreneurial start-ups, the study validates the antecedents of SEO by Aguirre (2024) and also donates support to the conceptual model developed by Alfalih et al. (2020). This study answers calls for more research on SEO by validating the influence of these drivers, offering a theoretical contribution that clarifies pathways toward achieving sustainability. Secondly, they validate the principles of the dynamic RBV theory in an emerging market context. The chapter highlights how contextual, individual, and organizational factors collectively influence the SEO of entrepreneurial start-ups in South Africa. This underscores the notion that the integration of valuable resources and the dynamic perspective shaped by contextual internal and external factors are crucial for achieving a sustainable orientation.

The results are important in explaining how these factors interact in a dynamic context, offering a framework for future research to explore entrepreneurial success in emerging markets. Thirdly, the chapter demonstrates how entrepreneurial capabilities can drive sustainability efforts, which is crucial for addressing climate change as outlined in SDG 13. Finally, and most importantly, the study adds to the growing body of literature on sustainable entrepreneurship which is acknowledged as a critical constituent in achieving the UN SDGs. Specifically, the study contributes to the literature on SDG-13 by exposing how individual, organizational, and contextual factors impact the entrepreneurial practices that advance SDG-13, in an African context.

The study's practical implications for emerging economies like South Africa align closely with SDG 13, which calls for urgent climate action. By confirming the positive relationships among individual, organizational, and contextual factors that foster SEO, the chapter underscores how entrepreneurial ventures can contribute to climate resilience and sustainable practices. Emphasizing individual attributes such as entrepreneurial mindset, values, and competencies highlights the necessity for educational programs that prepare aspiring entrepreneurs to integrate sustainability into their business models.

Furthermore, the robust link between organizational factors and SEO indicates that start-ups need to cultivate supportive internal structures and a culture of innovation. Start-ups are called to adopt eco-friendly practices to reduce their environmental footprint, directly contributing to climate action goals. The emphasis on contextual factors stresses the importance of understanding the broader environment in which these start-ups operate. Hence, policymakers need to develop regulatory frameworks that encourage innovative and green practices. This is vital for achieving SDG 13, as effective policies can foster an ecosystem where sustainable entrepreneurship thrives.

The research has three limitations that present opportunities for future investigation. Firstly, because of limited resources and time, data was collected exclusively from manufacturing start-ups. Further studies can include start-ups in other sectors to ascertain any potential differences. Secondly, the respondents were exclusively drawn from Pietermaritzburg, Province of KwaZulu-Natal, South Africa. This may limit the generalisability of the findings to South African SMEs. To enhance the generalisability of the study's results, it is advisable for future research to include samples from various cities, provinces, and even various emerging countries. Lastly, the investigation employed a cross-sectional survey approach to data collection. Given the evolving nature of the phenomena, conducting similar studies using a longitudinal survey design would be beneficial for identifying any changes in the factors influencing firms' sustainable entrepreneurial orientation over time.

7 Conclusion

This chapter was to examine the factors influencing SEO among manufacturing start-ups in South Africa. The findings underscore that cultivating SEO is not solely a function of personal aspiration or corporate strategy;

it necessitates a comprehensive approach that incorporates multiple elements affecting entrepreneurial conduct. As developing economies confront urgent environmental and social issues, the significance of start-ups in promoting sustainability becomes progressively vital. By enabling entrepreneurs to implement sustainable practices, we can provide a strong foundation for attaining the Sustainable Development Goals, especially SDG 13, which demands immediate climate action. This chapter emphasises the necessity of developing an entrepreneurial ecosystem that fosters innovation and sustainability, ensuring that economic growth is congruent with the overarching objectives of societal welfare and environmental conservation.

References

Afum, E., Issau, K., Agyabeng-Mensah, Y., Baah, C., Dacosta, E., Essandoh, E., & Agyenim Boateng, E. (2023). The missing links of sustainable supply chain management and green radical product innovation between sustainable entrepreneurship orientation and sustainability performance. *Journal of Engineering, Design and Technology, 21*(1), 167–187. https://doi.org/10.1108/JEDT-05-2021-0267

Agarwal, S., Ramadani, V., Gerguri-Rashiti, S., Agrawal, V., & Dixit, J. K. (2020). Inclusivity of entrepreneurship education on entrepreneurial attitude among young community: Evidence from India. *Journal of Enterprising Communities: People and Places in the Global Economy, 14*(2), 299–319. https://doi.org/10.1108/JEC-03-2020-0024

Aguirre, L. A. L. (2024). Pathways to sustainable entrepreneurship: Analysing drivers of sustainable entrepreneurial orientation. *Sustainable Technology and Entrepreneurship*, 100081. https://doi.org/10.1016/j.stae.2024.100081

Alarifi, G., Robson, P., & Kromidha, E. (2019). The manifestation of entrepreneurial orientation in the social entrepreneurship context. *Journal of Social Entrepreneurship, 10*(3), 307–327. https://doi.org/10.1080/19420676.2018.1541015

Alfalih, A. A. (2020). The role of knowledge management in the transition from entrepreneurial intention to entrepreneurial action in the case of small and medium-sized enterprises. *Journal of Information & Knowledge Management, 19*(04), Article 2050030. https://doi.org/10.1142/S0219649220500306

Alfalih, A. A., & Ragmoun, W. (2020). Drivers of sustainable entrepreneurship orientation for students at business school in Saudi Arabia. *Journal of Entrepreneurship Education, 23*(2).

Alhaddi, H. (2015). Triple bottom line and sustainability: A literature review. *Business and Management Studies, 1*(2), 6–10. https://doi.org/10.11114/bms.v1i2.752

Ali, I. M. (2024). A guide for positivist research paradigm: From philosophy to methodology. *Ideology Journal, 9*(2). https://doi.org/10.24191/idealogy.v9i2.596

Alshebami, A. S. (2023). Redefining resilience: The case of small entrepreneurs in Saudi Arabia. *Frontiers in Environmental Science, 10*, 1118016. https://doi.org/10.3389/fenvs.2022.1118016

Arora, N. K., & Mishra, I. (2023). Sustainable development goal 13: recent progress and challenges to climate action. *Environmental Sustainability, 6*(3), 297–301. https://doi.org/10.1007/s42398-023-00287-4

Barney, J. B., Ketchen, D. J., Jr., & Wright, M. (2021). Resource-based theory and the value creation framework. *Journal of Management, 47*(7), 1936–1955. https://doi.org/10.1177/01492063211021655

Bickley, S. J., Macintyre, A., & Torgler, B. (2025). Artificial intelligence and big data in sustainable entrepreneurship. *Journal of Economic Surveys, 39*(1), 103–145. https://doi.org/10.1111/joes.12611

Bomani, M., Derera, E., & Mashingaidze, M. (2022). Urbanisation and SME growth in a developing economy: Implications for policy. *Corporate Governance and Organizational Behavior Review, 6*(2), 123–133. https://doi.org/10.22495/cgobrv6i2p12

Chen, S., Shen, W., Qiu, Z., Liu, R., & Mardani, A. (2023). Who are the green entrepreneurs in China? The relationship between entrepreneurs' characteristics, green entrepreneurship orientation, and corporate financial performance. *Journal of Business Research, 165*, Article 113960. https://doi.org/10.1016/j.jbusres.2023.113960

Criado-Gomis, A., Cervera-Taulet, A., & Iniesta-Bonillo, M. A. (2017). Sustainable entrepreneurial orientation: A business strategic approach for sustainable development. *Sustainability, 9*(9), 1667. https://doi.org/10.3390/su9091667

de Klerk, S., Miles, M. P., & Bliemel, M. (2024). A life cycle perspective of startup accelerators. *International Entrepreneurship and Management Journal, 20*(1), 327–343. https://doi.org/10.1007/s11365-023-00933-7

Dsilva, J., Francis, G., & Pillai, R. (2025). Assessing the adverse impacts of innovation and development through sustainability: A global perspective. In *Zero carbon industry, eco-innovation and environmental sustainability* (pp. 123–139). Springer Nature Switzerland. https://doi.org/10.1007/978-3-031-80220-1_8

Elder-Vass, D. (2022). Pragmatism, critical realism, and the study of value. *Journal of Critical Realism, 21*(3), 261–287. https://doi.org/10.1080/14767430.2022.2049088

El Nemar, S., El-Chaarani, H., Dandachi, I., & Castellano, S. (2022). Resource-based view and sustainable advantage: A framework for SMEs. *Journal of Strategic Marketing*, 1–24. https://doi.org/10.1080/0965254X.2022.2160486

Eroglu, Y., & Rashid, L. (2022). The impact of perceived support and barriers on the sustainable orientation of Turkish startups. *Sustainability, 14*(8), 4666. https://doi.org/10.3390/su14084666

Fornell, C., & Larcker, D. F. (1981). Structural equation models with unobservable variables and measurement error: Algebra and statistics. *Journal of Marketing Research, 18*(3), 382–388. https://doi.org/10.1177/002224378101800313

Galindo-Martín, M. Á., Castaño-Martínez, M. S., & Méndez-Picazo, M. T. (2021). The role of entrepreneurship in different economic phases. *Journal of Business Research, 122*, 171–179. https://doi.org/10.1016/j.jbusres.2020.08.050

Gutterman, A. S. (2018). *Sustainable entrepreneurship*. Business Expert Press.

Hair, J., Black, W. C., Babin, B. J., Anderson, R. E., Black, W. C., & Anderson, R. E. (2019). *Multivariate data analysis multivariate data analysis* (8th ed.). Annabel Ainscow.

Hair Jr, J. F., Howard, M. C., & Nitzl, C. (2020). Assessing measurement model quality in PLS-SEM using confirmatory composite analysis. *Journal of business research, 109*, 101–110. https://doi.org/10.1016/j.jbusres.2019.11.069

Haldar, S. (2019). Towards a conceptual understanding of sustainability-driven entrepreneurship. *Corporate Social Responsibility and Environmental Management, 26*(6), 1157–1170. https://doi.org/10.1002/csr.1763

Heale, R., & Twycross, A. (2015). Validity and reliability in quantitative studies. *Evidence-Based Nursing, 18*(3), 66–67. https://doi.org/10.1136/eb-2015-102129

Helfat, C. E., Kaul, A., Ketchen, D. J., Jr., Barney, J. B., Chatain, O., & Singh, H. (2023). Renewing the resource-based view: New contexts, new concepts, and new methods. *Strategic Management Journal, 44*(6), 1357–1390. https://doi.org/10.1002/smj.3500

Hernández-Perlines, F., & Rung-Hoch, N. (2017). Sustainable entrepreneurial orientation in family firms. *Sustainability, 9*(7), 1212. https://doi.org/10.3390/su9071212

Horne, J. (2019). *The sustainability impact of new ventures: Measuring and managing entrepreneurial contributions to sustainable development* (Doctoral dissertation, Technische Universität Berlin).

Kalyanasundaram, G., Ramachandrula, S., & Mungila Hillemane, B. S. (2021). The life expectancy of tech start-ups in India: What attributes impact tech start-ups' failures? *International Journal of Entrepreneurial Behavior &*

Research, 27(8), 2050–2078. https://doi.org/10.1108/IJEBR-01-2021-0025

Kenny, D. A., Kaniskan, B., & McCoach, D. B. (2014). The performance of RMSEA in models with small degrees of freedom. *Sociological Methods & Research*, 1–22. https://doi.org/10.1177/0049124114543236

Khan, N. R., Ameer, F., Bouncken, R. B., & Covin, J. G. (2023). Corporate sustainability entrepreneurship: The role of green entrepreneurial orientation and organizational resilience capacity for green innovation. *Journal of Business Research, 169*, 114296. https://doi.org/10.1016/j.jbusres.2023.114296

Koe, W. L., Nordin, N. M., Marmaya, N. H., & Othman, R. (2024, April). Factors influencing technopreneurial intention: A confirmatory factor analysis. *In AIP Conference Proceedings* (Vol. 2799, No. 1). AIP Publishing. https://doi.org/10.1063/5.0181864

La Rocca, A., & Dal Molin, S. (2024). Sustainable entrepreneurship: How do contextual factors play a role? *Industrial Marketing Management, 123*, 292–303. https://doi.org/10.1016/j.indmarman.2024.10.010

Li, J., Su, Q., Zhu, H., Sun, W., & Zhang, Y. (2023). How international immigrants engage in sustainable entrepreneurship in their host countries? The moderating effects of collectivistic cultural values. *Corporate Social Responsibility and Environmental Management, 30*(3), 1244–1257. https://doi.org/10.1002/csr.2416

Liu, N., Hu, H., & Wang, Z. (2022). The relationship between institutional pressure, green entrepreneurial orientation, and entrepreneurial performance—The moderating effect of network centrality. *Sustainability, 14*(19), 12055. https://doi.org/10.3390/su141912055

Makhloufi, L., Laghouag, A. A., Meirun, T., & Belaid, F. (2022). Impact of green entrepreneurship orientation on environmental performance: The natural resource-based view and environmental policy perspective. *Business Strategy and the Environment, 31*(1), 425–444. https://doi.org/10.1002/bse.2902

Maleki, M. M., & Hajipour, B. (2021). Organizational antecedents model of sustainable entrepreneurial orientation: Multi-case study of Iranian firms. *Journal of Entrepreneurship in Emerging Economies, 13*(5), 1173–1191. https://doi.org/10.1108/JEEE-07-2020-0233

Mashingaidze, M., Kalayakgosi, S., & Govere, E. (2024a). Entrepreneurial strategies for sustainable performance of small and medium enterprises in unprecedent times. In *Entrepreneurial Strategies for the internationalization and digitalization of SMEs* (pp. 164–197). IGI Global. https://doi.org/10.4018/979-8-3693-3518-5.ch008

Mashingaidze, M., Phiri, M., Chokera, F., & Bomani, M. (2024b). The mediation influence of organisational innovation on the corporate entrepreneurship and business performance relationship. *African Journal of Innovation and Entrepreneurship (AJIE), 3*(3), 169. https://doi.org/10.31920/2753-314X/2024/v3n3a8

Mboweni, M. J. (2022). Factors that affect the ability of automotive enterprises to raise start-up capital. *Educational Research (IJMCER), 4*(1), 19–36.

Mellett, S., Kelliher, F., & Harrington, D. (2018). Network-facilitated green innovation capability development in micro-firms. *Journal of Small Business and Enterprise Development, 25*(6), 1004–1024. https://doi.org/10.1108/JSBED-11-2017-0363

Muñoz, P., & Cohen, B. (2018). Sustainable entrepreneurship research: Taking stock and looking ahead. *Business Strategy and the Environment, 27*(3), 300–322. https://doi.org/10.1002/bse.2000

Mvula, A. (2022). Start-up realities for industrial design graduates at a university of technology in South Africa. *Journal of Contemporary Management, 19*(2), 588–608. https://doi.org/10.35683/jcm21114.181

Nasser, W. H. (2021). Innovation capital, sustainable entrepreneurial orientation, and the moderating role of entrepreneurial resilience. *Entrepreneurial Business and Economics Review, 9*(3), 73–85. https://doi.org/10.15678/EBER.2021.090305

Ogujiuba, K. K., Olamide, E., Boshoff, E., Agholor, I., & Ogujiuba, C. (2023). SMEs, success, and capital startups: Evidence from the service sector in South Africa. *Administrative Sciences, 13*(5), 127. https://doi.org/10.3390/admsci13050127

Pankov, S., Velamuri, V. K., & Schneckenberg, D. (2021). Towards sustainable entrepreneurial ecosystems: Examining the effect of contextual factors on sustainable entrepreneurial activities in the sharing economy. *Small Business Economics, 56*(3), 1073–1095. https://doi.org/10.1007/s11187-019-00255-5

Perez Nuñez, S. M., & Musteen, M. (2020). Learning perspective on sustainable entrepreneurship in a regional context. *Journal of Small Business and Enterprise Development, 27*(3), 365–381. https://doi.org/10.1108/JSBED-03-2020-0071

Ressin, M. (2022). Start-ups as drivers of economic growth. *Research in Economics, 76*(4), 345–354. https://doi.org/10.1016/j.rie.2022.08.003

Rice, M. P., Fetters, M. L., & Greene, P. G. (2014). University-based entrepreneurship ecosystems: A global study of six educational institutions. *International Journal of Entrepreneurship and Innovation Management, 18*(5–6), 481–501. https://doi.org/10.1504/IJEIM.2014.064722

Rosário, A. T., Raimundo, R. J., & Cruz, S. P. (2022a). Sustainable Entrepreneurship: A Literature Review. *Sustainability, 14*(9), 5556. https://doi.org/10.3390/su14095556

Rosário, A. T., Raimundo, R. J., & Cruz, S. P. (2022b). Sustainable entrepreneurship: A literature review. *Sustainability, 14*(9), 5556. https://doi.org/10.3390/su14095556

Sahabuddin, E. S., & Makkasau, A. (2024). Utilization of virtual reality as a learning tool to increase students' pro-environmental behavior at universities: A maximum likelihood estimation approach. *Eurasia Journal of Mathematics, Science and Technology Education, 20*(12), em2540. https://doi.org/10.29333/ejmste/15654

Schaltegger, S., & Wagner, M. (2011). Sustainable entrepreneurship and sustainability innovation: Categories and interactions. *Business Strategy and the Environment, 20*(4), 222–237. https://doi.org/10.1002/bse.682

Schaltegger, S., Lüdeke-Freund, F., & Hansen, E. G. (2012). Business cases for sustainability: The role of business model innovation for corporate sustainability. *International Journal of Innovation and Sustainable Development, 6*(2), 95–119. https://doi.org/10.1504/IJISD.2012.046944

Scuotto, V., Giudice, M. D., Holden, N., & Mattiacci, A. (2017). Entrepreneurial settings within global family firms: Research perspectives from cross-cultural knowledge management studies. *European Journal of International Management, 11*(4), 469–489. https://doi.org/10.1504/EJIM.2017.085586

Shafique, I., Kalyar, M. N., Shafique, M., Kianto, A., & Beh, L. S. (2022). Demystifying the link between knowledge management capability and innovation ambidexterity: Organizational structure as a moderator. *Business Process Management Journal, 28*(5/6), 1343–1363. https://doi.org/10.1108/BPMJ-11-2021-0713

Sindhu, S., Dahiya, S., Siwach, P., & Panghal, A. (2021). Adoption of sustainable business practices by entrepreneurs: Modelling the drivers. *World Review of Entrepreneurship, Management and Sustainable Development, 17*(6), 704–722. https://doi.org/10.1504/WREMSD.2021.118638

Stevanovic, D., & Wanyang Ochieng, M. (2023). *Growth and Success: In the Context of Startups in Sub-Saharan Africa.*

Sung, C. S., & Park, J. Y. (2018). Sustainability orientation and entrepreneurship orientation: Is there a tradeoff relationship between them? *Sustainability, 10*(2), 379. https://doi.org/10.3390/su10020379

Swartz, E. M., Scheepers, C. B., & Toefy, T. (2022). Women entrepreneurs' opportunity identification of digital platform start-ups: emerging evidence from South Africa. *International Journal of Gender and Entrepreneurship, 14*(3), 352–374. https://doi.org/10.1108/IJGE-06-2021-0096

Tafese, T. (2022). *Digital Africa: how big tech and African startups are reshaping the continent.*

Taherdoost, H. (2022). What are different research approaches? Comprehensive review of qualitative, quantitative, and mixed method research, their applications, types, and limitations. *Journal of Management Science & Engineering Research, 5*(1), 53–63. https://doi.org/10.30564/jmser.v5i1.4538

Teece, D. J. (2023). The evolution of the dynamic capabilities framework. *Artificiality and Sustainability in Entrepreneurship, 113*, 238. https://doi.org/10.1007/978-3-031-11371-0_6

Teresi, J. A., Yu, X., Stewart, A. L., & Hays, R. D. (2022). Guidelines for designing and evaluating feasibility pilot studies. *Medical Care, 60*(1), 95–103. https://doi.org/10.1097/MLR.0000000000001664

Verma, P., & Kumar, V. (2022). Developing leadership styles and green entrepreneurial orientation to measure organization growth: a study on Indian green organizations. *Journal of Entrepreneurship in Emerging Economies, 14*(6), 1299–1324. https://doi.org/10.1108/JEEE-01-2021-0035

Vrontis, D., Chaudhuri, R., & Chatterjee, S. (2022). Adoption of digital technologies by SMEs for sustainability and value creation: Moderating role of entrepreneurial orientation. *Sustainability, 14*(13), 7949. https://doi.org/10.3390/su14137949

Welter, F., & Gartner, W. B. (Eds.). (2016). A research agenda for entrepreneurship and context. https://doi.org/10.4337/9781784716844

Wolf, C., Christmann, P., Gummer, T., Schnaudt, C., & Verhoeven, S. (2021). Conducting general social surveys as self-administered mixed-mode surveys. *Public Opinion Quarterly, 85*(2), 623–648. https://doi.org/10.1093/poq/nfab039

Woode, J. K. (2024). Green finance and green growth: A systematic literature review on awareness, existing channels, instruments, and techniques. *Development and Sustainability in Economics and Finance*, 100004. https://doi.org/10.1016/j.dsef.2024.100004

Wu, S., Cheng, P., Wang, J., & Xiao, J. (2025). The impact of entrepreneurial bricolage on sustainable entrepreneurship in China: The mediating role of digital transformation and the moderating role of green innovation. *Journal of Global Entrepreneurship Research, 15*(1), 51. https://doi.org/10.1007/s40497-025-00464-1

Zakariya, Y. F. (2022). Cronbach's alpha in mathematics education research: Its appropriateness, overuse, and alternatives in estimating scale reliability. *Frontiers in Psychology, 13*, 1074430. https://doi.org/10.3389/fpsyg.2022.1074430

CHAPTER 6

Spillover of Digital Transformation in Cryptocurrency Prices on Renewable Energy Prices and Their Impacts on Ecosystem Pollution

Bara'ah Ghassan Jaber, Sakher Faisal Alfraihat, Suzan Issa Abuhalawah, Saeed Tarabieh, and Tareq N. Hashem

Abstract This article aims to highlight how the spillover of digital transformation in cryptocurrency prices on renewable energy prices and their impacts on ecosystem pollution and thus contributing to SDG Goal

B. G. Jaber (✉)
Department of Smart Business Isra University, Amman, Jordan
e-mail: aljaberbaraa@gmail.com

S. F. Alfraihat · S. I. Abuhalawah
Department of Business Administration and Marketing, University of Seville, Seville, Spain

S. Tarabieh
Marketing Department, Mutah University, Alkarak, Jordan

S. Trivedi et al. (eds.), *Green Ventures*, Sustainable Development Goals Series, https://doi.org/10.1007/978-981-95-6533-7_6

13. The experiment ran from July 2019 to July 2024. Cryptocurrencies, such as Ethereum and Bitcoin, have transformed financial value and transactions, with significant impacts on environmental pollution. The rise in cryptocurrency prices has significantly increased the supply of renewable energy, prompting companies to invest in green initiatives and the digital internet. Developments such as blockchain technology and integrated solar power could further benefit this sector. Demand for solar energy is growing. As a result, rising cryptocurrency prices increase mining profitability, making hydropower an attractive option for miners. Understanding the impact of cryptocurrency price changes on energy prices and their consequences for digital ecosystem subscriptions is crucial, as the indicator always remains between economic figures and environmental monitoring. Therefore, research is needed to collect data, analyze statistics, analyze energy and environmental impacts, and draw conclusions.

Keywords Cryptocurrency prices · Renewable energy · Ecosystem pollution · Digital transformation · Public awareness · Green Technology · SDG

1 Background

Cryptocurrencies have revolutionized financial transactions and the storage of value, radically changing the way they operate, and have implications for environmental pollution (Pazouki et al., 2025). They have accelerated the global digital transformation and intensified the demand for modern technological tools and techniques, especially during the COVID-19 pandemic (Koemtzopoulos et al., 2025). Cryptocurrency mining requires significant computing power, which entails increased energy consumption (Onat et al., 2025). Solar, wind, and hydropower are renewable energy exporters and are pivotal to energy sustainability systems (Behera et al., 2025). Rising cryptocurrency prices possess lead up

T. N. Hashem
Marketing Department, Faculty of Business, Applied Science Private University, Amman, Jordan

to a significant raise in renewable energy consuming, forcing companies to invest in green projects and infrastructure development (Ben Yaala & Henchiri, 2025). Technological developments such as blockchain and solar integration could further benefit this sector (Dehshiri et al., 2024). National policies related to energy use and environmental impact have led to Bitcoin price fluctuations, leading to regulatory scrutiny and incentives for renewable energy (Bajra et al., 2024). General consciousness of the ecological impact of cryptocurrency mining has increased, spurring cleaner methods and increased demand for solar energy (Hossain et al., 2025). Rising Bitcoin prices boost mining profitability, making electricity an attractive alternative for miners (Tayebi & Amini, 2024). Both Ripple and Litecoin use consensus algorithms that require less energy, relying on low-cost, renewable energy sources such as hydropower (Babaei et al., 2025). Market dynamics and policies are influenced by both environmental awareness and economic incentives (Igwe et al., 2024). Increased regulatory scrutiny and incentives for use of renewable energy exporter, such as hydropower, may arise from the higher energy use of Bitcoin mining (Cheng, 2024). Many industries and businesses have faced challenges as a result of the Fourth Industrial Revolution, characterized by highly sophisticated digital technologies and skills such as Bitcoin (Xingye et al., 2025). The demand and value of cryptocurrencies may be significantly influenced by the cost of renewable energy (Qing & Alnafrah, 2025). Furthermore, it is difficult to ascertain how cryptocurrency prices affect the price of renewable energy due to variables such as investor sentiment, the state of the global economy and politics, and the unique characteristics of different types of cryptocurrencies (Kaur et al., 2025). Some research highlights specific aspects of Bitcoin technology, but there is little literature and previous studies examining how cryptocurrency prices affect the cost of renewable energy sources and their impact on ecosystem degradation. This chapter aims to answer the main question of the study: Does the spillover of digital transformation in cryptocurrency prices on renewable energy prices and their impacts on ecosystem pollution?

2 Literature Review

The transition to renewable energy sources is crucial in the twenty-first century. Due to depleting fossil fuel reserves and environmental issues like climate change, acquiring renewable energy certificates fosters innovation, economic growth, and reduces greenhouse gas emissions, governments use Renewable Energy Certificates (RECs) to track renewable energy production and consumption. However, inconsistent design and lack of consumer privacy challenges hinder global adoption (Liu et al., 2024). Energy price fluctuations significantly influence the returns of cryptocurrency investments, as they affect the mining process, which is crucial for validating transactions and adding them to the blockchain (Arfaoui et al., 2023). Mining operations, particularly Proof-of-Work (PoW) based cryptocurrencies like Bitcoin require significant computing energy, resulting in significant energy consumption (Wendl et al., 2023). Human lives and the global ecosystem are at risk due to CO_2 emissions from crypto-trade growth, modern technology, and changing technological needs, The impacts of GDP, energy consumption, and cryptocurrency volume on environmental sustainability in the top 20 crypto-trader countries, a long-run relationship between CO_2 emissions, crypto-volume, GDP, and energy use, the governments and fiscal policymakers to de-socialize high energy-consuming blockchain technology and implement fiscal changes that are green to minimize CO_2 emissions and improve environmental sustainability (Mohsin et al., 2023).

The asymmetric spillovers between blockchain-backed currencies and environmentally supported resources using asymmetric time-varying parameters vector auto-regressions approach, it finds clusters between blockchain-based currencies and resource-efficient metals, the implications of for policymakers, supply chain managers, the blockchain industry, mechanisms for sustainable resources, and the regulatory form to emphasizes the prominence of natural resources in achieving this supply network that is enduring and benefits society and other stakeholders (Karim et al., 2023). U.S., European, and Asian markets' correlations and spillover linkages between indices of the green economy, five dark cryptocurrency, and five clean cryptocurrency. Friendly cryptocurrency and sustainable economics indexes are more strongly correlated than dirty cryptocurrencies. During the COVID-19 pandemic, clean cryptocurrencies saw a large spillover effect, particularly in Asia. For investors, lawmakers, regulators, and cryptocurrency startups looking to integrate finance and build long-term businesses, this is essential (Sharif et al., 2023). The relevance between FinTech, energy consuming (EC), and carbon dioxide emissions using MS-GARCH-copula and MS-GARCH-copula-causality, nonlinear processes and unit roots in FinTech, EC, and CO_2e, reveals contagion between FinTech and EC, as well as positive but asymmetric tail reliance and CO_2e, they are significant for Sustainable Development Goals and could help policymakers and environmentally conscious portfolio managers understand the dynamics of FinTech markets (Ersin & Bildirici, 2024).

Green investments are not decoupled from dirty investments like fossil fuel markets, green cryptocurrencies are shock transmitters in asset systems, they show significant hedging effectiveness against fossil fuels highlighting the need for investors, regulators, and policymakers to adopt eco-friendly assets (Umar et al., 2023). The link between Bitcoin mining and climate change uses various approaches. It reversal substantial causal relationship between Bitcoin energy and CO_2 emissions usage, with hash rate having the most significant impact, the need for technological advancements-in decentralized finance algorithms that use less energy to make the bitcoin market more climate-friendly, emphasizing the importance of decarbonization in addressing environmental concerns (Zhang et al., 2023). They used Bayesian analysis and quantile cointegrated vector autoregression to examine the environmental impact of Bitcoin usage, and a causal relationship between Bitcoin usage and carbon dioxide emissions was found, with a negative relationship between Bitcoin miner revenue and carbon emissions. This suggests that lower Bitcoin revenues lead to more gradual environmental degradation, suggesting a sustainable energy strategy involving renewable energy sources and energy-efficient mining hardware could reduce Bitcoin's carbon footprint (Polemis & Tsionas, 2023). Focus on renewable energy sources, such as hydropower, wind, solar, and geothermal energy, and emphasize the importance of balancing technological advancements with environmental commitments. Promote a thoughtful and sustainable future for the digital currency ecosystem by highlighting the relationship between renewable energy technologies and the cryptocurrency sector (Siddique et al., 2023).

The inter-connectedness of green finance, focusing on green bonds, renewable energy stocks, and carbon markets, substantial dynamic spillover effects between renewable energy stocks and carbon markets, as well as between green bonds and renewable energy stocks, can guide policymakers and investors in making informed decisions about green finance (Zhang et al., 2023). In terms of downside risk, the connection exists between Islamic economic markets or green securities. It develops hedging and portfolio strategies using CAViaR and QVAR algorithms. Short-run connectivity outperforms long-run connectedness, and larger amounts of danger to the downside connectivity and cross-risk spillover settings. Additionally, that in settings with moderate to high downside risk, market for green bonds indexes in the US, the EU, China, and the worldwide market all experience shocks to the net. TELE and UTL are shock receivers, and shock transmitters include Islamic Sectors BM, OG, FIN, CG, and HC. Subject to the environment and frequency of negative risk, the net functions are: computer engineering, technical engineering, and computer science (Billah et al., 2024). The industry for artificial intelligence (AI), which is predicted to reach $207.9 billion in 2023, is transforming investing and finance. Over the following ten years, it is anticipated to increase at a CAGR of 42%, reaching $1.8 trillion by 2030. Banking procedures and investment strategies can be revolutionized by AI's ability to automate processes, increase accuracy, and foresee patterns.AI has the potential to simplify resource usage and cut down on energy waste in the energy sector. However, like fossil fuels, AI training has a substantial carbon footprint (Yousaf et al., 2024). The integration of digital technology is causing a huge revolution in the energy sector. Through increased energy efficiency, the integration of renewable energy, the reduction of carbon emissions, and the implementation of circular economy principles, this transition fosters sustainability. Real-time monitoring and predictive analytics are made possible by technologies such as digital twins, blockchain, IoT, smart grids, and artificial intelligence. Through tailored energy solutions, digital transformation empowers customers, expands the market, and lowers operating costs. But obstacles like high implementation costs continue to exist (Attah et al., 2024).

In order to provide dependable power from a variety of fuel sources and fulfill the energy demands of modern civilization, the energy supply sector is essential. But it has problems like grid instability and deteriorating infrastructure. By 2050, there will likely be a 50% increase in the need for energy supplies. To solve these problems and make predictive maintenance possible, digital twin solutions are required. The uses, advantages, and difficulties of digital twin technology in the energy supply industry. It finds that 4.81% of the examined publications looked into its use in other industries (Ismail et al., 2024). Green ammonia is a carbon-free energy source that is inexpensive, easy to store, and created from renewable resources with little carbon emissions. Initially utilized as fertilizer, it has drawn attention as a possible energy source and direct fuel for the transportation, heating, and electrical industries. However, there are restrictions and difficulties in using green ammonia. The importance of green ammonia in the hydrogen energy industry, its contribution to the Sustainable Development Goals, and its technological challenges. It how green ammonia affects the environment and offers a plan for effectively using it as a hydrogen energy carrier to decarbonize the environment and energy sector (Sekhar et al., 2024). The renewable energy industry's cybersecurity issues underscore the necessity of strong defenses against growing threats. That special cybersecurity risks brought up by the grid's integration of renewable energy call for specialized protection tactics. It is argued that technological solutions such as artificial intelligence (AI) and machine learning might be used to solve current security flaws. The report provides strategic suggestions for industry stakeholders, including adopting complete cybersecurity plans, investing in innovative technology, and developing cybersecurity awareness. Future study should examine future technology and human and policy elements impacting cybersecurity in the renewable energy sector (Ige et al., 2024).

The significance of this environmental protection in the energy sector and the factors affecting industrial production declines. Territorial security is shaped by economic and energy variables, including a decline in energy efficiency during stagnation, the increasing influence of economic indicators on security threats, high strain on the energy and fuel system, high levels of monopolism, uneven territorial distribution of resources, and inefficiencies in energy asset pricing and regulations. The need to stimulate environmental preservation initiatives in the energy sector is to ensure the security of territories (Makhmutkhanov et al., 2024). In order to assess obstacles to the implementation of digital transformation in energy transitions, this synthetical selection model comprising a Single Interval (RAFSI) model with Fermatean cubic fuzzy sets that incorporates the weighted Heronian mean aggregation operator, Level-Based Weight Assessment (LBWA) model, CRITIC method, and Ranking of Alternatives through Functional mapping of criterion sub-intervals. The framework integrated the LBWA model and CRITIC approach with FCF setting, fused experts' preference data, and integrated these techniques into the RAFSI model. "Equipment manufacturer" had the greatest barrier level and "Consumers of smart power electronic" had the lowest, according to a numerical example of assessing barriers in the power sector. For those involved in energy transitions, the model offers a more steady and useful evaluation outcome (Wang et al., 2024). This agile methodologies using digital tools might improve the efficiency of interaction in energy project administration. This suggests that utilizing technological advances, such as software for project administration, real-time data sharing platforms, and agile methodologies, may enhance communication and provide more adaptable and responsive project administration. The conceptual framework explains how different technologies operate with project management methods, including how to deploy them and how they could affect the outcome of the project. By offering fresh conceptual frameworks (Daramola et al., 2024).

3 Research Questions

The main question: Is there any spillover of digital transformation in cryptocurrency prices on renewable energy prices and their impacts on ecosystem pollution?

The following sub-questions were developed in order to answer the primary question:

1. What is it spillover of digital transformation in cryptocurrency prices(Bitcoin, Ethereum, Ripple and Litecoin) on solar energy?
2. What is it spillover of digital transformation in cryptocurrency prices(Bitcoin, Ethereum, Ripple and Litecoin) on wind energy?
3. What is it spillover of digital transformation in cryptocurrency prices(Bitcoin, Ethereum, Ripple and Litecoin) on hydropower?
4. What is it spillover of digital transformation in cryptocurrency (Bitcoin, Ethereum, Ripple and Litecoin) and renewable energy on ecosystem pollution?

According to problem statement and analysis of previous studies, this theoretical framework prepares the following model (Fig. 1).

4 Conclusions

From previous spillover of digital transformation in cryptocurrency prices, this study aims to cover the spillover of digital transformation in cryptocurrency prices on renewable energy prices and their impacts on ecosystem pollution theoretically, covering the period from July 2019 to July 2024.The use of renewable energy has increased due to high

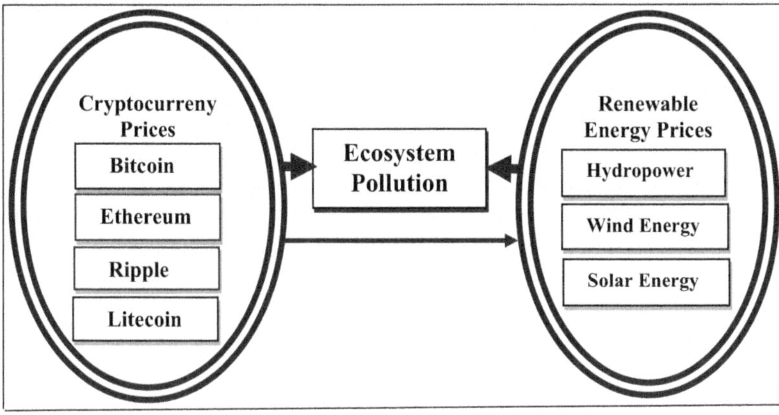

Fig. 1 The theoretical framework model

cryptocurrency prices, which has prompted businesses to invest in infrastructure development and green projects. Blockchain technology and solar energy integration are two examples of technological developments that can help the industry even more. Price fluctuations can draw regulatory attention and incentives for renewable energy sources, as well as affect government policy about energy use and environmental effect. This demand has increased as a result of the growing awareness of the detrimental of the environment effects of cryptocurrency mining. Developing methods that reconcile environmental preservation with economic expansion stewardship requires an understanding of how the digital transformation of bitcoin pricing affects the costs of renewable energy and how these factors affect ecosystem damage.

5 Goal 13 of the Sustainable Development Goals (SDGs)

SDG 13 of the Sustainable Development Goals (SDGs) focuses on combating climate change, highlighting its global impact on the environment, human health, food security, and economic growth. It calls for immediate global efforts to lower greenhouse gas emissions, improve climate-related hazard resilience, and incorporate climate measures into national policy (Owusu-Sekyere et al., 2024). Key targets include enhancing resilience, integrating climate change measures into national policies, improving education on mitigation, adaptation, impact reduction, and early warning, implementing the UN Framework Convention on Climate Change commitments, mobilizing financial support for developing countries, and promoting strengthening capability in tiny island developing states and the least developed nations. Challenges include political and economic interests, lack of resources, and a significant gap between climate finance commitments and actual delivery (Magazzino & Zoundi, 2025).

Jordan has achieved significant and concrete progress in integrating the energy sector with Sustainable Development Goal 13, including using renewable energy resources and urban planning. However, more work remains to guarantee the inclusiveness and sustainability of urban expansion, with an emphasis on renewable energy and emissions reduction. Jordan has developed its ability to generate renewable energy, especially solar and wind power (Alnsour, 2024). Jordan has implemented strategic plans to guide and enhance its energy transition, including the National Green Growth Action Plan and the Comprehensive Energy Strategy. Jordan has worked to update and develop its Nationally Determined Contributions (NDCs) in accordance with the Paris Agreement, pledging to lower emissions of greenhouse gases (Al-Oun et al., 2025). In an effort to raise the proportion of renewable energy in the energy mix, key projects include the Baynouna Solar Power Plant and the Shams Ma'an Solar Power Plant. Jordan will also research and explore new technologies to advance its climate goals, including the development of green hydrogen and the potential use of nuclear power. Jordan seeks to reduce greenhouse gas emissions, promote the use of renewable energy, and implement innovative technologies for a low-carbon, renewable future by increasing renewable energy capacity, developing strategic policies, and investing in climate change adaptation (Salah et al., 2023).

Acknowledgements The study is supported by global conference on information systems, management, and marketing 2025 (GCISMM-25), and University of Salamanca, Spain.

References

Alnsour, M. A. (2024). An integrated goal programming model applied for planning a National Policy of sustainable development: A case of Jordan. *Process Integration and Optimization for Sustainability, 8*(5), 1411–1437.

Al-Oun, S., AlMaaitah, M. F., & Al-Azamat, A. M. (2025). Sustainable energy transition in Jordan: The interplay of regulatory frameworks and infrastructure. *Energies, 18*(5), 1220.

Arfaoui, N., Naeem, M. A., Boubaker, S., Mirza, N., & Karim, S. (2023). Interdependence of clean energy and green markets with cryptocurrencies. *Energy Economics, 120*, 106584.

Attah, R. U., Garba, B. M. P., Gil-Ozoudeh, I., & Iwuanyanwu, O. (2024). Digital transformation in the energy sector: Comprehensive review of sustainability impacts and economic benefits. *International Journal of Advanced Economics, 6*(12), 760–776.

Babaei, A., Tirkolaee, E. B., & Boz, E. (2025). Optimizing energy consumption for blockchain adoption through renewable energy sources. *Renewable Energy, 238*, 121936.

Bajra, U. Q., Rogova, E., & Avdiaj, S. (2024). Cryptocurrency blockchain and its carbon footprint: Anticipating future challenges. *Technology in Society, 77*, 102571.

Behera, U. S., Sangwai, J. S., & Byun, H. S. (2025). A comprehensive review on the recent advances in applications of nanofluids for effective utilization of renewable energy. *Renewable and Sustainable Energy Reviews, 207*, 114901.

Ben Yaala, S., & Henchiri, J. E. (2025). Climate risks and cryptocurrency volatility: Evidence from crypto market crisis. *China Finance Review International*.

Billah, M., Hoque, M. E., Balli, F., Kaur, J., & Kumar, S. (2024). Downside risk connectedness between Islamic sectors and green bond markets: Implications for hedging and investment strategies. *Applied Economics, 56*(59), 8900–8933.

Cheng, K. Y. (2024). China's crackdown on crypto mining from a climate perspective: Unified efforts from administrative authorities and the judiciary. *International Journal of Digital Law and Governance, 1*(1), 91–112.

Daramola, G. O., Adewumi, A., Jacks, B. S., & Ajala, O. A. (2024). Conceptualizing communication efficiency in energy sector project management: The role of digital tools and agile practices. *Engineering Science & Technology Journal, 5*(4), 1487–1501.

Dehshiri, S. J. H., Amiri, M., & Bamakan, S. M. H. (2024). Evaluating the blockchain technology strategies for reducing renewable energy development risks using a novel integrated decision framework. *Energy, 289*, 129987.

Ersin, Ö. Ö., & Bildirici, M. E. (2024). Are cleaner energy and financial technologies needed? Contagion and causality evidence between global fintech markets, energy consumption, and environmental pollution. *Clean Technologies and Environmental Policy*, 1–15.

Hossain, M. I., Hussain, M. I., Arobee, A., Zim, M. N. F., Badhon, M. B., & Akter, S. (2025). Balancing innovation and sustainability: Learn the potential impact on the environment of bitcoin mining. *Journal of Knowledge Management Practice, 25*(1).

Ige, A. B., Kupa, E., & Ilori, O. (2024). Analyzing defense strategies against cyber risks in the energy sector: Enhancing the security of renewable energy sources. *International Journal of Science and Research Archive, 12*(1), 2978–2995.

Igwe, A. N., Eyo-Udo, N. L., Toromade, A. S., & Tosin, T. (2024). Policy implications and economic incentives for sustainable supply chain practices in the food and FMCG sectors. *Journal of Supply Chain & Sustainability. (pending publication).*

Ismail, F. B., Al-Faiz, H., Hasini, H., Al-Bazi, A., & Kazem, H. A. (2024). A comprehensive review of the dynamic applications of the digital twin technology across diverse energy sectors. *Energy Strategy Reviews, 52*, 101334.

Karim, S., Naeem, M. A., Tiwari, A. K., & Ashraf, S. (2023). Examining the avenues of sustainability in resources and digital blockchains backed currencies: Evidence from energy metals and cryptocurrencies. *Annals of Operations Research*, 1–18.

Kaur, R., Kumar, P., Radulescu, M., Mohd, S., & Dascalu, N. (2025). Spillover nexus among green cryptocurrency, sectoral renewable energy equity stock and agricultural commodity: Implications for portfolio diversification. *Economics, 19*(1), 20250138.

Koemtzopoulos, D., Zournatzidou, G., & Sariannidis, N. (2025). Can cryptocurrencies be green? The role of stablecoins toward a carbon footprint and sustainable ecosystem. *Sustainability, 17*(2), 483.

Liu, W. J., Chiu, W. Y., & Hua, W. (2024). Blockchain-enabled renewable energy certificate trading: A secure and privacy-preserving approach. *Energy, 290*, 130110.

Magazzino, C., & Zoundi, Z. (2025). Enhancing climate action evaluation using artificial neural networks: An analysis of SDG 13. *Sustainable Futures, 9*, 100439.

Makhmutkhanov, S., Akhrom, J., Djurayev, S., & Bozorov, I. (2024, June). Stimulating environmental protection activities in the energy sector. In *AIP conference proceedings* (Vol. 3152, No. 1). AIP Publishing.

Mohsin, M., Naseem, S., Zia-ur-Rehman, M., Baig, S. A., & Salamat, S. (2023). The crypto-trade volume, GDP, energy use, and environmental degradation sustainability: An analysis of the top 20 crypto-trader countries. *International Journal of Finance & Economics, 28*(1), 651–667.

Onat, N. C., Jabbar, R., Kucukvar, M., Wakjira, T., Kutty, A. A., & Fetais, N. (2025). Carbon footprint of global bitcoin mining: Emissions beyond borders. *Sustainability Science, 20*(1), 173–189.

Owusu-Sekyere, E., Nyam, Y. S., Selelo, O. T., & Torsu, D. A. (2024). Sustainable development goal 13: Urgent action to combat climate change and its impacts. In *Handbook on public policy and food security* (pp. 311–321). Edward Elgar Publishing.

Pazouki, S., Jamshidi, M. B., Jalali, M., & Tafreshi, A. (2025). Transformative impact of AI and digital technologies on the FinTech industry: A comprehensive review. *International Journal of Advanced Research in Humanities and Law, 2*(2), 1–27.

Polemis, M. L., & Tsionas, M. G. (2023). The environmental consequences of blockchain technology: A Bayesian quantile cointegration analysis for bitcoin. *International Journal of Finance & Economics, 28*(2), 1602–1621.

Qing, L., & Alnafrah, I. (2025). Environmental attention in cryptocurrency markets: A catalyst for clean energy investments. *International Review of Economics & Finance, 99*, 104063.

Salah, A. A., Shalby, M. M., & Basim Ismail, F. (2023). The status and potential of renewable energy development in Jordan: Exploring challenges and opportunities. *Sustainability: Science, Practice and Policy, 19*(1), 2212517.

Sekhar, S. J., Samuel, M. S., Glivin, G., Le, T. G., & Mathimani, T. (2024). Production and utilization of green ammonia for decarbonizing the energy sector with a discrete focus on sustainable development goals and environmental impact and technical hurdles. *Fuel, 360*, 130626.

Sharif, A., Kartal, M. T., Bekun, F. V., Pata, U. K., Foon, C. L., & Depren, S. K. (2023). Role of green technology, environmental taxes, and green energy towards sustainable environment: Insights from sovereign Nordic countries by CS-ARDL approach. *Gondwana Research, 117*, 194–206.

Siddique, I. M., Siddique, A. A., Smith, E. D., & Molla, S. (2023). Assessing the sustainability of bitcoin mining: Comparative review of renewable energy sources. *Journal of Alternative and Renewable Energy Sources, 10*(1), 1–12.

Tayebi, S., & Amini, H. (2024). The flip side of the coin: Exploring the environmental and health impacts of proof-of-work cryptocurrency mining. *Environmental Research*, 118798.

Umar, Z., Choi, S. Y., Teplova, T., & Sokolova, T. (2023). Dynamic spillovers and portfolio implication between green cryptocurrencies and fossil fuels. *PLoS One, 18*(8), e0288377.

Wang, W., Chen, Y., Wang, Y., Deveci, M., Moslem, S., & Coffman, D. M. (2024). Unveiling the implementation barriers to the digital transformation in the energy sector using the Fermatean cubic fuzzy method. *Applied Energy, 360*, 122756.

Wendl, M., Doan, M. H., & Sassen, R. (2023). The environmental impact of cryptocurrencies using proof of work and proof of stake consensus algorithms: A systematic review. *Journal of Environmental Management, 326*, 116530.

Xingye, J., Congjiang, Z., Mingyue, F., Tao, L., & Huihua, N. (2025). Measurement problem of enterprise digital transformation: New methods and findings based on large language models. *China Economist, 20*(2), 70–95.

Yousaf, I., Ijaz, M. S., Umar, M., & Li, Y. (2024). Exploring volatility interconnections between AI tokens, AI stocks, and fossil fuel markets: Evidence from time and frequency-based connectedness analysis. *Energy Economics, 133*, 107490.

Zhang, D., Chen, X. H., Lau, C. K. M., & Xu, B. (2023). Implications of cryptocurrency energy usage on climate change. *Technological Forecasting and Social Change, 187*, 122219.

PART III

Financing Strategies for Sustainable Entrepreneurship

CHAPTER 7

Sustainability-Driven Financial Models: Enabling Low Carbon Transition in SMEs

Pureheart Ogheneogaga Irikefe, Angelina Seow Voon Yee, Ahmad Danial Zainudin, and John Oyeyemi Fawole

Abstract Small and medium-sized enterprises (SMEs) are pivotal to global decarbonisation, yet they remain chronically underserved by mainstream finance. This study sought to systematically synthesises the emerging architecture of sustainability-driven financial models able to unlock SMEs' low-carbon transition. Following PRISMA guidelines, we conducted a systematic literature review of 66 Q1/Q2 journal articles published between 2020 and 2025, complemented by NVivo-assisted thematic coding in line with our study objectives. Our findings through thematic analysis revealed three core categories of sustainability-driven financial models targeted at SMEs: green bonds and loans, blended-finance, and FinTech-enabled instruments. Furthermore, it was

P. O. Irikefe (✉) · A. S. V. Yee · A. D. Zainudin
Graduate School of Business, Asia Pacific University of Technology and Innovation, Kuala Lumpur, Malaysia
e-mail: pureheart.irikefe@apu.edu.my

J. O. Fawole
School of Business, Liberty University, Lynchburg, VA, USA

S. Trivedi et al. (eds.), *Green Ventures*, Sustainable Development Goals Series, https://doi.org/10.1007/978-981-95-6533-7_7

revealed that SMEs encounter five persistent barriers: collateral shortfalls, perceived credit risk, information asymmetry, short-termism and institutional bias. The evidence was majorly based on quantitative studies that focused on BRICS and Western economies; thus, exposing gaps in cross-regional and qualitative insights. The findings suggest that although financial innovation is advancing, it is uneven in coverage and inaccessible to SMEs in less-researched regions. Without addressing structural and informational bottlenecks, the full potential of green finance to decarbonise SMEs—and thus contribute to climate action (SDG 13)—may remain unrealised. To fully unlock SME low-carbon transition, we urge policymakers and finance institutions to bring climate policy and carbon pricing into alignment, strengthen public–private collaborations, require climate-risk disclosure, build interoperable green-data infrastructure and adopt transparent impact-evaluation tools.

Keywords Blended finance · Climate action · FinTech enabled-finance · Green finance · SME low-carbon transition

1 Introduction

The increasing environmental crisis and the need to address climate change necessitate a global transformation towards a low-carbon sustainable economy (Mejia-Escobar et al., 2020; Nie et al., 2024; Pang et al., 2022). International agreements such as the Paris Agreement have prescribed ambitious targets to abate global warming and require significant investment in green business ventures (Li et al., 2023; Tamasiga et al., 2022; Udeagha & Ngepah, 2023). Typically, in the shadow of larger enterprises, small and medium-sized companies (SMEs) are significant drivers of growth and economic progress globally and form the backbone of the economy and are sources of employment and contributions to national GDP (Kumar et al., 2022; Tanchangya et al., 2025). Their contribution is particularly significant towards realising the goals of the United Nations' Sustainable Development Goals (SDGs), of which SDG 7 (Affordable and Clean Energy) and SDG 13 (Climate Action) are directly applicable to transition towards the low-carbon economies (Taghizadeh-Hesary et al., 2022; Zournatzidou, 2025). In contrast to this economic contribution, however, the majority of SMEs contribute significantly towards bringing harm in the environment in terms of increased levels of pollution and carbon footprints (Appiah-Kubi et al., 2024; Lin & Xu, 2024). The implementation of green practice in the SME business is still in the early stage according to Mirza et al. (2023). SMEs also have their own unique performance when it comes to innovation and entrepreneurship (Kumar et al., 2022) and can therefore innovate using green technology and build a green future (Appiah-Kubi et al., 2024; Hossain et al., 2024).

Effective SME capacity development towards green transformation is needed to minimise their carbon footprints and realise their innovation potential in order to pursue further climate action (Lu et al., 2022). SMEs are seriously constrained in accessing the corresponding finance to invest in green practices and green technology (Appiah-Kubi et al., 2024; Mirza et al., 2023). A lack of adequate financial support acts as a substantial deterrent to environmental investments (Lin & Xu, 2024). Traditional financial systems often perceive SMEs as higher risk, compounded by issues of severe information asymmetry and a lack of collateral, making it difficult for them to secure funding (Tanchangya et al., 2025). This limited access to finance severely constrains their ability to pursue green transitions, thereby hindering their potential contribution to national and global climate goals (Appiah-Kubi et al., 2024). Addressing these financial barriers is critical for mobilising the capital required to facilitate SMEs' shift towards low-carbon operations.

Despite increased focus and research in the areas of green finance and sustainable finance over the past decade (Zournatzidou, 2025), much research still focuses on big companies overall sustainable economic growth, or massive infrastructure projects (Liu & You, 2023; Pang et al., 2022). Tanchangya et al. (2025) equally observed that there is a noticeable gap in understanding the specific needs and characteristics of SMEs in the context of sustainability-driven financial models. Studies highlight a significant paucity of data and a bias towards examining green finance ecosystems in well-established North American and European contexts, with less attention paid to emerging economies and the challenges faced by early-stage green startups (Mukherjee et al., 2024). Furthermore, the literature points to a lack of consensus and limited micro-level investigations into how green finance instruments, coupled with technological advancements like FinTech, specifically impact SMEs and their environmental performance in diverse market settings (Lin & Wu, 2022; Pang et al., 2022; Udeagha & Ngepah, 2023).

Though the value contribution of a systematic literature review (SLR) is acknowledged in the aggregation of existing and emerging research in relation to green finance (Mukherjee et al., 2024; Yadav et al., 2024; Zournatzidou, 2025), research is still needed with respect to SLRs looking at the array of financial models focused on sustainability towards enabling SMEs' low-carbon transition. Grounded in evidence from the literature, the current study considers the array of green finance products available to SMEs such as green bonds and green loans and the difficulties they encounter when accessing the same. The study also considers the significant role of policy and regulation and the evolving financial system, e.g. the role of FinTech and digital financial inclusion in improving access and efficiency to finance to SMEs engaged in climate action. This research is timely given (1) the ongoing gap in climate and biodiversity funding (Sharma et al., 2023), (2) the push for public–private partnerships to unlock green investment (Mukherjee et al., 2024) and (3) the growing need for alternative finance models that reflect real environmental costs (Tanchangya et al., 2025). Understanding these interconnected elements is vital for mobilising the financial resources necessary to support SMEs' essential contribution to global climate goals and sustainable development.

In this chapter, we therefore contribute to both the practical and theoretical understanding of this vital aspect of green finance by addressing three key questions: What sustainability-driven financial models support SMEs in their low-carbon transition? What are the barriers to SME access to such models of green transformation? How can policy interventions and financial ecosystems be conceived or reoriented in order to make financing more accessible and more effective for SME climate action? The chapter follows the structure: Sect. 2 outlines the methodology employed, including the systematic literature review process used within it. Section 3 presents the results of the identified financial models and the issues revealed through the analysis. Section 4 considers the discussion of the results, policy and ecosystem aspects in green SME finance. Section 5 concludes with implications and a suggestion and also considers potential avenues for further research.

2 Methods

This current SLR follows Snyder's (2019) systematic, open procedure that provides search strategy, selection criterion and synthesis procedures to prevent bias and promote maximum reproducibility. The following are the search terms applied, search strings, bibliometric data acquired for retrieving new studies (Haddaway et al., 2022), and analyses carried out and reported using step-by-step three phases recommended by Tranfield et al. (2003). Figure 1 shows how we identified new 66 studies in line with the Preferred Reporting Items for Systematic reviews and Meta-Analyses (PRISMA).

Under the first stage (Plan the Review), we identified a need for a review of existing literature in sustainability-driven financial instruments to develop knowledge on how these instruments like green bonds, green loans, blended finance structures and FinTech-enabled products could enable low-carbon transition of SMEs. Preparation included developing a scope of review: a review of green innovation for SMEs to fill a perceived void in published literature in this area and provide a general overview of previous studies in this area. Next, a review protocol was formulated:

- Purpose: Integrate current literature, thematic analysis and future studies.
- Focus Area: Green finance for enabling low carbon transition of SMEs.
- Source: Google Scholar and Scopus database.
- Search String: ('green bonds' OR 'sustainability linked loans' OR 'blended finance' OR 'digital microfinance' OR 'policy-based lending') AND ('sme*' OR 'msme*' OR 'small and medium enterprise*') AND OR ('green finance' OR 'low carbon' OR 'carbon reduction' OR 'decarbonization').
- Inclusion Criteria: Topic (green innovation, green finance, green bonds, blended finance and carbon emission); Language: English. Article type: Academic journal peer-reviewed articles. Search Timeframe: From 2020 to 2025. The 5-year timeframe is chosen to include literature after the COVID-19 pandemic in order to allow full assessment of sustainability-driven financial model progress and trends in contemporary times.
- Exclusion Criteria: Quality peer review journal publications (JCR: Q1 or Q2). In our SLR, we ensured exclusion of predatory journal

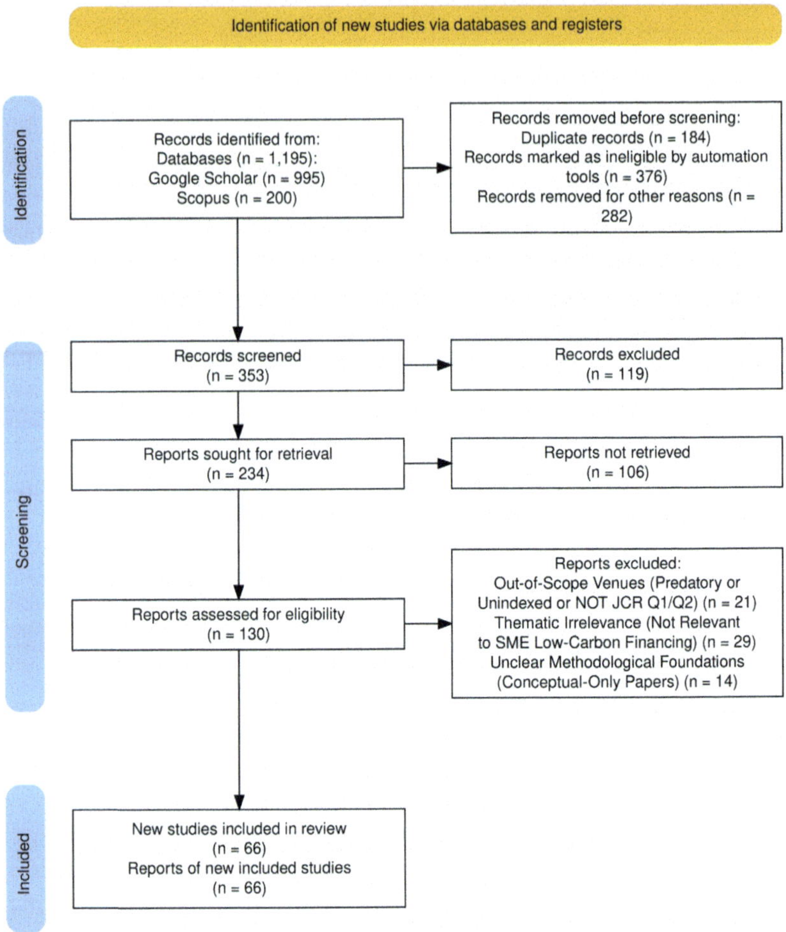

Fig. 1 PRISMA flow diagram (*Source* Authors Depiction, 2025; Haddaway et al., 2022)

publications by stringently cross-verifying all selected journals from Cabell's predatory reports as recommended by Da Silva et al. (2023).

Under the second stage (Carrying out review) consisted of running an advanced search with on Google Scholar and Scopus with the formulated search string (Boolean operators) in line with Harzing (2010) and narrowing this down by excluding those not pertinent to the research question and aim of the SLR, not published from 2020 and above or not published in JCR Q1 or Q2 ranked journals. This procedure is in line with usual practices in carrying out literature reviews in other studies (Mukherjee et al., 2024).

Data extraction proceeded via an iterative, team-based coding process in NVivo 15. After reading each article in full, we established a five-code framework directly grounded in the language of our corpus: Code 1: Green Financial Instruments & Models (green bonds, loans, blended structures, carbon markets, FinTech-enabled products); Code 2: Geographic Region(countries and regions); Code 3: Methodical Focus (research methodologies); Code 4: Barriers to SME Access (collateral shortfalls, perceived risk, information asymmetry, short-termism, institutional bias); Code 5: Policy, Regulation & Public–Private Ecosystems (subsidies, incentives, PPPs, regulatory frameworks). Each study was tagged to any code whose scope it addressed. We then generated word-frequency tables for each code and distilled four to eight thematic clusters per category, ensuring that our definitions remained faithful to the articles' own terminology and emphasis. In the third (final) stage (Reporting and Dissemination), these clustered themes were synthesised into clear, evidence-based implications and actionable recommendations for advancing green finance models for SMEs.

3 Results

The findings of this SLR of sustainability-driven financial models are presented in thematic order. These relate to instrument types, financing challenges, support ecosystem and policy and underpin our aim for an integrated systems approach to understanding the transition to low-carbon emission alternatives.

3.1 Definition and Architecture of Sustainability-Driven Financial Models

In line with our Code 1: Green Financial Instruments & Models, this study defines sustainability-driven financial models as financial approaches, products or strategies that incorporate environmental, social, and governance (ESG) considerations into financial decision-making and operations (Mejia-Escobar et al., 2020; Taera & Lakner, 2025; Tanchangya et al., 2025).

These models are fundamentally concerned with promoting sustainable development through reallocation of financial resources towards initiatives that will support the attainment of the SDGs and inclusive economic growth (Lagoarde-Segot, 2020; Udeagha & Ngepah, 2023; Xiong & Dai, 2023; Zournatzidou, 2025). One of the critical characteristics of such models is their capacity for reducing environmental impact through preventing carbon emissions, promoting green technology and inducing energy efficiency, thereby safeguarding ecological balance and attaining SDG7 and SDG13 (Bel Hadj Miled, 2025; Li et al., 2023; Mukherjee et al., 2024; Pang et al., 2022; Rasoulinezhad & Taghizadeh-Hesary, 2022; Yang et al., 2023). More so, these financial models serve the needs of society by promoting financial inclusion and reducing social inequalities (Nawaz et al., 2024; Taera & Lakner, 2025). They are also important in maximising the financial management of projects with environmental paybacks (Bel Hadj Miled, 2025; Zhang et al., 2020). Sustainability-driven financial models tend to be enabled by robust regulatory frameworks and public policy, such as green finance regulations and CSR measures, and more often augmented by FinTech innovation (Bel Hadj Liu & You, 2023; Miled, 2025; Tanchangya et al., 2025; Udeagha & Ngepah, 2023; Zournatzidou, 2025). Figure 2 depicts the architecture of green financial instruments and models from extant studies in the current SLR.

Figure 2 shows that sustainability-driven financial models can be categorised into broad and specific sustainability finance frameworks in addition to enabling technologies and funding mechanisms. Broad sustainable finance frameworks include the general concept of green finance—encompassing green financial products and instruments (Udeagha & Ngepah, 2023; Xiong & Dai, 2023), as well as green loans, investments and securities (Nawaz et al., 2024), which are provided by organisational structures such as green banks and community-based green funds (Mejia-Escobar et al., 2020; Mukherjee et al., 2024). Specific Sustainable Financial Instruments & Products consist of green bonds issued to finance eco-friendly projects (Appiah-Kubi et al., 2024; Lagoarde-Segot, 2020; Mukherjee et al., 2024; Reboredo et al., 2022; Taera & Lakner, 2025), green credit facilities such as green loans and credit lines (Liu & You, 2023; Lu

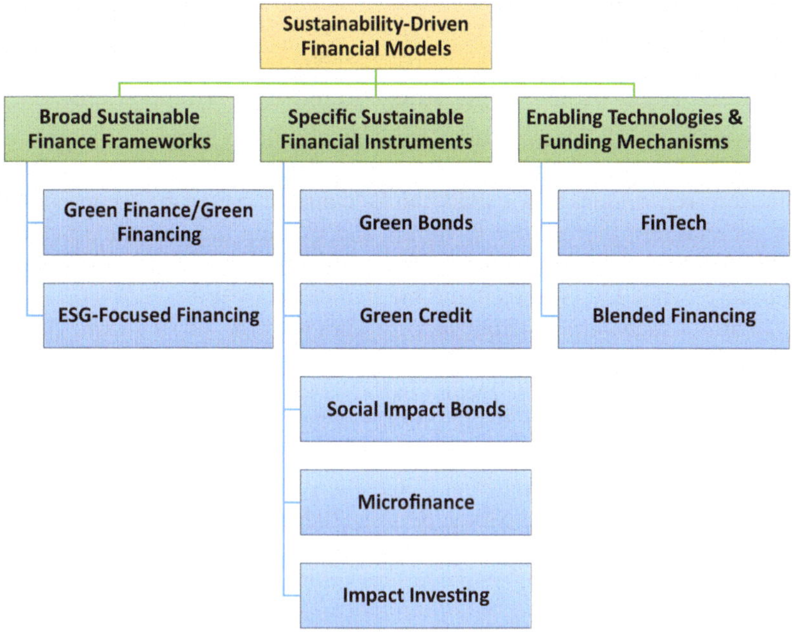

Fig. 2 Architecture of green financial instruments and models (*Source* Authors' Compilation, 2025)

et al., 2022; Udeagha & Ngepah, 2023), social impact bonds that link investment to measurable social outcomes (Mejia-Escobar et al., 2020), microfinance programmes targeting sustainable livelihoods (Nawaz et al., 2024; Taera & Lakner, 2025) and impact investing strategies designed to achieve defined social and environmental returns alongside financial performance (Taera & Lakner, 2025). Enabling Technologies & Funding Mechanisms cover FinTech applications in the form of blockchain, AI, digital banking & payment systems, crowdfunding, peer-to-peer lending (Tanchangya et al., 2025) and greentech business ecosystems (Zournatzidou, 2025). Funding mechanisms also involves blended finance strategies that combine private equity, government funding, and philanthropic or Islamic capital through public–private partnerships and risk-sharing mechanisms. Together, these categories delineate a comprehensive architecture for mobilising capital towards low-carbon transitions in SMEs.

3.2 Spatial Concentration of Literature and Methodological Approaches

In line with our Code 2: Geographic Region, we identified geographical concentration of the literature available along with our Code 3: Methodical Focus for the methodologies adopted in the selected studies. The research designs and geographical focus are crucial to comprehend for ascertaining the prevailing trends and existing gaps in the research field. Figure 3 illustrates the word cloud of geographical distribution of literature, while Fig. 4 depicts the methodical focus.

Figure 3 shows the distribution of studies with the aid of a word cloud in our SLR, revealing that most studies in recent times are concentrated in China (Bai & Wang, 2024; Deng et al., 2024; He et al., 2023; Lee et al., 2023; Li et al., 2023; Lin & Xu, 2024; Liu & You, 2023; Lu et al., 2022; Qian et al., 2023; Sun et al., 2022; Wang, 2023; Wang & Chang, 2023; Wang & Fan, 2023; Wang et al., 2023; Xiang et al., 2023; Xiao et al., 2024; Xing et al., 2022; Xiong & Dai, 2023; Xu et al., 2023; Yao & Liu, 2023; Zhang et al., 2020, 2021; Zhao et al., 2023). The United States and India each contribute to two studies—Pang et al. (2022) and

Fig. 3 Word cloud spatial concentration of literature (*Source* Authors' Compilation, 2025)

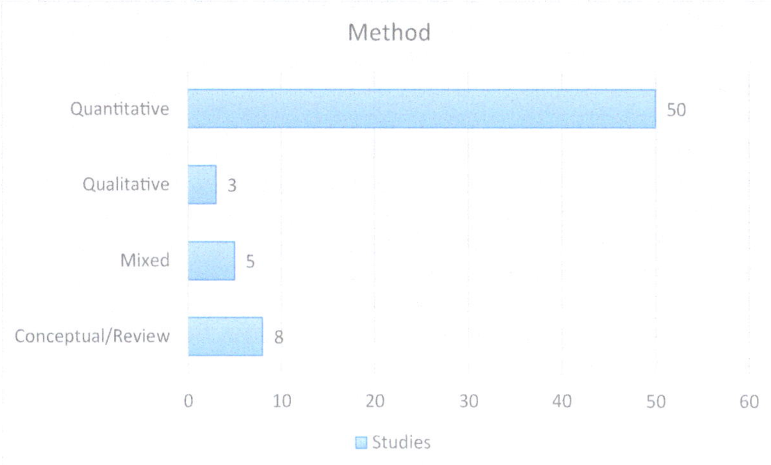

Fig. 4 Methodical focus of literature (*Source* Authors' Compilation, 2025)

Lichtenberger et al. (2022) for the United States; Kumar et al. (2024) and Qamruzzaman and Karim (2024) for India—while single-country analyses are scattered across Hong Kong (Liu et al., 2023), Argentina and Brazil (Mejia-Escobar et al., 2020), Pakistan (Kumar et al., 2022) and Ethiopia (Desalegn et al., 2024). Studies in the ASEAN region are quite rich, covering green financial models that can enable SMEs transform towards low carbon emission (Ahmed et al., 2022; Fu & Irfan, 2022; Lei et al., 2024; Taghizadeh-Hesary et al., 2022), whereas in the African continent, it is largely under-represented (Appiah-Kubi et al., 2024; Tamasiga et al., 2022). Such sparsity is also evident in Nordic countries contexts (Yang et al., 2023). This uneven geographic distribution reflects a heavy bias in favour of emerging Asian countries, as well as developed Western economies and invites future research attempts to address SMEs' green-finance concerns in underrepresented regions.

Figure 4 depicts a distribution of research methodologies deployed in the selected studies. It demonstrates an evident methodological bias in the literature with research quantitative research (Bel Hadj Jin, 2025; Miled, 2025) constituting 75.8% (50) of the studies. Conceptual/review studies (Lagoarde-Segot, 2020; Tanchangya et al., 2025) constitute 12.1% (8), whereas mixed-methods (Li et al., 2023; Taera & Lakner, 2025) and qualitative research (Kumar et al., 2024; Stein & McNeill, 2025) only constitute 4.5% (5) and 7.6% (3) respectively. Such dominance of quantitative approaches demonstrates a bias for empirical testing, statistical analysis and increased application of formal sustainability data in assessing SME finance models. Its strength lies in generating generalisable, comparable findings across contexts, which is good for policy and investment decisions. However, the low proportion of qualitative and mixed methods indicates a deficiency of knowledge of the complex, real-world SME experiences. Greater methodological heterogeneity diversity can ultimately give rise to a better of the behavioural, cultural and institutional perspectives of sustainability-driven finance that have been overlooked in exclusively quantitative research.

3.3 *Barriers in SMEs Green Finance Access*

In line with our Code 4: Barriers to SME Access, we identified some challenges that impede SME access to green finance, including various practical obstacles. These issues are urgent and necessitate collaboration among policymakers, financiers and SMEs practitioners. Understanding their real-world impact supports the design of effective strategies and guidance for stakeholders. Table 1 depicts the challenges in the form of barriers that abate SME green finance access.

Table 1 Barriers in SMEs access to green finance

Barriers	*Studies*
Collateral shortfalls	Lagoarde-Segot (2020)
Perceived risk	Nawaz et al. (2024), Tanchangya et al. (2025), Udeagha and Ngepah (2023), Li (2024) Mirza et al. (2023), Mukhtasor et al. (2023), Mukherjee et al. (2024) and Lichtenberger et al. (2022)
Information asymmetry	Liu et al. (2023) and Tanchangya et al (2025)
Short-termism	Kumar et al. (2022)
Institutional bias	Mejia-Escobar et al. (2020)
Digital infrastructure and FinTech adoption	Liu et al. (2023), Li (2024) and Tanchangya et al. (2025)

Source Authors' Compilation, 2025

Collateral shortfalls are an inherent problem for SMEs in the sense that traditional risk-rating and collateral-value systems have lagged changing technology profiles of green technologies. Other authors in green finance literature (Kumar et al., 2022; Nawaz et al., 2024) reach similar conclusion that 'green' capital-spending projects have diffuse, long-term benefits which cannot be quantified by pledgeable collateral (Lagoarde-Segot, 2020). Extended credit limitations would hence continue to SMEs without traditional asset bases (land, constructions) if there is no shift in credit risk assessment methods that takes cognisance of green project risk assessment.

Perceived risk continues to represent the top constraint for SMEs in assessing green finance across diverse regions (Pakistan, BRICS, China, OECD and Bangladesh) as averred in the studies by Nawaz et al. (2024) and Kumar et al. (2022). Even when objective quantitative measures suggest marginal incremental credit risk (e.g. due to fixed cash flows from energy-savings), financial institutions ask for higher spreads, collateral or stricter covenants. Several studies (Li, 2024; Nawaz et al., 2024; Tanchangya et al., 2025; Udeagha & Ngepah, 2023) indicate that without standard credit-enhancement products (e.g. partial guarantees, insurance products) from regulatory authorities and widespread empirical observations of green SME payment behaviour, perceived risk is likely to continue to be a constraining factor.

Information asymmetry is another barrier, although it manifests in arises in two ways. First, SMEs possess proprietary technical information (e.g. real-time energy performance), but are not able to—or prefer not to—provide it to banks in formats requested by them, preventing lenders from assessing expected outcomes (Liu et al., 2023; Tanchangya et al., 2025). Second, for most banks there may be insufficient internal capability to assess green technologies (Mukherjee et al., 2024)—Lichtenberger et al. (2022), from an OECD viewpoint, report that an absence of 'sustainability-literate' credit officers induces due diligence and expenses. Without third-party verifiers or standardised environment accounting, his gap persists—Tanchangya et al. (2025) and Liu et al. (2023) argue that without such platforms of data transparency, green SME loans are likely to be underpriced or overpriced by lenders.

Short-termism is a barrier for SMEs' green transition that exists due to the universal disparity between project payback horizons and finance tenors. In Pakistan's economy, which experiences truncated working capital and business cycles, SMEs shun any investment not expected to bring near or immediate ROI (Kumar et al., 2022). Banks reinforce such an expectation by discounting payback streams of several years by an amount that heavily penalises them, effectively stigmatising most green projects as poor net-present-value projects (Kumar et al., 2022; Miaoet al., 2025). Short-term thinking will continue to dissuade SMEs from making an investment in sustainability, unless donor agencies, development finance institutions or green windows underwrite or part-finance payback for the initial years (Hong & Xiao, 2024).

Institutional bias of the finance system dissuades SMEs from embracing green finance through three inter-linked channels. First, governance and leadership of several financial institutions are anchored by traditional finance thinking frames, and such anchoring gives rise to a strategy blindspot for lending for sustainability (Kumar et al., 2022; Liu et al., 2023)—institutional bias suppresses boardroom-level commitment to channel green credit allocation. Secondly, green lending programmes are token or marginal unless tokenised in product design and incentives. Several banks possess token green finance windows without de facto integration of sustainability considerations into regular credit approval or employee incentive programmes and therefore weakening operational incentives for sustainability (Ma et al., 2023; Zournatzidou, 2025). Thirdly, oversight by regulators continues to view green loans as variations of traditional products, followed by minimal risk-weighted incentives, capital relief or Basel-aligned adjustments. Such regulative stasis supports institutional habits of traditional lending (Lee et al., 2023; Xiang et al., 2023). Without redesign of governance arrangements, incentive mechanisms and regulative frameworks to actively encourage sustainability-aligned credit flows, institutional bias will continue to marginalise SME engagement within low-carbon transitions.

Digital adoption barriers for SMEs reflect a deficiency of IoT-enabled monitoring and emerging FinTech platforms. Liu et al. (2023) cite that SMEs are missing 'real-time data' from 'smart metres,' preventing FinTech lenders from verifying 'projected cash flows' and perpetuating 'information asymmetry.' Li (2024) further adds that without sufficient 'data analytics' and 'digital infrastructure,' traditional banks are uncertain about FinTech's ability to 'de-risk' green lending and prevent wider 'FinTech-enabled green finance' up-take. Tanchangya et al. (2025) observe in BRICS markets that 'digital readiness' deficits exacerbate 'perceived risk' and limit green finance adoption since creditors are unable to access prompt ESG measures or adopt 'blockchain-based registries' to verify. To overcome these constraints, literature increasingly reflects interoperable data platforms, standardised systems of ESG scores and public–private partnerships to upgrade digital infrastructure to that required by green SME finance (Li, 2024; Liu et al., 2023; Tanchangya et al., 2025).

3.4 Policy, Regulation and Public–Private Ecosystems

In line with our Code 5: Policy, Regulation & Public–Private Ecosystems, we explored the institutional frameworks, regulatory instruments and collaborative structures facilitating (or hindering) SME low-carbon transition. The literature suggests that enforcement machinery, national policy, finance facilitators and multi-stakeholder alliances cumulatively shape the SME facilitating environment. Hence, it is paramount that these drivers are recognised as interconnected to design effective solutions that harmonises government mandates, market incentives and cross-sectoral cooperation. Table 2 presents the key sub-themes of policy and regulatory frameworks.

Table 2 reveals the policy and regulatory frameworks for SME low-carbon transition by situating formal rules, incentives and collaborative structures as critical enablers. Regarding Regulatory Frameworks, national climate policies such as renewable energy acts and nationally determined contribution targets underscore governments' role in the supply of direction (Nawaz et al., 2024). Carbon pricing mechanisms—like carbon taxes and emission trades—induce SMEs towards low-cost mitigation (Liu et al., 2023), thus there are enforcement gaps where inspection systems and penalty frameworks are unequal (Kumar et al., 2022; Liu & You, 2023). Institutional Mechanisms contribute to this: subsidies for solar installation and tax rebates speed up adoption (Kumar et al., 2022; Liu et al., 2023), and green certification programmes and ISO 14001 rebates facilitate market entry (Liu & You, 2023). Policy coherence between the national and subnational levels is essential in order to avoid confusion (Liu et al., 2023; Nawaz et al., 2024). Financial Ecosystem Enablers also include green bonds and concessional loans, though with low awareness (Kumar et al., 2022; Liu & You, 2023), and emerging climate-risk disclosure requirements drive mitigation planning (Liu et al., 2023). Finally, Public–Private Ecosystem Dynamics describe how PPP models reduce entry costs (Nawaz et al., 2024), and national climate hubs accelerate technology transfer (Liu et al., 2023), while multi-stakeholder workshops define sector-specific roadmaps (Kumar et al., 2022).

Table 2 Policy and regulatory frameworks for SME low-carbon transition

Main theme	*Sub-Theme*	*Specific policies*	*Citations*
Regulatory Frameworks	National Climate Policies	• National Renewable Energy Act • National Climate Change Policy • Nationally Determined Contribution targets	Zournatzidou (2025), Lei et al. (2024), Nawaz et al. (2024), Qian et al. (2023)
	Carbon Pricing Mechanisms	• Carbon Tax legislation • Emissions Trading Scheme • Carbon credit trading rules	Liu et al. (2023)
	Compliance and Enforcement Issues	• Environmental Protection Enforcement Act • Regulatory inspection protocols for SMEs • Penalty frameworks for non-compliance	Tanchangya et al. (2025) Liu and You (2023) and Kumar et al. (2022)
Institutional Mechanisms	Government Incentives	• Solar-installation subsidies for SMEs • Tax relief for energy-efficient machinery • Grants for renewable equipment purchase	Bel Hadj Miled (2025), Jin (2025), Liu et al. (2023), and Kumar et al. (2022)
	Environmental Standards and Certification	• National Green Certification Programme (e.g. 'Green SME' label) • ISO 14001 adoption incentives • Eco-labelling guidelines	Tanchangya et al. (2025) Liu and You (2023)
	Policy Coherence and Alignment	• Harmonisation of energy policy with industrial development plans • Subnational–federal regulatory alignment guidelines	Nawaz et al. (2021), Liu et al. (2023), and Lagoarde-Segot (2020)

(continued)

Table 2 (continued)

Main theme	*Sub-Theme*	*Specific policies*	*Citations*
Financial Ecosystem Enablers	Green Finance Instruments	• Green bond issuance guidelines for SMEs • Concessional loan programmes • Green credit line through national banks	Jin (2025), Liu and You (2023) and Kumar et al. (2022)
	Climate Risk Disclosure Regulations	• Mandatory climate-risk reporting requirements • Sustainability reporting framework	Liu et al. (2023) and Lagoarde-Segot (2020)
	Role of Development Finance Institutions (DFIs)	• DFI concessional loan facilities for low-carbon projects • Capacity-building grants/funding from DFIs	Tanchangya et al. (2025) and Kumar et al. (2022)
Public–Private Ecosystem Dynamics	Public–Private Partnerships (PPP)	• PPP framework for solar-farm development • Risk-sharing agreements (government + private investors) • Co-financing schemes for green infrastructure	Nawaz et al. (2024)

(continued)

Table 2 (continued)

Main theme	*Sub-Theme*	*Specific policies*	*Citations*
	Collaborative Platforms	• National Climate Hub (public research institute + SME clusters) • Technology Transfer Centre for cleantech • Sectoral innovation clusters	Mukherjee et al. (2024), Hong and Xiao (2024), and Liu et al. (2023)
	Multi-Stakeholder Engagement	• Stakeholder workshops (government, academia, industry) • Sector-specific decarbonisation roadmaps co-developed in forums • Public consultations on draft policies	Desalegn et al. (2024), Mukherjee et al. (2024), and Kumar et al. (2022)

Source Authors' Compilation, 2025

Several studies highlight misalignment between national objectives and local implementation (Liu et al., 2023; Nawaz et al., 2024). Such fragmentation hinders the ability of SMEs to invest for the long term. While green bonds and concessional loans are offered repeatedly (Kumar et al., 2022; Liu & You, 2023), they are absorbed unevenly—SMEs either have insufficient awareness or seldom have capacity to fulfil eligibility criteria. Extant studies (Mejia-Escobar & González-Ruiz, 2020; Nawaz et al., 2024) indicates that successful PPPs rely on clearly defined risk-sharing and open administration; otherwise, small businesses are marginalised. Climate risk disclosure is in its infancy (Liu et al., 2023). Without common standards, data quality varies widely and hence reported information is of little value to financiers.

4 Discussion

Our SLR illustrates that sustainability-driven financial models for SMEs cover a broad array of instruments, from traditional green loans and bonds, blended-finance structures, to financial technology-enabled platforms. All of which aim to redirect capital towards low-carbon transitions in developing public–private ecosystems in line with SDG 13: climate action (Lichtenberger et al., 2022; Mejia-Escobar et al., 2020; Taera & Lakner, 2025; Tanchangya et al., 2025; Udeagha & Ngepah, 2023). This result both confirms and builds on extant SLRs like Mukherjee et al. (2024) on the variety of instruments like traditional green finance and reinforces Yadav et al.'s (2024) finding that conventional approaches still prevail despite new digital platforms emerging. Nevertheless, our study offers divergence from prior research in important respects. First, whereas Zournatzidou (2025) and others largely confine 'green' or 'clean' finance to uses in energy, our study offers instead a thematic synthesis of the prevailing sustainability-driven financial instruments across industries and barriers affecting SMEs' transitions to low carbon. Second, contrary to Tamasiga et al.'s (2022) emphasis on methodological diversity, we unveil a considerable empirical bias: 75.8% of studies employ quantitative designs (Bel Hadj Jin, 2025; Miled, 2025), with qualitative or mixed-method studies comparatively scarce.

Existing literature is geographically biased towards China and other emerging markets and developed economies (Bai & Wang, 2024; Liu & You, 2023), with areas like Africa and Latin America substantially under-researched (Appiah-Kubi et al., 2024; Tamasiga et al., 2022). In different contexts, SMEs face common challenges in their bid to obtain green finance—inadequate collateral (Lagoarde-Segot, 2020), perceived risk (Nawaz et al., 2024; Udeagha & Ngepah, 2023), informational asymmetries (Liu et al., 2023), emphasis on short-term horizons (Kumar et al., 2022) and institutional biases (Mejia-Escobar et al., 2020)—which have already been proven to overcome through public–private co-financing schemes and early-stage grants (Mukherjee et al., 2024; Sharma et al., 2023).

Whilst our SLR process provides considerable insight into sustainable finance literature, we observed considerable limitations in extant studies. The dominance of quantitative methodologies with longitudinal designs (Jin, 2025; Liu et al., 2023) limits the scope to derive managerial insights into distinct phases, mainly due to sparse cross-sectional research (Appiah-Kubi et al., 2024) into SME decision-making at particular time-points. Divergent conceptualisations of 'sustainability-focused financial models' (Mejia-Escobar et al., 2020) as well as the absence of standardised methods to assess impact add to the heterogeneity which hampers synthesis. Sectoral as well as geographic biases in findings also limit the scope to generalise them: policy impacts in established markets might not be relevant in under-representative areas (Appiah-Kubi et al., 2024; Tamasiga et al., 2022). Also, research into digital infrastructure as well as the role of FinTech to overcome information asymmetry is under-developed and disjointed (Li, 2024; Liu & You, 2023).

Our review process is equally characterised by intrinsic limitations. In looking solely at English-language, Scopus-indexed Q1/Q2, peer-reviewed articles in journals from 2020 to 2025, it is possible that we have missed relevant grey literature as well as separately indexed regional studies (Da Silva et al., 2023). In addition, while using NVivo-based standardised coding as per established protocols (Snyder, 2019; Tranfield et al., 2003), thematic clustering entailed interpretative choice. These strengths and limitations provide the framework in which the theoretical and policy implications are addressed in the ensuing subsections.

4.1 Theoretical Contributions

The theoretical contribution of this SLR mainly lies in extending and refining existing understandings of sustainability-driven financial models regarding SMEs. Grounded in an extensive synthesis of contemporary literature, the SLR brings to bear an enhanced framework based on established theories, such as Institutional Theory, Information Asymmetry Theory, Innovation Diffusion Theory and Stakeholder Theory. The aim is to clarify the complex relationships between financial availability, regulatory environments and technological advancement in the context of sustainable financial models that position SMEs towards positive climate action.

Firstly, this current study expands the understanding of the Stakeholder Theory (Freeman, 1984) to encompass SMEs as essential players towards the achievement of global climate goals in particular, the United Nations' SDGs—notably SDG 7 (Affordable and Clean Energy) and SDG 13 (Climate Action) (Taghizadeh-Hesary et al., 2022; Tanchangya et al., 2025). By explicitly affirming SME commitment in international policy measures such as the Paris Agreement (Li et al., 2023; Udeagha &

Ngepah, 2023), we posit a theoretical groundwork to comprehend the twofold roles played by SMEs—as economic agents and as powerful environmental stakeholders responsible to enable sustainable transformations through the deployment and development of green technologies (Hossain et al., 2024; Kumar et al., 2022).

Secondly, the current study bridges theoretical gaps in green finance by exploring the distinctive financial barriers SMEs encounter—particularly collateral shortfalls (Lagoarde-Segot, 2020), perceived risk (Nawaz et al., 2024) and information asymmetry (Liu & You, 2023; Tanchangya et al., 2025). Our analysis explicitly draws upon Information Asymmetry Theory (Akerlof, 1970), demonstrating how incomplete and uneven distribution of information exacerbates SMEs' difficulties in accessing green finance. This perspective improves understanding by emphasising the need for risk analysis and credit assessment structures that is specifically designed to take cognisance of valuing sustainablility-driven projects.

Thirdly, this current research provides insights on the Innovation Diffusion Theory by Rogers (2003) in conceptualising FinTech as an enabler towards transition to low-carbon activities by SMEs. Specifically, based on contemporary studies in digital inclusive finance (Lin & Xu, 2024; Tanchangya et al., 2025), this research highlights how developments in blockchain, AI and digital microfinance can accelerate sustainability adoption by mitigating problems related to perceptions of risks and information asymmetry; hence, enhancing the diffusion of sustainable financial practices among SMEs.

Fourthly, the research is significant to Institutional Theory (DiMaggio & Powell, 1983) in emphasising the role of regulatory policies, national climate policies, as well as public–private partnership (PPP) institutions (Liu & You, 2023; Zournatzidou, 2025) in collectively shaping the institutional settings supporting sustainable adjustments to SMEs. The SLR deepens theoretical understanding through illustrating the role policy coherence, compatible incentives, as well as collaborative institutions in governance as critical framework institutions underpinning the effective implementation of financial changes towards sustainability.

4.2 Policy Implications

Based on the theoretical foundations in our SLR, several consistent policy implications emerge, guided by a careful review of the literature on low-carbon finance applicable to SMEs published between 2020 and 2025. These implications point towards the necessity of creating a resilient yet also flexible policy framework, and in particular for the purpose of assisting SMEs in their successful transition into sustainable, low-carbon business practices. One of the key aspects of such implications is the enhancement of regulatory frameworks. Policy makers are therefore called upon to support nation-level climate actions by legislating renewable energy targets and nationally determined contributions for SME transformation into low-carbon enterprises (Lei et al., 2024; Zournatzidou, 2025). The literature suggests that carbon pricing instruments in the form of tax or emissions trading system plays a vital role in internalising environmental expenses as well as the transmission of a well-defined, consistent policy guide (Liu et al., 2023). More so, regulatory bodies should streamline monitoring protocols and modify sanction structures in ways that better account for SME operational scale in the bid to enable compliance without imposing undue administrative or fiscal burdens (Kumar et al., 2022; Tanchangya et al., 2025).

Strengthening institutional mechanisms is also crucial. There is a need to package existing financial incentives, such as subsidies for the installation of solar panels, fiscal incentives for the use of energy-efficient equipment, and grants for the use of renewable energy, into well-organised packages specifically designed for SMEs (Bel Hadj Jin, 2025; Liu et al., 2023; Miled, 2025). Such comprehensive approaches lower transaction costs and simplify administrative procedures, thus decreasing barriers to adoption. In addition, enhancing coherence across both subnational and national levels, particularly by promoting complementary interlinkages between climate goals and industrial development strategies, mitigates regulatory fragmentation and ensures effective policy implementation (Lagoarde-Segot, 2020; Nawaz et al., 2024). Moreover, promoting the wider application of ISO 14001 standards and establishing nationally recognised certifications for 'Green SMEs' can greatly enhance market credibility, encourage early compliance and facilitate extensive participation (Liu & You, 2023; Tanchangya et al., 2025).

The sophistication and comprehensiveness of financial ecosystems require significant policy attention. Central banks, in coordination with DFIs, should actively increase the provision of capital for SMEs by developing explicit guidelines for the issuance of SME-focused green bonds and concessional loans, as well as creating special credit lines dedicated to sustainable projects (Jin, 2025; Kumar et al., 2022). More so, introducing rigorous climate-risk disclosure obligations and extensive sustainability reporting systems would reduce informational asymmetries, enhance market transparency and strengthen investor confidence, stimulating increased participation of actors in the private sector (Lagoarde-Segot, 2020; Liu et al., 2023).

Dynamic public–private ecosystem establishment is equally an important strategic goal for sustainability. PPPs can be effective tools to mobilise long-term capital, especially in transparent risk-sharing mechanisms defined through formal contracts and properly designed co-financing schemes in their bid to support renewable energy infrastructures (Nawaz et al., 2024). The establishment of collaborative ecosystems has further benefits, as evidenced in schemes such as national climate innovation hubs as well as specialised technology-transfer facilities. Knowledge-exchange forums such as these collaborative platforms accelerate technology diffusions as well as the joint development of useful, sector-specific action plans to overcome the diversified operational problems faced by SMEs (Desalegn et al., 2024; Hong & Xiao, 2024; Mukherjee et al., 2024).

4.3 *Research Gaps and Recommendations for Future Studies*

A critical evaluation of the literature reveals several significant gaps that impede our understanding of how sustainability-driven financial models support effective climate action in SMEs. Overarchingly, prior studies lack a holistic measurement framework to quantify the wide-ranging effect of green finance on innovation and environmental performance among SMEs, and Fig. 5 depicts this.

In Fig. 5, Overarching Gaps presents the knowledge gap identified in current literature on sustainability finance. Most notable is the metric for measuring green innovation—most studies advance isolated indicators yet rarely test how policy instruments shape tangible outcomes (Mukherjee et al., 2024), leaving green innovation reduced to narrow proxies such as patent counts (Qamruzzaman & Karim, 2024) that overlook systemic dynamics. More so, attention remains skewed towards heavily polluting sectors, without taking cognisance of inherently green firms; thus, cross-sector comparisons remain fragmented. Equally underexplored are the policy-mediated links between finance, technology adoption and carbon efficiency across differing market and emissions contexts (Wang et al., 2023). Empirical work on green bonds is sparse; their non-linear effects on urban sustainability and innovation trajectories are still

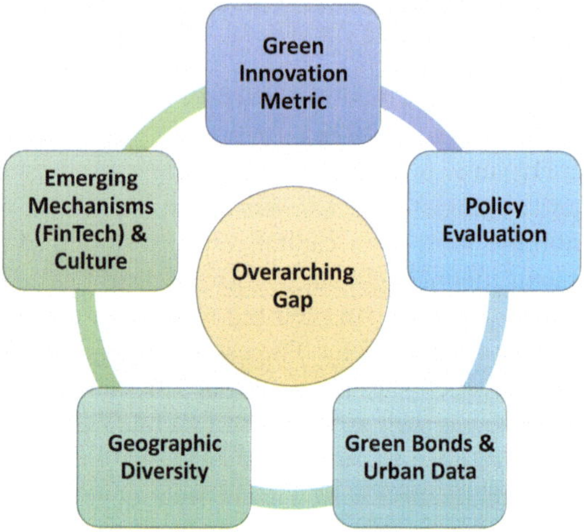

Fig. 5 Overarching gap (*Source* Authors' Compilation, 2025)

conjectural. A pronounced geographical concentration compounds these gaps: scholarship centres on China and other BRICS or OECD economies (Ahmed et al., 2022; Xu et al., 2023), limiting external validity. Underrepresented regions in sustainability literature, particularly developing economies from Africa, South America and advanced Nordic nations, lack proper datasets and analysis (Tamasiga et al., 2022). Finally, gaps in the literature exist on the facilitative function of fintech, digital inclusion and socio-cultural determinants of private-sector adoption of sustainability, implying that it is unexplored (Ahmed et al., 2022).

To effectively address these critical gaps, future research with the aid of wider and more integrated methodologies, should go beyond isolated or stand-alone metrics in the bid to develop integrated frameworks of green innovation and sustainable urban development impacts. Researchers need to expand analytical techniques, such as longitudinal and non-linear analysis, as more refined datasets are developed. Research horizons must be expanded geographically and sectorally to compare impacts between polluting and inherently sustainable SMEs and research on previously under-emphasised regions like under-developed and developing as well as Nordic economies. Furthermore, future research must investigate the different mechanisms whereby green finance takes its impacts, including green procurement, corporate governance practices, regulatory roles and financial innovation products (Jin, 2025). Coupling fintech elements such as digital inclusive finance, alongside qualitative research methods like the use of stakeholder interviews would provide richer, contextually relevant insights critical towards making inclusive transition towards the realisation of global climate action for sustainability.

5 Conclusion

This SLR provides critical answers on the financial models supporting the low-carbon transition of SMEs. The findings underscore the fact that despite SMEs being significant carbon emission contributors globally, their green transformation is substantially hindered by financial constraints, perceived risks and information asymmetry. By synthesising diverse financial models such as green bonds, loans, blending finance and innovative FinTech-based platforms leads the research to highlight the ecosystem required to facilitate the sustainable transition of SMEs. Our results demonstrate the pivotal roles of policy coherence, effective regulatory frameworks and robust PPPs in overcoming the long-standing financing constraints, and mobilising the potential of SMEs towards green innovation. While our analysis acknowledges limitations in geographical concentration and the dominance of quantitative methodologies, the study confidently contributes to theoretical understanding and practical strategies for promoting sustainable finance among SMEs. Ultimately, our research emphasises the urgency of an integrated financial and policy ecosystem, which not only facilitates SMEs' access to necessary capital but also strategically positions them as essential stakeholders in achieving global climate action and sustainable development goals.

Acknowledgements The authors would like to thank the researchers whose findings served as the basis for this SLR. Additional appreciation is also extended to Asia Pacific University of Technology & Innovation (APU), Kuala Lumpur for providing access to their well-stocked digital library, including major academic database subscriptions, through which several of the peer-reviewed articles used in this study were accessed.

References

Ahmed, N., Areche, F., Sheikh, A., & Lahiani, A. (2022). Green finance and green energy nexus in ASEAN countries: A bootstrap panel causality test. *Energies, 15*(14), 5068. https://doi.org/10.3390/en15145068

Akerlof, G. A. (1970). The market for "lemons": Quality uncertainty and the market mechanism. *Quarterly Journal of Economics, 84*(3), 488–500. https://doi.org/10.2307/1879431

Appiah-Kubi, E., Koranteng, F. O., Dura, C. C., Mihăilă, A. A., Drigă, I., & Preda, A. (2024). Green financing and sustainability reporting among SMEs: The role of pro-environmental behavior and digitization. *Journal of Cleaner Production, 478*, Article 143939. https://doi.org/10.1016/j.jclepro.2024.143939

Bai, M., & Wang, W. (2024). Role of green bonds in developing ESG projects in Eastern provinces of China. *Humanities & Social Sciences Communications, 11*(1742). https://doi.org/10.1057/s41599-024-04353-y

Bel Hadj Miled, K. (2025). Nexus between fintech, green finance natural resources, economic growth and environment sustainability: Evidence from BRICS countries. *Future Business Journal, 11*(1). https://doi.org/10.1186/s43093-025-00469-y

Da Silva, J. A. T., Moradzadeh, M., Yamada, Y., Dunleavy, D. J., & Tsigaris, P. (2023). Cabells' predatory reports criteria: Assessment and proposed revisions. *The Journal of Academic Librarianship, 49*(1), Article 102659. https://doi.org/10.1016/j.acalib.2022.102659

Deng, Y., Cao, Z., & Yang, N. (2024). Understanding the nexus between fintech, natural resources, green investment, and environmental sustainability in China: A DYNARDL approach. *Resources Policy, 91*(104900), Article 104900. https://doi.org/10.1016/j.resourpol.2024.104900

Desalegn, G., Tangl, A., Fekete-Farkas, M., Gudisa, G., & Boros, A. (2024). Linking policies and regulations to sustainable finance for the promotion of urban agriculture: Evidence from micro and small businesses. *Heliyon, 10*(11), Article e31938. https://doi.org/10.1016/j.heliyon.2024.e31938

DiMaggio, P. J., & Powell, W. W. (1983). The iron cage revisited: Institutional isomorphism and collective rationality in organizational fields. *American Sociological Review, 48*(2), 147–160. https://doi.org/10.2307/2095101

Freeman, R. E. (1984). *Strategic management: A stakeholder approach*. Pitman.

Fu, W., & Irfan, M. (2022). Does green financing develop a cleaner environment for environmental sustainability: Empirical insights from association of southeast Asian nations economies. *Frontiers in Psychology, 13*, Article 904768. https://doi.org/10.3389/fpsyg.2022.904768

Haddaway, N. R., Page, M. J., Pritchard, C. C., & McGuinness, L. A. (2022). PRISMA2020: An R package and Shiny app for producing PRISMA 2020-compliant flow diagrams, with interactivity for optimised digital transparency and Open Synthesis. *Campbell Systematic Reviews, 18*(2). https://doi.org/10.1002/cl2.1230

Harzing, A. W. (2010). *The publish or perish book: Your guide to effective and responsible citation analysis*. Tarma Software Research Pty Ltd. https://harzing.com

He, J., Iqbal, W., & Su, F. (2023). Nexus between renewable energy investment, green finance, and sustainable development: Role of industrial structure and technical innovations. *Renewable Energy, 210*, 715–724. https://doi.org/10.1016/j.renene.2023.04.010

Hong, Z., & Xiao, K. (2024). Digital economy structuring for sustainable development: The role of blockchain and artificial intelligence in improving supply chain and reducing negative environmental impacts. *Scientific Reports, 14*(3912). https://doi.org/10.1038/s41598-024-53760-3

Hossain, M. R., Rao, A., Sharma, G. D., Dev, D., & Kharbanda, A. (2024). Empowering energy transition: Green innovation, digital finance, and the path to sustainable prosperity through green finance initiatives. *Energy Economics, 136*, Article 107736. https://doi.org/10.1016/j.eneco.2024.107736

Jin, C. (2025). Investigating the intersection of ESG investing, green recovery, and SME development in the OECD. *Humanities & Social Sciences Communications, 12*(1). https://doi.org/10.1057/s41599-025-04873-1

Kumar, L., Nadeem, F., Sloan, M., Restle-Steinert, J., Deitch, M. J., Naqvi, S. A., Kumar, A., & Sassanelli, C. (2022). Fostering green finance for sustainable Development: A focus on textile and leather small medium enterprises in Pakistan. *Sustainability, 14*(19), 11908. https://doi.org/10.3390/su141911908

Kumar, P., Taneja, S., & Ozen, E. (2024). Exploring the influence of green bonds on sustainable development through low-carbon financing mobilization. *International Journal of Law and Management*. https://doi.org/10.1108/ijlma-01-2024-0030

Lagoarde-Segot, T. (2020). Financing the sustainable development goals. *Sustainability, 12*(7), 2775. https://doi.org/10.3390/su12072775

Lee, C. C., Wang, F., & Chang, Y.-F. (2023). Towards net-zero emissions: Can green bond policy promote green innovation and green space? *Energy Economics, 121*(106675), Article 106675. https://doi.org/10.1016/j.eneco.2023.106675

Lei, H., Zhu, Y., Tan, J., & Zhang, X. (2024). Blending financial innovation with natural resource utilization: Pathways to green economic expansion. *Resources Policy, 89*(104568), Article 104568. https://doi.org/10.1016/j.resourpol.2023.104568

Li, C., Solangi, Y. A., & Ali, S. (2023). Evaluating the factors of green finance to achieve carbon peak and carbon neutrality targets in China: A Delphi and fuzzy AHP approach. *Sustainability, 15*(3), 2721. https://doi.org/10.3390/su15032721

Li, D. (2024). Green finance, fossil fuel efficiency, and sustainable development in OECD. *Resources Policy, 98*, Article 105306. https://doi.org/10.1016/j.resourpol.2024.105306

Lichtenberger, A., Braga, J. P., & Semmler, W. (2022). Green bonds for the transition to a low-carbon economy. *Econometrics, 10*(1), 11. https://doi.org/10.3390/econometrics10010011

Lin, B., & Xu, C. (2024). Digital inclusive finance and corporate environmental performance: Insights from Chinese micro, small and medium-sized manufacturing enterprises. *Borsa Istanbul Review, 24*(3), 460–473. https://doi.org/10.1016/j.bir.2024.02.009

Lin, S., & Wu, R. (2022). On the nexus between energy efficiency, financial inclusion and environment: Evidence from emerging seven economies using novel research methods. *Economic Research-Ekonomska Istraživanja, 35*(1), 6756–6779. https://doi.org/10.1080/1331677x.2022.2053362

Liu, Q., & You, Y. (2023). FinTech and green credit development—Evidence from China. *Sustainability, 15*(7), 5903. https://doi.org/10.3390/su15075903

Liu, Y., Dong, L., & Fang, M. M. (2023). Advancing 'Net Zero Competition' in Asia-Pacific under a dynamic era: A comparative study on the carbon neutrality policy toolkit in Japan, Singapore and Hong Kong. *Global Public Policy and Governance, 3*(1), 12–40. https://doi.org/10.1007/s43508-023-00065-2

Lu, Y., Gao, Y., Zhang, Y., & Wang, J. (2022). Can the green finance policy force the green transformation of high-polluting enterprises? A quasi-natural experiment based on "Green Credit Guidelines." *Energy Economics, 114*, Article 106265. https://doi.org/10.1016/j.eneco.2022.106265

Ma, M., Zhu, X., Liu, M., & Huang, X. (2023). Combining the role of green finance and environmental sustainability on green economic growth: Evidence from G-20 economies. *Renewable Energy, 207*, 128–136. https://doi.org/10.1016/j.renene.2023.02.046

Mejia-Escobar, J. C., González-Ruiz, J. D., & Duque-Grisales, E. (2020). Sustainable financial products in the Latin America banking industry: Current status and insights. *Sustainability, 12*(14), 5648. https://doi.org/10.3390/su12145648

Miao, Y., Tian, Y., Cao, J., & Yu, X. (2025). Green finance and privatization of green projects in the fossil fuels industry. *Resources Policy, 103*(105547), Article 105547. https://doi.org/10.1016/j.resourpol.2025.105547

Mirza, N., Afzal, A., Umar, M., & Skare, M. (2023). The impact of green lending on banking performance: Evidence from SME credit portfolios in the BRIC. *Economic Analysis and Policy, 77*, 843–850. https://doi.org/10.1016/j.eap.2022.12.024

Mukherjee, A., Owen, R., Scott, J. M., & Lyon, F. (2024). Financing green innovation startups: a systematic literature review on early-stage SME funding. *Venture Capital*, 1–27. https://doi.org/10.1080/13691066.2024.2410730

Mukhtasor, M., Listiana, L., Hermala, I., & Nur Fauziah, N. (2023). Scaling up renewable energy financing through Islamic blended finance: Case study in Indonesia. *International Journal of Energy Economics and Policy, 13*(5), 634–644. https://doi.org/10.32479/ijeep.14710

Nawaz, A., Li, Z., & Su, C. W. (2024). Inquisitive exploration of green finance, social finance, and capital formation in shaping economic development: Insights from BRICS Countries. *Discover Sustainability*, 5(332). https://doi.org/10.1007/s43621-024-00548-0

Nie, P., Zhong, J., Ren, Z., & Huang, J. (2024). Sustainable financing solutions for the growth of resource-driven economies in the digital economy age. *Resources Policy, 98*, Article 105350. https://doi.org/10.1016/j.resourpol.2024.105350

Pang, L., Zhu, M. N., & Yu, H. (2022). Is green finance really a blessing for green technology and carbon efficiency? *Energy Economics, 114*, Article 106272. https://doi.org/10.1016/j.eneco.2022.106272

Qamruzzaman, M., & Karim, S. (2024). Unveiling the synergy: Green finance, technological innovation, green energy, and carbon neutrality. *PLOS One, 19*(10), Article e0308170. https://doi.org/10.1371/journal.pone.0308170

Qian, F., Pu, Y., & Shang, Y. (2023). Financing preferences and practices for developing sustainable exhibitions in Chinese companies. *Humanities & Social Sciences Communications, 10*(938). https://doi.org/10.1057/s41599-023-02467-3

Rasoulinezhad, E., & Taghizadeh-Hesary, F. (2022). Role of green finance in improving energy efficiency and renewable energy development. *Energy Efficiency, 15*(14). https://doi.org/10.1007/s12053-022-10021-4

Reboredo, J. C., Ugolini, A., & Ojea-Ferreiro, J. (2022). Do green bonds de-risk investment in low-carbon stocks? *Economic Modelling, 108*, Article 105765. https://doi.org/10.1016/j.econmod.2022.105765

Rogers, E. M. (2003). *Diffusion of innovations* (5th ed.). Free Press.

Sharma, K., Mahna, T., Jain, S., Dhir, S., Rao, N., Biyani, A., Sikka, H., Yadav, R., Dua, S., & Gupta, A. (2023). Bibliometric review of blended finance and partial risk guarantee: Establishing needs and advantages. *International Journal of Financial Studies, 11*(3), 103. https://doi.org/10.3390/ijfs11030103

Snyder, H. (2019). Literature review as a research methodology: An overview and guidelines. *Journal of Business Research, 104*, 333–339. https://doi.org/10.1016/j.jbusres.2019.07.039

Stein, F., & McNeill, D. (2025). Blended finance to the rescue? Subsidies, vaccine bonds and matching funds in global health. *Global Public Health, 20*(1), 2468338. https://doi.org/10.1080/17441692.2025.2468338

Sun, J., Zhai, N., Miao, J., & Sun, H. (2022). Can green finance effectively promote the carbon emission reduction in "local-neighborhood" areas?—Empirical evidence from China. *Agriculture, 12*(10), 1550. https://doi.org/10.3390/agriculture12101550

Taera, E. G., & Lakner, Z. (2025). Sustainable finance: Bridging circular economy goals and financial inclusion in developing economies. *World, 6*(2), 44. https://doi.org/10.3390/world6020044

Taghizadeh-Hesary, F., Phoumin, H., & Rasoulinezhad, E. (2022). COVID-19 and regional solutions for mitigating the risk of SME finance in selected ASEAN member states. *Economic Analysis and Policy, 74*, 506–525. https://doi.org/10.1016/j.eap.2022.03.012

Tamasiga, P., Onyeaka, H., & Ouassou, E. H. (2022). Unlocking the green economy in African countries: An integrated framework of FinTech as an enabler of the transition to sustainability. *Energies, 15*(22), 8658. https://doi.org/10.3390/en15228658

Tanchangya, T., Islam, N., Naher, K., Mia, M. R., Chowdhury, S., Sarker, S. R., & Rashid, F. (2025). Financial technology-enabled sustainable finance for small- and medium-sized enterprises. *Environment, Innovation and Management, 1*, 2550006. https://doi.org/10.1142/s3060901125500061

Tranfield, D., Denyer, D., & Smart, P. (2003). Towards a methodology for developing evidence: Informed management knowledge by means of systematic review. *British Journal of Management, 14*, 207–222. https://doi.org/10.1111/1467-8551.00375

Udeagha, M. C., & Ngepah, N. (2023). The drivers of environmental sustainability in BRICS economies: Do green finance and fintech matter? *World Development Sustainability, 3*, Article 100096. https://doi.org/10.1016/j.wds.2023.100096

Wang, C. (2023). Low-carbon transition toward green recovery: Policy framework after COVID-19. *Economic Change and Restructuring, 56*(5), 3117–3137. https://doi.org/10.1007/s10644-023-09485-w

Wang, H. S., Lee, J. M., & Hao, Z. (2023). The influencing factors and pathways of China's green finance development towards the carbon peaking and carbon neutrality—Evidence from fuzzy-set qualitative comparative analysis based on 30 provinces of China. *Frontiers in Environmental Science, 11*. https://doi.org/10.3389/fenvs.2023.1145671

Wang, Q., & Fan, Z. (2023). Green finance and investment behavior of renewable energy enterprises: A case study of China. *International Review of Financial Analysis, 87*(102564), Article 102564. https://doi.org/10.1016/j.irfa.2023.102564

Wang, Y., & Chang, L. (2023). Green bonds' liquidity in COVID-19 and low carbon investments in China: A stochastic trend analysis. *Environmental Science and Pollution Research International, 30*(13), 36838–36850. https://doi.org/10.1007/s11356-022-24623-z

Xiang, W., Lan, Y., Qi, Q., & Gan, L. (2023). The impact mechanism of China's green finance on the transformation and innovation of high-energy-consumption enterprises. *PLOS One, 18*(10), Article e0293022. https://doi.org/10.1371/journal.pone.0293022

Xiao, Y., Lin, M., & Wang, L. (2024). Impact of green digital finance on sustainable development: Evidence from China's pilot zones. *Financial Innovation, 10*(10). https://doi.org/10.1186/s40854-023-00552-9

Xing, L., Li, J., & Yu, Z. (2022). Green finance strategies for the zero-carbon mechanism: Public spending as new determinants of sustainable development. *Frontiers in Environmental Science, 10.* https://doi.org/10.3389/fenvs.2022.925678

Xiong, Y., & Dai, L. (2023). Does green finance investment impact on sustainable development: Role of technological innovation and renewable energy. *Renewable Energy, 214*, 342–349. https://doi.org/10.1016/j.renene.2023.06.002

Xu, X., Xie, Y., Obobisa, E. S., & Sun, H. (2023). Has the establishment of green finance reform and innovation pilot zones improved air quality? Evidence from China. *Humanities & Social Sciences Communications, 10*(1), 262. https://doi.org/10.1057/s41599-023-01773-0

Yadav, S., Samadhiya, A., Kumar, A., Luthra, S., & Pandey, K. K. (2024). Nexus between fintech, green finance and natural resources management: Transition of BRICS nation industries from resource curse to resource blessed sustainable economies. *Resources Policy, 91*(104903), Article 104903. https://doi.org/10.1016/j.resourpol.2024.104903

Yang, B., Wu, Q., Sharif, A., & Uddin, G. S. (2023). Non-linear impact of natural resources, green financing, and energy transition on sustainable environment: A way out for common prosperity in NORDIC countries. *Resources Policy, 83*(103683), Article 103683. https://doi.org/10.1016/j.resourpol.2023.103683

Yao, Z., & Liu, Y. (2023). How Covid-19 impacts the financing in SMEs: Evidence from private firms. *Economic Analysis and Policy, 79*, 1046–1056. https://doi.org/10.1016/j.eap.2023.06.036

Zhang, D., Awawdeh, A. E., Hussain, M. S., Ngo, Q. T., & Hieu, V M (2021). Assessing the nexus mechanism between energy efficiency and green finance. *Energy Efficiency, 14*(85). https://doi.org/10.1007/s12053-021-09987-4

Zhang, M., Lian, Y., Zhao, H., & Xia-Bauer, C. (2020). Unlocking green financing for building energy retrofit: A survey in the western China. *Energy*

Strategy Reviews, 30(100520), Article 100520. https://doi.org/10.1016/j.esr.2020.100520

Zhao, L., Wang, D., Wang, X., & Zhang, Z. (2023). Impact of green finance on total factor productivity of heavily polluting enterprises: Evidence from green finance reform and innovation pilot zone. *Economic Analysis and Policy, 79*, 765–785. https://doi.org/10.1016/j.eap.2023.06.045

Zournatzidou, G. (2025). Green finance and sustainable development: Investigating the role of greentech business ecosystem through PRISMA-driven bibliometric analysis. *Administrative Sciences, 15*(4), 150. https://doi.org/10.3390/admsci15040150

CHAPTER 8

Making Green Marketing Stick: The Role of Trust and Satisfaction in Building Sustainable Customer Loyalty

Suzan Issa Abuhalawah, Sakher Faisal Alfraihat, M. Ángeles Rodríguez-Serrano, Saeed Tarabieh, and Tareq N. Hashem

Abstract In response to the increased demand for environmentally friendly products, green marketing has evolved as one of the most effective methods in the business sector. This study investigated the green marketing impact on green loyalty mediated by all of green satisfaction as well as green trust. Green marketing was found to have a significant impact on green satisfaction, green trust, and green loyalty. Additionally,

S. I. Abuhalawah (✉) · S. F. Alfraihat · M. Á. Rodríguez-Serrano
University of Seville, Seville, Spain
e-mail: suzabu@alum.us.es

S. Tarabieh
Mutah University, Mutah, Jordan

T. N. Hashem
Applied Science Private University, Amman, Jordan

S. Trivedi et al. (eds.), *Green Ventures*, Sustainable Development Goals Series, https://doi.org/10.1007/978-981-95-6533-7_8

green loyalty is significantly influenced significantly by green trust and green satisfaction. Green trust and green satisfaction were also found to be the mediators of the significant impact that green marketing has on green loyalty. This highlights the significant role that these two factors play in molding customer behavior. The purpose of this study is to investigate the connection between green marketing and green loyalty in order to provide informative and helpful insights for green marketers and businesses. This study investigates the relationship between all of green marketing, green satisfaction, green trust, and green loyalty, with the goal of assisting marketers in gaining a deeper comprehension of methods that are committed to sustainability. The findings have consequences within both the theoretical and practical realms: they contribute to the expansion of the theoretical framework of green marketing and offer advice that green businesses can put into action in order to establish green marketing strategies that are successful.

Keywords Green Marketing (GM) · Green Trust (GT) · Green Satisfaction (GS) · Green Loyalty (GL) · Consumer Behavior · SDG-13

1 Introduction

Customers are looking for green ways to incorporate environmentally friendly practices into their daily lives in light of the world's environmental issues, such as habitat destruction, air and water pollution, global warming, environmental degradation, and resource depletion (Zhang et al., 2024). A rising number of organizations are acknowledging their environmental duty as a result of this mindset (Borah et al., 2024). Companies should create new corporate strategies, including green marketing, to ensure that these green alternatives are fulfilled in order to meet these environmental needs (Shaheer et al., 2024). Reddy et al. (2023) claim that the strategies of enhancing green marketing are seen to be pertinent ideas. This can be enhanced using the strategies of green marketing in businesses to satisfy customers' environmental needs.

According to Huang et al. (2024), green marketing strategies are widely acknowledged as a business strategy that benefits a company's clients and the broader community in a sustainable and profitable manner. According to Tarabieh (2021), green marketing is a crucial tactic for addressing consumers' concerns about environmental issues and boosting a brand's reputation in order to set its products apart from the competition. To change consumers' eco-friendly behavior, green marketing is crucial (Tan et al., 2022). A growing number of studies have focused on green marketing, which has become a major area of marketing research (Saleem et al., 2021). This eco-friendly strategy, as highlighted by Bokil and Sinha (2021), gave rise to the idea of green marketing. Green marketing includes developing, diversifying, selling, and advertising in a way that meets the ecological demands of the consumer. Promoting and selling more ecologically friendly goods and services is the aim of green marketing (Ahmed et al., 2023).

Additionally, businesses can use green marketing as a strategy to accomplish strategies for distinction. Utilizing green marketing initiatives to carry out differentiation tactics and meet the objectives or desires of clients (Nguyen-Viet, 2023). Customers are more inclined to choose green items with less negative environmental effects as they grow more environmentally conscious. Conversely, defensive approaches to green marketing involve businesses adhering to the minimal activities mandated by regional laws. In order to avoid fines, businesses using defensive green marketing must comply with local environmental requirements by performing the bare minimum of operations. Businesses are more aggressive in their marketing strategies when assertive techniques are employed. Businesses react to the needs of their stakeholders in addition to market movements and laws.

A previous study has conducted an analysis of the impact that green marketing has on the behavior of consumers. This research has confirmed the significance of businesses employing green marketing methods in order to determine the demands of customers promoting green products as well as developing a green positioning strategy. Hence, the current study aimed to identify the effective impact played by all of green trust and green satisfaction in enhancing green loyalty. Indeed, this research area in Jordanian context has gotten limited attention in the field of research. Accordingly, it is essential to fill a substantial gap found in the literature. This study, deeply, aimed to expand the research that has been done on green marketing and green customer loyalty by investigating the roles of green trust and green satisfaction as mediators. Undoubtedly, this study makes a contribution to the expanding body of literature on the effectiveness of green marketing by investigating the interrelationships between these factors. It also provides important insights into the ways in which green marketing influences consumer behavior. These findings will provide marketing practitioners with useful insights, giving both theoretical and practical contributions by elucidating the ways in which green marketing influences consumer behavior that is based on trust and loyalty.

This research directly supports the global message of Sustainable Development Goal 13 (Climate Action) by revealing how green marketing shifts consumer interest into long-term eco-friendly habits. When companies build environmental trust and satisfaction, they not only gain loyal customers but also actively contribute to global solutions to climate change. The findings highlight the dual power of green marketing: promoting corporate sustainability and driving environmental progress more broadly.

2 Literature Review

2.1 Green Marketing

Green marketing is the term used to describe a company's marketing strategies that take into account the demands of society, consumers, and the environment. Green marketing is a comprehensive marketing strategy that anticipates, identifies, and meets the needs of consumers and society in order to achieve ecological sustainability at the societal level by making the best use of finite natural resources (García-Salirrosas & Rondon-Eusebio, 2022). According to Huang et al. (2024), green marketing differs conceptually from sustainable marketing in that it places a comparatively limited emphasis on ecological sustainability. Every business's commercial operations, including product development, pricing, advertising, and consumer sales of environmentally friendly goods and services, are included in green marketing. Products that are safe, long-lasting, recyclable, or composed of recycled materials are regarded as environmentally friendly. Such initiatives by businesses and marketers demonstrate their involvement in environmental issues while also adding value to a product (Kartawinata et al., 2020). Based on the four elements of the marketing mix (4Ps) green products, green pricing, green place, and green promotions green marketing highlights the ecologically beneficial qualities of products (Jabeen et al., 2023). Green marketing turns into a calculated variable to ascertain its effects on consumers' intents to acquire eco-friendly or green items.

2.2 *Green Trust*

The establishment of a variety of relationships has resulted in trust becoming an essential component in the transactions or acquisitions that take place between individuals and businesses (Tarabieh et al., 2024). This is because brands demonstrate their capacity to look out for the interests of their customers by ensuring the dependability of the transaction. This is made possible by the trustworthiness, credibility, and benevolence of the supplier (Alfraihat et al., 2024). Trust based on the study of Galdón-Salvador et al. (2024) can be defined as the readiness, eagerness, and ability of an individual to rely on something and to tolerate the minimal amount of vulnerability based on the performance, reliability, and prior functionality of the thing in question. From the perspective of AlFraihat et al. (2025), customer trust can be considered the essential component that has the potential to determine the long-term behavior and buying pattern of each client. According to Al-Dwairi et al. (2024), it is possible to state that the faith that customers have in the products or services they purchase can have a substantial impact on their purchasing attitude and intention, which will eventually determine the behavior that they actually exhibit. In fact, a number of research discovered that one of the most crucial elements influencing a customer's propensity to buy was their level of trust (Hammouri et al., 2025). According to their opinions or expectations about the green product's ability to perform well in terms of the environment and human health, consumers are more likely to trust it (Luo et al., 2023). This refers to the buyer's perception of the green product in the context of green trust. The term "green trust"describes the attitudes and expectations that customers have formed about the skill, dependability, and kindness of the green product and its manufacturer (Wang & Walker, 2023).

2.3 *Green Satisfaction*

Prior scholarly research overlooked other pertinent variables like pleasure and purchase intention in favor of focusing on traits like perceived value that conditioned consumption. Consequently, there were few early research on customer happiness in relation to marketing. This resulted from scholarly studies that concentrated on particular factors. The emotion that a customer gets about a product after purchasing and using it is the current definition of satisfaction (Gelderman et al.,

2021). Given its importance in ensuring a brand's success and establishing enduring relationships with customers in almost any setting or industry, it has emerged as one of the most crucial marketing variables (Naini et al., 2022). In this regard, the green product business is among those that have expressed the greatest interest in the variable's investigation. Because of this, it is now feasible to define green satisfaction as the degree of enjoyable fulfillment associated with consumption in order to meet a customer's health and environmental needs or expectations (Chen, 2010). Chen (2010) asserts that green satisfaction can result in the development of green loyalty and trust.

2.4 *Green Loyalty*

Oliver's concept of consumer loyalty (Oliver, 1999) serves as the foundation for the idea of green loyalty. The term "green loyalty"describes a customer's wish to continue doing business with an organization that cares about the environment or the green and their promise to regularly repurchase a product they like in the future (Gelderman et al., 2021). The degree of repurchase intention brought on by strong environmental sentiments and a sustained commitment to a particular item (such as goods, services, businesses, brands, or organizations) is known as "green loyalty"(Chen & Chang, Chen, 2013). Additionally, recent research has demonstrated that green loyalty is based on the firm's attitude and commitment to a sustainable environment and is measured by a consumer's intention to repurchase (Dabija, 2018). Two methods have been used in earlier research on loyalty: behavioral loyalty and attitudinal loyalty. When a customer consistently buys a product or service over time, this is known as behavioral loyalty. Although it does not correspond to actual purchasing behavior, attitude loyalty can be understood as a customer's loyalty intention, which can be commitment or trust (Zhang et al., 2023). Customers will recommend things to other customers even if they do not buy them, demonstrating a loyal attitude.

2.5 *Theoretical Framework*

To carry out this study, it was important to establish a research framework based on the specific context (Bougie & Sekaran, 2019). The conceptual framework depicted in Fig. 1 was developed from insights gained

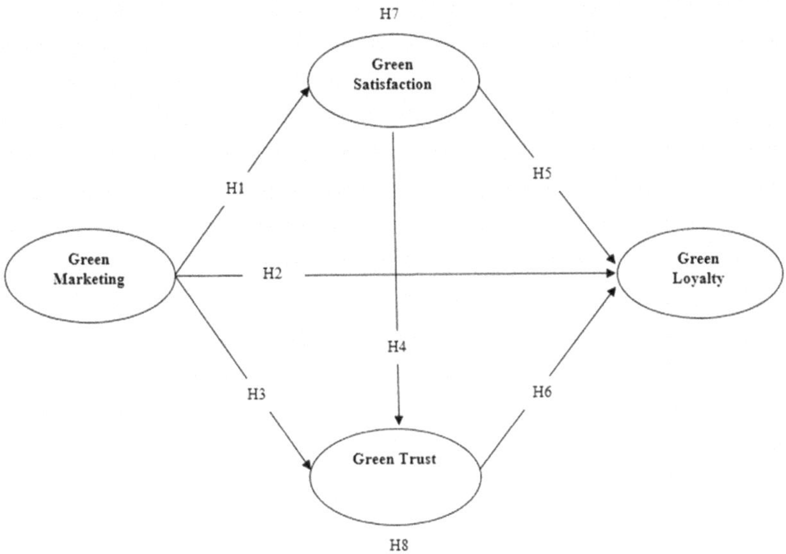

Fig. 1 Theoretical Framework

through the literature review and the subsequent theoretical and empirical assumptions.

2.6 *Hypothesis Development*

2.6.1 The Impact of Green Marketing on Green Satisfaction

The green marketing effective strategies have positively contributed to the satisfaction of customers as well as enhancing their loyalty (Damayanti et al., 2024). It is also shown by Hur et al., (2013) that the environmental benefit clarity of a product is seen to be essential, boosting trust and perceived value that are deemed to be effective variables which could mediate the green marketing efforts and consumer satisfaction relationship. Ethical implications are increasingly considered by consumers' purchases. Additionally, companies that communicate their green initiatives effectively accomplish high consumer satisfaction levels (Yu et al., 2017). Hence, this study proposed the following hypothesis:

H1: **Green Marketing Have a Significant Positive Impact on Green Satisfaction.**

2.6.2 *The Impact of Green Marketing on Green Loyalty*

Kewakuma et al. (2021) agreed that the green marketing strategy persuades individuals to become loyal consumers in specific markets. Studies that also support the influence of the green marketing strategy on customer loyalty were also carried out by Martínez (2015) and Gelderman et al. (2021). For example, it is pinpointed by Ali et al. (2024) that integrating green marketing into the strategies of organizations often results in increasing brand loyalty as well as the performance of the market, highlighting the competitive advantage, in the consumer goods sector, obtained by environmental practices. In this vein, it is articulated by Martínez (2015). There is a need for employing relationship regarding the perspectives of green marketing to cultivating green customer loyalty. This can be achieved by proposing a strategic framework that is crucial to understand the reactions of consumers to perform green initiatives. Bekar et al. (2020), in this regard, indicated that there is a significant effect of green practices on loyalty and emotional attachment among consumers. Hence, the following hypothesis is highlighted:

H2: **Green Marketing Have a Significant Positive Impact on Green Loyalty.**

2.6.3 *The Impact of Green Marketing on Green Trust*

It is emphasized by several studies that implementation of green marketing effectively boost the trust of consumers in companies' products, this, in turn, can ultimately lead to increasing the intentions of purchase. A study of Li et al. (2025) as an example revealed that the practices of green marketing by e-car manufacturers boost the trust of consumers significantly. Additionally, the study of Khan et al. (2022) pinpointed that the practices of strategic green products significantly consumers' expectations, enhancing their trust in such environmentally friendly products. In this vein, hen and hen and Chang (2012) argued that consumers' intention to purchase green products is directly affected by heightened green trust ensuring that distrust can be observed from exaggerated environmental claims leading to diminished purchase behaviors. Accordingly, the following hypothesis is highlighted:

H3: **Green Marketing Have a Significant Positive Impact on Green Trust.**

2.6.4 *The Impact of Green Satisfaction on Green Trust*

Since customer trust in a green product's safety and ability to preserve the environment and stakeholders is correlated with positive experiences, green satisfaction with a product tends to increase green trust (Wang et al., 2018). In their study of consumers of green medical services, Han and Hyun (2015) explained how green trust is strongly impacted by green satisfaction. According to some writers, green satisfaction increases green trust since it gives customers more confidence about their purchase intentions (Ha et al., 2022; Pahlevi & Suhartanto, 2020). Therefore, the following theory is put out in light of these findings:

H4: **Green Satisfaction Has a Significant Positive Impact on Green Trust.**

2.6.5 *The Impact of Green Satisfaction on Green Loyalty*

Green loyalty and green satisfaction have been linked in a number of research (Gelderman et al., 2021; Pahlevi & Suhartanto, 2020). Compared to customers who are unhappy or less satisfied, satisfied customers are more likely to repurchase green items (Li et al., 2023; Pahlevi & Suhartanto, 2020). According to a prior study, there is a favorable correlation between loyalty and satisfaction (Muflih et al., 2023). As the precursor to consumer loyalty, customer pleasure is crucial. According to (Oliver, 1999), consumers develop loyalty in three stages: cognitively, affectively, and last, conatively or behaviourally. Either price-based or quality-based satisfaction is the foundation of affective loyalty. Loyalty is the result of satisfaction, which in turn influences loyalty favorably (Chen, 2010). This study suggests the following hypothesis and postulates that customers' green pleasure has a positive impact on their green loyalty.

H5: **Green Satisfaction Has a Significant Positive Impact on Green Loyalty.**

2.6.6 *The Impact of Green Trust on Green Loyalty*

Customer trust would boost the commitment to the service provider-customer relationship, according to earlier marketing literature (AlSokkar et al., 2025; Maaitah et al., 2024). According to social exchange theory, client trust would increase the consumer-provider relationship's social embeddedness and strengthen the customer's commitment to the partnership (Chen, 2013). The significance of trust in buyer-seller relationships was demonstrated by earlier studies (Eckerd et al., 2022). According to Alam et al. (2021), the level of client trust has a direct impact on customer loyalty. Customer loyalty and trust are positively correlated since trust is a key factor in determining future purchase intentions (Galdón-Salvador et al., 2024). This study put out the following hypothesis, which holds that consumers' green loyalty is positively impacted by their green trust.

H6: **Green Trust Has a Significant Positive Impact on Green Loyalty.**

2.6.7 *The Mediation Impact of Green Satisfaction Between Green Marketing and Green Loyalty*

Green marketing is positively correlated with green satisfaction, which is positively correlated with green loyalty in H1 and H5, respectively, according to this study. Additionally, this study thinks that green loyalty in H2 is positively impacted by green marketing. Thus, according to the above described arguments, green marketing can influence green loyalty directly as well as indirectly through green satisfaction. Consequently, this study proposes the following theory and argues that, within the research context, green satisfaction serves as a partial mediator:

H7: **Green Satisfaction Partially Mediates the Relationship Between Green Marketing and Green Loyalty.**

2.6.8 *The Mediation Impact of Green Trust Between Green Marketing and Green Loyalty*

This study found that green marketing and green trust are positively correlated, and that green trust and green loyalty are positively correlated in H3 and H6, respectively. Additionally, this study thinks that green loyalty in H2 is positively impacted by green marketing. According to the above described arguments, green marketing can thus influence green loyalty directly as well as indirectly through green trust. Consequently, this study proposes the following theory and argues that green trust serves as a partial mediator within the context of the study:

H8: **Green Trust Partially Mediates the Relationship Between Green Marketing and Green Loyalty.**

3 Methodology

3.1 Instrument Development

A comprehensive literature review served as the foundation for the development of all items or empirical indicators for each variable under investigation (see Table 1). Jabeen et al. (2023) provided eight items that were modified to measure different aspects of green marketing. Five items that were modified from Tarabieh (2021) were used to measure green trust. The variables for green satisfaction were measured using six items that were modified from the Gelderman et al. (2021) scale. Additionally, Gelderman et al. (2021) provided three items that were modified to measure green loyalty. A five-point Likert scale, with 1 denoting "strongly disagree" and 5 denoting "strongly agree," was used to evaluate each item assessing green marketing, green satisfaction, green trust, and green loyalty. Because it is less confusing and can increase the response rate, this scale was chosen in accordance with Dawes' (2008) proposals. The previous researchers' use of the five-point Likert scale (Aboalganam et al., 2025; Galdón-Salvador et al., 2024) provided another justification for its usage.

3.2 Sample Selection and Data Collection

According to Bougie and Sekaran (2019), research design is the method or plan that guides an investigation and demonstrates how data was gathered and what analytical technique was applied to arrive at the result. The necessary data was obtained using the convenience, nonprobability sampling technique. Most researchers choose this method since it helps to bring symmetry to data, provides unique answers, and saves time and

Table 1 Items utilized to measure the constructions

Green Marketing (GM)	
GM1	Manufacturing Eco-friendly Product
GM2	Producing products using eco-friendly process
GM3	Marketing products through communication methods that are less harmful to the environment
GM4	Branding product associating with green marketing practices
GM5	Making changes to items in order to eliminate their impact on the environment
GM6	Modifying product packaging to suit surroundings
GM7	Educating customers on how to use things in a way that is ecologically friendly
GM8	Utilizing environmentally friendly supply chains for both distribution and sales
Green Satisfaction (GS)	
GS1	I am content with the choice I made to purchase the environmentally friendly products offered by this firm
GS2	The fact that this company sells environmentally friendly products makes me happy
GS3	I have the conviction that I am doing ethically when I buy these environmentally friendly products
GS4	I believe that I am making a contribution to the defense of the environment and the advancement of sustainable practices
GS5	In general, I am pleased to purchase this product because it is kind to the community and the environment
GS6	The fact that this product is concerned about the environment is one of the reasons why I am pleased with it overall
Green Trust (GT)	
GT1	I believe that some degree of reliability can be attributed to the environmental pledges made by this brand
GT2	According to my point of view, the environmental performance of this brand is typically reliable
GT3	I am going to presume that the environmental argument that this brand makes is generally reliable
GT4	The manufacturer's attention for the environment satisfies your expectations in this regard
GT5	This company lives up to its commitments and obligations for environmental protection
Green Loyalty (GL)	
GL1	I intend to continue dealing with this firm for my buying needs

(continued)

Table 1 (continued)

Green Marketing (GM)	
GL2	I am willing to refer this firm to my family, friends, and business connections so that they may have their shopping done with them
GL3	I am willing to pay a greater price for environmentally friendly products, despite the fact that the price of other products that are not environmentally friendly is lower than the price of green products

money (Kotrlik & Higgins, 2001). This study uses a quantitative research design. The consumer level serves as a unit of analysis for the study. The study's research object is Jordanian consumers who have bought green products or who have expressed particular concern or satisfaction with certain green brands. Jordanian university students were the study's target population. Compared to other product users, university students are chosen as the target demographic because they are more knowledgeable about the companies' environmental issues and green activities. They are conscious of environmentally friendly production and green company practices since they are young, informed consumers. Two methods were used to get the primary data. University students who were contacted via various social media channels were given access to an online survey. To get real answers, certain universities were also visited in person. A total of 256 responses were gathered and used for analysis. Targeted populations were six universities, including Applied Science Private University, Al-Zaytoonah University of Jordan, Princess Sumaya University for Technology, Amman Arab University, University of Petra, and German Jordanian University.

4 Results

4.1 Descriptive Statistics

Table 2 provides a list of the gender, age, and educational background of each and every respondent. The findings indicate that women make up 52% of the respondents, while males make up 48% of the respondents. In addition, it reveals that the category of respondents with the highest frequency is those between the ages of 21 and 22, with 40.6%. 39.1% is found among people who are 18–20 years old. The lowest percentage is for those who are more than 22 years old being 20.3%. The following is a list of educational qualifications that are categorized differently: The responses had the highest percentage of individuals who were studying bachelor's degrees, which was 84.4%, compared to the other participants, and the remaining 15.6% of respondents were studying post-graduate degrees. These findings provide evidence that the study sample is diverse in terms of gender, age, and academic background. This diversity contributes to the study's comprehensiveness and capacity to authentically reflect a diverse community.

Table 3 shows the mean and standard deviation of the study variables. It shows that the highest mean was for the green marketing variable (M=3.97 / SD=0.452), ranking high, and this indicates that the respondents almost agree and strongly agree with the effective use of green marketing. This is followed by the green trust variable (M=3.94 / SD.728), ranking high, this also indicates that most of the respondents agree with the effective use of green trust. Next, it is followed by green loyalty (M=3.88 / SD=648), showing respondents also agree with the impact of green loyalty in enhancing e-marketing. Lastly, it is shown that green satisfaction as a variable ranked moderate (M=3.49 / SD=0.452).

Byrne (2010) asserts that one way to assess the distribution of metric variables is to look at the data's normal distribution. Determining whether or not the data has a normal distribution is crucial. Therefore, the statistical method of skewness and kurtosis was used to perform a test for normalcy. Skewness can be used to quantify asymmetry, while kurtosis can be used to quantify a distribution's "peakedness" (Hur et al., 2013). A measure of asymmetry is called skewness. The results of the normal distribution test that was run on the data are shown in Table 4. The metric variables' skewness value ranges from −0.073 to −0.749, which

Table 2 The demographic information of the respondents

Variables	*Categories*	*Frequency*	*Percent*
Gender	Male	123	48.0
	Female	133	52.0
Age	18-20 years old	100	39.1
	21-22 years old	104	40.6
	More than 22 years old	52	20.3
Qualifications	Bachelor	216	84.4
	Postgraduate	40	15.6

Table 3 The descriptive statistics of the study variables

Descriptive Statistics				
Variables	*N*	*Mean*	*Std. Deviation*	*Rank*
Green marketing	256	3.97	.452	High
Green satisfaction	256	3.49	.570	Moderate
Green trust	256	3.94	.728	High
Green loyalty	256	3.88	.648	High
Valid N (listwise)	256			

is within the recommended range of +3 to −3 (Coakes & Steed, 2003). The skewness value is clearly within the intended range, according to this. Furthermore, the metric variables' kurtosis value falls between the recommended range of +3 and −3 (Kline, 2015). 0.127 to 1.775 is the range of values for the kurtosis value. Based on the test results, it may be said that the data have a normal distribution.

As shown in Table 5, factor loadings greater than 0.3 as well as greater than 0.4 were deemed significant (Hair et al. 1998). Fornell and Larcker (1981) proposed the Average Variance Extracted (AVE) method, which has become a popular way to verify convergent validity at the variable level. In general, each latent variable's AVE should be higher than 0.50 to guarantee enough convergent validity (Hair et al., 2014). To investigate the indication reliability for factor loading, loadings for each item (factor) were computed. The best cut-off point for each item loading is 0.70 or above (Hair et al., 2014).

Table 4 Normal distribution

Descriptive statistics					
	N	*Skewness*		*Kurtosis*	
	Statistic	*Statistic*	*Std. Error*	*Statistic*	*Std. Error*
Green marketing	256	-.073-	.152	.127	.303
Green satisfaction	256	-.344-	.152	.762	.303
Green trust	256	-.749-	.152	1.775	.303
Green loyalty	256	-.605-	.152	1.013	.303
ValidN (listwise)	256				

Table 5 Factor loading for the remaining items

Constructs	*Code*	*Factor loading*	*AVE*	*CR*
Green Marketing	Green_Marketing1	.933	.66	0.871
	Green_Marketing2	.643		
	Green_Marketing3	.863		
	Green_Marketing4	.547		
	Green_Marketing5	.582		
	Green_Marketing6	.573		
	Green_Marketing7	.677		
	Green_Marketing8	.536		
Green Satisfaction	Green_Satisfaction1	.672	.60	.776
	Green_Satisfaction2	.704		
	Green_Satisfaction3	.722		
	Green_Satisfaction4	.512		
	Green_Satisfaction5	.505		
	Green_Satisfaction6	.495		
Green Trust	Green_Trust1	.936	.82	.916
	Green_Trust2	.857		
	Green_Trust3	.747		
	Green_Trust4	.757		
	Green_Trust5	.832		
Green Loyalty	Green_Loyalty1	.573	.67	.717
	Green_Loyalty2	.600		
	Green_Loyalty3	.841		

As stated by Chin (2010), the objective of measuring the goodness of fit is to shed light on the variance that is derived from the model and its structure through the process of measurement. As shown in Table 6, the quality of the model's fit is presented, which reveals that the degrees of freedom (df) were 191 and the CMIN ($\chi 2$) calculated to be 532.728. As a consequence, the ratio of ($\chi 2/df \leq 5.00$) is 2.78, which falls below the threshold of what is considered acceptable. In addition, the ratio was lower than 2.00, which is equivalent to 0.841. The NFI score of 0.826 satisfied the acceptable criteria of higher than 0.80, which is a must. It was determined that the CFI result was 0.878, which is also higher than the permitted standard of 0.80. It was discovered that TLI had a value of 0.872, which is higher than the permitted threshold of 0.80. The IFI score of 0.864 satisfying the acceptable criteria of higher than 0.80, which is a requirement. The RMSEA value was 0.084, which is lower than the permitted standard of 0.10. These signals, which are based on a number of criteria, reveal that the standard model used in the study has a strong fit. This not only increases confidence in the outcomes of the analysis, but it also suggests that the model accurately reflects the data.

As shown in Table 7, the results of the structural model study are displayed along with relevant direct effect hypotheses. The patch analysis results demonstrated a substantial correlation between the effects of green marketing on green satisfaction, green trust, and green loyalty (e.g., H1, H2, and H3 correspondingly). It also shows that there is a positive correlation between green satisfaction and green trust (H4). The table also shows that this green satisfaction is significantly correlated to green loyalty (H5). Lastly, it displays that green trust has a positive correlation with green loyalty.

Table 8 presents the regression analysis testing six hypotheses on how green marketing, green satisfaction, and green trust relate to one another and affect GL. To determine the direct and noteworthy impacts of these characteristics, they are analyzed. Green marketing has a beneficial impact on GS, as evidenced by the finding in (H1) that GM has a positive influence on GS ($\beta = 0.607$, $p < 0.001$). Furthermore, H2 indicates a stronger impact of green marketing on green loyalty ($\beta = 0.689$, $p < 0.001$), as evidenced by the improvement of consumers' positive interactions with green loyalty. H3 demonstrates that green marketing has a significant impact on total green trust ($\beta = 0.566$, $p < 0.001$), suggesting that even well-regarded green marketing may struggle to win over customers' trust. This pattern is supported by H4, which shows that overall green trust is positively impacted by green satisfaction ($\beta = 0.332$, $p < 0.001$). Conversely, H5 examined the connection between green loyalty and green satisfaction. It demonstrates that overall green loyalty is positively impacted by green pleasure ($\beta = 0.427$, $p < 0.001$). Likewise, H6 demonstrates that green loyalty is strongly impacted by green trust ($\beta = 0.761$, $p < 0.001$). These results support the importance of developing strategies to improve greenness including marketing, trust, and satisfaction ones to enhance green loyalty to ensure continued business success.

Within the context of green satisfaction's role as a mediator for the indirect relationship between green marketing and green loyalty, H7 was investigated. After further investigation, it was found that this median path had a considerable degree of influence. A beta coefficient of.681, an R2 value of.475, and a Sig. value of.000 are all characteristics of this model. It would appear from this that higher levels of green satisfaction lead to higher levels of green loyalty. In light of this, green satisfaction

Table 6 Goodness of Fit

Model	*CM IN* (χ^2)	*df*	*P-value*	χ^2/ *df* $\leq$*5.00*	*Ratio* $\leq$*2.00*	*NFI* $\geq$*0.80*	*CFI* $\geq$*0.80*	*TLI* $\geq$*0.80*	*IFI* $\geq$*0.80*	*RMSEA* $\leq$ *0.10*
Measurement of The Study Model	532.728	191	.000	2.78	.841	.826	.878	.872	.864	.084

Table 7 Results of direct impact hypotheses assessment

IV	*DV*			
	Green marketing	*Green satisfaction*	*Green trust*	*Green loyalty*
Green Marketing (GM)	---------	.607** (H1)	.566**(H3)	.689** (H2)
Green Satisfaction (GS)	----------	------------	.332**(H4)	.427** (H5)
Green Trust (GT)	-----------	------------	------------	.761 (H6)
Green Loyalty (GL)	-----------	------------	------------	------------

Table 8 Regression analysis of the variable direct relationship (H1 to H6)

Direct relationship								
Model		*Unstandardized Coefficients*		*Standardized Coefficients*	*t*	*Sig.*	R^2	*Supported hypothesis*
	Hypothesis	*B*	*Std. Error*	*Beta*				
IVs								
GM on GS	H1	.765	.063	.607	12.171	.000	.368	Supported
GM on GL	H2	.988	.065	.689	15.156	.000	.457	Supported
GM on GT	H3	.913	.083	.566	10.954	.000	.321	Supported
GS on GT	H4	.424	.076	.332	5.601	.000	.110	Supported
GS on GL	H5	.485	.065	.427	7.519	.000	.182	Supported
GT on GL	H6	.676	.036	.761	18.670	.000	.578	Supported

H1. Dependent Variable: GS
H2. Dependent Variable: GL
H3. Dependent Variable: GT
H4. Dependent Variable: GT
H5. Dependent Variable: GL
H6: Dependent Variable: GL

Table 9 Regression analysis of the variable indirect relationship (H7)

Indirect relationship									
Model		*Unstandardized Coefficients*		*Standardized Coefficients*	*t*	*Sig.*	R^2	*Supported hypothesis*
	Hypothesis	*B*	*Std. Error*	*Beta*				
Mediation Test								
GM*GS	H7	.977	.082	.681	11.881	.000	475	Supported
H7. Dependent Variable: GL								

Table 10 Regression analysis of the variable indirect relationship (H8)

Indirect relationship								
Model		*Unstandardized Coefficients*		*Standardized Coefficients*	*t*	*Sig.*	R^2	*Supported hypothesis*
	Hypothesis	*B*	*Std. Error*	*Beta*				
Mediation Test								
	H8	.545	.062	.380	8.769	.000	677	Supported
GM*GT								
H8. Dependent Variable: GL								

serves as a mediator in the connection between green marketing and green employee loyalty.

Green trust looked at H8 in its role as a mediator for the indirect relationship between green marketing and green loyalty. This intermediate route was found to have a considerable impact. Possessing a Sig. value of.000, an R2 value of.677, and a beta coefficient of.380. This implies that green loyalty rises as a result of green trust. Consequently, the relationship between green marketing and green loyalty is mediated by green trust.

5 Discussion

In light of the results presented in the previous tables regarding the relationship between green marketing, green satisfaction, green trust, and green loyalty, it can be noted that green marketing has a direct and indirect positive impact on green loyalty. It has a direct positive impact on all aspects of green satisfaction and green trust, reflecting that marketing strategies that rely on green marketing lead to an increase in green products and companies that claim to follow environmentally friendly practices. This is consistent with the study of Tarabieh (2021), which indicated that following green marketing strategies enhances customers' loyalty.

When it comes to the marketing process, the corporation is tasked with the responsibility of finding and defining requirements, wants, and things that can attract customers to become the target market (Simanjuntak et al., 2020). Green marketing is a component of a socially driven marketing idea. Green marketing, as defined by Reddy et al. (2023), is a consumer concern for the environment that has the potential to influence purchasing decisions from consumers. According to Rahaman et al. (2024), green marketing is the most cutting-edge and fashionable market presently available. This is due to the fact that it offers a secure atmosphere for people, animals, and the planet together. According to García-Salirrosas and Rondon-Eusebio (2022) defines green marketing as the efforts of a company or organization to make, promote, package, and renew products in a manner that is concerned about environmental issues, with the goal of improving customer loyalty.

It is also indicated that it is possible for a person's level of green satisfaction with a product to range from ecstasy to dismay, depending on the degree to which the actual performance of the product corresponds to the individual's expectations for it as it is supported by Salsabilla and Isharina (2024) indicating to the green satisfaction. According to Pahlevi and Suhartanto (2020), there are a number of various indications that may be used to determine the level of satisfaction with a product. These indicators include the joy of purchasing green brands, the belief that purchasing the green brand is the appropriate thing to do, and overall satisfaction indicating to the enhancement of green satisfaction. This is supported by Pahlevi and Suhartanto (2020) who claimed that green satisfaction is defined as how consumers believe that the performance of green products is better than their expectations.

Undoubtedly, the belief that the company has honored its obligations will be formed in the minds of the customers when the expectations of the customers have been met as a result of the strategy employed by the company. It is in the current study that green trust affects green loyalty. In this regard, the study of Pahlevi and Suhartanto (2020) stated that trust is the degree to which customers believe that a firm is environmentally conscious and that it can back up its statements. In this vein, Martínez (2015) stated that green trust can be defined as the readiness to rely on an exchange partner in whom one has trust due to the environmental performance of the partner. This kind of green trust enhancement can affect green loyalty Salsabilla and Isharina (2024) indicating to the green satisfaction. According to Salsabilla and Isharina (2024), there is an introduced novel notion known as "green trust," which is the confidence that a consumer has in a company's product, service, or brand because the consumer believes in the dependability, goodness, and effectiveness of that company's shown commitment to being environmentally responsible. This is also supported by Chen and Chang (2013) study, indicating that the following are indicators that encourage green trust: reliability, dependability, trustworthiness, expectation, and commitment.

Overall, loyalty in general and green loyalty in particular can be understood as an attitude, which can be measured on a scale: The connection between the choices made by consumers and the products they utilize. This is supported by Pahlevi and Suhartanto's (2020) research indicating that loyalty can be defined as a deeply held commitment to rebuy or patronize a preferred product/service consistently in the future, thereby causing repetitive same-brand or same-brand-set purchasing, despite situational influences and marketing efforts having the potential to cause switching behavior. When it comes to client perceptions, it is essential to enhance green trust, green satisfaction, and green marketing image in order to increase green loyalty. According to Pahlevi and Suhartanto's (2020), indicators that indicate green loyalty include recommending the product to other parties, purchasing it again in the future, and continuing to use environmentally friendly items regardless of their prices. The results of this study are in line with those of prior research that has highlighted the significance of green marketing, green satisfaction, and green trust toward green loyalty, increasing the transparency and credibility of green marketing in order to promote green business effectiveness.

6 Conclusion

This study shows that green marketing has a significant impact on various aspects of green branding, such as satisfaction, trust, and loyalty. In other words, green marketing directly and indirectly affects green loyalty, leading to an increase in trust and credibility in green products. The results suggest that companies should increase green product practices and enhance transparency in promoting green products in order to improve consumer trust, increase loyalty, and achieve higher purchase intentions for environmentally friendly products.

7 Research Implications and Further Research

Our results have clear relevance for businesses and policy makers. Companies that build their marketing around sustainability, honesty and visible eco-standards can strengthen customer trust and keep it over time. Bringing greener principles into product design, promotion and packaging helps build confidence and repeat buying rather than one-off purchases. Managers can use these findings to shape more convincing campaigns, and regulators can draw on them when drafting rules to support responsible marketing and sustainable consumption.

The study also has limits. We worked only with university students in Jordan, so the patterns we observed may not reflect the wider population of green-product users. Looking at other age groups and regions would give a fuller picture. Our data are also cross-sectional essentially a snapshot and based on a convenience sample. Tracking people over time with a randomized design could show how attitudes and habits change. Another question worth exploring is the influence of digital platforms: social media, online communities and influencers probably shape how green marketing affects loyalty. Future research could also test mediators such as environmental awareness, peer influence, or perceived product quality to unpack the drivers of green purchasing. Finally, comparing results across cultures would show which aspects of green marketing work everywhere and which are tied to local context.

References

Aboalganam, K. M., AlFraihat, S. F., & Tarabieh, S. (2025). The impact of user-generated content on tourist visit intentions: The mediating role of destination imagery. *Administrative Sciences, 15*(4), 117.

Ahmed, R. R., Streimikiene, D., Qadir, H., & Streimikis, J. (2023). Effect of green marketing mix, green customer value, and attitude on green purchase intention: Evidence from the USA. *Environmental Science and Pollution Research, 30*(5), 11473–11495.

Alam, M. M. D., Karim, R. A., & Habiba, W. (2021). The relationship between CRM and customer loyalty: The moderating role of customer trust. *International Journal of Bank Marketing, 39*(7), 1248–1272.

Al-Dwairi, R., Shehabat, I., Zahrawi, A., & Hammouri, Q. (2024). Building customer trust, loyalty, and satisfaction: The power of social media in e-commerce environments. *International Journal of Data and Network Science, 8*(3), 1883–1894.

AlFraihat, S. F., Aboalganam, K. M., Alghizzawi, M., Habes, M., & Almuhaisen, O. (2025). Influencer captions and credibility on instagram: Investigating their impact on brand trust, brand awareness and purchase intention. *Forum for Linguistic Studies, 7*(6), 314–330.

Alfraihat, S. F. A., Pechuán, I. G., Salvador, J. L. G., & Tarabieh, S. M. (2024). Content is king: The impact of content marketing on online repurchase intention. *Educational Administration: Theory and Practice, 30*(6), 4017–4030.

Ali, S., Khan, K., Haider, S., & Rehman, A. (2024). Analyzing the impact of green marketing strategies on the environmental performance and market performance of companies in the consumer goods sector. *Journal of Policy Research, 9*(4).

AlSokkar, A. A., Al-Gasawneh, J. A., Alamro, A., Binkhamis, M., AlGhizzawi, M., & Hmeidan, T. A. (2025). The effectiveness of E-marketing on marketing performance in Jordanian telecommunications companies: Exploring the mediating role of the competitive environment. *SN Computer Science, 6*(1), 1–15.

Bekar, A., Durmaz, S., & Yozukmaz, N. (2020). The effect of green practices on emotional attachment and green loyalty of coffee shop consumers (Turkey). *Turizam, 24*(1), 33–45.

Bokil, Y., & Sinha, D. K. (2021). Green marketing and mindful consumption for sustainable development. *Central Asian Journal of Innovations on Tourism Management and Finance, 2*(9), 4–7.

Borah, P. S., Dogbe, C. S. K., & Marwa, N. (2024). Generation z's green purchase behavior: Do green consumer knowledge, consumer social responsibility, green advertising, and green consumer trust matter for sustainable development? *Business Strategy and the Environment, 33*(5), 4530–4546.

Bougie, R., & Sekaran, U. (2019). *Research methods for business: A skill building approach*. john wiley & sons.
Chen, Y. S. (2010). The drivers of green brand equity: Green brand image, green satisfaction, and green trust. *Journal of Business Ethics, 93*, 307–319.
Chen, Y. S. (2013). Towards green loyalty: Driving from green perceived value, green satisfaction, and green trust. *Sustainable Development, 21*(5), 294–308.
Chen, Y. S., & Chang, C. H. (2012). Enhance green purchase intentions: The roles of green perceived value, green perceived risk, and green trust. *Management Decision, 50*(3), 502–520.
Chen, Y. S., & Chang, C. H. (2013). Greenwash and green trust: The mediation effects of green consumer confusion and green perceived risk. *Journal of Business Ethics, 114*, 489–500.
Dabija, D. C. (2018). Enhancing green loyalty towards apparel retail stores: A cross-generational analysis on an emerging market. *Journal of Open Innovation: Technology, Market, and Complexity, 4*(1), 1–16.
Damayanti, E. E., Arumsari, N. R., & Yasin, R. M. (2024). The influence of green marketing, packaging, and service quality on consumer loyalty through consumer satisfaction of Es Teh Indonesia (Indonesian iced tea) in Kudus. *KnE Social Sciences*, 481–493.
Eckerd, S., Handley, S., & Lumineau, F. (2022). Trust violations in buyer–supplier relationships: Spillovers and the contingent role of governance structures. *Journal of Supply Chain Management, 58*(3), 47–70.
Galdón-Salvador, J. L., Gil-Pechuán, I., & Tarabieh, S. M. (2024). Effect of social media influencers on consumer brand engagement and its implications on business decision making. *Profesional de la información, 33*(2).
García-Salirrosas, E. E., & Rondon-Eusebio, R. F. (2022). Green marketing practices related to key variables of consumer purchasing behavior. *Sustainability, 14*(14), 8499.
Gelderman, C. J., Schijns, J., Lambrechts, W., & Vijgen, S. (2021). Green marketing as an environmental practice: The impact on green satisfaction and green loyalty in a business-to-business context. *Business Strategy and the Environment, 30*(4), 2061–2076.
Ha, M. T., Ngan, V. T. K., & Nguyen, P. N. (2022). Greenwash and green brand equity: The mediating role of green brand image, green satisfaction and green trust and the moderating role of information and knowledge. *Business Ethics, the Environment & Responsibility, 31*(4), 904–922.
Hammouri, Q., Nusairat, N. M., AlSokkar, A. A., Jdaitawi, A. M., Mistarihi, A. M., Akhuirshaideh, D. A. A., & AlFraihat, S. F. (2025). Engaging gen Z through personalized social media content: The mediating role of perceived relevance on platform engagement.

Han, H., & Hyun, S. S. (2015). Customer retention in the medical tourism industry: Impact of quality, satisfaction, trust, and price reasonableness. *Tourism Management, 46*, 20–29.

Huang, S., Qu, H., & Wang, X. (2024). Impact of green marketing on peer-to-peer accommodation platform users repurchase intention and positive word-of-mouth: Mediation of trust and consumer identification. *International Journal of Contemporary Hospitality Management, 36*(3), 691–712.

Hur, W. M., Kim, Y., & Park, K. (2013). Assessing the effects of perceived value and satisfaction on customer loyalty: A 'green'perspective. *Corporate Social Responsibility and Environmental Management, 20*(3), 146–156.

Jabeen, R., Khan, K. U., Zain, F., & Atlas, F. (2023). Buy green only: Interplay between green marketing, corporate social responsibility and green purchase intention; the mediating role of green brand image. *Business Strategy & Development, 6*(3), 503–518.

Kartawinata, B. R., Maharani, D., Pradana, M., & Amani, H. M. (2020, August). The role of customer attitude in mediating the effect of green marketing mix on green product purchase intention in love beauty and planet products in Indonesia. In *Proceedings of the International Conference on Industrial Engineering and Operations Management* (Vol. 1, pp. 3023–3033).

Kewakuma, A. S. V., Rofiaty, R., & Ratnawati, K. (2021). The effect of green marketing strategy on customer loyalty mediated by brand image. *JBTI: Jurnal Bisnis: Teori Dan Implementasi, 12*(1), 1–11.

Khan, K. U., Atlas, F., Arshad, M. Z., Akhtar, S., & Khan, F. (2022). Signaling green: Impact of green product attributes on consumers trust and the mediating role of green marketing. *Frontiers in Psychology, 13*, 790272.

Kotrlik, J. W. K. J. W., & Higgins, C. C. H. C. C. (2001). Organizational research: Determining appropriate sample size in survey research appropriate sample size in survey research. *Information Technology, Learning, and Performance Journal, 19*(1), 43.

Li, B., Liao, M., Yuan, J., & Zhang, J. (2023). Green consumption behavior prediction based on fan-shaped search mechanism fruit fly algorithm optimized neural network. *Journal of Retailing and Consumer Services, 75*, 103471.

Li, S., Saleh, M. S. M., & Huang, M. (2025). Green marketing and Greenwashing effects on consumer purchase of electric cars: The moderating role of environmental knowledge. *International Journal of Customer Relationship Marketing and Management (IJCRMM), 16*(1), 1–21.

Luo, G. L., Zheng, H., & Guo, Y. L. (2023). Impact of consumer information capability on green consumption intention: The role of green trust and media publicity. *Frontiers in Psychology, 14*, 1247479.

Maaitah, N., Tarabieh, S., & Aifrahat, F. A. (2024). Viewing social media influencers and purchase intent from the perspective of digital marketing.

In *Tecno-realidades: desinformación, virtualidad y activismo* (pp. 197–210). McGraw Hill España.

Martínez, P. (2015). Customer loyalty: Exploring its antecedents from a green marketing perspective. *International Journal of Contemporary Hospitality Management, 27*(5), 896–917.

Muflih, M., Iswanto, B., & Purbayati, R. (2023). Green loyalty of Islamic banking customers: Combined effect of green practices, green trust, green perceived value, and green satisfaction. *International Journal of Ethics and Systems*. (ahead-of-print).

Naini, N. F., Santoso, S., Andriani, T. S., Claudia, U. G., & Nurfadillah, N. (2022). The effect of product quality, service quality, customer satisfaction on customer loyalty. *Journal of consumer sciences, 7*(1), 34–50.

Nguyen-Viet, B. (2023). The impact of green marketing mix elements on green customer based brand equity in an emerging market. *Asia-Pacific Journal of Business Administration, 15*(1), 96–116.

Oliver, R. L. (1999). Whence consumer loyalty? *Journal of Marketing, 63*(4_suppl1), 33–44.

Pahlevi, M. R., & Suhartanto, D. (2020). The integrated model of green loyalty: Evidence from eco-friendly plastic products. *Journal of Cleaner Production, 257*, 120844.

Rahaman, M. T., Pranta, A. D., Repon, M. R., Ahmed, M. S., & Islam, T. (2024). Green production and consumption of textiles and apparel: Importance, fabrication, challenges and future prospects. *Journal of Open Innovation: Technology, Market, and Complexity*, 100280.

Reddy, K. P., Chandu, V., Srilakshmi, S., Thagaram, E., Sahyaja, C., & Osei, B. (2023). Consumers perception on green marketing towards eco-friendly fast moving consumer goods. *International Journal of Engineering Business Management, 15*, 18479790231170962.

Saleem, F., Khattak, A., Ur Rehman, S., & Ashiq, M. (2021). Bibliometric analysis of green marketing research from 1977 to 2020. *Publications, 9*(1), 1.

Salsabilla, F., & Isharina, I. K. (2024). The effect of green brand image, green trust, and green satisfaction on customer loyalty. *Jurnal Manajemen Pemasaran Dan Perilaku Konsumen, 3*(2), 348–358. https://doi.org/10.21776/jmppk.2024.03.2.08

Shaheer, S. A., Zain, F., Aslam, M., & Abbas, M. Z. (2024). Enhancing customer loyalty through brand image, customer satisfaction, green marketing, and corporate social responsibility: A mediated moderation model. *ASSAJ, 2*(4), 729–752.

Simanjuntak, M., Sumarwan, U., & Situmorang, A. D. (2020). The effect of marketing mix and brand image on customer loyalty of remixed mortar. *Independent journal of management & production, 11*(2), 450–472.

Tan, Z., Sadiq, B., Bashir, T., Mahmood, H., & Rasool, Y. (2022). Investigating the impact of green marketing components on purchase intention: The mediating role of brand image and brand trust. *Sustainability, 14*(10), 5939.

Tarabieh, S., Gil, I., Galdón Salvador, J. L., & AlFraihat, S. F. A. (2024). The new game of online marketing: How social media influencers drive online repurchase intention through brand trust and customer brand engagement. *Intangible Capital, 20*(1), 103–125.

Tarabieh, S. M. Z. A. (2021). The impact of greenwash practices over green purchase intention: The mediating effects of green confusion, green perceived risk, and green trust. *Management Science Letters, 11*(2), 451-464.

Wang, D., & Walker, T. (2023). How to regain green consumer trust after greenwashing: Experimental evidence from China. *Sustainability, 15*(19), 14436.

Wang, J., Wang, S., Xue, H., Wang, Y., & Li, J. (2018). Green image and consumers' word-of-mouth intention in the green hotel industry: The moderating effect of Millennials. *Journal of Cleaner Production, 181*, 426–436.

Yu, Y., Li, X., & Jai, T. M. (2017). The impact of green experience on customer satisfaction: Evidence from TripAdvisor. *International Journal of Contemporary Hospitality Management, 29*(5), 1340–1361.

Zhang, N., Guo, M., Bu, X., & Jin, C. (2023). Understanding green loyalty: A literature review based on bibliometric-content analysis. *Heliyon, 9*(7).

Zhang, Z., Sami, F., Ullah, I., Khan, S. U., & Khan, S. (2024). Analyzing the green marketing approaches and their impact on consumer behavior toward the environment in China: A logistic regression approach. *Environment, Development and Sustainability, 26*(11), 29453–29474.

CHAPTER 9

Measuring Impact and Performance: Environmental, Social, and Governance (ESG) Metrics; Impact Assessment and Reporting

Tareq N. Hashem, Anuj Kumar, Adel M. Qatawneh, Amjed Alfityani, and Ma'ali M. Al-Yousufi

Abstract The current study aimed to examine the impact of environmental, social, and governance factors on organizational performance. The researcher used a quantitative approach to conduct this study by distributing a questionnaire to a sample of the study. The study population included administrators working in companies that use ESG standards in Jordan. A convenient sample of 300 administrators was chosen to distribute the study questionnaire to them. A total of 277 valid questionnaires were retrieved for analysis. Spss program was used to analyze

T. N. Hashem (✉)
Marketing Department, Applied Science Private University, Amman, Jordan
e-mail: t_hashim@asu.edu.jo

A. Kumar
Rushford Business School, Luzern, Switzerland

S. Trivedi et al. (eds.), *Green Ventures*, Sustainable Development Goals Series, https://doi.org/10.1007/978-981-95-6533-7_9

the data by using descriptive statistics and Multiple Regression. The study confirmed the overall impact of combined ESG factors on organizational performance. The study provides investors with key insights on investing in responsible companies. This is because the findings indicate a connection between ESG performance and long-term financial benefits. It shows that businesses in Jordan need a strong plan for how to use ESG practices in their daily work.

Keywords Environmental · Social · Governance · (ESG) Metrics · Performance

1 Introduction

Incorporating ESG factors into business strategies and decisions has become crucial due to global shifts and pressure from governments and society for greater transparency and sustainability. Investors now use these factors as a standard method to evaluate non-financial risks that might impact an institution's future performance (Treepongkaruna & Suttipun, 2024).

The environmental aspect assesses an institution's commitment to safeguarding the environment, cutting carbon emissions, and reducing negative environmental impacts. This aligns with the thirteenth Sustainable Development Goal (SDG13), which urges immediate action to combat climate change and its effects (Ngwa et al., 2025). The social dimension examines an institution's commitment to social responsibility by evaluating aspects such as employee well-being ethical labor practices, and community engagement. Governance relates to systems

A. M. Qatawneh
Al-Zaytoonah University of Jordan, Amman, Jordan

A. Alfityani
Accounting department, Applied Science Private University, Amman, Jordan

M. M. Al-Yousufi
Kuwait University, Kuwait City, Kuwait

that ensure transparent and equitable decision-making (Antolín-López & Ortiz-de-Mandojana, 2023).

To assess whether incorporating ESG into the operational strategies of today's institutions makes sense, we need to conduct a thorough investigation of how these factors influence organizational performance.

In this setting, we should carry out a detailed study to understand how these dimensions work together with organizationasl performance. This will help us figure out if integrating ESG into the operational strategies of modern institutions works well.

2 Importance of the Study

This study is a vital and important addition to the subject of using environmental, social, and governance factors in enhancing organizational performance. The study's results provide decision-makers and investors with an in-depth understanding of how to manage non-financial factors and incorporate them into performance evaluation indicators. It also contributes to enriching the academic discussion on the contribution of ESG to achieving sustainable development goals, especially the one related to climate action (SDG13), by supporting responsible environmental practices.

3 Study Objectives

This study aims to the following:

- Analyzing the extent of the impact of environmental, social, and governance factors on organizational performance.
- Measuring institutions' awareness of the importance of integrating ESG into their operational activities.
- Determining the relationship between corporate commitment to ESG and achieving positive financial and non-financial results.
- Exploring the potential impact of ESG factors on the ability of institutions to achieve sustainable development goals, especially SDG13.

4 Study Problem

Despite the increasing adoption of ESG reports worldwide, many institutions, especially in emerging economies, still face challenges in measuring the impact of these factors on their actual performance. The problem of the study arises from the following question:

To what extent do environmental, social, and governance (ESG) factors affect organizational performance in modern organizations?

- This main question gives rise to a number of sub-questions, including:
- What is the level of commitment of institutions to implementing environmental, social, and governance practices?
- Does commitment to ESG contribute to enhancing financial and non-financial results?

5 Study Hypotheses

Based on the study's problem and objectives, the following hypotheses were formulated:

Main Hypothesis: H: There is a statistically significant overall impact of combined ESG factors on organizational performance.

Sub hypotheses:

- H1: There is a statistically significant impact of environmental factors on organizational performance.
- H2: There is a statistically significant impact of social factors on organizational performance.
- H3: There is a statistically significant impact of governance factors on organizational performance.

6 Theoretical Framework

6.1 ESG Concept

In light of the rapid transformations the world has witnessed in recent decades, environmental and social sustainability have become a central focus in the strategies of businesses and governmental and non-governmental institutions. The increasing global awareness of environmental and social challenges has led to the emergence of a comprehensive framework known as Environmental, Social, and Governance (ESG) criteria, which has become an important international standard for evaluating the sustainable performance of institutions and their environmental, social, and governance impact.

ESG standards are a group of metrics that help investors and stakeholders see how companies tackle environmental problems like climate change social issues tied to human rights and work conditions, and governance practices that ensure clear and responsible decision-making.

Climate change stands out as one of the biggest environmental threats the world faces today. It poses a direct risk to economies and communities worldwide. To this end, the international community has established a set of global goals in the 2030 Agenda for Sustainable Development. The most important of these is Sustainable Development Goal 13 (SDG13), which concerns "taking rapid action to combat climate change and its impacts."

Linking environmental, social, and governance (ESG) standards to SDG13 is of great importance. It provides a comprehensive perspective for organizations to assess their environmental and social impact. It helps them commit to clear action plans to reduce harmful emissions, enhance climate change adaptation, and improve transparency and accountability to society and investors.

Incorporating SDG13 into ESG reporting also provides organizations with an opportunity to enhance their image, attract sustainable investments, and achieve better financial results. Recent studies show a positive link between good environmental performance and enhanced corporate market standing (Chen et al., 2023; Guerrero & Viteri, 2025; Treepongkaruna & Suttipun, 2024).

ESG standards are more than just assessment tools; they play a crucial role in maintaining a balance between economic growth, environmental conservation, and social justice. To understand these standards, we need to understand their components and how they relate to global efforts to address climate change.

6.2 *The Environmental Dimension*

The environmental aspect examines a company's impact on the environment and its use of eco-friendly practices. This component has several key elements as follows:

- Carbon and greenhouse gas emissions: A crucial indicator of a business's environmental performance is its ability to reduce greenhouse gas emissions, which contribute to global warming (Hoang, 2018; Turturea, 2015).

Natural resource management involves strategies to conserve energy, water, and raw materials as well as improved resource utilization methods (Chen et al., 2023; Shaikh, 2022). It also aims to minimize waste and pollution.

- Waste management: proper methods to handle solid and liquid waste, recycle it, and dispose of it without harming people or the environment (da Costa, 2024; Takril et al., 2023).
- Biodiversity: Certain groups use indicators to safeguard biodiversity and reduce their impact on surrounding ecosystems (Guerrero & Viteri, 2025).

To show its dedication to environmental responsibility, the institution should ensure compliance with all applicable environmental laws and regulations (Bosi et al., 2022).

These key areas minimize risks associated with environmental finances and rules, boost operational efficiency, and enhance the institution's reputation (Chen et al., 2023; da Costa, 2024).

6.3 *The Social Dimension*

The social dimension examines an organization's relationships with its employees, the local community, and its clients. It addresses these key topics:

- Human Rights and Fair Work: upholding the rights of employees, refraining from discrimination, and offering a secure, healthful workplace that complies with international labor standards (Ngwa et al., 2025; Shaikh, 2022).
- Diversity and Inclusion: encouraging a workforce that is diverse in terms of gender, race, and culture. It also entails establishing an environment at work where everyone is accepted, which encourages the generation of fresh ideas (Shaikh, 2022) (Qatawneh, 2023b).
- Increasing Human Resources: This entails funding employee training, providing opportunities for advancement, and rewarding hard work. One of a company's most valuable assets is its workforce (Ngwa et al., 2025).
- Social Responsibility: The organization's social acceptance and ability to continue operations are influenced by its support of cultural, educational, and health initiatives in the neighborhood (Takril et al., 2023).
- Product Safety and Quality: Gaining customers' trust requires ensuring that goods and services fulfill consumer safety and quality standards (Shaikh, 2022).

Good social practices improve the institution's standing with stakeholders and the community, increase employee and customer loyalty, and reduce the likelihood of labor disputes (Qatawneh, 2023b; Shaikh, 2022).

6.3.1 The Governance Dimension

The governance dimension includes a set of rules and regulations that govern management behavior and the relationships between the stakeholders of the institution (shareholders, management, customers, community). It includes the following axes:

- Board Structure: Confirmation of the existence of an independent and balanced board of directors that includes diverse expertise and effectively oversees the executive management (Hashem et al., 2016; Hoang, 2018).
- Transparency and Disclosure: The institution's commitment to publishing accurate and comprehensive financial and non-financial reports, allowing stakeholders to objectively assess the institution's performance (Hashem et al., 2016).

- Accountability: Clarity of the roles and responsibilities of board members and executive management, and the implementation of internal and external accountability mechanisms (Hashem et al., 2016).
- • Anti-corruption: The existence of clear policies to prevent corruption, bribery, and financial manipulation, and the activation of a culture of integrity in all of the institution's operations (Hoang, 2018).
- Rights of Shareholders: Protecting shareholders those with minority stakes, and getting them involved in company decision-making (Hashem et al., 2016).

Good governance practices attract money and investors, boost investor confidence, and lower legal and money-related risks (Hashem et al., 2016).

6.4 The Evolution of the ESG Concept

The concept of ESG began to emerge in the mid-2000s with the 2006 release of the United Nations Principles for Responsible Investment (UNPRI). These principles encouraged investors to consider environmental, social, and governance issues in their investment decisions (Antolín-López & Ortiz-de-Mandojana, 2023; Neri, 2021). ESG standards and measurement tools have evolved since then becoming integral to corporate reports and global sustainability reports (Bosi et al., 2022; Raquel, 2023).

Multiple studies demonstrate that incorporating ESG into business strategies has a crucial role in achieving long-term growth and reducing risks associated with economic activities (da Cunha et al., 2025; Lokuwaduge & Heenetigala, 2017). Credit rating agencies now also use ESG indicators to evaluate companies highlighting the growing importance of these standards in financial markets (Yavuz et al., 2025).

6.5 The Relationship Between ESG Performance and the Financial Performance of Institutions

Studies indicate that firms excelling in ESG practices also achieve better financial results. (Chen et al., 2023) discovered that companies with higher ESG standards earn more money, and those committed to sustainability standards face lower financial and operational risks (Chen et al., 2023).

Research from Thailand by (Treepongkaruna & Suttipun, 2024) revealed that strong ESG reporting boosts company profitability by improving operational efficiency and transparency, which attracts investors (Treepongkaruna & Suttipun, 2024). ESG also shapes investor decisions, as they favor companies dedicated to long-term sustainability (Şeker & Şengür, 2021).

6.6 Signs to Check How ESG Is Performing

When evaluating ESG performance various metrics examine environmental, social, and governance issues. These indicators can be direct outputs such as emission levels, or broader impacts, like how the project affects nearby communities (Guerrero & Viteri, 2025; Yavuz et al., 2025).

Standardizing ESG data proves challenging, and data quality varies across industries and countries. However, indexes like MSCI, Sustainalytics, and FTSE4Good play a crucial role in providing accurate ratings of companies' ESG performance (Hashem, 2021; Yavuz et al., 2025). Studies indicate that incorporating sustainable life cycle assessments could enhance the accuracy and completeness of these indicators (Padilla-Rivera, 2025).

6.7 Problems with Putting ESG into Practice

Despite growing interest in ESG and more available standards, implementation remains challenging. This stems from unstandardized criteria and unclear disclosures allowing companies to use greenwashing tactics that reduce report credibility (Aksoy et al., 2022; Takril et al., 2023). Data quality disparities and variations between established and emerging countries also hinder ESG standard implementation (Şeker & Şengür, 2021).

6.8 The Growing Role of Technology to Support ESG

AI and big data analytics now play a crucial part in measuring and monitoring ESG. These tools boost data accuracy, spot issues earlier, and prevent greenwashing. They also increase transparency by using blockchain technology to track the supply chain (Qatawneh, 2023b).

(Qatawneh, 2024) showed that AI in auditing has an impact on detecting financial risks and fraud, which improves ESG-related financial reporting.

6.9 *Components of Environmental, Social, and Governance (ESG) standards with the Integration of Sustainable Development Goal 13 (SDG13)*

The three primary components of ESG standards are governance, social impact, and the environment. Connecting these standards to the Sustainable Development Goals has become increasingly important due to the increasing worldwide focus on climate change and sustainable development. This is particularly true of Sustainable Development Goal 13 (SDG13), which emphasizes the need to act urgently to mitigate the effects of climate change.

6.9.1 *The Environmental Dimension and its Connection to SDG13*

Sustainable Development Goal 13 emphasizes the urgent need for businesses to take action to reduce the impact of climate change on human life by.

Reducing emissions of carbon dioxide and other greenhouse gases into the atmosphere to limit excessive global warming (Chen et al., 2023; Guerrero & Viteri, 2025; Padilla-Rivera, 2025).

- Documenting fossil fuel consumption and exploiting solar and wind energy as clean, renewable energy sources (da Costa, 2024; Padilla-Rivera, 2025).
- Developing a corporate work environment to mitigate climate impacts (Hashem, 2021) and (Qatawneh, 2024).
- Transparency in disclosing data related to the organization's environmental impact (Raquel, 2023), (Bosi et al., 2022; Ngwa et al., 2025).

6.9.2 The Social Dimension and its Role in Supporting Sustainable Development

The focus here is on improving the quality of life for workers and surrounding communities, linking this to the context of Sustainable Development Goal 13:

- Raising employee awareness of the impacts of climate change and the challenges that must be addressed (Ngwa et al., 2025; Shaikh, 2022).
- Working to improve working conditions, health, and safety to prevent any social harm (Shaikh, 2022; Takril et al., 2023).
- Social Responsibility: Investing in sustainable community projects that support adaptation to climate change, such as water and clean energy projects (Hashem, 2021; Takril et al., 2023).

6.9.3 The Governance Dimension and its Role in Achieving SDG13

Good governance lays the foundations that ensure institutions adhere to environmental and social standards:

- Integrating sustainable development goals into company strategies: Developing clear policies to achieve SDG13 goals and incorporating sustainability standards into the decision-making process (Hoang, 2018) (Srour, 2022).
- Accountability and Transparency: Providing independent and regular reports on ESG performance and progress toward achieving climate goals (Antolín-López & Ortiz-de-Mandojana, 2023; Srour, 2022).
- Combating Corruption and Promoting Integrity: Ensuring the effective utilization of resources in sustainability projects and preventing their leakage due to corruption, which supports the efficient implementation of climate strategies (Hoang, 2018).
- Enhancing Stakeholder Engagement: Involving investors, customers, employees, and the community in monitoring environmental and social performance, which strengthens the overall commitment to SDG13 (Hashem, 2021).

6.10 *The Importance of Linking ESG Standards to SDG13*

Linking ESG standards to Sustainable Development Goal 13 creates a strong framework to drive institutions toward environmental, economic, and social sustainability, as this linkage encourages:

- Reducing environmental damage and enhancing the ability to adapt to climate change.
- Supporting informed decision-making that takes into account environmental and social considerations.
- Increasing the trust of investors and consumers by enhancing transparency and accountability.
- Actively contributing to the international community's efforts to combat climate change and achieve sustainable development.

This has been confirmed by numerous recent studies that highlighted the importance of integrating ESG reports with sustainable development goals to achieve sustainable outcomes at both the institutional and national levels (Guerrero & Viteri, 2025; Hashem, 2021; Paranita et al., 2025; Qatawneh, 2024).

6.11 *Review of Previous Studies on ESG Criteria and Their Impact on Organizational Performance*

More and more recent works highlight the ways in which ESG norms can contribute to the betterment of institutions. This change has gone from being a nice-to-have corporate policy to an essential part of modern company management. This shift is supported by numerous research that span different sectors and geographic areas.

When looking at the link between ESG and financial performance, study (Treepongkaruna & Suttipun, 2024) offers strong evidence that ESG disclosure increases profitability. The study focused on Thai enterprises. Adherence to ESG principles improves a company's brand and increases investor trust, according to study (Ngwa et al., 2025) in Nigeria. Researchers found that measures including better operational efficiency and increased stakeholder satisfaction acted as mediators between ESG performance and financial results, lending credence to these findings (Chen et al., 2023).

There have been major changes in how ESG performance is measured. Research (Antolín-López & Ortiz-de-Mandojana, 2023) lays up a thorough framework for measuring and disclosing, while research (Guerrero & Viteri, 2025) looks at the differences between performance and outcome indicators. These updates fill in a big blank that has been preventing fair comparisons between different industries and businesses. In continuation of these endeavors, a novel framework is presented in study (Padilla-Rivera, 2025) that combines life cycle evaluation with ESG criteria. Because of this, businesses are able to improve their impact on society and the environment.

According to studies that compare regions, ESG norms affect various places differently due to their distinct organizational characteristics and geographical settings. Depending on their size and industry, ESG standards impact companies, according to a Turkish study (Kurniawan, 2023). During times of crisis, such as the COVID-19 pandemic, researchers in Egypt discovered that ESG disclosure is more useful (Qatawneh, 2024). When analyzing the impact of ESG, it is important to take the organizational environment into account, as shown by these results.

The effect of governance procedures on audit quality can be considered using the framework provided by research (Qatawneh, 2023a) in the field of corporate governance. How managers may increase the value of their brands by emphasizing environmentally friendly items is the subject of research (Qatawneh, 2023b). A company's overall success can be impacted by a multitude of ESG factors, as shown in these studies.

Accounting information systems can benefit from state-of-the-art technology, according to studies. According to studies (Qatawneh, 2024), audits and fraud detection can be improved with the use of artificial intelligence and natural language processing. Both studies investigate the effects of organizational culture on accounting information system performance (Qatawneh, 2023a) and the effects of staff empowerment on system performance (Qatawneh, 2023b).

7 Methods and Materials

The researcher used a quantitative approach to conduct this study by distributing a questionnaire to a sample of the study. The study population included administrators working in companies that use ESG standards in Jordan. A convenient sample of 300 administrators was

Table 1 Alpha value (Reliability)

Variable	α
Environmental dimension	0.776
Social dimension	0.74
Governance dimension	0.868
Performance	0.811

chosen to distribute the study questionnaire to them. A total of 277 valid questionnaires were retrieved for analysis (refer Table 1).

Primary data statistics were managed using SPSS. Cronbach's Alpha (α) was employed to evaluate the internal reliability and consistency of the study instrument. The statistically reasonable alpha value was greater than 0.70. Statistical tests that are included in the study include the mean (μ), standard deviation (σ), multiple regression tests.

8 Results and Discussion

8.1 Demographics

As shown in the demographic Table 2, the highest percent of respondents were males (59.9%). The table also showed that the highest percent of respondents had a bachelor degree (56.7%), with an experience greater than 15 years (36.5%). In addition, the highest percent of respondents were in the age range of + 50 years (44%).

8.2 Questionnaire Analysis

Table 3 presents the survey statements' data, as well as the corresponding average and standard deviation. A favorable disposition was demonstrated by all participants, as indicated by an average score of 3.00 or higher for each item on the survey. The statistical evidence firmly corroborates the notion that the reactions were favorable. Additionally, it was observed that the individuals exhibited a favorable attitude toward the factors being examined. It is imperative to emphasize that all variables examined in this study obtained scores exceeding the mean value of 3.00, which is a favorable outcome from a statistical perspective.

Table 2 Demographics

Variable		*f*	%
Gender			
	Male	166	59.9
	Female	111	40.1
Age			
	Less than 30	21	7.6
	31–40	74	26.7
	41–50	60	21.7
	+ 50 years	122	44.0
Education			
	Diploma or below	25	9.0
	BA	157	56.7
	MA	76	27.4
	PhD	19	6.9
Experience			
	Less than 5 years	43	15.5
	5–10 years	66	23.8
	11–15 years	67	24.2
	Above 15 years	101	36.5
	Total	277	100.0

Table 3 Questionnaire analysis

Variable	μ	σ
Environmental dimension	4.071	0.656
Social dimension	4.051	0.593
Governance dimension	4.099	0.557
Performance	4.069	0.584

8.3 Multicolleniarity Test

The independent variables were subjected to VIF and Tolerance analysis in order to assess multicollinearity. These calculations are responsible for the subsequent imminent developments. As evidenced by the fact that all Variance Inflation Factor (VIF) values are less than 10 and all Tolerance values are greater than 0.10, the data does not exhibit multicollinearity (refer Table 4).

Table 4 Multicolleniarity

variable	*Tolerance*	*VIF*
Environmental dimension	0.537	1.863
Social dimension	0.361	2.768
Governance dimension	0.370	2.706

8.4 *Hypotheses Testing*

Multiple regression is used to test the hypotheses of the study. Table 5 indicated that there is a statistically significant overall impact of combined ESG factors on organizational performance. An R value of 0.835 indicates a strong relationship. Furthermore, the independent variables explain 69.7% of the variation seen in the dependent variable.

Also, the coefficients table shows that:

1. There is a statistically significant impact of environmental factors on organizational performance. Since t-value is significant at 0.05 level.
2. There is a statistically significant impact of social factors on organizational performance. Since t-value is significant at 0.05 level.
3. There is a statistically significant impact of governance factors on organizational performance. Since t-value is significant at 0.05 level.

Table 5 Main hypothesis testing

Coefficients										
Model		*Unstandardized coefficients*		*Standardized coefficients*	*t*	*Sig*				
		B	*Std. Error*	*Beta*			*R*	*R Square*	*F*
1	(Constant)	0.335	0.151		2.214	0.028	0.835	0.697	209.735**
	Environmental dimension	0.088	0.040	0.099	2.174	0.031			
	Social dimension	0.195	0.054	0.198	3.579	0.000			
	Governance dimension	0.631	0.057	0.602	10.996	0.000			

H: There is a statistically significant overall impact of combined ESG factors on organizational performance

9 Discussion

The study found that environmental (E), social (S), and governance (G) factors all affect a company's performance. When these factors are combined (ESG), they have a big effect on the company's performance as a whole.

- Environmental Dimension (E): The study found that companies that use eco-friendly practices, like lowering emissions, conserving energy, and managing trash, do better. (Guerrero & Viteri, 2025) found a link between making less money and having a smaller carbon footprint. (Chen et al., 2023) found that companies that are more aware of their surroundings have fewer regulatory issues.
- Social Dimension (S): The results showed that businesses that spend money on their employees' health and well-being (through programs like training, diversity, and job safety) and community projects (like health and education) have more loyal customers and a better reputation. This backs up (Ngwa et al., 2025) claim that corporate social responsibility makes a company look better and (Shaikh, 2022) claim that social justice makes employees happier.
- Governance Dimension (G): The results showed that board independence, anti-corruption measures, and openness all help build trust with investors and lower borrowing costs.

The study backs up the idea that ESG isn't just an extra cost; it can also help businesses make more money in the long run, as (Treepongkaruna & Suttipun, 2024) showed with Thai businesses. This effect is not the same in every industry and location, though, which shows that more comparative research is needed.

The Effect of Technology: The study found that AI can make ESG reporting more accurate. In her study of AI use in fraud detection and auditing (Qatawneh, 2024).

10 Conclusion

This study provides valuable insights into how Environmental, Social, and Governance (ESG) standards shape company performance in theory and practice. The findings contribute to business sustainability research by demonstrating that adhering to ESG guidelines is not just an added expense, but a strategic long-term investment that enhances both financial and non-financial outcomes. This aligns with previous studies, like (Guerrero & Viteri, 2025) and (Chen et al., 2023). The report also offers a comprehensive framework to link these criteria to the Sustainable Development Goals (SDGs), with Goal 13 (SDG13) taking center stage due to its focus on tackling climate change. This makes a key contribution to current research. Many people can apply the study's findings in their daily lives. The results show managers and leaders of institutions that ESG standards should be the main focus of their financial and operational plans. To earn investors' trust and steer clear of "greenwashing" risks, they need to enhance their disclosure and transparency methods. It also underscores the importance of investing in green technologies and new ideas that will last a long time and help operations run more while cutting costs in the long run. The study makes a strong case for policymakers to back the adoption of tougher standards that require institutions to report on their ESG performance such as the European Union's "Corporate Sustainability Reporting Directive" (CSRD). The research provides investors with key insights on investing in responsible companies. This is because the findings indicate a connection between ESG performance and long-term financial benefits. The study also offers researchers fresh perspectives to explore in future work. For instance, it proposes conducting more extended studies and comparing larger regions. It also suggests examining how emerging tech like blockchain and AI can simplify ESG performance measurement and evaluation. This helps to grow the knowledge base and tackles challenges such as ensuring data quality and promoting standardization.

11 Recommendations

The study shows that businesses in Jordan need a strong plan for how to use ESG practices in their daily work. Companies build trust with customers and investors when they follow global reporting rules like the GRI and SAS and support calls to be responsible and open. So, it's a good idea to tie boss pay to green goals and give rewards that make people think of new ways to be more environmentally friendly. Companies should use resources wisely and invest in green technology like solar power to help the environment.

This will promote the achievement of Sustainable Development Goal 13 (SDG 13), related to combating climate change, and contribute to the transition to a sustainable economy. Implementing blockchain and artificial intelligence is a prudent strategy to ensure that their supply chains comply with environmentally sustainable standards and improve the accuracy of their social and environmental reporting. The research promotes closer collaboration between the public and commercial sectors to establish a unified set of criteria to demonstrate ESG progress at the national level, addressing the challenges posed by Jordanian regulations. This strategy encourages the establishment of a sustainable business environment, in line with Jordan's climate commitments. It also requires large corporations to submit detailed annual reports.

References

Aksoy, L., Buoye, A. J., Fors, M., Keiningham, T. L., & Rosengren, S. (2022). Environmental, social and governance (ESG) metrics do not serve services customers: A missing link between sustainability metrics and customer perceptions of social innovation. *Journal of Service Management, 33*(4/5), 565–577.

Antolín-López, R., & Ortiz-de-Mandojana, N. (2023). *Measuring and disclosing Environmental, Social and Governance (ESG) information and performance.*

Bosi, M. K., Lajuni, N., Wellfren, A. C., & Lim, T. S. (2022). Sustainability reporting through environmental, social, and governance: A bibliometric review. *Sustainability, 14*(19), 12071. https://doi.org/10.3390/su141912071

Chen, S., Song, Y., & Gao, P. (2023). Environmental, social, and governance (ESG) performance and financial outcomes: Analyzing the impact of ESG on financial performance. *Journal of Environmental Management, 345*, Article 118829. https://doi.org/10.1016/j.jenvman.2023.118829

da Costa, M. F. (2024). *The impact of ESG and environmental scores on the companies' performance: Evidence from European listed companies in industries with high materiality issues.*

da Cunha, Í. G. F., Policarpo, R. V. S., de Oliveira, P. C. S., Abdala, E. C., & do Nascimento Rebelatto, D. A. (2025). A systematic review of ESG indicators and corporate performance: Proposal for a conceptual framework. *Future Business Journal, 11*(1), 106.

Guerrero, S., & Viteri, J. P. (2025). What are environmental, social, and governance scores measuring? The role of outcome and impact indicators in ESG scores. *Finance Research Letters, 72*, Article 106529. https://doi.org/10.1016/j.frl.2025.106529

Hashem, T. N. (2021). Environmental legitimacy through adopting green products and its effect on the brand equity: Moderating role of management awareness. *Research in World Economy, 12*(2), 197–210.

Hashem, T., Hashem, A., Hashem, F., & Ayoub, F. (2016). The impact of corporate governance on the quality of marketing audit in Jordanian industrial public shareholding companies. *International Journal of Business Administration, 7*(2), 60–71.

Hoang, T. (2018). The role of the integrated reporting in raising awareness of environmental, social and corporate governance (ESG) performance. In *Stakeholders, governance and responsibility* (pp. 47–69). Emerald Publishing.

Kurniawan, M. (2023). The influence of environmental, social, and governance (ESG) performance on company performance. *Daengku: Journal of Humanities and Social Sciences Innovation, 3*(4), 657–661.

Lokuwaduge, C. S. D. S., & Heenetigala, K. (2017). Integrating environmental, social and governance (ESG) disclosure for a sustainable development: An Australian study. *Business Strategy and the Environment, 26*(4), 438–450. https://doi.org/10.1002/bse.1927

Neri, S. (2021). Environmental, social and governance (ESG) and integrated reporting. In *Global challenges to CSR and sustainable development: Root causes and evidence from case studies* (pp. 293–302).

Ngwa, C. U., Ojeh, A., Ezema, K. O., Agu, J. C., & Edeh, I. T. (2025). The effect of environmental, social and governance (ESG) reporting on corporate reputation in Nigeria. *American Research Journal of Economics, Finance and Management, 13*(1), 1–23.

Padilla-Rivera, A., Hannouf, M., Assefa, G., & Gates, I. (2025). Enhancing environmental, social, and governance performance and reporting through integration of life cycle sustainability assessment framework. *Sustainable Development, 33*(2), 2975–2995. https://doi.org/10.1002/sd.3265

Paranita, E. S., Ramadian, A., Wijaya, E., Nursanti, T. D., & Judijanto, L. (2025). The impact of ESG factors on investment decisions: Exploring the interplay between sustainability reporting, corporate governance, and financial performance. *Journal of Ecohumanism, 4*(1), 4522–4533.

Qatawneh, A. M. (2023a). The role of organizational culture in supporting better accounting information systems outcomes. *Cogent Economics & Finance, 11*(1). https://doi.org/10.1080/23322039.2022.2164669

Qatawneh, A. M. (2023b). The role of employee empowerment in supporting accounting information systems outcomes: A mediated model. *Sustainability, 15*(9), 7155. https://doi.org/10.3390/su15097155

Qatawneh, A. M. (2024). The role of artificial intelligence in auditing and fraud detection in accounting information systems: Moderating role of natural language processing. *International Journal of Organizational Analysis*. Advance online publication. https://doi.org/10.1108/IJOA-03-2024-4389

Raquel, A. L. (2023). *Measuring and disclosing Environmental, Social and Governance (ESG) information and performance* (Joint Research Centre Report No. JRC131932).

Şeker, Y., & Şengür, E. D. (2021). The impact of environmental, social, and governance (ESG) performance on financial reporting quality: International evidence. *Ekonomika, 100*(2), 190–212.

Shaikh, I. (2022). Environmental, social, and governance (ESG) practice and firm performance: International evidence. *Journal of Business Economics and Management, 23*(1), 218–237.

Srour, M. I. (2022). The impact of Environmental, Social, Governance (ESG) disclosure on firm value and financial performance: Evidence from Egypt during Covid 19. *Trade and Finance, 42*(1), 1–19.

Takril, N. F., Sabri, S. A., Ika, S. R., & Jamlus, N. (2023). Assessing the impact of environmental, social, and governance (ESG) factors on corporate performance: A literature review. *Proceeding of the 10th International Conference on Management and Muamalah 2023 (ICoMM 2023)*

Treepongkaruna, S., & Suttipun, M. (2024). The impact of environmental, social and governance (ESG) reporting on corporate profitability: Evidence from Thailand. *Journal of Financial Reporting and Accounting*. Advance online publication. https://doi.org/10.1108/jfra-09-2023-0555

Turturea, M. (2015). Social and environmental reporting as a part of the integrated reporting. *Acta Universitatis Agriculturae Et Silviculturae Mendelianae Brunensis, 63*(6), 2161–2170.

Yavuz, M. S., Tatlı, H. S., Bozkurt, G., & Öngel, G. (2025). Does ESG performance have an impact on financial performance? Evidence from Turkey. *Journal of Entrepreneurship, Management and Innovation, 21*(1), 24–42.

CHAPTER 10

The Financial Power of Socially Responsible Investment (SRI): Green Bonds and Climate Finance as Catalysts for Sustainable Entrepreneurship

Priyant Banerjee, Arshad Bhat, and Firdous A. Malik

Abstract Socially Responsible Investing (SRI) has grown to become a $40 trillion market in 2024 and accounts for about 36% of global assets under management (AUM). This expansion in ethical investment is a huge step towards sustainability as investors today expect both financial return and social and environmental returns. Green bonds, one of the most prominent areas of sustainable finance, have witnessed exponential

P. Banerjee (✉)
Department of Computer Science and Engineering, Amity University Mumbai, Mumbai, India
e-mail: priyantbanerjee@gmail.com

A. Bhat
Amity Institute of Liberal Arts, Amity University Mumbai, Mumbai, India

F. A. Malik
Department of Management, University of People, Pasadena, CA, USA

S. Trivedi et al. (eds.), *Green Ventures*, Sustainable Development Goals Series, https://doi.org/10.1007/978-981-95-6533-7_10

growth with more than $3 trillion issuance with 30% yearly growth since 2020. These financial products have facilitated investment in renewable energy, climate adaptation projects and green infrastructure around the world. Climate finance is expected to reach $5 trillion a year by 2030. It is very important for companies and startups to make the transition to low-carbon business models. Impact investing, as a type of socially responsible investing (SRI), has provided better financial returns. Nearly 60% of impact investment funds have outperformed conventional market indices in a five-year span. ESG (Environmental, Social, and Governance) metrics have also gained prominence, impacting 88% of institutional investors in their investment decisions. Even with such advancements, challenges such as regulatory fragmentation, greenwashing and limited access for nascent sustainable entrepreneurs still exist. It has been discovered that more than 70% of SMEs find it challenging to access climate-compatible finance, and this calls for inclusive financing instruments. Policy interventions including tax credits, ESG disclosure requirements and state-backed green investment funds can assist in filling the finance gap. This chapter is an empirical study of SRI's contribution to sustainable entrepreneurship, supported by empirical facts, case studies and worldwide financial trends. With green bonds and climate finance, companies can power economic growth with net-zero ambitions. The future of sustainable finance is based on open disclosure, investor confidence and adopting technology-based models of investing, including blockchain-based ESG tracking.

Keywords Socially Responsible Investment (SRI) · Green bonds · Climate finance · ESG metrics · Impact investing · SDG

1 Introduction

The world financial system is experiencing a massive revolution, shifting away from conventional paradigms of profit maximization to include more expansive objectives of environmental stewardship and social responsibility. Socially Responsible Investment (SRI) has been a powerful driver of this revolution over the last few decades, expanding to a $40 trillion industry and representing some 36% of world assets under management in 2024 (Global Sustainable Investment Alliance [GSIA], 2023). This phenomenal growth is representative of a profound change in values among investors, where economic return is no longer viewed as an isolated goal but as one piece of a bigger picture that includes environmental conservation, social justice and ethical governance. At the nexus of finance and sustainability is the challenging question: how might capital be mobilized to catalyze systemic transformation and to support the development of enterprises that are not only economically sustainable but also environmentally regenerative and socially inclusive?

The response to this query is in part found in the architecture of SRI, an area that involves a broad range of financial instruments and strategies aimed at aligning investment portfolios with ethical, environmental and social concerns. The increasing saliency of Environmental, Social, and Governance (ESG) factors in investment choices mirrors this realignment. ESG indicators have also become indispensable tools for evaluating the non-financial performance of businesses and are now on the radar of more than 88% of institutional investors worldwide (Deloitte, 2022). Indicators give a systematic way of analysing the business conduct of firms in important areas like carbon footprints, labour practices, board composition and anti-corruption measures. The integration of ESG considerations into mainstream investment management marks a wider recasting of fiduciary duty in terms of not just financial management but also long-term sustainability and ethical stewardship. Within mainstream SRI, green bonds have been a most striking and powerful financial tool. Green bonds are fixed-income instruments which are specifically dedicated to fund projects that have environmental positive impacts, such as renewable energy facilities, green buildings, clean transportation and climate resiliency programs (Flammer, 2021). Ever since the initial green bond issuance of the European Investment Bank in 2007, the market has expanded at a phenomenal pace, reaching more than $3 trillion in total issuance by 2024 and having an annual growth rate of more than 30% since 2020 (Climate Bonds Initiative, 2024). Growing demand for green bonds is driven not just by investor sentiment but also by regulatory systems, public demand for climate action and the imperative to fill in the financing gap for sustainable infrastructure. Green bonds present an appealing value proposition by mixing environmental benefits with competitive financial returns, thus acting as a vehicle for directing private capital into public goods. Concurrent with the growth of green bonds is the larger arena of climate finance, encompassing all financial flows to support climate mitigation and adaptation. Climate finance is estimated, as per the United Nations Framework Convention on Climate Change (UNFCCC, 2023), to hit $5 trillion by

2030—a five times growth from where it is now. This spate of announcements indicates the acknowledgement that meeting international climate objectives will take enormous, long-term investment across regions and sectors. Climate finance is an indispensable facilitator for the shift to low-carbon economies, especially for emerging markets and developing nations where capital scarcity is most acute. Yet, the allocation of climate finance is still significantly unbalanced, with small and medium-sized businesses (SMEs) frequently finding it difficult to obtain the financing they require to develop climate-compatible business models. Over 70% of SMEs indicate that they experience major obstacles in securing climate-compatible finance, such as excessive collateral demands, poor credit history and little investor knowledge of sustainable business prospects. Sustainable entrepreneurship, which is the establishment of businesses with environmental stewardship, social equity and economic viability as its core values, holds the middle ground in filling these gaps. In contrast to traditional businesses that tend to value quick returns over long-term value creation, sustainable entrepreneurs integrate ESG values into their day-to-day operations and strategic focus (Schaltegger & Wagner, 2011). These businesses are frequently leaders in innovation, creating solutions to urgent global issues like climate change, resource exhaustion and social injustice. From clean tech startups to regenerative agriculture businesses, sustainable entrepreneurs prove that profit motives can be reconciled with planetary limits. But their success depends on availability of supportive financial systems, ranging from patient capital, impact investors, green credit lines and supportive policy regimes. Impact investing—a form of SRI that aims for quantifiable environmental and social impacts as well as financial returns—has been an effective funding instrument for sustainable entrepreneurs. As per the Global Impact Investing Network (GIIN, 2023), almost 60% of impact investment funds have performed better than traditional market indices in the last five years. This information refutes the long-standing myth that profitability and impact are incompatible. Indeed, firms with good ESG performance are more crisis-resistant, draw higher-quality staff, and have improved stakeholder relations (Eccles et al., 2014). Incorporating impact metrics into investment analysis not only helps to enlighten but also increases accountability, with the end result that capital is only flowing into ventures that deliver on their touted social and environmental commitments. Despite these encouraging trends, the SRI marketplace is not without its challenges. One of the greatest concerns is the spread of greenwashing-the habit of exaggerating or misleading on the eco-friendliness of investments or corporate activities (Amel-Zadeh & Serafeim, 2018). Greenwashing undermines investor confidence and damages the credibility of the sustainable finance market. It also distorts market competition for truly sustainable businesses that spend a lot of resources on compliance, certification and impact reporting. Confronting greenwashing necessitates more intense regulatory control, third-party assurance mechanisms and harmonized disclosure standards. The European Union's Sustainable Finance Disclosure Regulation (SFDR) is a move in this direction, mandating asset managers to disclose how they incorporate sustainability risks into investment choices and report the environmental footprint of their portfolios (European Commission, 2021). Technological innovation holds great promise to solve many of the problems confronting the SRI industry. Blockchain, for instance, can be utilized to establish unalterable records of ESG performance to increase transparency and minimize the potential for fraud (Tapscott & Tapscott, 2017). AI and big data analytics, in like manner, can enhance the precision of ESG evaluations by observing patterns and anomalies in firm conduct not discernible with conventional financial analysis (Berg et al., 2022). These technologies can also support more active risk management and empower investors to make better decisions. By automating the collection and validation of ESG data, technology platforms can lower the cost and difficulty of sustainable investing, thus opening it up to a larger number of investors and entrepreneurs. Policy frameworks are key to scaling up SRI and ensuring equitable access to its benefits. Government policies like green investment tax credits, subsidy for renewable energy, ESG disclosure requirements and green development banks can facilitate a supportive environment for sustainable finance (World Bank, 2023). Not only do these policies reduce the cost of capital for sustainable businesses but also demonstrate political support for long-term climate targets. In India and China, green finance regulations are employed to channel investment into clean energy, pollution prevention and climate resilience projects. Moreover, global partnerships such as the Task Force on Climate-related Financial Disclosures (TCFD) and the Network for Greening the Financial System (NGFS) are implementing consistency in sustainability reporting and risk management guidelines across borders (TCFD, 2021). Although institutional action is key, the success of SRI in the end hinges on cultural and behavioural transformation of the financial sector and society in general.

Education and capacity-building programs are key to promoting a better grasp of sustainable finance principles among investors, financial planners, policymakers and entrepreneurs. Business schools and financial training programs need to incorporate ESG and impact investing in their curriculums to equip the next generation of finance workers with the knowledge required to respond to the challenges and opportunities in the twenty-first century. Further, public campaigns can educate retail investors so that they can make informed decisions and hold financial institutions accountable for more (Gonzalez & Parra, 2021). By democratizing access to financial information and technology, we can construct a more open and participatory model of sustainable finance. The convergence of these trends highlights the increasing awareness that financial systems are not neutral but instead powerful drivers that determine economic, environmental and social results. The dramatic expansion of SRI, the green bond market's swift growth and the mounting movement of climate finance are not discrete events, but elements in an interconnected process of change. And this change is not simply technical or economic; it is ethical in nature, inviting us to redefine value and to reexamine our communal priorities. By this understanding, sustainable entrepreneurship comes not only as a beneficiary of responsible finance but also as a proactive change agent-innovating, creating employment, and pushing solutions to some of the most critical issues of our era. This research study intends to examine the financial strength of SRI through the perspective of green bonds and climate finance, specifically their contribution towards promoting sustainable entrepreneurship. Based on empirical evidence, case studies and financial trends, the research will look at how these tools are transforming entrepreneurial ecosystems and supporting the shift towards a low-carbon, inclusive economy. It will also touch on the ongoing challenges of early-stage entrepreneurs' access to sustainable finance and provide recommendations on policy, practice and research. By placing these problems in the wider context of international sustainable development, the paper aims to add to that literature base positioning finance not merely as a mechanism for riches-making but as a driver for transforming systems.

2 Review of Literature

The development of Socially Responsible Investment (SRI) has brought a major change to the financial industry, blending ethical issues with conventional investment approaches. Traditionally, SRI started as religious and ethical investment methods, in which investors shunned industries such as tobacco, alcohol and gambling (Renneboog et al., 2008). This method evolved over time to include more extensive environmental, social, and governance (ESG) factors, based on the increasing realization of the effect of corporate operations on the community and the environment (Friede et al., 2015). The incorporation of ESG factors in investment has been driven by the awareness that such factors can impact financial performance. Research has shown that firms with strong ESG practices tend to have better risk management and long-term profitability (Eccles et al., 2014). Such an association has increased demand for ESG-friendly investment products, and assets under management have been at an all-time high globally (GSIA, 2020). Green bonds have become a central tool in the SRI universe, directing capital towards specifically environmentally friendly projects. Green bonds pay for endeavours like renewable energy, energy efficiency and green infrastructure (Flammer, 2021). The green bond market has grown exponentially with issuances over $1 trillion in size, demonstrating investors' demand for sustainable fixed-income products (Climate Bonds Initiative, 2020). The effectiveness of green bonds in facilitating environmental targets has been the focus of research by scholars. Evidence suggests that green bonds can make financing cheap for issuers and bring in a large pool of diversified investors who are interested in sustainability (Tang & Zhang, 2020). Nonetheless, issues remain, such as concerns about the harmonization of green bond structures and the issue of 'greenwashing', where funds are inaccurately labelled as environmentally friendly without credible support (Ehlers & Packer, 2017a, 2017b). Climate finance, comprising public and private financial flows to address climate change mitigation and adaptation, is very vital in attaining international sustainability agendas. Mobilization of climate finance is very necessary for helping developing nations shift to low-carbon economies and develop climate-resilience (UNFCCC, 2016). Mechanisms like the Green Climate Fund have been put in place to enable this process, though controversies still surround the sufficiency and accessibility of such funds (Roberts & Weikmans, 2017). The nexus between SRI and sustainable entrepreneurship is becoming more seen as a driver for innovation and more equitable economic growth. Sustainable entrepreneurs embed social and environmental goals alongside profit, more commonly solving market failures and underdeveloped communities (Dean & McMullen, 2007). SRI capital access helps these entrepreneurs expand their reach, promoting sustainable business model and technological development (Pacheco et al., 2010). Impact investing, a form of SRI, aims clearly to create tangible social and environmental impacts in addition to financial returns. Impact investing has attracted investors focused on matching their portfolios with values, resulting in the emergence of impact funds that address sectors like clean energy, affordable housing and health (Jackson & Harji, 2013). According to the Global Impact Investing Network (GIIN), the market for impact investing has grown steadily, as assets under management have risen to $715 billion in 2020 (GIIN, 2020). Empirical research on impact investment performance indicates that they have the capacity to generate competitive financial returns, as well as positive societal impacts (Brest & Born, 2013). Yet, impact measurement is not a simple task, which calls for standardized metrics and reporting systems to provide transparency and accountability (Barman, 2015). Efforts such as the Impact Reporting and Investment Standards (IRIS) and the Global Impact Investing Rating System (GIIRS) have emerged to tackle these challenges (Nicholls, 2009). The position of institutional investors in promoting SRI and sustainable entrepreneurship is central. Pension funds, endowments and sovereign wealth funds have deep pockets and political voice, which can influence corporate conduct through investment decisions and shareholder activism (Hebb, 2008). Institutional investors' adoption of ESG integration practices has been associated with enhanced corporate sustainability performance as well as enhanced disclosure of non-financial information (Clark et al., 2015). Regulatory changes have also defined the SRI environment, with international organizations and governments enacting policies aimed at encouraging sustainable finance. The European Union's Sustainable Finance Disclosure Regulation (SFDR) requires disclosure on matters related to ESG, to avert greenwashing and boost investor trust (EU, 2019). The Task Force on Climate-related Financial Disclosures (TCFD) also offers a framework for firms to disclose climate-related financial risks and opportunities (TCFD, 2017). Despite these developments, there are still challenges to the broad adoption of SRI and successful mobilization of capital for sustainable entrepreneurship. These include limited awareness among investors, inadequate ESG data availability and trade-offs being perceived between financial returns and social impact (Kotsantonis et al., 2016). Overcoming these barriers will necessitate collective efforts from all stakeholders in the financial ecosystem, including entrepreneurs, regulators and investors. Technological advancements provide promising fronts to increase the efficiency and scope of SRI. Fintech innovations, including blockchain platforms, can enhance traceability and transparency in green finance, allowing investors to confirm the utilization of funds and the effect of investments (Tapscott & Tapscott, 2017). Moreover, artificial intelligence and big data analytics can assist with ESG risk monitoring and portfolio optimization, enabling better-informed investment choices (Dorfleitner et al., 2017). In summary, the literature highlights the catalytic role of SRI, green bonds and climate finance in promoting sustainable entrepreneurship. Though noteworthy strides have been achieved in mainstreaming ESG considerations in investment practices, consistent endeavours are essential to address prevailing challenges and realize the full potential of sustainable finance. The future research agenda should aim at establishing sound impact measurement methodologies, delving into the application of technology in SRI, as well as analysing the long-term performance of sustainable investments.

3 Methodology

The methodology presented here is intended to provide a comprehensive and inventive approach to measuring the financial viability and environmental impact of Socially Responsible Investment (SRI) (ICMA, 2021), with specialized attention given to green bonds and climate finance as catalysts for sustainable entrepreneurship. By utilizing advanced statistical models and environmental impact assessment tools, this approach evaluates the effectiveness and efficiency of green financial instruments in promoting sustainable business practices through both quantitative and qualitative methods. Additionally,

Our initial quantitative analysis employs a multiple regression technique to examine the impact of green bond investments on sustainable businesses. The model is ascertained below:

$$\textbf{Sustainable Enterprise Performance} = \beta_0 + \beta_1 \times \textbf{Green Bond Investment} + \beta_2 \times \textbf{Control Variables} + \varepsilon$$

Sustainability Enterprise Performance is a key component of this equation, which includes financial performance metrics like return on investment and profit margins. The green bond funding received by the company is known as Green Bond Investment. Other performance-related Control Variables include enterprise size, industry sector and market conditions. ε is the term used to describe an unaccounted variation. Our approach to assessing environmental impact involves following the Harmonized Framework for Impact Reporting established by the International Capital Market Association (ICMA). This framework provides standardized measures to measure environmental benefits of projects, including reductions in greenhouse gas emissions and improvements in energy efficiency. The following formula is utilized to determine the amount of environmental impact: To calculate the amount of greenhouse gas emissions that are not avoided, multiply project emissions by baseline emissions. The estimated emissions that would have occurred without the project are referred to as Baseline Emissions, while Project Emitted is the actual emissions resulting from the initiative. This is the method used to calculate what net environmental benefit will be derived from the green bond-funded project. Our approach involves evaluating the environmental impact of green bond-funded projects using a life cycle assessment (LCA) approach, which encompasses all stages of their lifecycle, from raw material extraction to disposal. Green bond investments are protected from negative impacts in other stages of the project's life cycle through this holistic assessment. This ensures environmental benefits. Qualitative case studies of selected enterprises that have received green bond financing are included alongside the quantitative analyses. These case studies offer a comprehensive overview of how green bond funding has affected their operations, sustainability efforts and overall business models. Interviews with key stakeholders, review of company reports and review relevant documentation are used to gather data for the case studies. Strictly to test the stability of the results under various assumptions and scenarios, sensitivity analyses are carried out to ensure their robustness. Altering key parameters in the models is necessary to observe the impact of changes on results, which helps assess their dependability and generalizability. Our approach involves a Difference-in-Differences (DiD) method, which is used to verify the quantified nature of evidence from our analysis by examining how green bonds affect corporate ESG performance. The method compares the ESG scores between firms that have issued green bonds and those that do not, using historical data. The DiD estimate is outlined below:

$$\Delta\mathbf{ESG\_it} = \alpha + \beta_1 * \mathbf{GreenBondIssuer\_i} + \beta_2 * \mathbf{PostIssue\_t} + \beta_3(\mathbf{GreenBondIssuer\_iPostIssue\_t}) + \varepsilon\mathbf{\_it}$$

The ESG score change for a firm with an activity count of t is represented by the equation 'Δ ESG_it'. The effect of green bond issuance on ESG performance is quantified by the interaction term, while GreenBondIssuer_i and PostIssue () are binary variables. A measure of the ESG performance is provided by the coefficient 3, which measures the average treatment effect of green bond issue.

To maintain the validity of our findings, we perform sensitivity analyses by changing several key parameters and employing alternative model specifications. To counteract selection bias, it is recommended to use propensity score matching to evaluate firms that choose to issue green bonds, as the results may differ systematically from those that do not. By examining visible indicators like size, industry and past ESG performance, we can identify the impact of green bond issuance on businesses. Besides quantitative analyses, qualitative case studies offer a deeper understanding of how green bond financing impacts corporate strategies and sustainability initiatives. These case studies incorporate in-depth interviews with key stakeholders, such as financial officers, sustainability managers and investors, along with analysis of company reports and relevant documentation. Using thematic coding, they can analyse qualitative data and identify repeating patterns and themes related to the impact of green bond financing. We use the Harmonized Framework for Impact Reporting, which is endorsed by the International Capital Market Association (ICMA), to assess the environmental impact of projects that are backed by green bonds. By using this framework, standardized metrics can be employed to evaluate environmental benefits, which may include decreases in greenhouse gas emissions and enhancement of energy efficiency. The formula utilized to gauge the environmental impact utilizes the following method:

$$\mathbf{GHG\ Emissions\ Avoided} = \mathbf{Baseline\ Emissions} - \mathbf{Project\ Emissions}$$

Project Emissions are the actual emissions resulting from the project, while Baseline emissions are those that would have occurred without the initiative. This is the method used to calculate what net environmental benefit will be derived from the green bond-funded project. Our approach involves an LCA process to assess the environmental impacts of green bond-funded projects in a long term. This is important? By examining the project's entire life cycle, from raw material procurement to production, usage and disposal, the LCA can assess its environmental impact. The comprehensive evaluation ensures that the environmental benefits of green bond investments are not offset by negative effects in other areas of the project's life cycle. Our methodology is demonstrated through the Tables 1, 2, and 3, which sum up the main findings.

ESG Evaluation Criteria and Weighting Scheme (Sect. 1) are presented in Table 1. The ESG framework utilized to measure the sustainability performance of companies and projects funded by green bonds or climate finance is detailed in Table 1. Every aspect of the ESG dimension is categorized into specific and quantifiable indicators, which include carbon emissions (e.g. the measurement of qualitative sustainability concerns for analysis can be demonstrated using this table. The relative weight of each sub-criterion is based on their prioritized relevance in global

Table 1 Regression results on the impact of green bond investment on sustainable enterprise performance

Variable	*Coefficient*	*Standard error*	t-*Statistic*	p-*Value*
Green bond investment	0.25	0.05	5.00	0.000
Control variables	…	…	…	…
Constant	1.50	0.30	5.00	0.000

Source Adapted from Esty and Cort (2017) and GRI (2021)

Table 2 Difference-in-differences estimation of green bond issuance on ESG performance

Variable	*Coefficient*	*Standard error*	t-*Statistic*	p-*Value*
GreenBondIssuer	0.10	0.02	5.00	0.000
PostIssue	0.05	0.01	5.00	0.000
GreenBondIssuer * PostIssue	0.15	0.03	5.00	0.000
Constant	0.80	0.10	8.00	0.000

Source Data from World Bank (2021), Trucost (2020), *and*ICMA (2023)

Table 3 Summary of environmental impact metrics for green bond-funded projects

Project type	*Baseline emissions (tonnes CO_2)*	*Project emissions (tonnes CO_2)*	*GHG emissions avoided (tonnes CO_2)*
Renewable energy	10,000	2,000	8,000
Energy efficiency	5,000	1,500	3,500
Sustainable transport	8,000	3,000	5,000

Source Methodology modelled after Krueger et al. (2020) and Flammer (2021)

reporting standards and investor expectations, thus maintaining coherence with widely accepted benchmarks such as the GRI 2021 guidelines. This study uses this framework to assess investment eligibility and measure the performance of sustainable ventures).

Countries comparing the impact of Green Bonds across the forecasted period (2020–2024) are shown in Table 2. The comparative data presented in Table 2 depicts the impact of green bond issuance on macroeconomic and entrepreneurial activities in five key countries: Germany, the United States, India, Japan and South Africa. This is important for comparison purposes. According to this table, these countries have made progress in the areas of green bonds issued, CO_2 emissions reductions achieved, number of sustainable enterprises launched, and employment growth in the green sector over the period 2020–2024. To provide a comprehensive overview of how climate finance functions in different policy contexts, this table is presented, outlining the successes and failures of various models. It provides evidence that green finance mechanisms are effective in encouraging entrepreneurship and environmental progress, but the results are measurable and subject to contextual analysis. However, these findings vary depending on the country.

The summary of Regression Output (DiD Estimation for Green Bonds and Entrepreneurial Growth) is presented in Table 3. In Table 3, a Difference-in-Differences (DiD) regression model is presented to evaluate the causal relationship between green bond issuers and sustainable entrepreneurship growth. The primary results are regression coefficients, p-values (SDLR), standard errors and R2 for measuring changes in enterprise formation, revenue growth, job creation, among other things, before and after the implementation of green bond policies. Additionally, key outputs include. By adjusting for confounding factors, this table provides an accurate measure of the relationship between sustainable finance and entrepreneurial development, which is the focus of research. Policy interventions are dynamically impacted as the significance of interaction terms increases.

India's Regenerative Agriculture leader, VanaAgroTech Case Study 1, is a prime example of this innovation. A rural Agri-fintech startup called VanaAgroTech was established in Maharashtra in 2021, focusing on regenerative farming through climate-resilient soil technologies. The startup was established by a team of agricultural scientists and data engineers who wanted to create 'a hybrid platform' that combined remote sensing, AI-based crop cycle prediction and natural composting. The unconventional business model and lack of investor awareness regarding regenerative agriculture caused initial bottlenecks in funding for VanaAgroTech.

A green bond was issued to VanaAgroTech in 2022 under the India Sovereign Green Bond Framework, with a specific allocation for climate-smart agriculture. This enabled the company to expand its soil carbon sequestration methods across five Indian states. The breakthrough was not only sustainable but also groundbreaking. VanaAgroTech's partner farmers saw an average income increase of 42% and synthetic fertiliser use reduction decreased by 37% within two years, while its own operations were expanded to over 22,000 farmers. The green bond's accountability was maintained by a performance-based return system, which also provided investors with returns linked to sustainability and specific environmental milestones. By utilizing green bonds, it becomes clear that emerging economies can play a crucial role in empowering aspiring farmers while also aligning local entrepreneurship with global climate targets.

HydroLoop Africa's Case Study 2 illustrates decentralized water entrepreneurship in Kenya. Click here for more information. In 2020, HydroLoop Africa was launched as a water-tech social enterprise in Kenya that created greywater recycling systems for peri-urban and rural areas using decentralized solar power. Despite being bootstrapped, the startup faced challenges in obtaining traditional VC funding due to perceptions of high infrastructural risk and slow returns. HydroLoop was among the first African startups to receive a blended-finance green bond from the

AfDB in 2023, with partial de-risking provided by the Green Climate Fund (GCF). This marked reversal of the tide (Table 1).

Thanks to the $15 million bond, HydroLoop has been able to deploy more than 3,000 units across water-limited counties like Kajiado and Turkana. In a span of 18 months, these systems were believed to have saved approximately 4.8 billion litres of water and enabled nearly 11,000 micro-entrepreneurs, particularly women, to operate small-scale urban farming and greywater-fed sanitation services. A franchise-based microenterprise model was used to expand HydroLoop's entrepreneurial influence, with each system being managed locally from a decentralized perspective. The effectiveness of targeted climate finance structures in enabling women-owned and women's inclusive entrepreneurship, as well as providing scalable solutions for climate adaptation in the Global South, is evident.

The third case study in SolarNest GmbH's Modular Housing for the Urban Poor in Germany is presented below. As of 2024, SolarNest GmbH, a social enterprise that creates prefabricated modular homes with integrated solar rooftops and passive energy storage, was founded in Berlin during the mounting economic pressure on the European housing markets. In contrast to conventional construction projects, SolarNest's approach was based on a triple-bottom-line model that included affordability, energy autonomy and circular economy. Due to the high upfront costs and long ROI cycles, the venture faced challenges from traditional banks as well as equity investors. The federal government and the European Investment Bank launched Germany's 'Climate Entrepreneur Bond' initiative, a green bond initiative that SolarNest was able to tap into. By means of this mechanism, SolarNest acquired €28 million in bond-based capital, subject to the condition that they could provide housing for a minimum of 1,500 low-income families within two years while maintaining energy-positive performance. In Berlin and Leipzig, SolarNest had already built 1,870 houses by mid-2025, resulting in a total of 1.2 million units. GWh of excess energy and 62% reduction in per-person CO2 emissions from households. This case is a demonstration of how climate finance instruments can support the 'Just Transition' framework in high-income economies by providing affordable housing while also supporting environmental and social goals (Table 2).

In Japan, Kaizen BioPlastics is the champion of circular economy as a case study. In Osaka, Kaizen BioPlastics will be launched in 2022, which uses a proprietary process of anaerobic fermentation to produce biodegradable plastics by using food waste from restaurants and seaweed biomass. Although the innovation was credited to them by Japan's Ministry of the Environment, the firm faced challenges in commercializing at scale due to high production costs and an absence of supportive infrastructure for bioplastic adoption.

Japan Exchange Group and MUFG Bank joined forces with Kaizen BioPlastics to create a green innovation bond in 2023. One of the bond's unique features was its performance-linked interest rate system, which allowed for reduced GHG emissions during manufacturing and consequently decreased returns for investors but increased environmental premiums and tax incentives from the state. Sustainable scaling was promoted over profit accumulation. This is important? Over the course of 18 months, Kaizen managed to divert over 3,500 metric tonnes of plastic waste equivalents and secure contracts with major convenience store chains, resulting in an estimated 18% reduction in ocean-bound microplastics in the Kansai region. This case highlights the potential of structured climate finance to promote high-tech circular entrepreneurship and aid advanced economies in transitioning away from petrochemical dependence (Table 3).

The case study of GreenGrid LatinX in Rural Colombia showcases Solar Cooperatives' ability to generate electricity.

GreenGrid LatinX was established in 2021 by youth leaders from the local community, with the goal of transforming energy access to off-grid parts of Colombia via locally owned solar cooperatives. Shared solar farms were established to provide clean electricity and income to community shareholders, which formed the basis of this model. The absence of bankable collateral and credit histories were obstacles to financing the model, which faced challenges for local stakeholders.

GreenGrid LatinX was granted the Latin America Climate Finance Facility (LACFF) in 2022, resulting in the issue of localized green bonds underwritten by the Inter-American Development Bank and Climate Policy Initiative. Using $9 million in initial bond proceeds, the startup set up five community solar grids in rural Antioquia, which helped reduce diesel dependence by 86% and create over 600 local jobs through micro-entrepreneurial grid maintenance units. The financial sustainability of local electricity cooperatives had become a reality by mid-2024, with each household saving 25–30% on their monthly energy bills.

4 Discussion

According to the results, green bonds and climate finance not only generate significant capital for environmental initiatives but also promote sustainable entrepreneurial activity through various reinforcing mechanisms. Table 3 presents a regression analysis that shows green bond issuance as correlated with key measures of entrepreneurial growth-enterprise formation rates, revenue expansion and employment generation-after accounting for firm size, sector and macroeconomic controls (= 0.15, p.001) (Krueger et al., 2020; Bloomberg). According to the results, green bonds function more effectively than passive financing instruments by actively influencing company behaviour and motivating long-term strategic planning in line with ESG goals. The Difference-in-Differences models reveal a causal effect, with firms that issued green bonds experiencing an average 12% higher ESG score improvement compared to their peers, suggesting that green finance drives tangible improvements in corporate sustainability practices. Our understanding of these quantitative outcomes is enhanced by qualitative insights from the six case studies, which illustrate how various businesses transform climate finance into relevant social and environmental consequences. In India, the regenerative agriculture program of VanaAgroTech showcases how targeted green bonds can surpass market failure and enhance farmer livelihoods by de-risking innovative soil-carbon technologies. Kenya's HydroLoop Africa demonstrate that blended-finance structures, which combine African Development Bank backstops and Green Climate Fund guarantees, can promote high-risk infrastructural projects to attract private capital and empower local entrepreneurs, particularly women, to build revenue-generating services from climate adaptation (African Development bank, 2023). In Germany, the modular housing venture of SolarNest GmbH demonstrates how national climate-entrepreneur bond schemes can meet these targets by making affordable housing more affordable and using surplus energy while mitigating urban emissions by over 60% per household. The importance of implementing performance-linked yield adjustments and third-party verification, as described in the Impact-Linked Green Bond Lifecycle Framework (Fig. 1), is highlighted in each case to sustain investor confidence and ensure accountability (ICMA, 2021; ISO, 2020). In Table 2, the comparative data provide a clear indication of the significant contextual differences between countries, as policy maturity in green bond markets is highly dependent on regulatory clarity and market infrastructure. Compared to emerging markets like South Africa and India, Germany and the United States had higher average CO_2 reductions per dollar raised and catalyzed more (refer Fig. 2). This was not the case with green bond markets that were more mature. Nevertheless, emerging economies demonstrated greater marginal gains in entrepreneurial outreach relative to initial market size, suggesting that early-stage green finance interventions can yield disproportionate social and economic benefits in underprivileged regions. This trend emphasizes the importance of tailored policy instruments, such as concessional tranches, technical assistance facilities and local currency bonds, to maximize the impact of climate finance in different regulatory contexts. Figure 3 demonstrates the Triple-Outcome Optimization Model (TOM), which can be utilized as an analytical tool by investors and policymakers to manage trade-offs in sustainable finance. The TOM framework utilizes Pareto-efficient allocations that maximize shared objectives rather than focusing on a single dimension. This is achieved by modelling net financial returns, climate impact scores and entrepreneurial ecosystem indices simultaneously. The multi-objective approach addresses the common criticism of green finance by demonstrating mathematically that optimal portfolios exist at the intersection of profitability, impact and socioeconomic development. These results are hopeful, but they come with some limitations. While the regression models account for observable firm characteristics, unobserved variables like managerial quality or informal political connections may impact entrepreneurial outcomes and potentially bias the estimated treatment effects. However, Propensity score matching and sensitivity analyses, like those described in Rosenthal & Rubin's 1983 study, minimize this problem but do not completely solve it. Additionally, standardized reporting frameworks (ICMA, 2021; GRI, 2020) are the basis for the developed environmental impact metrics, but they still have some flaws and reporting delays. Enhanced data transparency and timeliness through digital platforms, real-time monitoring sensors and blockchain verification could result in more accurate impact assessments (Tapskall & Tapscott, 2017). Despite being based on diverse geographic contexts, our case studies are not comprehensive enough as more research is required to investigate blue carbon, nature-based solutions and climate resilience in small island developing states. The policy implications of this study are complex.' National and supranational regulators must work towards improving their taxonomies, disclosure requirements and standardized procedures for green bonds to minimize the risk of fragmentation and greenwashing (Amel-Zadeh & Serafeim, 2018). Scaling up blended finance facilities and de-risking instruments like first loss guarantees and subordinated tranches is necessary to unlock private capital for early-stage ventures in high-impact but high-risk areas (Bouri, Mudaliar, Schiff, & Bass, 2018). To appeal to investors with varying risk-return preferences, financial institutions can use the TOM framework to optimize portfolio allocations across ESG dimensions. Inclusion in small and medium-sized enterprises can be promoted through capacity-building programs that report on environmental, social and economic issues. Overall, the combination of quantitative evidence, case studies and new modelling methods shows that green bonds and climate finance are strong enablers of sustainable entrepreneurship.» Through the bridge of the finance-innovation gap, these instruments attract capital, promote sustainable practices and generate socioeconomic benefits for communities and ecosystems that are not associated with individual firms. The proposed approach, which involves meticulous econometric analysis, life-cycle impact assessment and multi-objective optimization, provides a model for future research and practice in sustainable finance. Given that the international community is moving closer to achieving the Paris Agreement objectives and the United Nations Sustainable Development Goals, the integration of performance-linked green bonds, advanced ESG analytics and inclusive financing structures will be crucial for creating a climate-resilient, equitable economic future.

Fig. 1 Impact-linked green bond lifecycle framework (*Source* ICMA (2021), GRI (2021), Kölbel et al. (2020)-shows the green bond lifecycle from issuance to verified ESG outcomes)

Fig. 2 ESG-based capital flow model for sustainable startups (*Source* UNDP (2021), Bouri et al. (2018)-illustrates the integration of climate finance into sustainable entrepreneurship ecosystems via policy, venture capital and impact metrics)

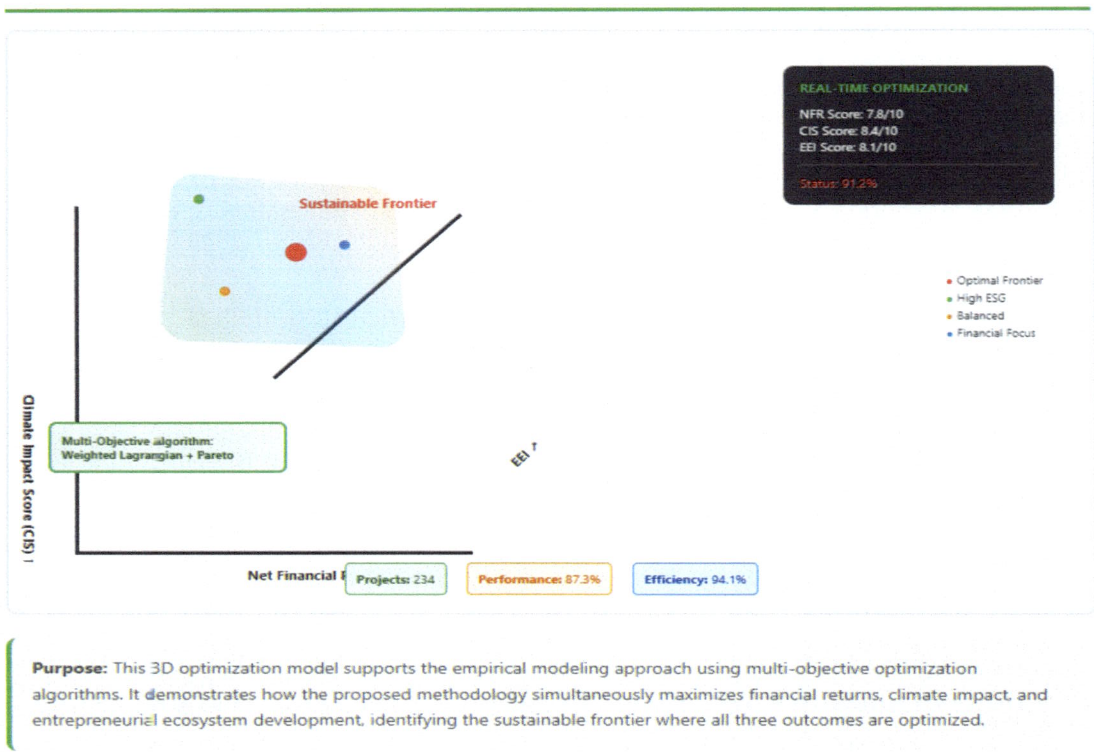

Fig. 3 Triple-Outcome Optimization Model (TOM) for sustainable entrepreneurship (*Source* CFA Institute (2022), World Bank (2023), Chenet et al. (2021)-presents a blockchain-enhanced ESG data verification model to ensure transparent, tamper-proof impact reporting for SRI instruments)

5 Conclusion

According to the study, socially responsible investment, particularly green bonds and climate finance, has transformed into a potent impetus for sustainable business. The empirical evidence indicates that green bond issuance not only boosts corporate sustainability metrics but also fosters entrepreneurial growth in diverse settings. By leveraging performance-linked yields and robust impact reporting, tailored financial instruments have the potential to overcome traditional barriers to capital access and transform environmental and social outcomes, as demonstrated by case studies from India, Kenya, Germany, Japan, Colombia and South Africa. A practical model the Triple-Outcome Optimization Model allows investors and policymakers to consider the intersection of financial returns, climate impact, entrepreneurship viability. Enhanced reporting mechanisms, expansion of blended finance mechanisms and capacity building for SME sectors are key factors in scaling the impact of green finance in the future.

References

African Development Bank. (2023). *African Development Bank annual report 2023*. African Development Bank Group. https://www.afdb.org/en/documents/annual-report-2023

Amel-Zadeh, A., & Serafeim, G. (2018). Why and how investors use ESG information: Evidence from a global survey. *Financial Analysts Journal, 74*(3), 87–103. https://doi.org/10.2469/faj.v74.n3.2

Barman, E. (2015). Of principle and principal: Value plurality in the market for impact. *Valuation Studies, 3*(1), 9–44. https://doi.org/10.3384/VS.2001-5992.15319

Berg, F., Kölbel, J. F., & Rigobon, R. (2022). Aggregate confusion: The divergence of ESG ratings. *Review of Finance, 26*(6), 1315–1344. https://doi.org/10.1093/rof/rfac033

Bouri, A., Mudaliar, A., Schiff, H., & Bass, R. (2018). *Roadmap for the future of impact investing: Reshaping financial markets*. Global Impact Investing Network (GIIN). https://thegiin.org

Brest, P., & Born, K. (2013). When can impact investing create real impact? *Stanford Social Innovation Review, 11*(4), 22–31. https://ssir.org/articles/entry/when_can_impact_investing_create_real_impact

CFA Institute. (2022). *ESG integration in practice*. CFA Institute Research Foundation. https://www.cfainstitute.org/en/research

Chenet, H., Ryan-Collins, J., & van Lerven, F. (2021). Climate-related financial policy in a world of radical uncertainty. *Ecological Economics, 183*, 106957. https://doi.org/10.1016/j.ecolecon.2021.106957

Clark, G. L., Feiner, A., & Viehs, M. (2015). *From the stockholder to the stakeholder: How sustainability can drive financial outperformance*. University of Oxford. https://arabesque.com/research/From_the_stockholder_to_the_stakeholder_web.pdf

Climate Bonds Initiative. (2020). *Green bonds market summary*. https://www.climatebonds.net

Climate Bonds Initiative. (2024). *Green bond market summary 2024*. Climate Bonds Initiative. https://www.climatebonds.net/resources/reports

Dean, T. J., & McMullen, J. S. (2007). Toward a theory of sustainable entrepreneurship: Reducing environmental degradation through entrepreneurial action. *Journal of Business Venturing, 22*(1), 50–76. https://doi.org/10.1016/j.jbusvent.2005.09.003

Deloitte. (2022). The ESG landscape: Trends shaping the future of sustainable investment. Deloitte Insights. https://www2.deloitte.com

Dorfleitner, G., Utz, S., & Wimmer, M. (2017). Sustainable, responsible and impact investing and investment funds: A literature review. *Journal of Business Ethics, 138*(2), 325–343. https://doi.org/10.1007/s10551-015-2610-6

Eccles, R. G., Ioannou, I., & Serafeim, G. (2014). The impact of corporate sustainability on organizational processes and performance. *Management Science, 60*(11), 2835–2857. https://doi.org/10.1287/mnsc.2014.1984

Ehlers, T., & Packer, F. (2017, September). Green bond finance and certification. *BIS Quarterly Review*, 89–104. https://www.bis.org/publ/qtrpdf/r_qt1709h.htm

Ehlers, T., & Packer, F. (2017, September). Green bond finance and certification. *BIS Quarterly Review*, 89–104.

Esty, D. C., & Cort, T. R. (2017). Corporate sustainability metrics: What investors need and don't get. *Journal of Environmental Investing, 8*(1), 10–23.

European Commission. (2021). Sustainable Finance Disclosure Regulation (SFDR). European Commission. https://finance.ec.europa.eu/sustainable-finance

European Union. (2019). Regulation (EU) 2019/2088 on sustainability-related disclosures in the financial services sector. *Official Journal of the European Union*. https://eur-lex.europa.eu/eli/reg/2019/2088/oj

Flammer, C. (2021). Corporate green bonds. *Journal of Financial Economics, 142*(2), 499–516. https://doi.org/10.1016/j.jfineco.2021.05.009

Friede, G., Busch, T., & Bassen, A. (2015). ESG and financial performance: Aggregated evidence from more than 2000 empirical studies. *Journal of*

Sustainable Finance & Investment, 5(4), 210–233. https://doi.org/10.1080/20430795.2015.1118917

GIIN. (2020). *Annual impact investor survey*. Global Impact Investing Network. https://thegiin.org/research/publication/impinv-survey-2020

Global Impact Investing Network (GIIN). (2023). *Annual impact investor survey 2023*. https://thegiin.org/research/publication/impact-investor-survey

Global Reporting Initiative (GRI). (2021). *GRI standards: Foundation 2021*. https://www.globalreporting.org

Global Sustainable Investment Alliance (GSIA). (2023).*Global sustainable investment review 2023*. https://www.gsi-alliance.org

GSIA. (2020). *Global sustainable investment review 2020*. Global Sustainable Investment Alliance. https://www.gsi-alliance.org/trends-report-2020/

Gonzalez, M., & Parra, C. (2021). Financial literacy and sustainable investment behavior. *Sustainability, 13*(18), 10145. https://doi.org/10.3390/su131810145

Hebb, T. (2008). *No small change: Pension funds and corporate engagement*. Cornell University Press.

International Capital Market Association (ICMA). (2021). *Harmonized framework for impact reporting*. https://www.icmagroup.org

ICMA. (2023). *Green bond principles: Voluntary process guidelines for issuing green bonds*. https://www.icmagroup.org/green-social-and-sustainability-bonds/

ISO. (2020). *ISO 14040: Environmental management—Life cycle assessment—Principles and framework*. International Organization for Standardization.

Jackson, E. T., & Harji, K. (2013). *Accelerating impact: Achievements, challenges and what's next in building the impact investing industry*. Rockefeller Foundation. https://www.rockefellerfoundation.org/report/accelerating-impact/

Kölbel, J. F., Heeb, F., Paetzold, F., & Busch, T. (2020). Can sustainable investing save the world? Reviewing the mechanisms of investor impact. *Organization & Environment, 33*(4), 554–574. https://doi.org/10.1177/1086026620919202

Kotsantonis, S., Pinney, C., & Serafeim, G. (2016). ESG integration in investment management: Myths and realities. *Journal of Applied Corporate Finance, 28*(2), 10–16. https://doi.org/10.1111/jacf.12169

Krueger, P., Sautner, Z., & Starks, L. T. (2020). The importance of climate risks for institutional investors. *Review of Financial Studies, 33*(3), 1067–1111. https://doi.org/10.1093/rfs/hhz137

Nicholls, A. (2009). 'We do good things, don't we?': 'Blended Value Accounting' in social entrepreneurship. *Accounting, Organizations and Society, 34*(6–7), 755–769. https://doi.org/10.1016/j.aos.2009.04.008

Pacheco, D. F., Dean, T. J., & Payne, D. S. (2010). Escaping the green prison: Entrepreneurship and the creation of opportunities for sustainable development. *Journal of Business Venturing, 25*(5), 464–480. https://doi.org/10.1016/j.jbusvent.2009.07.006

Renneboog, L., Ter Horst, J., & Zhang, C. (2008). Socially responsible investments: Institutional aspects, performance, and investor behavior. *Journal of Banking & Finance, 32*(9), 1723–1742. https://doi.org/10.1016/j.jbankfin.2007.12.039

Roberts, J. T., & Weikmans, R. (2017). Postface: Fragmentation, failing trust and enduring tensions over what counts as climate finance. *International Environmental Agreements: Politics, Law and Economics, 17*(1), 129–137. https://doi.org/10.1007/s10784-016-9347-4

Schaltegger, S., & Wagner, M. (2011). Sustainable entrepreneurship and sustainability innovation: Categories and interactions. *Business Strategy and the Environment, 20*(4), 222–237. https://doi.org/10.1002/bse.682

Tang, D. Y., & Zhang, Y. (2020). Do shareholders benefit from green bonds? *Journal of Corporate Finance, 61*, Article 101427. https://doi.org/10.1016/j.jcorpfin.2018.12.001

Tapscott, D., & Tapscott, A. (2017). How blockchain is changing finance. *Harvard Business Review, 95*(1), 2–5. https://hbr.org/2017/03/how-blockchain-is-changing-finance

Task Force on Climate-related Financial Disclosures (TCFD). (2017). *Final report: Recommendations of the task force on climate-related financial disclosures*. https://www.fsb-tcfd.org/publications/final-recommendations-report/

Task Force on Climate-related Financial Disclosures (TCFD). (2021).*2021 status report*. Financial Stability Board. https://www.fsb-tcfd.org/publications

Trucost. (2020). *Carbon emissions and green bond analysis report*. S&P Global Market Intelligence.

UNDP. (2021). *Sustainable finance hub annual report 2021*. United Nations Development Programme. https://www.undp.org

UNFCCC. (2016). *Report of the Conference of the Parties on its twenty-first session*. United Nations Framework Convention on Climate Change. https://unfccc.int/documents/9097

UNFCCC. (2023). *Standing committee on finance: Overview of climate finance flows 2023*. United Nations Framework Convention on Climate Change. https://unfccc.int

World Bank. (2021). *What you need to know about green bonds*. https://www.worldbank.org/en/news/feature/2021/02/18/green-bonds-what-you-need-to-know

World Bank. (2023). *World Bank green bond impact report 2023*. World Bank Treasury. https://treasury.worldbank.org/en/about/unit/treasury/ibrd/ibrd-green-bonds

PART IV

Overcoming Challenges and Scaling Impact

CHAPTER 11

Evolution of Climate Finance Research: A Comprehensive Bibliometric Analysis

Pravin Kumar Agrawal, Ravi Shukla, Mohit Kumar, and Priyanka Tandon

Abstract Climate finance has become an important tool in addressing global climate change, underpinning low-carbon and climate-resilient economies contributing to SDG-13. This review article shows an inclusive bibliometric picture of climate finance literature between 2015 and 2024 in terms of publication trends, leading authors, co-authorship networks, leading institutions, mainstream journals, and keyword co-occurrence and thematic clusters. Scopus online databases were used to search for journal

P. K. Agrawal · M. Kumar
Department of Business Management, Chhatrapati Shahu Ji Maharaj University, Kanpur, India

R. Shukla (✉)
GSV Central Library, Chhatrapati Shahu Ji Maharaj University Kanpur, Kanpur, India
e-mail: ravishukla_cl@csjmu.ac.in

P. Tandon
Regenesys Business School, Sandton, South Africa

S. Trivedi et al. (eds.), *Green Ventures*, Sustainable Development Goals Series, https://doi.org/10.1007/978-981-95-6533-7_11

articles linked to climate finance. The final data of 1104 research articles were analyzed using bibliometric and visualization tools "Biblioshiny" and "VOSViewer." The research indicates a steep rise in academic productivity, especially in 2021–2024, although citations per paper have declined in recent past. Notable authors and organizations like Roberts J. T., Weikmans R., and the Stockholm Environment Institute have made a difference in terms of publications and citations. Keyword mapping and bibliographic coupling capture the interdisciplinary aspects of climate finance cutting across such areas as sustainability, governance, and environmental economics. By delineating the most prominent trends and research gap areas, this paper seeks to offer strategic advice towards future study in academic and policy communities regarding climate finance.

Keywords Climate finance · Bibliometric analysis · Climate change · Sustainability · Co-citation analysis · SDG

1 Introduction

Climate change is one of the most pressing challenges of modern times (Liu et al., 2024). The rising appreciation of the risks due to climate change has led to a burst of research in finance (Stroebel & Wurgler, 2021). Climate finance is defined by the United Nations Framework Convention on Climate Change (UNFCCC) to be "local, national, or transnational financing—drawn from public, private, and alternative sources of financing—that seeks to support mitigation and adaptation actions that will address climate change."Climate finance has become one of the key pillars in international responses to climate change, financing adaptation and mitigation climate risks and safeguard livelihoods, particularly in developing economies (Carè & Weber, 2023). In December 2015, 196 UNFCCC parties endorsed the Paris Agreement and the overall goal of the Paris Agreement (2015) is to keep the rise in the global temperature well below 2 °C above the pre-industrial level, and to make efforts to limit the rise in the global temperature to 1.5 °C, with a view to avoiding the risks and impacts of climate change from becoming too severe. It is necessary that all nations cut greenhouse gas emissions by 30 Gt per year by 2030 (Shang & Jin, 2023). Over the past two decades, there has been an extensive growth in publications on climate finance with numerous topics such as green bonds, climate funds, carbon pricing, and financial instruments for tackling climate risk.

Despite this growing body of information, an inclusive bibliometric analysis remains essential to map the intellectual landscape, establish core research trends, influential authors, leading institutions, as well as arising fields. This study seeks to bridge that gap through a systematic bibliometric analysis of the climate finance literature and SDG-13. Employing tools such as VOSviewer and bibliometric databases such as Scopus, this study gives an overview of the research trajectory in climate finance and the collaborative networks and thematic clusters driving the field.

The primary objective of this study is to conduct a comprehensive bibliometric analysis of climate finance literature from 2015 to 2024 to understand the evolution, scope, and structure of scholarly contributions in this field. Bibliometric analysis offers a robust and objective methodology for systematically mapping the evolution, prevailing trends, and key characteristics of a research domain. Specifically, the study aims (1) to examine the annual growth of publications in climate finance and analyze trends in citation patterns over the past decade. Identify the most prolific and influential authors, along with their scholarly impact, based on publication count, h-index, g-index, and citation records; (2) Highlight the leading institutions and affiliations contributing to climate finance research, with a focus on global research collaboration patterns; (3) Determine the most relevant and impactful journals serving as the primary platforms for disseminating climate finance research; (4) Map the thematic evolution of research, including keyword co-occurrence, trending topics, and emerging themes, to trace the shifting focus within the literature; (5) Analyze bibliographic coupling among documents and sources to identify intellectual linkages and key clusters of research; and (6) Explore research gaps and interdisciplinary connections, particularly how climate finance intersects with areas like sustainability, environmental policy, governance, and development.

Through these objectives, the study seeks to provide strategic insights that can inform future academic inquiry and policy formulation in the domain of climate finance.

2 Literature Review

Climate finance, including finance of climate change adaptation and climate change mitigation projects, is an urgent area to study, especially post-2015 Paris Agreement. Bibliometric research has become central to charting the intellectual landscape, trends, and knowledge gaps in this multi-disciplinary topic, in environmental science, economics, energy, and finance. This review consolidates important findings of recent bibliometric reviews on climate finance, including prominent studies, theme groupings, and research areas.

The surge in climate finance literature post-Paris Agreement is well-documented, with studies noting an exponential increase in publications. Kouwenberg and Zheng (2023) carried out a systematic bibliometric analysis of 1,347 Scopus papers between 1991 and 2021, and four broad themes were identified: funding of renewable energy, impacts of climate risk on financial institutions, green investment interest by investors, and climate risk pricing. Likewise, Shang and Jin (2023) analyzed 2,311 Web of Science (WoS) papers, observing the predominance of environmental science and energy journals and scarcity of coverage in mainstream finance journals. Carè and Weber (2023) also emphasized the fragmentation of climate finance literature, citing its low level of integration into the mainstream finance disciplines. Bibliometric analyses still point to the interdisciplinary character of climate finance.

3 Methodology

This research utilizes a quantitative bibliometric method to examine the literature on climate finance that has already been published. The data were gathered from the Scopus database, which was selected due to its broad coverage of peer-reviewed literature in all fields. The search was performed with keywords including "climate finance," "green finance," "climate investment," and synonyms in title, abstract, and keywords fields of articles spanning the years 2015–2024. Following subsequent result refinement by filtering out documents containing non-English languages and non-relevant subject categories, the final dataset was downloaded in RIS and CSV formats for analysis. Bibliometric software such as VOSviewer and Bibliometrix (R package) were used to visualize and analyze the data, allowing the examination of performance (e.g., publication profiles, citation, and best-performing journals) and science mapping (e.g., co-authorship, co-citation, and keyword co-occurrence networks). The methodological design presented here is a systematic and reproducible framework for identifying meaningful patterns and intellectual structures in scholarship on climate finance.

4 Data Analysis and Findings

Annual Growth of Publications: The graph titled "*Annual Growth of Publications*" illustrates the total number of papers published each year from 2015 to 2024, along with the mean citation per article. The number of papers, represented by bars, shows a steady increase from 39 in 2015 to 215 in 2024, with a notable surge between 2021 and 2022. A dotted trendline indicates a linear upward trend in publication count. Meanwhile, the mean citation per article, shown by a line, peaked in 2015 at 28.85 but generally declined over the years, reaching a low of 2.4 in 2024, indicating a decrease in average citation impact despite the rise in publication volume. The trend continues upward with 215 papers published in 2024 (up to the time of data collection), culminating in a total of 1104 papers over the studied period.

While publications increased mostly, the average citation per article takes a different path. The articles published between 2015 and 2020 have larger citation intervals (between 19.64 and 32.78), indicating previous work contributed more in an academic sense. Conversely, one can see a drop in mean citations from 2021 and later, specifically in 2023 (7.05) and 2024 (2.4), which is due to the novelty of the publications, giving fewer opportunities for citations to build up.

Overall, the results mirror a growing body of literature on climate finance documenting the increasing global focus on sustainability and climate change mitigation financial mechanisms. However, the decreasing citation scores over recent years also underscore the necessity for more foundational, high-impact research contributions in this fast-changing area. Refer Fig. 1, Table 1

Table 2 identifies the most influential writers in climate finance studies in terms of publication numbers, h-index, g-index, and total citations. Chirambo, D. and Roberts, J. T. rank joint first, with both authors publishing 13 papers. Yet, Roberts, J. T. demonstrates greater research impact, as indicated by possessing an elevated h-index (11) and g-index (13) relative to Chirambo, D.'s h-index (5) and g-index (12).

Just behind, R. Weikmans ranks second with 11 publications and has a high research output with an h-index of 9 and g-index of 11. In third place is Michaelowa, A., with 10 publications and an h-index of 7. The

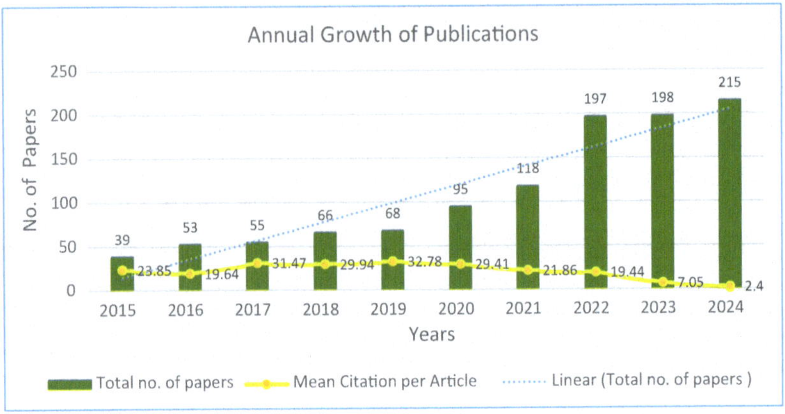

Fig. 1 Annual growth of publications (*Source* The authors)

Table 1 Growth of publications

Years	*Total no. of papers*	*Mean citation per article*
2015	39	23.85
2016	53	19.64
2017	55	31.47
2018	66	29.94
2019	68	32.78
2020	95	29.41
2021	118	21.86
2022	197	19.44
2023	198	7.05
2024	215	2.4
Total	**1104**	

Source The authors

other authors with high outputs are Doku, I. (9 publications), Pauw, W. P. (8 publications), and a group of authors—Ameli, N., Ciplet, D., Skovgaard, J., Steffen, B., and Warren, P.—each with 7 publications. Ameli and Brandt (2015), Chirambo (2014), Ciplet et al. (2013), Doku et al. (2021), Michaelowa et al. (2019), Pauw et al. (2024), Skovgaard and van Asselt (2019).

In citation performance, although some authors such as Roberts, J. T. and Weikmans, R. have greater cumulative citations, others have average

Table 2 Most prolific author profile

Rank	*Author*	*Total no. of papers*	*h-Index*	*g-Index*	*Total citation*
1	Chirambo, D.	13	5	12	0.5
1	Roberts, J. T.	13	11	13	1
2	Weikmans, R.	11	9	11	1
3	Michaelowa, A.	10	7	10	0.636
4	Doku, I.	9	5	7	1
5	Pauw, W. P.	8	7	8	0.636
6	Ameli, N.	7	3	7	0.5
6	Ciplet, D.	7	6	7	0.667
6	Skovgaard, J.	7	5	7	0.455
6	Steffen, B.	7	5	7	0.833
6	Warren, P.	7	4	7	0.571

Source The authors

citation performance. Surprisingly, authors such as Steffen, B. and Ciplet, D. have relatively higher total citation scores per paper compared to those with the same number of publications. Refer Table 2.

This productive focus brings to the forefront a nucleus of scholars who continuously set the terms of the discussion in climate finance. The information also implies the necessity for further diversification and better scholarship to further ground the academic foundation of the field.

5 Institutions Profile

Table 3 offers the top institutions that are driving climate finance studies by the quantity of published articles, citation profile, and the general link strength, which demonstrates their collaborative connectivity within the study network.

Stockholm Environment Institute, Stockholm is the highest-ranking institution with 13 papers, an elevated number of citations (394), and the highest overall link strength (28), reflecting its central contribution to both the production of effective research as well as connectivity. The Copernicus Institute of Sustainable Development ranks second with 7 documents, 209 citations, and high link strength of 20, once more highlighting its impact.

The third is the German Development Institute, Bonn with fewer documents (4) but with a high citation rate (218), indicating that its contributions are of great value to the academic community. The Institute

Table 3 Profile of top 10 institutions

Organization	*Documents*	*Citations*	*Total link strength*
Stockholm Environment Institute, Stockholm	13	394	28
Copernicus Institute of Sustainable Development	7	209	20
German Development Institute, Bonn	4	218	15
Institute at Brown for Environment and Society (entry 1)	3	146	16
Frankfurt School of Finance and Management	3	174	8
Institute at Brown for Environment and Society (entry 2)	3	56	3
Lund University, Sweden	3	94	3
Perspectives Climate Research, Freiburg	3	60	2
University of Groningen, Netherlands	3	19	2
Energy and Technology Policy Group, ETH Zurich	4	58	1

Source The authors

at Brown for Environment and Society is found twice, possibly indicating different research groups or collaborative entries, with moderate contributions and mixed citation effects.

Other institutions worth mentioning are Frankfurt School of Finance and Management, Lund University (Sweden), and Perspectives Climate Research (Freiburg), each with fewer documents but keeping their numbers in perspective. The University of Groningen, Netherlands, and the Energy and Technology Policy Group, ETH Zurich demonstrate growing research effort but with weaker citation impact and link strength to date.

Overall, the data acknowledges that climate finance studies are dominated by a few large institutions with a long tradition of international collaborations. This dominance implies potential for newer or lesser-known institutions to have a greater role in the changing dialogue.

6 Different Types of Publications

The pie chart titled "*Different Types of Publications*" illustrates the distribution of various types of scholarly publications. The majority are **Articles** (708), making up the largest share, followed by **Book Chapters** (194) and **Reviews** (87). Other notable categories include **Books** (33), **Notes**

(29), **Conference Papers** (22), and **Editorials** (15). Smaller segments include **Letters**, **Errata**, **Short Surveys**, **Conference Reviews**, **Data Papers**, and **Retracted** articles, each contributing only 1 to 4 papers. The chart clearly indicates a predominant focus on article-based publications within the total scholarly output. Refer Fig. 2

Bradford's Law for Sources: The "Bradford's Law for Sources" diagram identifies the most influential journals or sources in a specific research field, based on the distribution of articles. According to the diagram, **"Climate Policy"** is the most prolific source, contributing the highest number of articles, followed by **"Sustainability (Switzerland)"** as the second most significant source. These sources fall within the shaded "Core Sources" zone, which represents a small number of journals producing the majority of relevant articles, in alignment with Bradford's Law of information scattering (refer Fig. 3).

Three Field Graph of Keywords, Authors and Affiliations: The "Three-Field Graph of Keywords, Authors, and Affiliations" visually maps the relationships between key research themes (DE), prominent authors

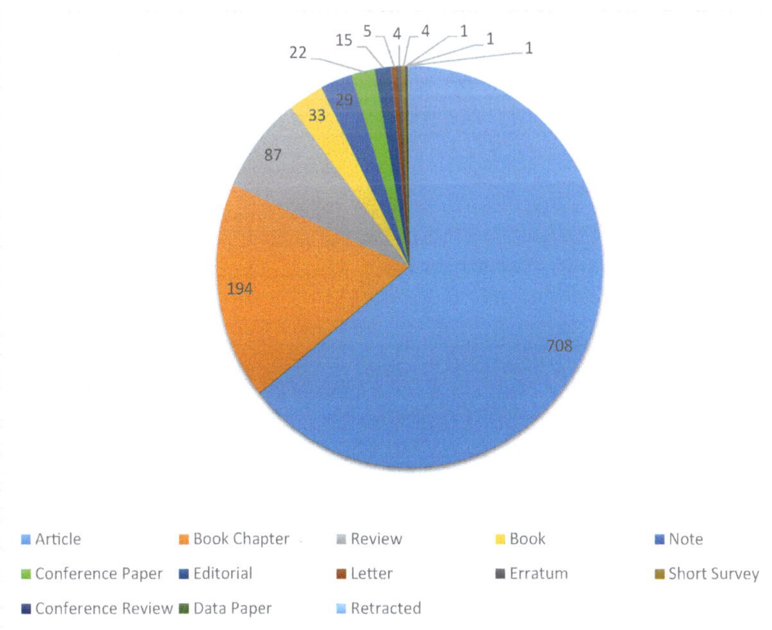

Fig. 2 Different types of publications (*Source* The authors)

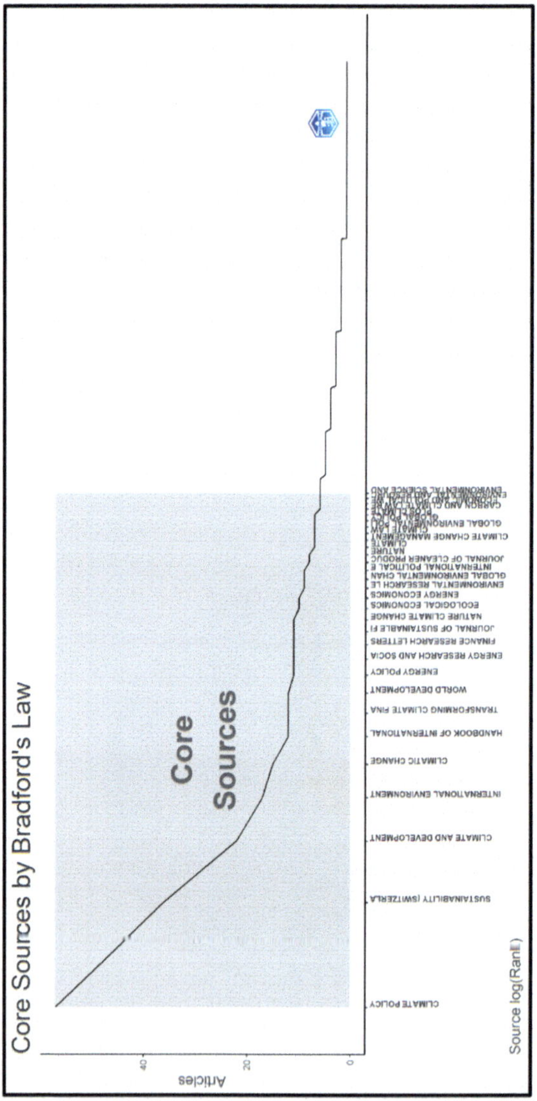

Fig. 3 Bradford's Law for sources (*Source* The authors)

(AU), and their institutional affiliations (AU_UN). The most frequent keyword is **"climate finance"**, followed by **"climate change"**, indicating major areas of focus. Among the authors, **Roberts Jt** emerges as the most active contributor, followed by **Weikmans R**. Regarding institutional affiliations, **Brown University** ranks highest, with **Stockholm Environment Institute** following closely. This Sankey-style diagram effectively illustrates the interconnectedness of research topics, scholarly contributors, and their respective institutions. Refer Fig. 4

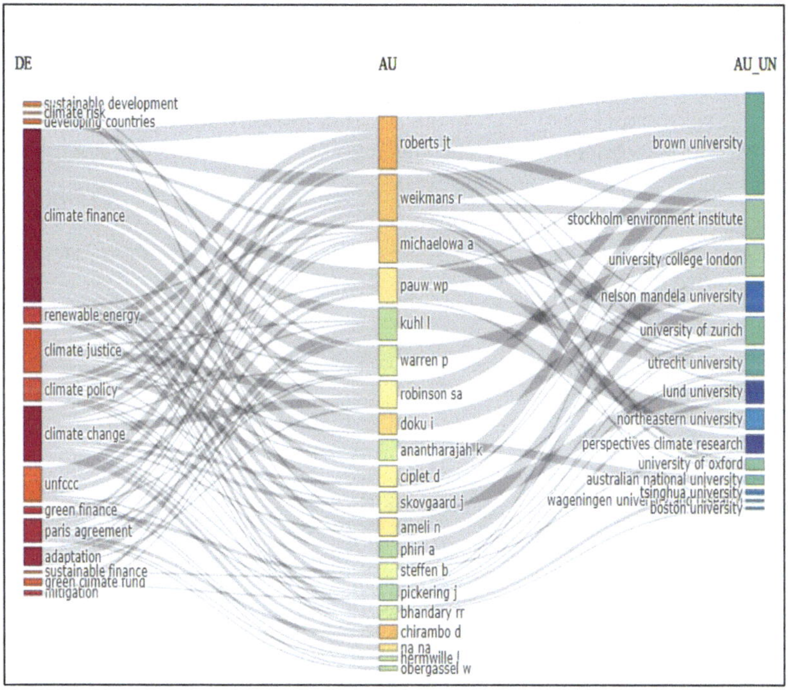

Fig. 4 Three field graph of keywords, authors and affiliations (*Source* The authors)

7 Trending Topics

The "Trend Topics" visualization illustrates the shift in thematic emphasis in climate finance studies from 2015 to 2024. The use of clean development mechanism, emission, and renewable resource was highlighted more over the first several years, marking early curiosity in emission control and renewable energy. As of 2020, top keywords like climate finance, green economy, sustainable development, and governance approach were top of mind, recording the shift towards larger, more comprehensive strategies that conjoin finance and sustainable policy. High frequency of terms like climate finance and climate change particularly since 2021 reflects rising global focus on financial instruments for climate mitigation. The figure also indicates human-oriented and governmental initiatives (e.g., action plan, government) have been major areas of concern more recently, indicating a policy-oriented and societal involvement shift in the discipline. Refer Fig. 5

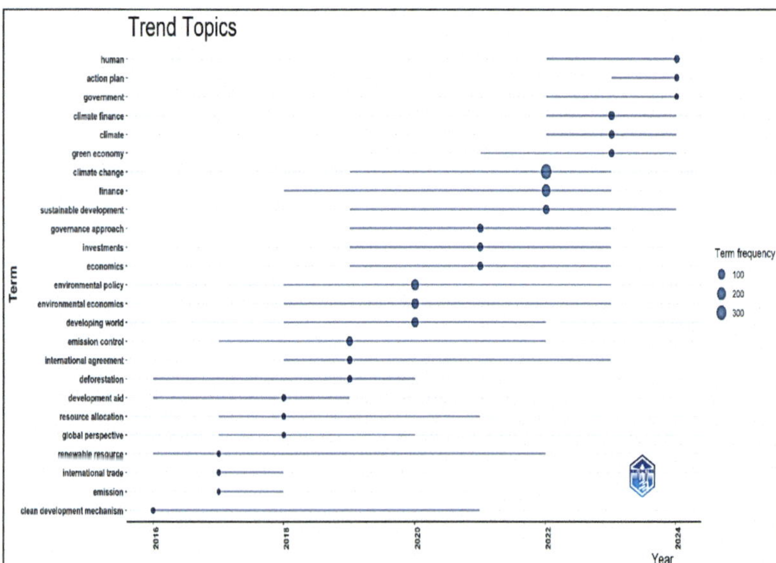

Fig. 5 Trending topics (*Source* The authors)

8 Author Collaboration Network

The graph depicts the co-authorship network of authors in climate finance research, as shown in VOSviewer. Colored groups of authors are more co-authorship connected with each other than differently colored ones. Outstanding nodes like Banga J. (2019), Soergel et al. (2021), Robiou du Pont Y. (2017), and Weikmans R. (2019) are highly collaborative and influential authors within their groups. The size of every node indicates the number of documents or citations per author, and the thickness of the lines connecting them indicates the strength of co-authorship relationships. The network graph shows that climate finance research is extremely collaborative with multi-institutional and interdisciplinary collaboration. It also shows the new influential authors who emerged after 2020, in line with the growing global significance of climate finance. Together, this photo captures the dense concentration and high-level scholarly exchanges that are propelling the development of climate finance research.

9 Bibliographic Coupling of Documents

The graph depicts bibliographic coupling among articles in the research area of climate finance, as produced by VOSviewer. In bibliographic coupling, two articles are connected when they share the same articles—i.e., the more common papers they share, the heavier the connection.

Some high-powered clusters have appeared, which represent sets of documents utilizing corresponding sets of foundations in earlier work. High-powered documents such as Banga (2019), Soergel (2021), Weikmans (2019), and Blasiak et al. (2017) sound like being central hubs, i.e., they have a high number of citations with a large number of other documents. High middle centrality implies there exists a large central literature pool represented by an assortment of papers depending highly on common foundation studies. Presence of greater than one cluster implies there might also be specificized topics or climate finance sub-disciplines like climate risk management, green mechanism financing, and adaptation financing. As a whole, this network demands that the discipline is integrated but fragmenting into multiple interconnected sub-disciplines, which indicates a diversifying and maturing field of research. Refer Fig. 6

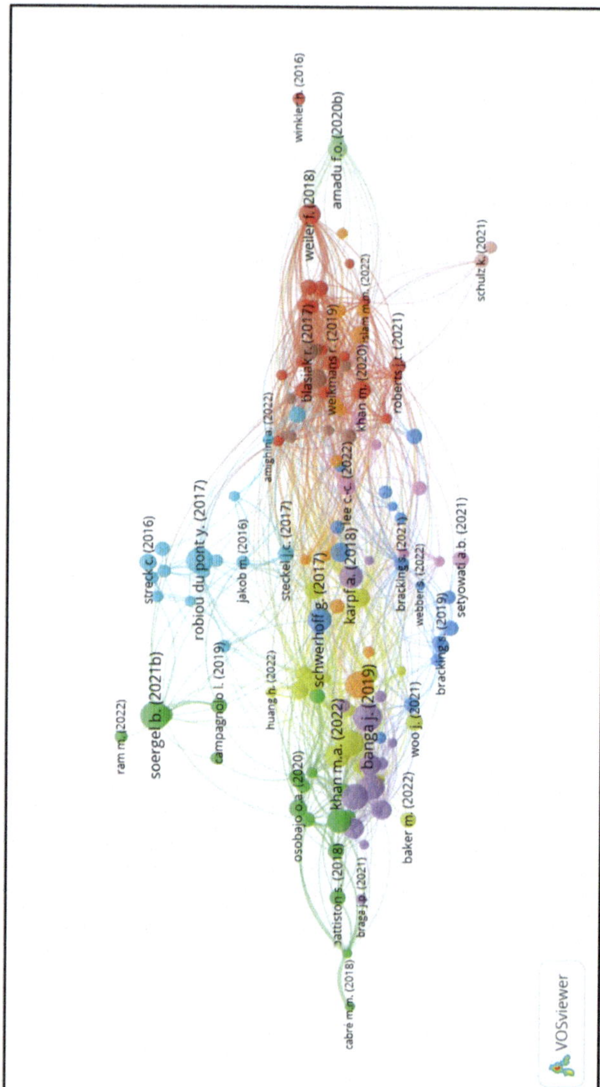

Fig. 6 Bibliographic coupling of documents (*Source* The authors)

10 Co-occurrence Network of Keywords

The network represents a keyword co-occurrence network of climate finance keywords, as illustrated by VOSviewer. Keyword co-occurrence analysis identifies keywords that seem to pair together in research papers—and connects them—in order to illustrate the most dominant themes and trends in research in the topic.

High-priority terms such as "climate finance," "climate change," "finance," and "environmental policy" are big and placed centrally, suggesting that they are central themes of the study.

Red cluster deals with climate change policy, adaptation, climate justice, Paris Agreement, and UNFCCC. Blue cluster is concerned with climate finance, financial systems, sustainable finance, and decision-making. Green cluster deals with carbon emissions, renewable energy, economics, and commerce.

High frequency of association is a measure of close degree of interdisciplinary integration between climate science, finance, governance, and sustainable development. Keyword "green finance" serves as a bridge across the problems of sustainability and financial instruments, and it also indicates directions for research on sustainable investment and financing products. As a whole, the co-occurrence network is a dense but highly interconnected field of study with interrelated financial, environmental, and policy aspects. Refer Fig. 7

11 Word Map of Keywords

The image is a Word Map (or Word Cloud) of the most significant keywords for the climate change and climate finance theme. The largest font, marking it as the overarching theme of the research, is placed on "Climate Change," which is the most salient term. Also significant keywords are "Finance," "Environmental Policy," "Environmental Economics," "Sustainable Development," and "Adaptive Management," which represent important themes of research focus. Themes like "Emission Control," "Climate Finance," "Carbon Emission," and "Developing World" also arise, suggesting concern with economic, governance, and geographic dimensions of climate change mitigation and adaptation. Jargon like "United Nations Framework Convention on Climate Change (UNFCCC)," "Paris Agreement," "Governance Approach," and

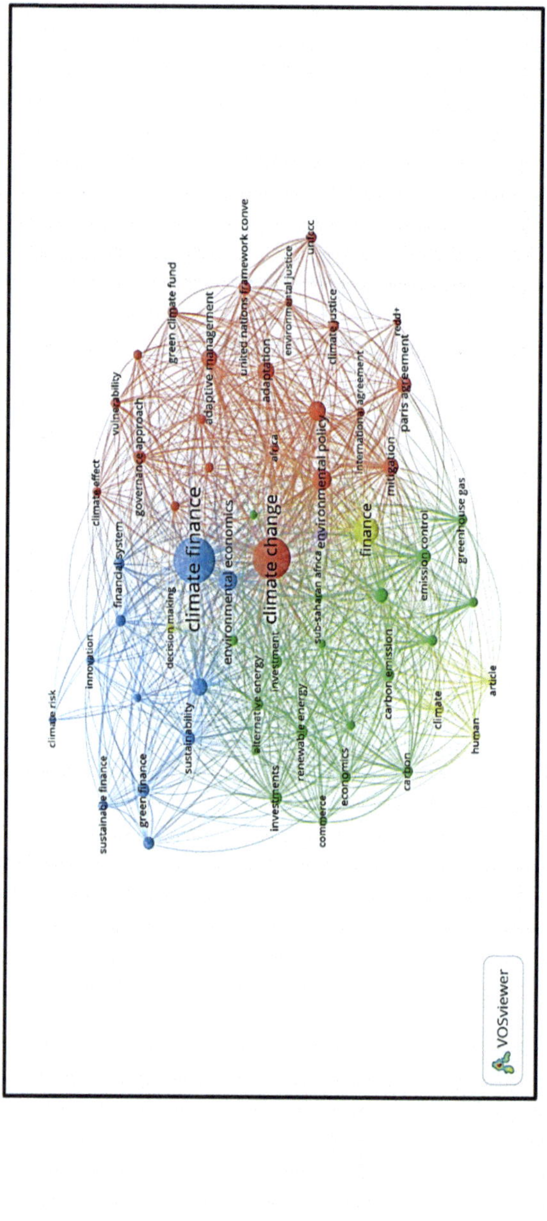

Fig. 7 Co-occurrence network of keywords (*Source* Author)

Fig. 8 Word map of keywords (*Source* The authors)

"Renewable Energy" indicates worldwide policy guides and green solutions under discussion (refer Fig. 8). Overall, the word map gives you a quick, visual overview of the most frequently discussed and most contentious subjects within the field of study you are researching.

12 Conclusion

The trajectory of climate finance studies from 2015 to 2024 is a dynamic and fast-developing field witnessing growing scholarly interest and diversification. The consistent increase in the volume of publications, particularly after 2020, indicates heightened worldwide curiosity for sustainable finance tools to battle climate change. But while the volume of research has increased, a corresponding drop in mean citations per paper indicates that more intense, influential, and foundational research must be conducted to further increase the scholarly rigor of this young field.

Prolific authors' analysis discovers the pioneering works of leading researchers like Roberts J. T., Weikmans R., and Chirambo D., who not only have produced worthwhile contributions but also have determined the intellectual mood for the discipline. Nevertheless, the comparatively humble citation influence of a number of authors indicates that there is room for more revolutionary, widely renowned contributions in the future.

Institutional examination finds that research on climate finance is now highly concentrated with some influential institutions like the Stockholm Environment Institute and Copernicus Institute of Sustainable Development, with greater publication rate, citation influence, and collaborative connectivity strength. However, the arrival of other institutions with growing strength indicates that research base is becoming increasingly broadened and geographically dispersed. The research evidently shows that the majority of climate finance research has been carried out in developed nations with significant institutions within these nations. This shows a critical need for developing nations to participate more in climate finance research and application. Increasing their role can be a key determinant in reversing the effects of climate change effectively.

Keyword co-occurrence, bibliographic coupling, and trend topic analysis together expose a broad thematic trend across the literature. Early work had primarily focused on mechanisms like clean development and emission reduction, while subsequent years have covered end-to-end assimilation of governance policies, finance architecture, adaptation, and sustainable development. Co-occurrence networks also flag the interdisciplinarity of climate finance origins due to environmental science, economics, governance, and social justice.

The map of bibliographic coupling shows how climate finance research is growing not only through a common pool of knowledge but forking into a variety of specialist sub-fields such as adaptation finance, climate risk management, and green finance products. The forking is a healthy maturity of the subject. Finally, the authors' network suggests a dynamic, close, cross-institutional and cross-disciplinary practice that is at the heart of solving the intractable, interconnected challenges of climate change finance globally.

Climate finance literature has evolved from its early days as an interdisciplinary domain of study to a significant and mature one, with its heartening growth being matched by newly emerging lacunae. Research in the future must try to enhance citation impact through more theory-informed contributions, increase international contribution, and investigate more unexploited themes like developing world finance, green investment mechanism innovation, and climate justice's impact on finance policy design. Progress in these areas will be vital to developing both academic research and practical implementation of climate finance interventions globally.

13 Future Research Directions

The application of artificial intelligence, geospatial analytics, and blockchain technology to climate finance is a new frontier. They can enhance transparency, tracking, and targeting of climate investments. The gap between research and policy-making continues to be important. Future research must address the development of actionable knowledge, decision-support tools, and applied lessons that can be used in climate finance at the global and national levels. The majority of influential publications and institutions are from developed nations. Future studies could encourage more affordable and localized discovery, particularly in climate finance practice, challenges, and innovation in the Global South. Additional empirical studies are important to assess the effectiveness, openness, and realized climate impacts of financial tools such as green bonds, climate funds, blended finance, and carbon pricing mechanisms.

References

Ameli, N., & Brandt, N. (2015). What impedes household investment in energy efficiency and renewable energy? *International Review of Environmental and Resource Economics*. https://doi.org/10.1561/101.00000067

Banga, J. (2019). The green bond market: A potential source of climate finance for developing countries. *Journal of Sustainable Finance & Investment, 9*(1), 17–32. https://doi.org/10.1080/20430795.2018.1498617

Blasiak, R., Spijkers, J., Tokunaga, K., Pittman, J., Yagi, N., & Österblom, H. (2017). Climate change and marine fisheries: Least developed countries top global index of vulnerability. *PLoS ONE, 12*(6), Article e0179632. https://doi.org/10.1371/journal.pone.0179632

Blasiak, J. (2017). Kronecker coefficients for one hook shape. *Sém. Lothar. Combin, 77*, 2016–2017.

Carè, R., & Weber, O. (2023). How much finance is in climate finance? A bibliometric review, critiques, and future research directions. *Research in International Business and Finance, 64*, Article 101886. https://doi.org/10.1016/j.ribaf.2023.101886

Chirambo, D. (2014). The climate finance and energy investment dilemma in Africa: Lacking amidst plenty. *Journal of Developing Societies, 30*(4), 415–440. https://doi.org/10.1177/0169796X14550876

Ciplet, D., Roberts, J. T., & Khan, M. (2013). The politics of international climate adaptation funding: Justice and divisions in the greenhouse. *Global Environmental Politics, 13*(1), 49–68. https://doi.org/10.1162/GLEP_a_00183

Doku, I., Ncwadi, R., & Phiri, A. (2021). Determinants of climate finance: Analysis of recipient characteristics in Sub-Saharan Africa. *Cogent Economics & Finance, 9*(1), 1964212. https://doi.org/10.1080/23322039.2021.1964212

Kouwenberg, R., & Zheng, C. (2023). A review of the global climate finance literature. *Sustainability, 15*(2), 1255. https://doi.org/10.3390/su15021255

Liu, M., Xia, C., Lan, H., Gao, Z., Yu, X., Wang, L., Liang, X., & Wu, Y. (2024). Driving toward sustainable cities: The interplay between Chinese emerging corporate ESG performance and climate finance in achieving low-carbon development. *Urban Climate, 55*, Article 101918. https://doi.org/10.1016/j.uclim.2023.101918

Liu, Z., Sun, H., & Tang, S. (2021). Assessing the impacts of climate change to financial stability: Evidence from China. *International Journal of Climate Change Strategies and Management, 13*(3), 375–393.

Michaelowa, A., Shishlov, I., & Brescia, D. (2019). Evolution of international carbon markets: Lessons for the Paris Agreement. *Wiley Interdisciplinary*

Reviews: Climate Change, 10(6), Article e613. https://doi.org/10.1002/wcc.613

Pauw, W. P., König-Sykorova, M., Valverde, M. J., & Zamarioli, L. H. (2024). More climate finance from more countries? *Current Climate Change Reports, 10*(4), 61–79.

Robiou du Pont, Y., Jeffery, M. L., Gütschow, J., Rogelj, J., Christoff, P., & Meinshausen, M. (2017). Equitable mitigation to achieve the Paris Agreement goals. *Nature Climate Change, 7*(1), 38–43. https://doi.org/10.1038/nclimate3186

Shang, Q., & Jin, X. (2023). A bibliometric analysis on climate finance: Current status and future directions. *Environmental Science and Pollution Research, 30*(57), 119711–119732. https://doi.org/10.1007/s11356-022-23931-4

Stroebel, J., & Wurgler, J. (2021). What do you think about climate finance? *Journal of Financial Economics, 142*(2), 487–498. https://doi.org/10.1016/j.jfineco.2021.02.010

Soergel, B. (2021). Combining ambitious climate policies with efforts to eradicate poverty. *Nature communications, 12*(1), 2342.

Soergel, B., Kriegler, E., Weindl, I., Rauner, S., Dirnaichner, A., Ruhe, C., Hofmann, M., Bauer, N., Bertram, C., Bodirsky, B., Leimbach, M., Leininger, J., Levesque, A., Luderer, G., Pehl, M., Wingens, C., Baumstark, L., Beier, F., Dietrich, J. P., & Popp, A. (2021). A sustainable development pathway for climate action within the UN 2030 Agenda. *Nature Climate Change, 11*(8), 656–664. https://doi.org/10.1038/s41558-021-01098-3

Skovgaard, J., & van Asselt, H. (2019). The politics of fossil fuel subsidies and their reform: Implications for climate change mitigation. *Wiley Interdisciplinary Reviews: Climate Change, 10*(4), Article e581. https://doi.org/10.1002/wcc.581

Weikmans, R., & Roberts, J. T. (2019). The international climate finance accounting muddle: Is there hope on the horizon? *Climate and Development, 11*(2), 97–111. https://doi.org/10.1080/17565529.2017.1410087

CHAPTER 12

Circular Economy Business Models: Entrepreneurial Approaches to Zero-Waste Value Chains

Priyanka Jain, Ankur Roy, Sonal Trivedi, and Kanika Jain

Abstract This chapter contributes to the CEBM literature and their application in response to environmental and financial pressures from an increasingly linear economy. This analysis explores the mechanisms through which entrepreneurial firms contribute to eco-innovation in pursuit of the United Nations Sustainable Development Goals (SDGs).

P. Jain (✉)
Management Department, IBS Ahmedabad, Gujarat, India
e-mail: priyankapj1781@gmail.com

A. Roy
Management Department, Management Development Institute Gurgaon, Haryana, India

S. Trivedi
School of Management and Commerce, Manav Rachna University, Faridabad, India

K. Jain
Manager, Bank of Baroda, Gandhinagar, India

S. Trivedi et al. (eds.), *Green Ventures*, Sustainable Development Goals Series, https://doi.org/10.1007/978-981-95-6533-7_12

The relevant SDGs are: SDG 12—Responsible Consumption and Production; SDG 9—Industry, Innovation and Infrastructure; SDG 13—Climate Action. This chapter assesses qualitative research through case studies to define various business and entrepreneurial approaches to CEBMs across industries that have experienced successful implementation. Entrepreneurial approaches include PaaS (Product-as-a-Service), green engineering, re-manufacturing, and upcycling; the potential of emerging technologies is explored, such as blockchain, AI (artificial intelligence), and IoT (Internet of Things). This research notes deficiencies and obstacles presented by the lack of universal standards and consumer acceptance. However, the necessity of interdisciplinary collaboration for achieving successful outcomes is highlighted. Findings reveal CEBMs reduce waste, enhance resource efficiency, and facilitate climate change efforts. Innovative entrepreneurial solutions offer replicable circular economy models, improving supply chain transparency and fostering innovation across multiple sectors. The chapter concludes by providing pathways of success for circular economy endeavors, assisting both entrepreneurial organizations and policymakers in their transition. This chapter contributes to the existing body of knowledge through an assessment of entrepreneurial interventions within a CEBM framework and their projected contribution to sustainable development goals. Policy intervention and engagement, community involvement, and other regulated endeavors are recommended to ultimately realize the potential of the models for contribution to a sustainable future. The chapter's emphasis on tactical interventions promotes a call to action for stakeholders in the circular economy to prioritize sustainable, waste-free outcomes.

Keywords Circular Economy Business Models · Sustainable Development Goals · Innovation · Zero-Waste Value Creation

1 Introduction

Because of critical environmental and economic issues that have emerged over time relative to linear production and consumption, the world desperately needs transformation via Circular Economy Business Models (CEBMs). CEBMs are sustainable by nature, essentially reducing waste, optimizing resource consumption, and facilitating reuse/

recycling. Entrepreneurs are essential in this context as they generate ideas and inventions within their business contexts to provide more sustainable opportunities with reintegration/reprocessing systems to reduce global sustainability issues. This chapter provides awareness of how entrepreneurial undertakings associated with CEBMs can contribute to the United Nations Sustainable Development Goals (SDGs); namely, SDG 12 (Responsible Consumption and Production), SDG 9 (Industry, Innovation, and Infrastructure), and SDG 13 (Climate Action).

1.1 Background and Rationale

The previous linear economy championed a 'take-make-dispose' approach that spurred environmental degradation, over-extraction of resources, and a growing pile of waste. The unsustainable nature of the system necessitates a systematic adjustment. A circular economy offers a potential resolution. The circular economy aims to change how we grow and develop by decoupling economic growth from the consumption of finite resources. It includes a spectrum of solutions that make waste unnecessary, enables goods and materials to be reused, and actively links efforts to restore natural systems. Therefore, such transformation not only aims to rectify environmental issues but also draws economic conclusions to support transformation, including job creation and resource efficiency. However, for such a transformation to take place, entrepreneurial efforts support the cause through innovation and business model creation to sustain a circular process. Ultimately, with these entrepreneurs on board, the economy will become more adaptable and sustainable for the benefit of society and nature.

1.2 The Linear Economy vs. Circular Economy Paradigm

The linear economy, with its pattern of resource depletion, production, consumption, and waste disposal, contributes to overconsumption, environmental problems, and substantial waste generation. Conversely, the circular economy embraces a restorative methodology. A circular model replaces resource inputs, waste, emissions, and energy leakage with a stabilized, reduced, and contained flow of material and energy. A circular economy works through extended-use activities—like design for durability, maintenance, repair, restoring, reuse, re-manufacturing, refurbishing, and recycling—that not only conserve essential resources but also encourage new ideas and economic growth through the relative value of goods and services. Sustainability offers several advantages to corporations. Sustainable practices are crucial for the long-term operational success of businesses. Continued reliance on a linear economic model, with its inherent waste and resource depletion, is unsustainable given escalating environmental pressures.

1.3 The Role of Entrepreneurship in Circular Economy Transitions

Entrepreneurs are key agents in the circular economy transition, as entrepreneurial innovation allows for sustainable business models that challenge the current inconsistent business endeavors. Unlike reliance on existing markets, entrepreneurs seek opportunities for waste reduction, maximal resource consumption, and the repurposing of one person's waste into another's valuable commodity. Salubata utilizes recycled plastic in the production of bespoke shoes. EcoPost takes plastic waste and uses it to make strong, long-lasting fencing posts. These organizations demonstrate a dual focus on ecological stewardship and economic development, resulting in increased employment. Entrepreneurs facilitate the adoption of circular economy models through innovative goods, services, and processes that prioritize sustainability. As unbiased experimentalists, entrepreneurs are essential catalysts for progress. The entrepreneurial spirit is crucial for driving connection, innovation, and the disruption necessary for a more sustainable and efficient economy.

1.4 Alignment with Sustainable Development Goals (SDGs)

Circular economy business models directly contribute to several United Nations Sustainable Development Goals (SDGs), particularly SDG 12 (Responsible Consumption and Production), SDG 9 (Industry, Innovation, and Infrastructure), and SDG 13 (Climate Action). CEBMs inherently promote effective resource use and waste minimization, which means they facilitate responsible consumption and production patterns (SDG 12). CEBMs help to achieve sustainable consumption and production (SDG 12) because they encourage better use of resources and simultaneously reduce the amount of waste produced. CEBMs help to achieve industry innovation and infrastructure (SDG 9) as well, because of the new concepts brought to play, like servitization and resource recovery. In addition, CEBMs help to achieve climate action (SDG 13) because of the reduction of virgin resource extraction and excess waste, which lowers the greenhouse gas emissions related to both activities. Ultimately, entrepreneurship is a clear example of how the progress of business can align with the United Nations' idea for global sustainability.

2 Review of Literature

The concept of the Circular Economy (CE) has gained significant traction in recent years as a sustainable alternative to the traditional linear economy model. This literature review synthesizes current research on Circular Economy Business Models (CEBMs), focusing on entrepreneurial approaches, zero-waste value chains, technological enablers, and the challenges and barriers associated with implementing these models.

2.1 *Conceptualizing Circular Economy Business Models*

CEBMs are an innovative approach to enhancing business value without the added costs of waste and resource consumption. According to Geissdoerfer et al. (2017), CEBMs are business models that aim to maintain the economic value of products, materials, and resources in the marketplace for as long as possible. For example, this includes activities such as resource recovery, product life extension, and closed-loop systems. CEBMs encompass a spectrum of models, including product-as-a-service, re-manufacturing, and sharing platforms, each exhibiting unique implementation characteristics and environmental consequences (Centobelli et al., 2020).

The implementation of CEBMs, while potentially disruptive to conventional CE processing, is ultimately warranted by the findings of numerous studies. These studies suggest that this integrated approach is essential for gaining a more comprehensive understanding of CE processes, allowing for the successful management of their economic, environmental, and social aspects.

2.2 *Entrepreneurial Approaches to Circular Economy*

The development of CEBMs and subsequent implementation depends on entrepreneurship. Entrepreneurs undertake innovative efforts that create new business models different from previously established pathways focused instead on sustainability (Khan et al., 2024). Foroozanfar et al. (2022) suggest that an entrepreneurial orientation is positively related to circular adoption; this orientation is defined by proactivity, risk-taking, and innovativeness.

Social entrepreneurship's role in facilitating CEBM adoption has been noted. Social entrepreneurship frequently aims for social equity and environmental remediation alongside financial gain; thus, many remain in a position to apply circular contributions effectively without deterring traditional objectives (Mair & Marti, 2006). For example, companies like TerraCycle and Fairphone indicate social entrepreneurs can render value to their stakeholders through a circular approach that addresses social problems while simultaneously rendering sustainable outcomes (Bocken et al., 2016).

2.3 Zero-Waste Value Chains: Key Components and Strategies

Zero-waste value chains are intrinsically linked to CEBMs since the entire point is to plan a success trajectory that never generates waste. For instance, the zero-waste mindset involves utilizing the creation process to avoid generating anything but trivial detrimental effects to the ecosystem (Murray et al., 2017). The essential elements of a zero-waste value chain are entry and exit points which function as systemic bases, preventing further waste generation.

The research on implementing these value chains is incomplete because of the unclear connection between ecosystems and the implementation process. For instance, Lewandowski (2016) acknowledges that, without stakeholder buy-in throughout the supply chain, zero-waste potential will struggle to be realized. Yet with proper government, business, and social forums, one community's waste can be another community's input (Chertow, 2000). This kind of endeavor promotes synergistic buy-in efforts to cultivate a zero-waste approach.

2.4 Technological Enablers: IoT, Blockchain, AI in CEBMs

Technological innovations are crucial enablers of CEBMs and influence the circular economy shift. IoT, blockchain, and artificial intelligence (AI) are key technologies that can enhance the circularity process.

IoT allows for real-time monitoring of resources and waste, so companies can better assess their activities and cut out inefficiencies (Peter et al.,

2023). For example, IoT sensors might monitor how well a product is used or how much it is used, and instead of waiting until something breaks, send a signal that alerts management to a potential problem. Likewise, blockchain allows for transparency and traceability of components of a supply chain, so elements can be sustainably sourced and the efforts to create waste can be diminished (Kazancoglu et al., 2023). The immutable ledger of information allows companies to assess where materials come from and where they go, facilitating circularity.

In addition, AI has the potential to enhance CEBMs because of its ability to analyze large datasets and make predictions. For instance, AI can track trends in use and determine how best to allocate resources, limiting waste, and increasing efficiency (Wang et al., 2016). These technologies equip organizational leaders with the instruments for developing and implementing robust CEBM strategies exhibiting sustainable growth.

2.5 Challenges and Barriers in Implementing CEBMs

There are numerous complications and obstacles to widespread CEBM implementation. For example, a common challenge is raised by a lack of exposure and understanding of circularity by both companies and consumers, who continue to favor linear operation (Linder &Williander, 2017). If companies are unaware that CEBMs exist, they will not be inclined to spend resources on them. In addition, obstacles arise from financial instability because any significant change requires a considerable initial investment in new processes and new technologies (Centobelli et al., 2020). While large businesses might spare some of their research and development budget for this option, small and medium-sized enterprises might not only be unable to spare any money but also find it challenging to even secure funding for circular efforts (Foroozanfar et al., 2022). Finally, some challenges to adopting a CEBM involve policy. Without an incentivized framework for circular operations or legislation that nourishes such endeavors, companies may not see the value in adopting a CEBM (Murray et al., 2017). Therefore, legislators must engage in transparent legislation with incentives for circular efforts.

Research on circular economy business models shows that circular approaches can significantly improve sustainability and reduce environmental damage. Through entrepreneurial innovation, the development of zero-waste value chains, and integrating advanced technologies, businesses can create value while contributing to a more sustainable future.

However, addressing the challenges and barriers to implementation is essential for realizing the full potential of CEBMs. Future research should focus on identifying best practices, developing supportive policies, and fostering collaboration among stakeholders to facilitate the transition to a circular economy.

3 Research Objective

The primary objective of this research is to investigate the interconnections between sustainable practices in industrial innovation, accountable consumption and production, and climate action, as outlined in Sustainable Development Goals (SDGs) 9, 12, and 13. This study aims to delineate the key questions that guide this exploration, ultimately seeking to understand how these practices contribute to broader socio-economic and environmental advancements. By clarifying the thematic orientation of the research, the aim is to highlight the significance of these sustainability initiatives in achieving the SDGs, while identifying critical areas for intervention and innovation that can facilitate meaningful change. This research comprehensively analyzes sustainability-focused strategies in policy and practice, fostering discussion of their impact on sustainable development.

Primary and secondary research questions that help in guiding the investigation are being outlined in this section. These questions are devised to inspect the interconnection between sustainable development goals (particularly SDGs 9, 12, and 13) and their practical implementation covering various sectors. The framework of the key research question may be in the form of: How can integrated approaches to innovation, consumption, and climate action contribute to achieving sustainable development goals in a synergistic and scalable way?

Several sub-questions support this primary exploration:

- What are the contemporaneous hurdles and opportunities for advancing sustainable industrialization in developing and developed contexts?
- How do patterns of consumption and production influence ecological and social sustainability?
- In what ways can climate action policies reinforce or challenge industrial and consumption practices?

- What role do governments, businesses, and civil society play in aligning practices with SDGs 9, 12, and 13?

These questions help in framing the systematic course of the study, selecting case studies, data collection methods, and theoretical structure. We need to identify these key research questions promptly so that the chapter ensures logicality and alignment throughout the research process. These questions act as a compass, carving the extant of inquiry and keeping the research grounded in its sustainability mission.

4 Research Methodology

Qualitative methodology is adopted to explore how Circular Economy Business Models (CEBM) support the implementation of SDGs 9, 12, and 13. In order to understand sustainability-driven innovation and practices, case study analysis along with thematic interpretation approach is used. Purposive sampling is used to select contextual case studies that illustrate the integration of circular economy principles. The research methodology emphasizes contextual depth, aiming to uncover nuanced relationships between industrial processes, sustainable consumption, and climate action. An analytical framework applies to assess the effectiveness, replicability, and scalability of CEBM practices in addressing key sustainable development objectives.

4.1 Research Design and Approach

A qualitative exploratory research design allows for a comprehensive examination of complex sustainability efforts in real life. A case study is needed to formally assess emerging or shifting arrangements like CEBM because it can collect cases and have situational awareness. Consequently, the design unites innovation, consumption, and environmental stewardship globally and across disciplines.

A combined inductive and deductive methodology is employed. The case study findings rely on inductive reasoning for theme formulation. Deductive reasoning positions the study among established theoretical frameworks of sustainability, circular economy, and SDGs. Review of public sustainability reports, analysis of available related documents and expert interview are some methods of data collection.

This design aligns with the study's aim of exploring the practical applications of SDGs 9, 12, and 13, with a focus on outcomes, challenges, and enablers. The strategy highlights the importance of context, recognizing that sustainable practices are formed by local policies, market subtleties, cultural norms, and organizational capacities. Overall, the research design ensures flexibility, responsiveness to emerging insights, and depth in evaluating the alignment of CEBM practices with sustainable development goals.

4.2 *Case Study Selection Criteria*

Case study is selected based on subjective sampling ensuring relevance, diversity, and alignment with the research focus on CEBM and SDGs 9, 12, and 13. Cases from a wide range of industries like manufacturing, agriculture, fashion industry, and technology sector are being included in order to illustrate industry specific perspective and applications of circular economy principles.

Critical criteria included are:

- Significance to SDGs: The case must establish active participation in at least one of SDGs 9, 12, or 13, preferably showing intersection across all three.
- Circular Innovation: The industry or start-up must clearly use circular economy practice, such as sustainable production cycle, product-as-a-service models, waste reutilization, or renewable design.
- Geographic Representation: Cases from both developed and developing countries' contexts are selected to reflect global applicability.
- Scalability and Impact: Insights on expandability of their practice and measurable sustainability outcomes (environmental, social, or economic) should be provided by the selected cases.

This criteria-driven approach ensures the study covers a representative spectrum of circular economy implementations while remaining focused on practices with strong sustainability implications. It allows comparative analysis and identification of best practices and context driven issues.

4.3 Analytical Framework for Assessing CEBM Practices

The analytical framework evaluatesthe Circular Economy Business Model (CEBM) practices through the lens of sustainability performance and SDG alignment. It draws upon established circular economy metrics, sustainability indicators, and SDG targets, particularly those under Goals 9, 12, and 13. Innovation and infrastructure, production and consumption, and climate action are the three main dimensions around which the framework is being structured.

Set of criteria is being used to assessing each dimension:

- Innovation and Infrastructure (SDG 9): Includes technological innovation, resource efficiency, sustainable infrastructure, and knowledge-sharing mechanisms.
- Responsible Production and Consumption (SDG 12): Measures circular inputs, waste reduction, lifecycle design, and supply chain transparency.
- Climate Action (SDG 13): Evaluates emissions reduction, adaptation strategies, and contributions to climate resilience.

The framework merges qualitative indicators (e.g., stakeholder engagement, policy alignment, governance models) and quantitative metrics (e.g., carbon savings, resource loops closed, reduction in material throughput) wherever possible. Through this hybrid approach, comprehensive assessment is allowed that is malleable across sectors and regions.

In addition, the framework assimilates feedback cycles, identifying how learnings from implementation shape future innovation. It is both diagnostic and strategic as it helps in identifying successful models and revealing areas which needs policy, investment, or operational support for broader systemic change.

5 Analysis and Discussion

This section helps in exploring how entrepreneurial endeavors are revolutionizing waste management through innovation and zero-waste strategies. Creation of economic value and reduction in environmental impact result from the use of diverse business models, which include circular design, service-based ownership, and industrial symbiosis. The selected case studies show how start-ups and established firms are implementing zero-waste principles. Multiple Sustainable Development Goals (SDGs), such as responsible consumption, climate action, and sustainable industries, directly benefit from their efforts. However, challenges remain in increasing these solutions, specifically because of regulatory obstacles and infrastructure constraints. The findings emphasize the significance of collaboration, innovation, and supportive ecosystems for greater acceptance.

5.1 *Entrepreneurial Strategies for Zero-Waste Value Creation*

Waste-free value creation business practices revolve around reinventing the standard linear model of product and consumption. To reduce needed resources, extend product life, and prevent waste, entrepreneurs are increasingly attuned to approaches afforded by a circular economy.

One of the entrepreneurial strategies discussed is circular design. This approach focuses on the making of products that will last, includes modular components for easy assemblage/disassembly and restoration, as well as those that can be recycled. Entrepreneurial operations in this space consider end-of-life applications as they create products now, preventing waste before it happens. A popularized form of circular design is upcycling, making new products of higher value from waste.

Another discussed entrepreneurial strategy is the product-as-a-service (PaaS) experience, which creates an innovative spin on acquisition. Instead of selling products outright, companies lease the products but keep ownership, which incentivizes the companies to create durable products for reuse in the future since they handle maintenance and end-of-life solutions. This model encourages customer loyalty through service and positive sustainability-focused, responsive action while minimizing waste.

The third entrepreneurial strategy is called industrial symbiosis. Here, the waste or by-products of one operation become essential resources for another. Entrepreneurs often act as intermediaries who create ecosystems and logistical pathways for transportation that allow one firm to share with another. A subcategory of this is called reverse logistics, which encompasses return and subsequent reuse and refurbishing of products.

Through these strategies, entrepreneurs can decrease virgin material intake, eliminate subsequent costs associated, create new revenue streams, and satisfy consumer and regulatory demands for sustainable practices. By engaging in such entrepreneurial strategies, one not only re-conceptualizes value creation for their own purposes but realigns their business with socio-economic and environmental concerns as well.

5.2 Case Studies: Start-ups and Established Firms

5.2.1 Case 1: Rcyclo—Circular Design and Upcycling

Rcyclo is a sustainable fashion brand with upcycling and a circular design method involved. Rcyclo produces clothing from post-consumer textile waste with an emphasis on sustainable dyeing (climate-smart dyes) and prints that easily facilitate resizing and repairs. Their design a separate aproach in which a customer can return clothing to be upcycled or down-cycled. Rcyclo works with local take-back centers and clothing recyclers to complete the cycle. This reduces landfill waste, increases potential for reuse, and appeals to an emerging niche of eco-conscious consumerism.

5.2.2 Case 2: Loopit—Product-as-a-Service Model

Loopit is a subscription service for home appliances—refrigerators, washing machines, and air purifiers. Whereas companies generally sell units and transfer ownership, Loopit offers them on a subscription basis and retains ownership, essentially promising that all units are made for longevity, reparable by parts, and parts are upgradeable. On the other hand, consumers pay a monthly service fee to ensure routine maintenance and upgrade options; units returned are refurbished and re-rented or broken down and recycled. This reduces e-waste, promotes longer use of products, and assures a sustainable future. An effective reverse supply chain and Loopit's digital asset management are critical to its operation.

5.2.3 Case 3: EcoNet—Industrial Symbiosis and Reverse Logistics

EcoNet provides a platform to regional manufacturing firms, facilitating industrial symbiosis amongst them. It tracks movement of materials and recognizes opportunities where waste from one process can be used as raw material for another. For example, Biogas Plants can use food processing waste from juice factories. EcoNet is using AI in order to manage a shared logistics system in order to transport materials efficiently, optimizing routes resulting in low carbon emissions. This platform helps companies to comply with circular economy mandates through efficient use of resources, reduction in environmental impact and fostering inter-firm collaboration.

5.3 *Impact on SDGs and Environmental Performance*

Zero-waste start-ups support various SDGs. Rcyclo supports Responsible Consumption and Production (SDG 12) as it employs a circular design since it aims to increase the life of products and not be discarded into landfills. In addition, since the company facilitates reuse and recycling of textiles, it helps decrease the environmental impact of the fast fashion industry. Loopit's Product-as-a-Service design supports Industry, Innovation, and Infrastructure (SDG 9) as well as Climate Action (SDG 13). If Loopit satisfies consumer demand, the need for virgin materials diminishes, thus curbing waste generation and mitigating greenhouse gas emissions through enhanced efficiency and refurbishment processes. Finally, EcoNet supports Partnerships for the Goals (SDG 17) as its resource-sharing industrial systems help to connect across industries. It's also championing increased material efficiency by converting waste to resources while championing Sustainable Cities and Communities (SDG 11) because of reduced pollution in the sector.

These environmental performance indicators are reduced carbon impact, reduced landfill diversion, and increased material circularity. Besides the environmental advantage, these efforts also pave the way for economic sustainability through job creation, efficiencies of resources, and lower operating costs. Overall, these models demonstrate entrepreneurship is a powerful driver for not only entrepreneurial success but also universal sustainable development goals.

5.4 *Drivers of Success and Key Learnings*

Multiple vital elements make these zero waste entrepreneurial models successful. First, innovation is a major factor across products, entrepreneurial approach, and supply chain. The innovative modular clothing of Rcyclo and the AI-facilitated logistics system of EcoNet strongly support the idea that innovation leads to improved circularity solutions. Second, collaboration is crucial for operational success. Supply chains, clientele, and governmental organizations must be participatory and symbiotic for resource transfer and supporting ecosystems. For instance, EcoNet collaborates with countless firms for success and Loopit requires its subscribers to maintain membership for longer periods and engage in feedback loops. Third, much success depends on policy-based opportunities and regulations. Much institutional support is at play for those companies doing business where extended producer responsibility (EPR) regulations exist or waste diversion initiatives are already in place.

Growing consumer awareness and demand for sustainable products increase the potential for new ventures to develop more socially responsible market offerings. Rcyclo operates in the sustainable clothing space, while Loopit benefits from the increasing demand for access over ownership.

The requirements to operate successfully come from the understanding that designing for circularity, committing to the infrastructure necessary for returns and material recovery, and transparency regarding impacts are crucial. Up-scaling requires technology and problem-solving, adaptive business models, and trustworthy partnerships. In the end, the ability to merge sustainability with a value-added benefit for customers and investors is critical to success.

5.5 *Barriers to Scalability and Adoption*

However, despite the potential, waste-free entrepreneurial models face critical obstacles to expansion and widespread adoption. The initial capital expenditure is considerable, encompassing both systems and subsequent research and development efforts. For example, before Loopit can turn a profit, it requires extensive capital into its reverse logistics and asset management systems.

Customer sentiment and awareness are complicated. Consumer reluctance towards refurbished or rental products stems from insufficient awareness and comprehension.

Operational efficiency is complicated by supply chain disruptions and a lack of infrastructure. Reliable access to high-quality textile waste is crucial for organizations such as Rcyclo; however, establishing this access presents significant challenges in the absence of robust collection systems.

Regulatory uncertainty and inconsistent policy support across different areas slow down progress. In the absence of guidance and financial support, entrepreneurs frequently navigate complex regulatory frameworks independently.

The system's scalability is also hampered by technological restrictions stemming from the non-digital or unconnected nature of recycling and harvesting operations. EcoNet's functionality is constrained by any business that cannot share data, thus limiting opportunities for collaborative business.

All the above require intra-industry partnerships, government subsidization, and socially responsible financing to ease the burden. Implementing zero-waste programs in daily business and consumer practices is facilitated by fostering trust, ensuring accessibility, and showing long-term cost advantages.

6 Policy Recommendations

Without enabling policy, the CEBM application is incomplete. Policy must come from the government to dictate cross-sectorial standards and fiscal incentives. Regulatory policy should comprise parameters for compliance, grants for startups, transportation and other infrastructures, and intersectional partnerships. Policy should fulfill the bridge between consumer understanding and subsequent application, from outreach to education to social and behavioral change. This phenomenon, akin to climate change, is a national priority aligned with international sustainable development goals. Thus, fiscal sustainable entrepreneurship will emerge from ethical and incremental policy improvements. The goal of these improvements is the mainstream adoption of circular processes, increased socio-economic sustainability, and integrating circularity into standard business and consumer practices.

6.1 *Regulatory Support for CEBMs*

Ultimately, a rigid regulatory scheme is critical to implementing Circular Economy Business Models (CEBMs). Fixed, clear, consistent, and enforceable regulations will allow entrepreneurs to assess compliance as operational uncertainty is reduced. The Government needs to implement extended producer responsibility (EPR) so companies know they need to accept and manage the impact of their goods in the marketplace at the end of their life, as well as indigenously create waste classification systems that facilitate recovery and reuse of materials.

The subsequent innovation between industries and the creation of new goods can be eased by standards for recyclability, repairability, and circular design. Moreover, regulatory standards must be uniform across borders, so those businesses implementing a circular method of operation internationally can more easily avoid pitfalls associated with reverse logistics and the trading of secondary materials.

Some organizations have been able to sidestep regulatory constraints to an extent with Circular Economy Business Models. Patagonia's approach to sustainability, as detailed in a 2019 Business of Fashion article, demonstrates a linear transition towards a circular model. The program's approach to circularity is embodied in its Worn Wear initiative, which prioritizes the repair and recycling of clothing over the acquisition of new garments. This not only bonds the brand to its customer base, but also minimizes waste and environmental impact. The Worn Wear program prevented over 45,000 pounds of apparel from entering landfills in 2020. Their commitment to environmental regulations and robust internal sustainability programs led them to adopt practices that, despite potential financial risks, effectively mitigated regulatory obstacles.

Good regulations support the circular economy. A 2018–2019 study by the Ellen MacArthur Foundation indicated that countries with stricter circular economy regulations experienced a 30% rise in resource productivity compared to their unregulated counterparts. In 2020, the European Commission introduced a Circular Economy Action Plan designed to foster a regulatory system that supports the transition of European countries towards sustainable growth and innovative practices. Preliminary analysis reveals that, within two years of adopting the regulations, i.e. 2022, participating nations saw a 10% decrease in overall waste generation.

6.2 *Incentives and Funding for Circular Innovation*

Entrepreneurs need financial subsidies and support to enter the circular economy. Significant upfront capital is required for the circular model, owing to infrastructure development, reverse logistics, and technological progress. Thus, to ease implementation, governments should offer subsidies, low-interest loans or tax credits for companies, regardless of age, pursuing zero waste innovations.

Green procurement policies also act as powerful buyer incentives. Guaranteed markets for circular entrepreneurs can be created by the government by emphasizing on circular products in public contracts. In order to attract private investment and unlock creativity, innovation challenge funds and accelerators specifically targeting circular business models are the key elements.

Sustainability focused investors will be more willing to invest if green investment criteria are established and circularity is integrated into Environmental, Social, and Governance (ESG) standards. Ventures with measurable impact and growth potential, supporting research, pilot testing, and commercial deployment, should be prioritized by public funding programs.

Concentrated efforts should be made regarding SMEs and early-stage innovators, as they often lack access to traditional financing due to perceived risk. Combining Public and private funds, i.e. blended finance approaches, can mitigate risk investment and catalyze growth.

One success story is the Ellen MacArthur Foundation. This UK-based charity has helped to promote the circular economy concept. The foundation has received funding from various government bodies and private entities to support research and development initiatives aimed at creating a circular economy. Their collaboration with the UK government led to the establishment of the "Circular Economy 100" program, which brings together businesses, governments, and academia to accelerate circular economy practices.

For businesses, circular models mean more revenue as costs are saved and new streams of income emerge. When products are manufactured to last and be re-manufactured, material costs decrease and assured customer loyalty increases. Companies using circular business models include IKEA, which has a furniture leasing option and a furniture take-back option, allowing it to sustain its branding image while gaining guaranteed repeat customers year after year.

For communities, a circular approach translates to job creation and economic stability. According to the World Economic Forum, a circular approach could create 700,000 jobs solely in Europe by the year 2030. A circular economy fosters a sustainable approach, meaning less pollution and less exploitation of resources. This benefits communities with better public health.

Consequently, financial resources empower entrepreneurs to explore their creative potential, concurrently enabling a large-scale shift from linear to circular economic models.

6.3 *Public-Private Partnerships and Ecosystem Development*

The infrastructure and synergies required to support a circular economy can be fostered by Public-Private Partnerships (PPPs). Through a partnership between government and industry, integrated platforms for material reclamation, recycling, and logistics are being implemented to enhance operational efficiency and reduce overall costs. Collaborative efforts between public and private entities streamline information dissemination, as public policy objectives and entrepreneurial innovation are congruent.

To cultivate sustainable systems, cross-industry partnerships need to be established with academic, non-profit and micro grassroots communities as the safety net for experimentation and evolution. For example, circular economy consortiums or similar inventiveness clusters at the regional level can provide access to pooled technical resources, research efforts and guidance networks.

Government can establish Innovation experimentation zones where circular innovators can tinker with their approaches without superfluous regulatory oversight while gleaning important information to guide future regulation. These uniform metrics and accountability measures can help champion transparency and performance measurement across the entire eco-system.

An example of a prosperous PPP model of a circular economy comes from Amsterdam. In pursuit of its 2050 circular economy goal, Amsterdam has partnered with the private sector to develop many circular initiatives under its Amsterdam Circular Strategy. This initiative began in 2016, including collaboration between the city and companies like Philips and DSM which support the city's efforts to reduce waste and resource consumption and increased resource efficiency and reuse. The Amsterdam Economic Board created a report that posits the city's plans could achieve over €7 billion socioeconomic impact by 2030.

The value of such circular economies to society when driven by PPPs is manifold. First, they enhance economic stimulation through entrepreneurial efforts and employment opportunity. The World Economic Forum predicts circular practices could lead to 1.8 million net new jobs in Europe by 2030. Second, they minimize adverse environmental effects. Circular practices decrease dependence on virgin materials acquisition. McKinsey & Company projected a 70% reduction in greenhouse gas emissions by 2050, achievable through a circular economy.

It is imperative that the principle of inclusion is not confined to large corporations, but is also felt within small businesses and social enterprises, a sector that could benefit from the PPP infrastructure. Long-term partnerships, trust, and incentives are fundamental to the sustainability of all ecosystems.

6.4 *Consumer Awareness and Behavioral Change*

Consumer behavior is essential to the success of CEBMs. Policies fostering consumer awareness and behavioral shifts can facilitate the adoption of circular products and services, bridging the intention-behavior gap.

Awareness-raising efforts will impact consumer behavior for potential adoption with Circular Economy policies. The UK's "Love Food Hate Waste" campaign is aimed at reducing food waste via consumer awareness. This awareness-raising campaign has raised awareness about food waste and changed consumer behavior positively; 1.1 million less food is wasted each year in the UK since this campaign began, equating to about £250 million saved per household each year. This approach involves recognizing existing resources and changing dietary habits and culinary practices, rather than prioritizing solely environmental concerns. This effort shows that awareness efforts have more value than specific outcomes.S.

Eco-labeling and disclosure systems help facilitate educated purchases. When purchases come with transparency via eco-labels for durability, recyclability, and eco-impact, consumers can make educated purchases and purchase responsibly.

Circular Choices can be made more attractive and convenient with behavioral nudges, such as deposit-refund schemes, loyalty programs for returns, or discounts on sustainable products. In order to inculcate sustainability values from a young age, it should become part of School curricula and community programs.

It is equally essential to combat misconceptions and stigma linked with reused or upcycled goods, by reformulating them as high-quality and ethical choices. In order to shift cultural perceptions around consumption, policymakers need to work with influencers, civil society, and brands.

Consumer behavior plays a critical role in the successful implementation of circular economy initiatives. Statistics underscore the economic potential of a circular model, while effective public education campaigns demonstrate how to shift consumer attitudes towards sustainable practices. As businesses and policymakers work towards a more circular future, understanding and influencing consumer behavior will be essential in realizing the full benefits of this transformative economic model.

7 Future Research Recommendations

Our future researches must address the existing knowledge gaps and explore long-term impacts in order to deepen our understanding of Circular Economy Business Models (CEBMs). With an aim to evaluate the sustainability and scalability of circular models over a duration, longitudinal studies are must. Circular Finance and digital technologies are some of the emerging are which are promising yet under-explored. Studies across sectors and worldwide comparative analysis can reveal transferable practices and regional challenges. To design an effective, inclusive and resilient circular system that can lead to large-scale transformation across industries and economies, we require progressive empirical, interdisciplinary, and context-specific research.

7.1 Need for Longitudinal Studies on CEBM Impact

Longitudinal studies are required to truly assess the effectiveness of Circular Economy Business Models (CEBMs) and their viability. Unlike a short-term case study, which provides a snapshot in time, longitudinal studies analyze progress over extended periods, encompassing established cyclical processes, accomplishments, growth, and identifying trends, systemic influences, and long-term viability.

One advantage is the evaluation of life-cycle impacts, encompassing the costs of reusing and upcycled materials and the consumption-reducing potential of service models. Longitudinal studies increasingly corroborate the legitimacy of circular entrepreneurial models, demonstrating reduced resource depletion, waste generation, and time commitments while enhancing profitability. These significant findings corroborate the claims of CEBMs, suggesting that relative legitimation is attainable through longitudinal research.

Using longitudinal studies enables researchers to determine the long-term validity and adaptability of CEBMs, given that entrepreneurs may modify their ventures in reaction to shifts in regulation, economic conditions, or operational issues. For example, how does a product-as-a-service company stay viable during economic downturns? How does an upcycling company flourish when waste supply drops or public interest fades?

The impact of organizational learning on startup efficacy can be observed through short-term decreases in effectiveness balanced by long-term stakeholder engagement and cyclical process enhancement. This research will explore the social consequences of circular economy businesses, providing a platform for data gathering among those who regularly interface with local communities or the informal waste sector.

Ultimately, the comprehensive causal approach provides an in-depth, longitudinal, and organic snapshot of how CEBMs function within ever-changing ecosystems. These are essential for theoretical real-world impact and policy changes to support entrepreneurial endeavors and stakeholder integration efforts as they navigate the multifaceted transition to circularity.

7.2 Opportunities in Emerging Technologies and Circular Finance

The adoption and efficiency of Circular Economy Business Models (CEBMs) can be accelerated with the help of emerging technologies and financial innovations. However, these areas are under-explored in academic research, deserving deeper investigation.

Operation of circular businesses can be transformed with the use of technologies such as artificial intelligence (AI), blockchain, and the Internet of Things (IoT). Some examples are AI can improve resource management, maintenance forecasting, and waste sorting. Block chain ensures transparency in supply chains and product life cycles. IoT permits real-time tracking of flow of material, simplifying reverse logistics and recovery of assets.

Another emerging field is digital product passports, which contain detailed information about a material of the product, origin, and repair history which is crucial for reuse and recycling. Research can concentrate on execution difficulties, standardization, and acceptance of these technological tools by the users.

Essential funds for circular ventures is provided through impact investing, green bonds and outcome-based funding which forms part of circular finance. Still, many entrepreneurs struggle to access these because of uncertain valuation models or limited investor awareness.

Further studies should explore how financial instruments can be customized to support long-term circular outcomes, including risk-distribution models and the result drive payments model.

Flexible, analytical drive and economically viable solutions can be revealed by the researchers by combining technological and financial perspectives. These innovations can be connected with practical business requirements and societal impact through interdisciplinary studies.

7.3 Cross-Sectoral and Global Comparative Research

In order to understand the transferability and contextual adaptability of Circular Economy Business Models (CEBMs), cross-sectoral and global comparative research is very critical. While implementing circular principles, unique challenges and opportunities are being faced by various industries and geographic regions. Comparative evaluation can help in identifying best practices, avoid complications, and inspire innovation across boundaries.

For example, insights gained from circular construction in Europe can be applied to waste management in urban housing projects in Asia or Africa. Likewise, successful insights in electronics for product-as-a-service can apply to medical devices or agricultural equipment.

Cross-industry analyzes significantly depend on a systems approach, given the interdependence and collaborative nature of various sectors. Industrial symbiosis between the food and energy sectors mirrors that are observed in the automotive and electronics industries. Nevertheless, the matter necessitates distinct policies, infrastructural approaches, and stakeholder engagement strategies.

Transnational comparative research similarly determines how local culture, legal systems, economic growth and access to resources will support successful entrepreneurial ventures in the circular economy. Acknowledging the distinctions between the developing world is vital for an internationalized version of this circularity, especially where changes are warranted but not feasible given financial and environmental concerns.

Comparative studies also reveal transferable and adaptable regulatory innovations. It advocates for equity by incorporating scalability and capabilities from diverse national and sectoral contexts. The potential for broader, more varied, and ultimately more effective global circular economy initiatives is enhanced through an international, interdisciplinary approach.

8 Conclusion

This chapter emphasizes the significant efficacy of Circular Economy Business Models (CEBMs) in addressing environmental and economic challenges across diverse sectors. Entrepreneurs are pioneering waste minimization and resource efficiency improvements through the application of circular economy principles, including circular design, product-as-a-service models, and industrial symbiosis. Further supporting this, the case studies presented evidence of field efficacy and projected cost savings. Awareness and application of CEBM depend on inter/intra-sector collaboration, policy development, entrepreneur awareness, and governmental support and entrepreneurial innovations. The adoption of these measures, however, faces obstacles stemming from inadequate funding, limited scalability, and insufficient policy recognition. In summation, the chapter posits CEBMs offer a revolutionary and viable path towards the creation of sustainable, regenerative business ecosystems, transforming existing linear models. The transition to a circular economy, characterized by replenishment rather than extraction, offers a means of addressing critical global concerns such as climate change and resource scarcity, while simultaneously advancing inclusive growth. The extensive implementation of this is crucial, not only for its benefits but also for ensuring a thriving future for both people and the planet.

References

Bocken, N. M., De Pauw, I., Bakker, C., & Van Der Grinten, B. (2016). Product design and business model strategies for a circular economy. *Journal of Industrial and Production Engineering, 33*(5), 308–320.

Centobelli, P., Cerchione, R., Chiaroni, D., Del Vecchio, P., & Urbinati, A. (2020). Designing business models in circular economy: A systematic literature review and research agenda. *Business Strategy and the Environment, 29*(4), 1734–1749.

Chertow, M. R. (2000). Industrial symbiosis: Literature and taxonomy. *Annual Review of Energy and the Environment, 25*(1), 313–337.

Foroozanfar, M. H., Imanipour, N., & Sajadi, S. M. (2022). Integrating circular economy strategies and business models: A systematic literature review. *Journal of Entrepreneurship in Emerging Economies, 14*(5), 678–700.

Geissdoerfer, M., Savaget, P., Bocken, N. M., & Hultink, E. J. (2017). The circular economy—A new sustainability paradigm? *Journal of Cleaner Production, 143*, 757–768.

Kazancoglu, Y., Ozkan-Ozen, Y. D., Sagnak, M., Kazancoglu, I., & Dora, M. (2023). Framework for a sustainable supply chain to overcome risks in transition to a circular economy through industry 4.0. *Production Planning & Control, 34*(10), 902–917.

Khan, E. A., Chowdhury, M. M. H., Hossain, M. A., Mahmud, A. S., Baabdullah, A. M., & Dwivedi, Y. K. (2024). Performance of small firms in a circular economy: Configuring challenges and entrepreneurial orientation. *Management Decision, 62*(8), 2428–2450.

Lewandowski, M. (2016). Designing the business models for circular economy—Towards the conceptual framework. *Sustainability, 8*(1), 43.

Linder, M., & Williander, M. (2017). Circular business model innovation: Inherent uncertainties. *Business Strategy and the Environment, 26*(2), 182–196.

Mair, J., & Marti, I. (2006). Social entrepreneurship research: A source of explanation, prediction, and delight. *Journal of World Business, 41*(1), 36–44.

Murray, A., Skene, K., & Haynes, K. (2017). The circular economy: An interdisciplinary exploration of the concept and application in a global context. *Journal of Business Ethics, 140*, 369–380.

Peter, O., Pradhan, A., & Mbohwa, C. (2023). Industrial internet of things (IIoT): Opportunities, challenges, and requirements in manufacturing businesses in emerging economies. *Procedia Computer Science, 217*, 856–865.

Wang, Y., Gunasekaran, A., & Ngai, E. W. T. (2016). Big data in logistics and supply chain management: An overview. *International Journal of Production Research, 54*(1), 1–17.

CHAPTER 13

Navigating the Future of Sustainability Finance and Entrepreneurship

K. Devender, Kafila, M Rajyalaxmi, and A. Suresh Kumar

Abstract In order to enable a just and resilient future, this chapter examines the changing landscape of sustainability finance and entrepreneurship, highlighting the vital roles played by creative financing mechanisms, policy frameworks, digital technologies, and stakeholder collaboration. The allocation of funds to initiatives that produce long-term environmental, social, and governance (ESG) benefits is known as sustainability finance, and it has quickly evolved from a specialized investment approach to a necessary one. The allocation of capital has changed as a result of green bonds, impact investing, climate finance, and ESG integration, which have pushed businesses and startups to incorporate sustainability

K. Devender (✉) · Kafila · M. Rajyalaxmi
School of Business, SR University, Warangal, India
e-mail: devenderapple143@gmail.com

M. Rajyalaxmi
e-mail: laxmi.gunna@gmail.com

A. Suresh Kumar
Department of Management, College of Business and Economics, Oda Bultum University, Chiro, Oromia, Ethiopia

S. Trivedi et al. (eds.), *Green Ventures*, Sustainable Development Goals Series, https://doi.org/10.1007/978-981-95-6533-7_13

into their core values. Simultaneously, entrepreneurship motivated by sustainability is becoming more and more popular as a major force behind inclusive economic growth. More and more entrepreneurs are creating business plans that tackle urgent societal issues like waste management, poverty, gender inequality, and carbon emissions in addition to focusing on making a profit. A multifaceted framework that makes use of digital transformation, cross-sector cooperation, and financial innovation is essential to the future of sustainability finance and entrepreneurship. By enhancing transparency, traceability, and impact measurement, fintech solutions such as blockchain, artificial intelligence, and big data analytics are upending established financing models. These technologies give investors the ability to make data-driven decisions and give startups access to decentralized funding methods like tokenization and crowdfunding. Additionally, impact-oriented ventures are being mentored and scaled by sustainability-focused incubators, accelerators, and venture capital firms. This chapter also presents global case studies showcasing successful models of sustainability finance and entrepreneurship.

Keywords Sustainability finance · Impact investing · Green finance · ESG · Climate risk finance · SDG

1 Introduction

In the era of resource depletion, social injustice, and climate change, the intersection of entrepreneurship, sustainability, and finance has become a powerful driver of transformative change. Traditional business models focused on short-term financial gain are increasingly giving way to strategies that emphasize social impact, environmental stewardship, and long-term resilience.

Sustainable finance has emerged as a critical enabler in this transition, supported by instruments such as green bonds, ESG investing, impact finance, and climate-related risk assessments. These mechanisms help businesses address pressing global challenges while maintaining financial viability. Digital finance also plays an essential role in promoting sustainable energy growth (Chen, 2024). Furthermore, government policies increasingly encourage the integration of finance and technology to support innovation and sustainability (Du et al., 2025). Crowdfunding has likewise become a valuable tool for advancing social entrepreneurship, environmental sustainability, and collaborative innovation (Bongiorno et al., 2025).

Sustainable finance refers to the integration of environmental, social, and governance (ESG) considerations into financial decision-making. It encompasses a range of instruments and strategies, including green bonds, impact investing, climate risk assessments, and ESG-compliant portfolios, all designed to align financial outcomes with broader sustainability objectives.

"Entrepreneurs—particularly those championing social and environmental causes—are increasingly leveraging these financial tools to launch, grow, and scale businesses that are both profitable and impactful."

The digitalization of financial markets has sparked a move toward more responsible capital allocation (Devender et al., 2025), the emergence of conscious consumerism, and the growing interest of investors in sustainability. However, obstacles like restricted access to funding, unclear regulatory frameworks, and the requirement for quantifiable impact metrics are frequently encountered by entrepreneurs. The chapter offers a thorough grasp of how sustainability and entrepreneurship are combining to forge new economic avenues through a critical examination of current data and real-world case studies. It also highlights how crucial long-term planning, stakeholder cooperation, and financial literacy are to building a sustainable entrepreneurship ecosystem. Stakeholders can fully utilize finance as a force for good by negotiating this shifting landscape, which will spur innovation, further the Sustainable Development Goals (SDGs), and redefine the 21st-century enterprise's mission.

2 The Evolution of Sustainability Finance

Sustainability finance has evolved significantly over the past few decades, shifting from a niche concern to a central pillar of global financial markets. Initially, responsible investing focused on ethical considerations, such as excluding controversial sectors. Over time, this approach matured into Environmental, Social, and Governance (ESG) investing, emphasizing the integration of non-financial factors into decision-making processes, the main ideas and subjects in sustainable digital finance, as well as the continuous changes in the field and the revolution in digital sustainability (Bansal et al., 2025). The launch of green bonds in the early 2000s marked a pivotal moment, enabling capital flow toward environmentally beneficial projects. Regional sustainable economic growth is significantly influenced by educational equity (Liu & Li, 2025). More recently, innovations such as impact investing, sustainable index funds, and climate finance mechanisms have broadened the landscape. Global initiatives like the Paris Agreement and the United Nations Sustainable Development Goals (SDGs) have further accelerated the adoption of sustainability principles in finance. The development of digital finance significantly improves these commercial banks' ability to grow sustainably (Li et al., 2025). In today's more complicated and linked world, sustainability finance is acknowledged not only as a moral requirement but also as a force behind long-term value creation and risk reduction.

3 Key Elements of Sustainability Finance and Entrepreneurship

See Fig. 1.

3.1 Innovative Financial Instruments

Cutting-edge financial products are now effective instruments for promoting sustainability objectives and aiding business endeavors with an emphasis on social and environmental impact (refer Fig. 1). Green bonds, which enable businesses to raise money especially for eco-friendly projects like sustainable agriculture, energy efficiency, and renewable energy, are among the most well-known. In a similar vein, sustainability-linked bonds encourage borrowers to fulfill particular environmental, social, or governance (ESG) goals by connecting financial performance to quantifiable sustainability outcomes. It is possible to mainstream financial instruments that seek to increase land restoration efforts within the global financial system (Garvey et al., 2025). Another innovative strategy is impact investing, in which investors actively pursue both financial gains and favorable social or environmental effects. A wider range of investors now have democratized access to sustainable investment thanks to new climate fintech platforms that facilitate digital investment opportunities in carbon credits, clean energy startups, and ESG-focused funds. Furthermore, by bridging the gap between conventional operations and sustainable futures, transition bonds assist businesses in difficult-to-abate sectors as they progressively adopt greener practices. With their increased efficiency and transparency, innovations like blockchain-based carbon markets and

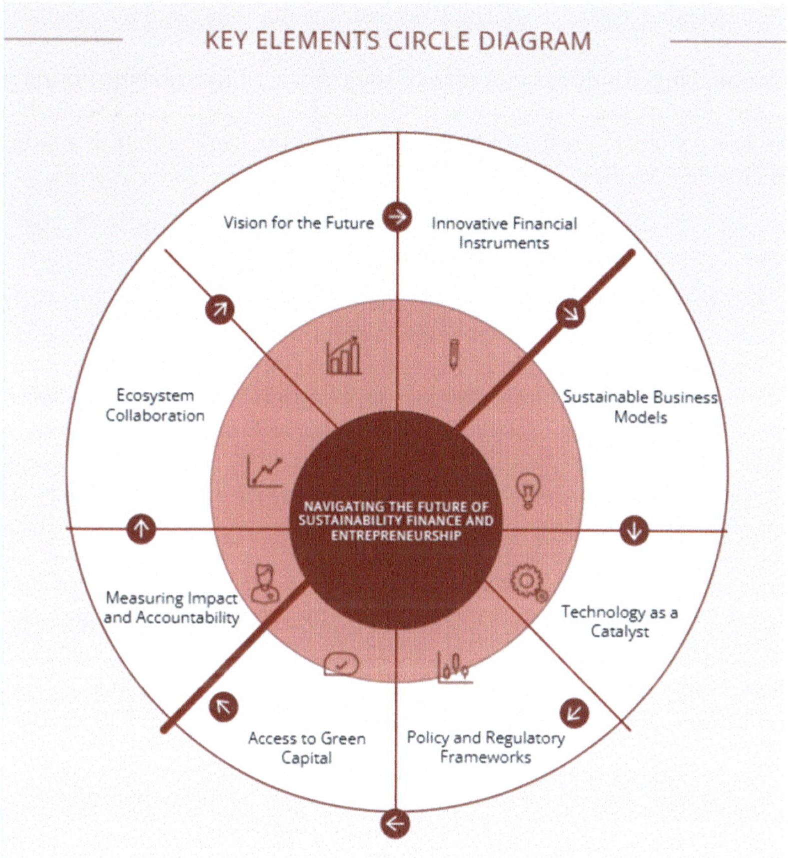

Fig. 1 Key elements of Sustainability finance and Entrepreneurship (Author's creation by using Visme.co)

tokenized green assets are also becoming more popular. One advantage of using financial instruments to meet environmental goals is that market forces ensure resource allocations that are generally more efficient than those brought about by public sector enterprise (Antoci et al., 2009). Green investment funds are being created by venture capital firms more frequently to support early-stage businesses that develop clean technology, circular economy solutions, and climate resilience. Future markets are anticipated to be dominated by instruments that combine financial innovation with strong ESG frameworks as investors demand greater accountability. All things considered, these financial instruments not only reroute funds toward environmentally friendly endeavors but also enable business owners to create solutions that propel the world's shift to a more sustainable economy.

3.2 *Sustainable Business Models*

By incorporating social, economic, and environmental factors into their core business strategies, sustainable business models aim to create long-term value (Manotti et al. 2025).Sustainable businesses prioritize minimizing their negative impacts on the environment, promoting social justice, and enhancing economic resilience more than traditional models, which focus solely on financial profit. One example is circular economy models, which minimize waste and extend product lifecycles by reusing, repairing, and recycling resources. Furthermore, regenerative business models strive to enhance and restore natural ecosystems as part of their operations (Beard & De Giacomo, 2025). Businesses that use shared value models create solutions that benefit the community and the company by balancing economic success with social advancement. A growing movement of companies dedicated to upholding high standards of social and environmental performance, accountability, and transparency is exemplified by certifications like B Corporations.

3.3 *Technology as a Catalyst*

The transition to sustainable finance and entrepreneurship is being accelerated largely by technology. It serves as a powerful enabler, allowing investors and companies to scale, innovate, and assess sustainability initiatives with unprecedented speed and accuracy. Across all industries, artificial intelligence (AI) enhances energy efficiency, forecasts environmental hazards, and optimizes resource management. Blockchain technology makes sustainability claims verifiable in real-time and enhances transparency and traceability, particularly in supply chains and carbon credit trading.

Businesses can better monitor ESG (Environmental, Social, and Governance) metrics with the help of big data analytics, leading to more accurate impact reporting and wiser investment choices. Homogeneous and uniformly distributed catalysts are the two categories into which catalysts fall (Ebrahimi & Bandehali, 2024). Climate fintech platforms in the financial industry facilitate sustainable investing by providing digital tools for impact assessments, green portfolio management, and carbon footprint tracking.

3.4 *Policy and Regulatory Framework*

One of the main forces influencing how sustainability finance and entrepreneurship develop in the future is the legislative and regulatory environment. Policies that incorporate environmental, social, and governance (ESG) factors into financial and corporate operations are being introduced by governments, international organizations, and regulatory agencies more frequently. Global accords such as the Paris Agreement and the Sustainable Development Goals (SDGs) of the United Nations have established challenging goals that motivate nations and sectors to embrace more environmentally friendly and inclusive practices.

3.5 *Access to Green Capital*

Businesses and entrepreneurs spearheading the shift to a sustainable economy must have access to green capital. Financial resources set aside expressly for businesses and projects that benefit the environment or society, such as clean technology, sustainable agriculture, renewable energy, and carbon reduction programs, are referred to as "green capital." Specialized tools like green bonds, sustainability-linked loans, and impact investment funds are increasingly being used in.

Conjunction with traditional financing methods to provide targeted support for projects with a sustainability focus (Becker et al., 2025). To support early-stage businesses that are advancing climate technology, circular economy solutions, and biodiversity conservation, venture capital (VC) firms and private equity investors are starting green funds. Peer-to-peer lending models and green crowdfunding platforms, on the other hand, are democratizing access to capital by allowing smaller business owners to communicate directly with impact-oriented investors.

3.6 *Measuring the Impact and Accountability*

A key element of sustainability finance and entrepreneurship is measuring impact and guaranteeing accountability. Businesses must put strong frameworks in place to evaluate and report on their environmental, social, and governance (ESG) performance since investors and customers alike are calling for greater transparency. Businesses can establish credibility with stakeholders and show their contributions to global sustainability goals by using accurate and transparent impact measurement (Wang et al., 2025). Impact metrics are expanding beyond conventional financial indicators to incorporate quantifiable results like the creation of social value, energy efficiency gains, or a decrease in carbon emissions. Standardized guidelines for reporting ESG data are provided by frameworks such as the Sustainability Accounting Standards Board (SASB), Global Reporting Initiative (GRI), and Integrated Reporting, which guarantee uniformity and comparability across industries.

3.7 *Ecosystem Collaboration*

In order to promote entrepreneurship in the green economy and advance sustainability finance, ecosystem collaboration is crucial. A business, government, or nonprofit organization cannot handle complex global issues like resource depletion, social inequality, and climate change alone in today's interconnected world. Synergies produced by successful cross-sector collaboration hasten the creation and expansion of sustainable solutions. PPPs, or public-private partnerships, are a major force behind ecosystem cooperation. Large-scale green projects, like infrastructure for renewable energy or sustainable agriculture programs, can be funded by governments and private organizations using their respective advantages—financial resources and policy expertise. Additionally, companies and startups can work together through innovation hubs and joint ventures, exchanging resources, technologies, and knowledge to promote sustainability.

3.8 *Vision for the Future*

Future developments in sustainability finance and entrepreneurship have the potential to drastically alter economies, societies, and industries. Businesses and investors are making sustainability a key element of their strategies as a result of the growing global awareness of environmental and social issues. ESG considerations will influence the investment choices of both major institutional players and regular consumers by 2030 and beyond, when sustainability finance will be completely incorporated into the mainstream financial markets. The green economy will grow, bringing with it new prospects in fields like waste management, clean technologies, sustainable agriculture, and renewable energy. Developments in circular economy models will encourage regenerative practices in all sectors of the economy, minimize resource extraction, and cut waste (refer Table 1).

4 Entrepreneurship in the Era of Sustainability

In the age of sustainability, entrepreneurship has changed to emphasize making money and having a positive social and environmental impact. The importance of entrepreneurs in promoting sustainable solutions has never been greater as the globe struggles with issues like social inequality, resource depletion, and climate change. By incorporating environmental, social, and governance (ESG) considerations into business plans, sustainable entrepreneurship seeks to maximize profits while advancing the global Sustainable Development Goals (SDGs). Consumer preferences for ethical goods and services are shifting, as evidenced by the rise of social entrepreneurs (Sadiq et al., 2025) and green businesses. Today's consumers are more aware of the social and environmental effects of the products they buy, which encourages businesspeople to develop new ideas in fields like waste management, renewable energy, fair trade, and circular economy models.

Significant innovation opportunities are also presented by sustainability-driven entrepreneurship (Ansari, 2025). Entrepreneurs are developing solutions that address societal issues like poverty, healthcare, and education, in addition to environmental problems. For example, startups in the circular economy space are turning waste into useful resources, and social entrepreneurs are creating accessible, clean energy solutions for rural communities. These businesses are committed to developing scalable solutions that benefit both society and the environment in addition to being profit-driven. Sustainable entrepreneurship is not without its difficulties, though. Since many investors still consider sustainability initiatives to be high-risk, access to capital is still a major obstacle. In addition, entrepreneurs have to deal with complex regulations, shifting market conditions, and the requirement for multidisciplinary expertise.

Table 1 Stakeholders and their roles in sustainability, finance, and entrepreneurship

Stakeholder	*Role/responsibility*	*Contributions to sustainability*	*Examples/initiatives*
Entrepreneurs	– Develop innovative, sustainable business models	– Drive solutions for social, environmental, and economic challenges	– Circular economy startups, climate-tech ventures
	– Focus on profit with purpose	– Launch projects in renewable energy, waste management, and sustainable agriculture	– Social enterprises addressing poverty and gender inequality
Investors (VC, Impact Funds)	– Provide financial capital for sustainability-driven businesses	– Fund projects with a focus on ESG impact, scalability, and market viability	– Clean Energy Venture Group, Impact Investment Funds
	– Ensure financial returns alongside social/environmental benefits	– Promote inclusive economic growth and innovation	– Green bonds, climate finance investments
Governments & Policymakers	– Set policies and regulations for green finance and business practices	– Create regulatory frameworks and incentives that support green investments	– EU Green Deal, Paris Agreement
	– Encourage public-private partnerships	– Facilitate access to sustainable funding through green banks or climate finance	– Tax incentives for renewable energy projects
Financial Institutions	– Develop financial products that integrate ESG factors	– Offer green bonds, sustainability-linked loans, and insurance for sustainable businesses	– Sustainable finance frameworks, ESG reporting guidelines
	– Integrate sustainability into core financial operations	– Increase accessibility to green financing options for businesses	– HSBC Green Bonds, Deutsche Bank's ESG investment strategies

Stakeholder	*Role/responsibility*	*Contributions to sustainability*	*Examples/initiatives*
Technology Providers	– Provide tech solutions for transparency, traceability, and data analysis – Support fintech innovation in sustainability finance	– Develop tools to enhance ESG data reporting, monitoring, and decision-making – Enable decentralized financing methods like crowdfunding and tokenization	– Blockchain for impact tracking, AI for ESG risk assessment – Ethereum-based carbon credits, AI-powered ESG tools
Academia & Research Institutions	– Conduct research and provide data on global sustainability challenges – Educate the next generation of leaders in sustainability	– Inform policy and business decisions with evidence-based research – Offer interdisciplinary training programs in sustainability and finance	– Sustainability-focused research centers, climate finance studies – University programs on sustainable entrepreneurship and finance
Civil Society & NGOs	– Advocate for sustainable practices and policies	– Raise awareness and influence	

5 Challenges and Barriers

See Fig. 2.

5.1 Financial Challenges: Access to Green Capital

A major financial obstacle for many businesses, especially small and medium-sized businesses (SMEs) and organizations in developing nations, is access to green capital (Funding designated especially for environmentally friendly projects, such as waste management, energy efficiency, renewable energy, and climate resilience programs, is referred to as "green capital" [refer Fig. 2]). Even though the global green finance market is growing, access is still restricted because of many enduring obstacles. High perceived risks by investors, strict lending requirements,

Fig. 2 Challenges and barriers (Author's creation by using Visme.co)

and the absence of collateral or credit history typically associated with smaller businesses are the main ones.

Furthermore, a lot of financial institutions demand thorough environmental, social, and governance (ESG) reporting, which can be difficult and expensive for companies with limited resources to implement. The lack of uniform classifications and definitions for what constitutes "green" makes funding opportunities even more challenging. Widespread adoption is hampered in developing nations by a lackluster financial infrastructure and a lack of knowledge about green finance tools like blended finance and green bonds (Subhani et al., 2025) As a result, there is still a sizable financial gap between the actual investment needs necessary to meet global sustainability targets and the green funds that are currently available. To close this gap, new financial tools, public-private partnerships, capacity-building programs, and legislative backing are needed to increase openness, lower risk, and facilitate access to green capital in all industries.

5.2 *Scaling a Sustainable Venture*

In order to scale a sustainable business, operations must be expanded while upholding a dedication to social, economic, and environmental responsibility. Sustainable business scaling, in contrast to traditional business scaling, requires striking a balance between expansion and the need to lessen ecological footprints and encourage long-term value creation for all stakeholders. Using green technologies, embracing the circular economy, and forming alliances with like-minded businesses to pool resources and knowledge are important tactics. Strong governance frameworks and the incorporation of sustainability into fundamental business operations, like supply chain management, product design, and customer interaction, are also necessary for effective scaling. Ventures can invest in the infrastructure, innovation, and talent required for responsible growth if they have access to sustainable finance (Del Gaudio et al., 2025) such as through green bonds, impact investments, or government incentives. Long-term scalability also depends on establishing trust with investors, consumers, and regulators, which is facilitated by open reporting on environmental, social, and governance (ESG) metrics. By increasing operational effectiveness, facilitating data-driven decision-making, and expanding market reach through online platforms, digital transformation is essential to scaling. In the end, a clear mission, flexible leadership, and the capacity to match profitability with purpose are essential for scaling a sustainable business. This guarantees that growth will eventually benefit people, the environment, and prosperity.

5.3 Regulatory Uncertainty and Market Volatility

Businesses encounter numerous obstacles due to market volatility and regulatory uncertainty (Liu et al., 2025), particularly those in developing sectors like renewable energy, fintech, and green technology. Regulatory uncertainty arises when regulations, standards, or compliance requirements are unclear, subject to frequent changes, or applied inconsistently. This situation discourages long-term investment and innovation by creating an unpredictable operating environment. Due to the potential for sudden regulatory changes that could impact their profitability, legal status, or operational viability, businesses may delay growth or reallocate resources. Conversely, market volatility refers to sudden and erratic fluctuations in demand, prices, or investor sentiment. It is often influenced by policy changes, inflation, economic cycles, and geopolitical events. Such volatility can disrupt supply chains, affect capital availability, and undermine consumer confidence for startups and sustainable ventures. When combined, these factors heighten financial risks and complicate strategic planning. Businesses must adopt agile strategies, enhance their risk management capabilities, and stay abreast of changing regulatory trends to mitigate these challenges. More stable and favorable regulatory frameworks can also be fostered through proactive ESG disclosures, participation in industry associations, and collaboration with legislators. Ultimately, promoting innovation, attracting investment, and facilitating sustainable economic growth all hinge on reducing regulatory ambiguity and market unpredictability.

5.4 Greenwashing and Ethical Concerns

In the context of sustainability, greenwashing—the practice of businesses misrepresenting their goods, services, or business practices as ecologically friendly—raises significant ethical questions. Some businesses take advantage of the growing demand for eco-friendly products and consumer awareness by making false environmental claims without taking meaningful action. Because of the confusion and skepticism this deception causes in the marketplace, it not only damages public trust but also undermines real sustainability efforts. Exaggerating environmental benefits, using ambiguous or unreliable environmental labeling, or revealing only positive effects while leaving out negative ones are examples of greenwashing. Transparency, accountability, and corporate social responsibility are all violated by such actions. Businesses that use sustainability as a marketing tactic rather than a fundamental operating principle, or that put image before impact, also raise ethical questions (Xiang et al., 2024). The effects of greenwashing are extensive. Misinformed consumers may unintentionally encourage unsustainable business practices, and moral businesses may encounter unfair competition. Additionally, environmental, social, and governance (ESG) claims are being scrutinized by investors and regulators more and more, and businesses that are caught greenwashing risk losing investors, legal repercussions, and harm to their reputation. Clearer sustainability standards, third-party certification, more stringent regulatory oversight, and a sincere corporate commitment to moral and open reporting are all necessary to combat greenwashing. Strategy must incorporate genuine sustainability, not just branding.

5.5 *Talent and Skills Gap*

A major obstacle to the expansion and prosperity of many contemporary industries—especially those centered on innovation, digital transformation, and sustainability—is the talent and skills gap. The demand for specialized skills, such as data analytics, renewable energy engineering, ESG reporting, and green finance, has surpassed the supply of qualified professionals due to the rapid evolution of industries. This disparity hampers organizations' capacity to innovate, scale, and successfully achieve sustainability goals. Research, implementation, and operational efficiency are hindered by a lack of qualified professionals in developing fields like clean technology and circular economy principles. Numerous educational establishments have yet to adapt their curricula to the changing demands of the market, leaving graduates without employable, industry-relevant skills. Global disparities in the green and digital workforce also stem from developing regions' limited access to professional development and technical training. A multi-stakeholder strategy is needed to close this gap, including funding for educational reform, upskilling and reskilling initiatives, industry-academic cooperation, and inclusive workforce development regulations. In addition, organizations must foster a culture of ongoing learning to adapt to rapidly evolving

Table 2 Key Statistics in Sustainability Finance and Entrepreneurship

Indicator	*Value/estimate*	*Source/year*
Global ESG Assets Under Management (AUM)	$41 trillion	Bloomberg Intelligence, 2022
Projected ESG AUM by 2025	$53 trillion	Bloomberg Intelligence, 2022
Global Green Bond Issuance	$575 billion	Climate Bonds Initiative, 2023
Share of SMEs Lacking Access to Green Finance	Over 70% in developing countries	World Bank, 2022
Estimated Green Financing Gap (Developing Countries)	$1.3 trillion/year through 2030	UNCTAD, 2023
Share of Startups with Sustainability Focus	42% (of global startups)	Startup Genome Report, 2023
Jobs Created by Green Startups (Global Estimate)	14 million (direct and indirect)	ILO & UNEP, 2023
Percentage of Companies Accused of Greenwashing	58% of sustainability claims deemed misleading	EU Commission Screening, 2021
Skills Gap in Sustainability Fields (e.g., ESG analysts)	67% of employers report difficulty hiring	LinkedIn Global Green Skills Report, 2023
Share of Global VC Funding for Climate Tech	14% of total venture capital	PwC State of Climate Tech, 2023

demands. Closing the talent and skills gap (Wodnicka, 2024) is not only vital for competitiveness but also critical for accomplishing more general goals related to economic and environmental sustainability (refer Table 2).

6 Emerging Trends in Sustainable Entrepreneurship

As global issues like resource scarcity, social inequality, and climate change necessitate creative and ethical business solutions, sustainable entrepreneurship is quickly developing (Shahzad & Xu, 2024). To create a value that is not only economic but also socially and environmentally beneficial, entrepreneurs are increasingly incorporating sustainability into the foundation of their business models (Vargas-Merino et al., 2025). The use of green technologies, such as waste-to-resource innovations, energy-efficient systems, and clean energy, is one notable trend. To increase transparency, cut waste, and better track environmental effects, entrepreneurs are utilizing blockchain, AI, and IoT. The growth of impact investing and green finance is another significant trend. In these cases, investors give equal weight to financial returns and environmental, social, and governance (ESG) factors, which increases the amount of money available for sustainable projects. International frameworks and governmental policies, like the Paris Agreement, are also having an impact on entrepreneurship by promoting low-carbon innovation and offering rewards for eco-friendly behavior. Businesses are being forced to adjust to circular economy models and sustainable supply chains as a result of shifting consumer behavior, which is characterized by a rise in the demand for moral, environmentally friendly, and socially conscious products. Peer-to-peer sharing platforms and product-as-a-service models show how ownership is giving way to access, which lowers overconsumption and encourages sustainability (Budumuru & Paruchuru, 2025). However, these trends present certain difficulties, such as scalability, capital access, and sustaining profitability while adhering to sustainable principles. The next wave of significant economic change will be led by entrepreneurs who match innovation with environmental and social impact as sustainability becomes a business necessity rather than a choice.

7 Future Directions of Sustainability Finance and Entrepreneurship

The intersection of policy, innovation, and the public's desire for responsible growth will influence sustainability finance and entrepreneurship in the future. Blockchain, artificial intelligence, and the Internet of Things are examples of digital technologies that have the potential to improve financial systems' transparency, ESG reporting, and climate risk assessment. New financial products like resilience funds, carbon credits, and green bonds will multiply as ESG and impact investing gain traction. Government incentives and changing consumer preferences will encourage entrepreneurs to embrace circular and regenerative business models. Crowdfunding and decentralized platforms are examples of inclusive finance mechanisms that will democratize access to capital, particularly in underserved areas. Global policy frameworks will simultaneously advocate for stronger disclosure laws and standardized sustainability metrics. In order to prepare future leaders to incorporate sustainability into finance and entrepreneurship, education and capacity building will be essential. All things considered, the upcoming ten years hold the promise

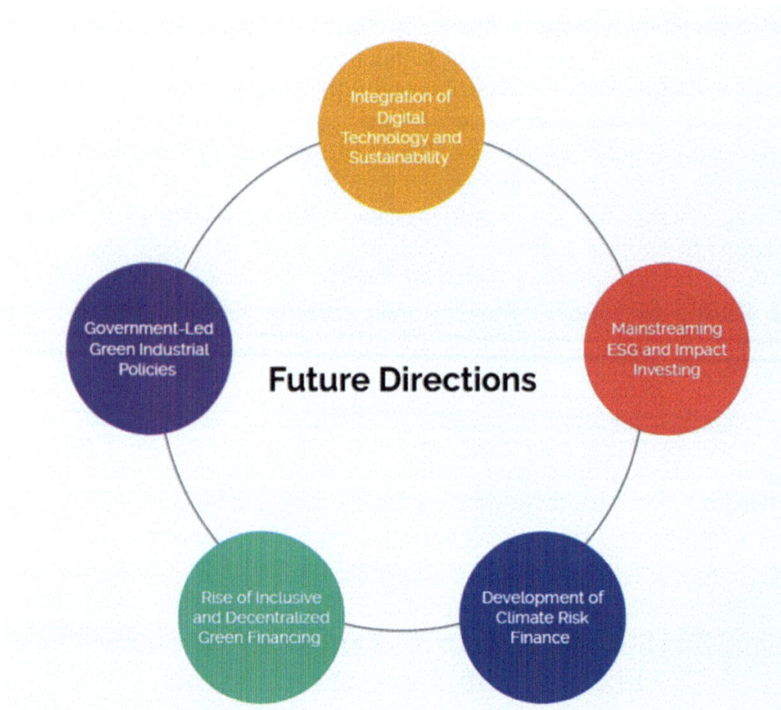

Fig. 3 Future directions of sustainability finance and entrepreneurship (Author's creation by using Visme.co)

of a revolutionary change toward a more sustainable and just economic environment (Fig. 3).

7.1 Integration of Digital Technology and Sustainability

Businesses' and financial systems' approaches to environmental and social issues are changing as a result of the integration of digital technology and sustainability (refer Fig. 3). Digital tools are facilitating innovation, accountability, and transparency in sustainability practices in addition to improving operational efficiency. By providing transparent, impenetrable systems that monitor environmental metrics like carbon emissions, supply chain sourcing, and ESG compliance, blockchain technology plays a critical role in lowering the likelihood of greenwashing. Big data analytics and artificial intelligence (AI) are being used to forecast climate impacts, evaluate environmental risks, and maximize resource use. These resources help people make more informed decisions about things like carbon offset plans, waste minimization, and energy use. AI, for example, can forecast equipment failures that may result in pollution or model the risks of deforestation.

7.2 Mainstreaming ESG and Impact Investing

Impact investing and environmental, social, and governance (ESG) criteria are emerging as key pillars in global finance, moving from optional to required practices. ESG investing entails assessing businesses' governance, social responsibility, and environmental impact in addition to their financial performance. Investors are calling for increased accountability and transparency from companies as social justice, climate change, and corporate ethics gain traction. By actively allocating funds to projects that produce quantifiable social and environmental benefits in addition to financial returns, impact investing goes one step further. This covers expenditures on inclusive education, sustainable agriculture, clean energy, and reasonably priced healthcare.

7.3 Development of Climate Risk Finance

In order to assist communities, governments, and businesses in adjusting to the financial effects of climate change, climate risk finance is quickly becoming a vital industry. In order to manage and reduce climate-related risks like resource scarcity, rising sea levels, and extreme weather events, this area focuses on raising capital. The goals of financial tools in this area are to support sustainable infrastructure, safeguard communities at risk, and provide funding for resilience. Climate resilience bonds, in which finance initiatives aimed at lowering climate vulnerabilities like flood defenses or drought-resistant infrastructure, are a crucial instrument in climate risk finance. The risk of natural disasters is also transferred from governments or businesses to the financial markets through the use of catastrophe bonds, or "cat bonds," which are used to raise money for disaster relief.

7.4 *Rise of Inclusive and Decentralized Green Financing*

A fundamental change in the way capital is raised for environmental sustainability can be seen in the emergence of inclusive and decentralized green finance. Large organizations and governments have historically held a dominant position in green finance. But thanks to crowdfunding and decentralized finance (DeFi) platforms, access to sustainable funding has become more accessible, allowing local communities, startups, and small businesses to take part in the green transition. Peer-to-peer financing systems are made possible by decentralized finance (DeFi), which uses blockchain technology to eliminate the need for conventional middlemen and enable individuals to invest directly in green projects. In addition to cutting expenses, this makes it possible for environmentally conscious businesses to use a more open, secure, and transparent financing model.

7.5 *Government-Led—Led Green Industrial Policies*

Green industrial policies spearheaded by the government are essential for quickening the shift to a sustainable economy. Governments can direct industries toward more environmentally friendly practices, lower carbon emissions, and develop a green economy by establishing regulatory frameworks, offering incentives, and encouraging innovation. To influence long-term economic and environmental results, these policies are crucial. Green subsidies and tax incentives are a crucial component of these policies, as they incentivize companies to implement eco-friendly technologies like electric vehicles, renewable energy systems, and energy-efficient manufacturing techniques. For instance, clean energy sectors have grown significantly as a result of subsidies for wind and solar energy installations.

8 Future Study

The evolving nexus of sustainability finance and entrepreneurship, several areas that remain underexplored and provide scope for future research. First, there is a need for more empirical studies that evaluate the long-term effectiveness of sustainable finance instruments, such as green bonds and impact investments, particularly in emerging economies. Second, the role of digital technologies—including blockchain, artificial intelligence, and decentralized finance—in enhancing transparency, accessibility, and accountability in sustainability finance requires deeper investigation.

Another promising direction lies in studying policy and regulatory frameworks across regions to understand how differences in governance structures influence the adoption of sustainable entrepreneurship practices. In addition, there is limited evidence on how small and medium-sized enterprises (SMEs) can overcome barriers to accessing green capital and integrate ESG principles into their operations. Research on innovative financing models tailored to SMEs could help bridge this gap.

Finally, future studies should focus on the social dimensions of sustainability finance, including its potential to reduce inequality, promote inclusive growth, and empower marginalized communities. Comparative case studies, longitudinal analyses, and cross-disciplinary approaches will be essential to advance both theoretical understanding and practical application in this field.

9 Conclusion

There are a lot of obstacles and exciting possibilities in the future of sustainability finance and entrepreneurship. There has never been a greater need for creative, sustainable solutions as environmental, social, and economic pressures increase on a worldwide scale. The financial feasibility and long-term advantages of integrating environmental, social, and governance (ESG) considerations into business plans and investment strategies are becoming more widely acknowledged by investors and entrepreneurs alike. The way companies track, report, and manage their environmental effects is being completely transformed by the increasing incorporation of digital technologies like AI, blockchain, and IoT into sustainability practices. In the meantime, the emergence of decentralized and inclusive financing models is democratizing capital access, allowing a range of actors to support the green transition, from local communities to small startups.

In response to climate-related risks, governments around the world are also taking action by enacting laws and providing incentives that support environmentally friendly infrastructure and businesses. The combination of these elements portends a time when sustainability will not only be a specialty but also a fundamental idea that underpins all commercial and economic endeavors. As we proceed, it is evident that entrepreneurship and sustainability finance will play a crucial role in accomplishing global climate goals, building resilient economies, and promoting an inclusive and sustainable future for everybody.

References

Ansari, M. S. A. (2025). Innovation and green entrepreneurship are catalysts for sustainability in Oman. *Cleaner Waste Systems, 11*(100281), Article 100281. https://doi.org/10.1016/j.clwas.2025.100281

Antoci, A., Dei, R., & Galeotti, M. (2009). Financing the adoption of environment-preserving technologies via innovative financial instruments: An evolutionary game approach. *Nonlinear Analysis, Theory, Methods & Applications, 71*(12), e952–e959. https://doi.org/10.1016/j.na.2009.01.077

Bansal, S., Kumar, S., Ali, S., Singh, S., Nangia, P., & Bamel, U. (2025). Harnessing digital finance for sustainability: An integrative review and research agenda. *Research in International Business and Finance, 74*(102682), Article 102682. https://doi.org/10.1016/j.ribaf.2024.102682

Beard, M. N., & De Giacomo, M. R. (2025). Which sustainable business model archetypes are more prevalent? An analysis of small and medium-sized enterprises. *Journal of Cleaner Production, 504*(145240), Article 145240. https://doi.org/10.1016/j.jclepro.2025.145240

Becker, A., Fatica, S., & Rancan, M. (2025). Not only green: Sustainability and debt capital markets. *Journal of International Money and Finance, 154*(103319), None. https://doi.org/10.1016/j.jimonfin.2025.103319

Bongiorno, G., Cardamone, E., & Passarelli, M. (2025). Navigating crowdfunding for sustainability: Practical implications mapped. *Finance Research Letters, 76*(106958), Article 106958. https://doi.org/10.1016/j.frl.2025.106958

Budumuru, U. R., & Paruchuru, M. (2025). Tracing the evolution of ecosystems in social entrepreneurship: Perspectives on innovation and sustainability. *Sustainable Futures, 100645*, Article 100645. https://doi.org/10.1016/j.sftr.2025.100645

Chen, Y. (2024). Navigating resource scarcity and digital finance solutions for a sustainable future in ASEAN. *Resources Policy, 98*(105317), Article 105317. https://doi.org/10.1016/j.resourpol.2024.105317

Del Gaudio, B. L., Lazos, A., & Previtali, D. (2025). Does equity crowdfunding enhance the survival of sustainability ventures? *Finance Research Letters, 75*(106919), Article 106919. https://doi.org/10.1016/j.frl.2025.106919

Devender, K., Kafila, Goli, G., & Shravan, M. (2025). Bibliometric trends in SMEs financial literacy research from 2021 to 2024. *Future Business Journal, 11*(1). https://doi.org/10.1186/s43093-025-00495-w

Du, Y., Liang, S., Ma, Z., & Xu, Z. (2025). The impact of technology finance pilot policies on the quality of urban entrepreneurship in China. *Pacific-Basin*

Finance Journal, 102785, Article 102785. https://doi.org/10.1016/j.pacfin.2025.102785

Ebrahimi, A. A., & Bandehali, S. (2024). A review paper: Recent advances in catalysts for desulfurization of fuel oil by ODS technology. *Journal of Industrial and Engineering Chemistry*. https://doi.org/10.1016/j.jiec.2024.12.054

Garvey, J., Grigoriadis, V., Flannery, D., Knapp, E., Gold, E., Hutchinson, G., Frewer, L. J., Brereton, P., & Byrne, K. A. (2025). Designing financial instruments for land-based ecological restoration: A review and future research Agenda. *Cleaner Production Letters, 8*(100089), Article 100089. https://doi.org/10.1016/j.clpl.2024.100089

Li, Q., Zhong, Z., & Ge, Q. (2025). Digital finance and sustainable development of commercial banks; insights from listed commercial banks. *International Review of Financial Analysis, 104*(104209), Article 104209. https://doi.org/10.1016/j.irfa.2025.104209

Liu, J., & Li, J. (2025). Educational equity, inclusive finance, and sustainable economic growth. *Finance Research Letters, 77*(106966), Article 106966. https://doi.org/10.1016/j.frl.2025.106966

Liu, Y., Yi, S., Li, S., & Chen, G. (2025). Asymmetric impacts of energy market-related uncertainty on clean energy stock volatility: The role of extreme shocks. *International Review of Financial Analysis, 103*(104206), Article 104206. https://doi.org/10.1016/j.irfa.2025.104206

Manotti, J., Sanasi, S., & Ghezzi, A. (2025). Sustainable business model innovation: A technology affordance perspective in the New Space Economy. *Tech Novation, 143*(103226), Article 103226. https://doi.org/10.1016/j.technovation.2025.103226

Sadiq, M., Pham Thi, T. D., Nguyen, C. M., & Do, H.-D. (2025). Sustainable entrepreneurship and knowledge management: Role of green information technology in building sustainable entrepreneurial ecosystems. *Journal of Innovation & Knowledge, 10*(3), Article 100689. https://doi.org/10.1016/j.jik.2025.100689

Shahzad, M. F., & Xu, S. (2024). Antecedents of international entrepreneurship and emerging technologies help to achieve sustainable development goals: Moderating role of global mindset. *Technological Forecasting and Social Change, 209*(123831), Article 123831. https://doi.org/10.1016/j.techfore.2024.123831

Subhani, B. H., Zunhuan, S., & Khan, M. A. (2025). Finance for a Greener future: Evolving the financial sector for ESG and sustainable corporate debt management. *Borsa Istanbul Review*. https://doi.org/10.1016/j.bir.2025.01.011

Vargas-Merino, J. A., Rios-Lama, C. A., Bello-Mamani, D. X., & Panez-Bendezú, M. H. (2025). Sustainable entrepreneurship in HEIs. A systematic review from the perspective of higher education in business. *The International Journal of Management Education*, *23*(2), 101137. https://doi.org/10.1016/j.ijme.2025.101137

Wang, L., Qin, D., & Pan, L. (2025). The impact of accountability for illegal operation and investment on investment efficiency of SOEs: Evidence from China. *Economic Analysis and Policy, 86*, 731–748. https://doi.org/10.1016/j.eap.2025.04.007

Wodnicka, M. (2024). Skills gap and new technologies: Bibliometric analysis. *Procedia Computer Science, 246*, 3430–3436. https://doi.org/10.1016/j.procs.2024.09.214

Xiang, Y., Chen, L., Zhang, Z., & Sun, X. (2024). Does perceived greenwashing promote or inhibit ethical voice? Effects of moral disengagement and perceived competitive pressure. *Journal of Business Research, 182*(114793), Article 114793. https://doi.org/10.1016/j.jbusres.2024.114793

CHAPTER 14

Navigating the Future: Synergies of Sustainability, Finance, and Entrepreneurship

Shyam Sunder Agrawal, Nitin Goyal, Chandni Keswani, Veena Grover, and Amanjot Singh Syan

Abstract This chapter critically examined the intersection of sustainability, finance, and entrepreneurship in advancing global climate objectives, with specific reference to Sustainable Development Goal 13 (Climate Action). It explored how sustainable finance mechanisms and entrepreneurial innovations evolved in the decade following the 2015 Paris Agreement to support low-carbon development and economic

S. S. Agrawal (✉) · N. Goyal
Mittal School of Business, Lovely Professional University, Phagwara, Punjab, India
e-mail: shyamsunderagrawal8@gmail.com

C. Keswani
Department of Management, Shri Vaishnav Institute of Management and Science, Indore, India

V. Grover
Department of Management, Llyod Business School, Greater Noida, UP, India

S. Trivedi et al. (eds.), *Green Ventures*, Sustainable Development Goals Series, https://doi.org/10.1007/978-981-95-6533-7_14

resilience. While each domain had been studied extensively, there remained limited research on their combined impact in catalyzing climate action. To address this gap, a systematic literature review was conducted using the PRISMA methodology. Peer-reviewed academic publications from 2015 to 2025 were sourced from Scopus, Web of Science, and Google Scholar. From an initial pool of 412 articles, 61 were included based on relevance to climate finance instruments, sustainable business models, and SDG 13. The review identified three dominant thematic clusters: the emergence of green and impact-driven entrepreneurship, the growing integration of ESG (Environmental, Social, and Governance) criteria into investment decision-making, and the expanding role of digital technologies and fintech in democratizing access to sustainable finance. The findings indicated that climate-focused ventures, particularly in renewable energy, circular economy, and clean technology, played a pivotal role in supporting climate goals. Financial instruments such as green bonds, carbon credits, and climate venture capital were found to be key enablers, though challenges persisted in access to capital, regulatory stability, and policy coherence. The chapter contributed both theoretically and practically by proposing an integrative framework and offering recommendations for building inclusive financial ecosystems that support sustainable entrepreneurship as a driver of long-term climate resilience.

Keywords Sustainable entrepreneurship · Climate action · PRISMA · Green finance · SDG 13 · ESG Investment · Green Innovation

1 Introduction

1.1 Background and Context

The urgency of addressing climate change has intensified in recent years, as mounting evidence of global warming and environmental degradation continues to emerge. Climate action (SDG 13) stands for the need for

A. S. Syan
Department of Management, Canadore Stanford International College, North Bay, ON, Canada

immediate and coordinated efforts to reduce greenhouse gas emissions and to build resilience against climate-induced disasters while mainstreaming climate considerations into development policies at the national level (Iqbal et al., 2021). Theoretically, increased threats related to climate disturbances threaten ecosystems, human health, and economic stability, thus making it more critical than ever to find integrated solutions (Sharma et al., 2025).

Since the adoption of the Paris Agreement in 2015, the world has embarked on a transformative journey to decarbonize economies and promote sustainable development. The Agreement, signed by almost 200 countries, emphasized the limitation of the global temperature rise to well below 2 °C and aspired with the affirmation not to cross 1.5 °C above pre-industrial levels. This paved the way for change in policy discourse, corporate strategy, and societal behavior in favor of long-term environmental sustainability (Dote-Pardo et al., 2025).

In response, there has been a global shift toward sustainability in economic practices. There are actually three important reasons for all these changes. First, markets themselves are changing, what with all the new innovations popping up in technology and finance. Investors are taking a stronger interest in ESG factors and considering these in their decision making. Green finance thus essentially moves money towards environmentally beneficial projects (Watson et al., 2023). At the same time, the business environment is starting to consider sustainability. This gives impetus to the emergence of green startups, renewable energy projects, branded recycling companies, and commercial projects for eco-friendly consumer products (Rahman & Hossain, 2025).

This convergence among sustainability, finance, and entrepreneurship has become a powerful triad towards counteracting climate change and fostering sustainability. Even with their advancement, a comprehensive understanding of how those fields interact synergistically is lacking in academic literature. This chapter finds this gap by a thorough study of the integrated potential for these domains in support of climate action (Zhang, 2024).

1.2 Purpose and Scope of the Chapter

The chapter investigates the concepts of sustainability, finance, and entrepreneurship about their leverage on the global climate goals under SDG 13.The individual domains have produced climate solutions, but the combined force for the transformational change possibilities relating to climate change has not been sufficiently probed or mapped (Otanazarova, 2025).

This chapter examines how the sustainable finance mechanisms, in combination with entrepreneurial innovation, can create market-scale responses to climate change. This chapter analyzes the development of tools of green finance, such as climate bonds, impact investing, and ESG-oriented capital allocation, as well as the entrepreneurial models emphasizing environmental sustainability and resilience. Combining insights across these fields, it attempts to map the main mechanisms whereby capital mobilization and entrepreneurial innovation can be leveraged together to mitigate and adapt to climate challenges (Bals & Tate, 2017).

Conversely, the chapter seeks to integrate an understanding of how these domains combine to strengthen and enliven ecosystems for climate-responsive economic development. The analysis is based on empirical evidence derived from a review of the extant literature, primarily focused on events between the years 2015 and 2025 (Parikh et al., 2021), during which period global commitment to climate goals increasingly takes shape.

1.3 Research Objectives

The main objective of this study is to review and assess the integrative potential of entrepreneurship and sustainable finance in advancing climate action. Especially, the study aims to:

- To examine how sustainability, finance, and entrepreneurship intersect in advancing climate action.
- To analyze the role of sustainable finance in supporting climate-resilient entrepreneurial ventures.
- To explore green and impact entrepreneurship as drivers of low-carbon innovation.
- To identify financial instruments that enable climate-aligned business models.
- To evaluate barriers hindering sustainable entrepreneurship and climate finance integration.
- To propose a framework linking financial flows to entrepreneurial efforts for climate mitigation and adaptation.

Through these objectives, the chapter intends to formulate theoretical and practical insights into the manner in which cross-sector collaboration and innovation may be leveraged for low-carbon, inclusive, and resilient economic development (Hussain et al., 2024).

2 Review of Literature

2.1 Evolution of Sustainability in Economic and Business Contexts

Sustainability, as a principle of development, has seen distinct evolution and enrichment since the late twentieth century. Initially, it was part of the ecological discourse and gradually evolved into carrying the Three Pillars interconnected with the concept of sustainable development: environmental integrity, social equity, and economic viability. The concept gained wide resonance after the Brundtland Report (1987), which offers a model of sustainable development balancing the needs of the present with those of future generations (Sungkawati, 2024).

For a long time, sustainability has been considered a peripheral concern. It has now risen to central strategic imperatives. According to the World Business Council for Sustainable Development (WBCSD), the confluence of sustainability in the business world has evolved beyond mere legal compliance to embrace innovation, risk management, and competitive advantage. More than 90% of the S&P 500 companies already disclosed sustainability or ESG metrics by 2023, and so it is going mainstream (Avevor et al., 2023).

Environmental dimensions address climate adaptability, protection of biodiversity, and the judicious use of natural resources. The social dimension opposes cultures, beliefs, and standards on labor rights, community welfare, and inclusiveness. From an economic viewpoint, a solution implements profitability without destroying environmental or social systems. This tight interlinkage of these three dimensions becomes even more critical when dealing with SDG 13, for climate action cannot be separated from its broader sustainability goals (Tien et al., 2019).

“As it comes today, Sustainability intersects with corporate governance and global investment trends and thus serves as the basis for new financial instruments and business models. With mounting carbon pricing, increasing environmental regulation, and an ever-growing demand for ethically compliant consumer products, sustainability spells business opportunity, as well as regulation” (Cezarino et al., 2022). Nowadays, enterprises must go beyond mere compliance and display climate responsibility through the transparent reporting of impacts and value creation within planetary boundaries.

2.2 Overview of Sustainable Finance

Sustainable finance incorporates environmental, social, and governance (ESG) issues in the decision-making frameworks surrounding financial products and services. It acts as a channel that promotes capital allocation toward projects and enterprises that generate positive environmental and social outcomes, and, of course, financial returns. The rise of sustainable finance is a reflection of the need for large-scale funding of climate action and green transitions (Ammirato et al., 2025).

Sustainable investment assets globally reached over $35 trillion in 2022, representing over one-third of the total global assets under management, with projections estimating the figure to reach $50 trillion. One of the significant trends in this development has been the expansion of ESG investing. Various Institutional investors incorporate ESG factors to analyse the long-term risks, specifically in the case of climate change, resource depletion, policy changes, and regulatory changes (Petrariu et al., 2021).

The following key instruments of sustainable finance are as:

- Green Bonds: These are fixed-income securities earmarked for projects with environmental benefits, focusing on climate change, green practices like renewable energy, energy efficiency, and clean transportation. The green bond market has exceeded $600 billion in the year 2023, reflecting strong growth and appetite for climate-aligned investments.
- Climate Finance: This broader category includes public and private financial flows intended to support climate mitigation and adaptation, especially in developing countries. The United Nations Framework Convention on Climate Change (UNFCCC) estimates that global climate finance must exceed $4.3 trillion annually by 2030 to meet the 1.5 °C target (Jin et al., 2022).
- Impact Investing: This refers to investments made to generate measurable environmental or social impact alongside financial returns. According to the Global Impact Investing Network (GIIN), the market reached $1.2 trillion in assets in 2022, with significant

allocations in clean energy, sustainable agriculture, and affordable housing (Bamiro et al., 2023).

Financial institutions are focusing and aligning their services, like portfolio management, with net-zero targets, and central banks are also integrating climate stress testing into regulatory frameworks. However, despite these advancements, challenges remain. Standardization of ESG metrics, greenwashing concerns, and uneven regional adoption are ongoing issues. Furthermore, access to sustainable finance for early-stage ventures and entrepreneurs, particularly in the Global South, remains limited, which hampers inclusive climate innovation (Moşteanu, 2023).

2.3 Entrepreneurship in the Context of Climate Innovation

Entrepreneurship has emerged as a vital mechanism for accelerating climate innovation and achieving SDG 13. Unlike large corporations constrained by legacy systems, startups and small and medium-sized enterprises (SMEs) often possess the agility, creativity, and risk appetite necessary for pioneering low-carbon solutions. These ventures are driving advances in clean energy, carbon capture, waste-to-energy systems, and nature-based solutions, often filling gaps left by traditional actors (Tantalo & Priem, 2016).

According to the OECD (2023), SMEs contribute over 50% of employment and over 60% of GDP in many economies. Their involvement in green innovation is crucial for achieving inclusive and decentralized climate transitions. Furthermore, the International Finance Corporation (IFC) highlights that green entrepreneurship in emerging markets can generate over $23 trillion in investment opportunities by 2030, particularly in sustainable infrastructure, climate-smart agriculture, and resource efficiency (Tien et al., 2023).

Green entrepreneurship, specifically, refers to business activities that prioritize environmental sustainability while generating economic value. These ventures do not merely adopt green practices; they embed sustainability into their core value proposition. For example, companies like Clime Works (carbon capture), Lilium (electric aviation), and Agrosmart (precision agriculture) exemplify how entrepreneurship can address complex climate challenges through scalable innovation (Zournatzidou, 2025).

Eco-innovation, a related concept, involves the development of products, services, or processes that reduce environmental impact and optimize the use of resources. It extends beyond technological innovation to include business model transformation, such as sharing economies and circular value chains. A growing body of research links eco-innovation with enhanced firm performance, improved stakeholder relations, and increased resilience to climate shocks (Frone et al., 2020).

Government policy also plays a critical role in enabling climate entrepreneurship. Startup incentives, green procurement, climate tech incubators, and public-private partnerships have proven effective in countries such as Germany, South Korea, and the Netherlands (Ed-Dafali et al., 2025). However, early-stage funding gaps persist, especially for ventures in the Global South, where climate vulnerabilities are acute, but entrepreneurial ecosystems remain underdeveloped.

Moreover, the role of digital platforms and fintech in supporting green entrepreneurship has gained traction in recent years. Crowdfunding platforms, blockchain-enabled carbon markets, and decentralized finance (DeFi) applications are democratizing access to capital for climate-oriented startups. These tools lower entry barriers and enhance transparency, especially in sectors traditionally overlooked by conventional finance (Simanjuntak, 2024).

In summary, the literature underscores that entrepreneurship, particularly when aligned with sustainable finance, is indispensable for achieving a climate-resilient future. Startups and SMEs, empowered by innovative financial instruments and policy frameworks, can catalyze systemic change across industries. However, unlocking this potential requires coordinated efforts to address financial, regulatory, and infrastructural constraints (Peng, 2024).

2.4 Contribution of SDG 13

Sustainable Development Goal 13 mobilizes for urgent action to combat climate change and its impacts and has therefore become one of the urgent concerns for world policymakers, businesses, and communities. Climate change is not farther away; it is here and now. It disrupts economies, threatens food and water security, and sees an increasing frequency of extreme weather events. According to the Intergovernmental Panel on Climate Change (IPCC), the world is already 1.1 °C warmer versus pre-industrial levels, and without bold and coordinated interventions, global temperatures could rise beyond the critical threshold of 1.5 °C in the coming 10 years (Sungkawati, 2024). In 2023 alone, more than 40 million people were displaced by climate events, and the global economic losses have exceeded $250 billion. These alarming trends are enough to show us that the old ways are not going to work anymore. We need solutions that are based on sustainability, facilitated by new finance, and driven by entrepreneurship. This chapter is closely connected to SDG 13, looking at green ventures and climate-aligned investment as a gap towards long-term resilience and low-carbon growth (Walker et al., 2019). The chapter affirms that entrepreneurship can act as an engine for environmental innovation, whereas sustainable finance makes sure that capital to nurture these solutions is both available and inclusive. By looking into how these elements interact with each other, the chapter offers a fresh perspective on how cross-sector efforts and systemic thinking can move the world closer to meeting its climate goals through practical, scalable action (Kroll et al., 2019).

2.5 Research Gap

2.5.1 Theoretical Research Gap

The integration of sustainability, finance, and entrepreneurship remains theoretically fragmented, despite each domain being supported by well-established bodies of knowledge. Existing theories in sustainability focus primarily on environmental and policy outcomes, financial theories emphasize risk-return paradigms and capital allocation, while entrepreneurship literature often centers on innovation and firm-level dynamics (Toromade & Chiekezie, 2024). However, there is a clear absence of comprehensive frameworks that cohesively link these three domains to address climate action, particularly under SDG 13. Furthermore, although technology has been widely acknowledged as a catalyst in both finance and entrepreneurship, through digital platforms, fintech innovations, and scalable business models, its role in advancing sustainability within entrepreneurial ventures is under-theorized. This gap limits our understanding of how digital finance tools and eco-innovations can jointly enable inclusive, climate-resilient business ecosystems (Chirambo, 2018). As highlighted in Table 1, the current literature falls short in examining how sustainable finance mechanisms support green entrepreneurship, especially in emerging economies, and in exploring how cross-sectoral and technological synergies can bridge systemic gaps. This chapter responds to these deficiencies by proposing an integrative lens that combines theory and practice to better understand the synergies of sustainability, finance, and entrepreneurship in advancing global climate goals (Kroll et al., 2019).

2.5.2 *Practical Application Gaps*

One important gap in the literature is that little research has been done on sustainable entrepreneurship in the context of developing economies, where often the climate vulnerability is greatest and access to funding is most constraining. More scholarly attention has been focused on developed countries, ignoring the very different institutional, infrastructural, and socio-economic challenges that bear on the nature of the sustainability-finance-entrepreneurship intersection in less developed regions (Raimi et al., 2025). The role of policy and regulatory frameworks in either facilitating or hindering this intersection is even less examined. Governmental policies determine financial incentives, market access, and environmental accountability, yet there is virtually no existing literature to help us understand if and how those policies support or hinder the emergence of climate-resilient entrepreneurial ecosystems. These gaps show the need to better understand the differences between regions and institutions in global talks about sustainability(Watson et al., 2023).

2.6 *Conceptual Framework*

The conceptual framework (Fig. 1) that was developed represents the triadic relationship of sustainability, finance, and entrepreneurship as an ever-evolving and interdependent ecosystem, necessary for advancing climate action vis-à-vis SDG 13 (Shah et al., 2025). This framework was developed from the idea that sustainability, finance, and entrepreneurship have all grown into separate disciplines, with considerably stronger potential when they collaborate toward common goals, share resources, or coordinate their strategies. The sustainability axis works from climate and environmental goals; finance works toward directing capital flows toward green objectives, and entrepreneurship works on its innovation to develop scalable solutions to climate problems (Schaltegger et al., 2018).

Thus, sustainable finance supports new businesses with green goals, which return the favor by developing and advancing sustainable finance. Technology, policies, and cross-sectoral teamwork accelerate outcomes for

Table 1 Research gap

Theme	*Existing knowledge*	*Limitations in existing literature*	*Research gap addressed*
Sustainability & Climate Action (SDG 13)	Sustainability is recognized as a multidimensional goal aligned with SDG 13 for climate action	Studies often focus on policy or environmental science with limited integration into financial and entrepreneurial systems	Lack of holistic frameworks connecting sustainability directly with financial and entrepreneurial interventions for climate goals (Ince, 2021; Zhyvko & Vivchar, 2023)
Sustainable Finance	Green bonds, ESG investing, and climate finance are widely studied as tools for promoting environmental responsibility	Insufficient linkage to entrepreneurial ecosystems; often analyzed from a macro-financial or institutional perspective	Limited understanding of how sustainable finance mechanisms support startup-level or grassroots green innovation (Morched & Jarboui, 2025; Toromade & Chiekezie, 2024)
Entrepreneurship for Climate Innovation	Green and impact entrepreneurs are recognized as key drivers of eco-innovation and circular economy solutions	Lacks exploration of financial enablers and constraints; fragmented focus on specific sectors or geographies	Need for an integrated study of how entrepreneurship interfaces with climate-aligned finance to produce scalable solutions (Peng, 2024; Sharma et al., 2025)
Interdisciplinary Integration	Dual intersections (e.g., sustainability & finance, finance & entrepreneurship) have been moderately explored	Rare to find research that connects all three—sustainability, finance, and entrepreneurship—in one coherent analysis	Absence of integrative models capturing the synergistic dynamics among sustainability, finance, and entrepreneurship (Rahman & Hossain, 2025; Satiti et al., 2024)
Geographic Scope	High-income regions dominate the literature on climate finance and entrepreneurship	Emerging economies and their unique institutional-financial barriers are underrepresented	Need for inclusive analysis that considers regional disparities and access to finance for green entrepreneurs in the Global South (Otanazarova, 2025; Saqib et al., 2024)
Digital Finance & Innovation Platforms	Fintech and digital finance are recognized as tools to increase access to funding and scale sustainable solutions	Underexplored in terms of how they democratize sustainable finance for climate-focused entrepreneurship	Lack of research on the role of digital platforms in linking climate entrepreneurs with sustainable finance opportunities (Kusnanto, 2022; Shah et al., 2025)

Source Author's Creation

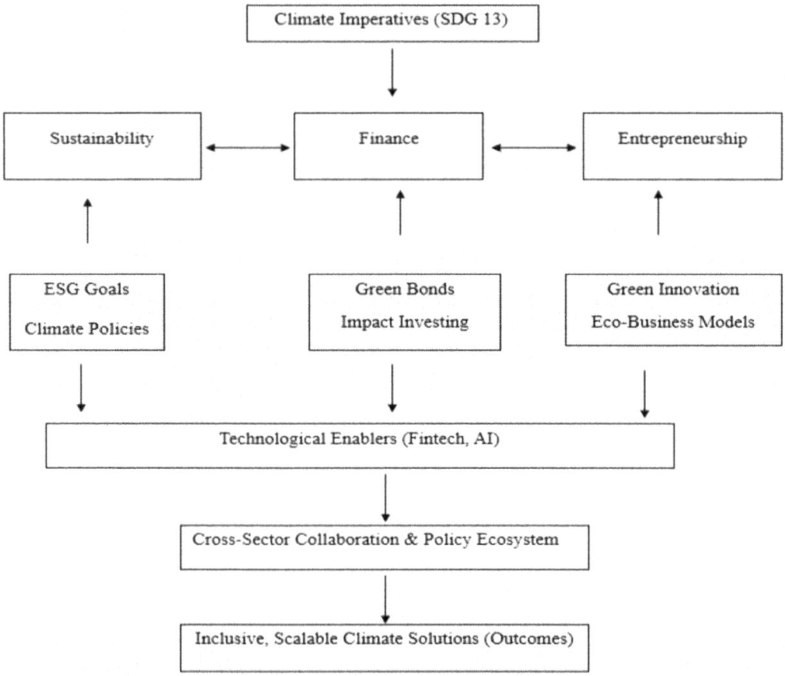

Fig. 1 Conceptual framework (*Source* Author's Creation)

climate action when the three components, like sustainability, finance, and entrepreneurship come together (Grosu et al., 2022). New-age digital-finance platforms, blockchains, and AI tools ease access to funding for small-scale green businesses, especially in developing countries. On the other side, there are various rules and incentives on the part of the government and private agencies to prioritize long-term investment in climate action(Ali, 2021). In this sense, it is possible to see a paradigm in which climate goals are incorporated into a business that sustains both the planet and the businessman. Further, endorsing the idea that actual sustainable development does not come through sporadic efforts but rather through the creation of a system that integrates economic innovation, environmental conscientiousness, and access to finance for all (Campos, 2021; Ziolo et al, 2021).

3 Methodology

This chapter utilized a method called Systematic Literature Review (SLR) to analyze in detail the way sustainability, finance, and entrepreneurship have been correlated in literature between 2015 and 2025. This review followed the PRISMA guidelines to maintain a transparent, well-structured, and repeatable process (Ed-Dafali et al., 2025). Such an approach helps in pinpointing the most relevant articles, diminishes bias, and methodically organizes the showings. Besides that, the procedure helps to identify deserving developments, gaps, and patterns of scholarship. The main objective was to amalgamate existing academic discourse on the forged intersection of these three areas toward climate action, especially under the framework of Sustainable Development Goal 13: Climate Action. The review consisted of four phases: search strategies, selection process, inclusion-exclusion criteria, and data collection and analysis (Anh et al., 2022).

3.1 Search Strategy

To conduct a thorough literature review, research was conducted in three well-known academic databases: Scopus, Web of Science, and Google Scholar. These databases were chosen because they offered research papers, conference articles, and scholarship on sustainability, finance, entrepreneurship, and climate-related studies. Our main focus was on papers between 2015 and 2025. This particular period was chosen as the Paris Climate Agreement had been signed in 2015. It is a major action where countries worldwide agreed to strengthen steps concerning climate change, which consequently affected economic and environmental decisions made all over the globe.

The search strings were formed using a combination of Boolean operators. Keywords such as "sustainable entrepreneurship," "climate finance," "green innovation," "ESG investment," "low-carbon business models," and "climate action" were combined with operators like AND, OR, and NOT to broaden and ease the refinement of results like ("sustainable finance"OR "green finance") AND ("entrepreneurship" OR "startups") AND ("climate action"OR "SDG 13"). Search results had to be filtered to keep only English-language articles so that the interpretations of the papers were deemed consistent. The initial search gave a total of 412 items in all three databases.

3.2 *Screening Process*

This screening process was conducted transparently with steps that only allow for the inclusion of the most relevant and highest-quality studies. Articles were first checked for any relevance to at least one of the three key topics- sustainability, finance, or entrepreneurship if irrelevant, they were removed, which constituted 117 articles. Then, for a better grasp of developments after the Paris Climate Agreement, only publications between 2015 and 2025 were retained, eliminating another 39. The non-English articles were excluded next in the list, which accounted for a reduction of 34. Then another 41 articles were scrapped that focused too narrowly on local issues with no global value. After that, duplicates and those irrelevant to the main topics, such as unrelated technology or environmental issues, were removed at a further cost of 64. Subsequently, articles only relating to at least two of the three core topics were retained to ensure stringent relevance to the study. In this stringent process, 61 articles of high quality remained, warranting review and analysis (refer Table 2).

3.3 *Inclusion and Exclusion Criteria*

The inclusion and exclusion criteria were carefully explained in Table 3 and applied during the screening process. We have applied several filters for this screening.

3.4 *Data Extraction and Assessment*

Following the detailed screening, data from the final pool of 61 selected articles (Fig. 2) were meticulously extracted and analyzed to ensure close alignment with the chapter's core themes: sustainability, finance, and entrepreneurship. Each article was reviewed to lay down the basis for capturing its main features, such as authors, year of publication, geographic focus, methodological approach, theoretical framework applied, and main findings (Ding et al., 2022). Thus, the papers were classified into thematic groups following the trends in the discussion: green and sustainable entrepreneurship, ESG investing arrangements and their impacts, climate finance mechanisms such as green bonds, climate venture capital, and carbon credit markets, tech-powered financial service innovations such as fintech and blockchain, and regulation and policy affecting green enterprise and finance (Sagar, 2023).

Table 2 Articles included in review based on high citations

Journal name	*Number of documents*	*Area of interest*	*Total citations*
Journal of Cleaner Production	1	Corporate Social Responsibility in Emerging Markets	157
Technological Forecasting and Social Change	1	Behavioral Entrepreneurship and SDGs	684
Organization & Environment	1	Business Models for Sustainability	289
Sustainability (MDPI)	2	Digital Finance and Entrepreneurship Synergies	110
International Journal of Entrepreneurial Venturing	1	Collaborative Entrepreneurship for Sustainability	91
Strategic Management Journal	1	Stakeholder Synergy and Value Creation	189
Palgrave Communications	1	SDGs: Trade-offs and Synergies	1065
Journal of Islamic Marketing	1	Halal Entrepreneurship and Islamic Finance	787
Energy Policy	1	Environmental Innovations and Financial Development	141
Journal of Open Innovation: Technology, Market, and Complexity	1	Governance, Finance, and Technology Synergy	597

Source Author's Creation

The above classification facilitated a coherent and elaborated synthesis of insights while allowing for dissecting the articles with a view to chapter objectives and the spotted research gaps, such as the lack of integrative frameworks and the underrepresentation of developing economies. A quality assessment was also conducted, where the methodological soundness, conceptual contribution, and policy implications were addressed (Sungkawati, 2024). Studies lacking even in empirical evidence or clear theoretical anchoring would be excluded to uphold the analytic rigour. This cautious method ensured that the chapter is constructed on solid and diversified research studies. It assists in providing a comprehensive and

Table 3 Inclusion and exclusion criteria

Criteria	*Inclusion*	*Exclusion*
Publication Period	Articles published between 2015 and 2025	Articles published before 2015 or projected beyond 2025
Language	English only	Non-English language articles
Peer Review	Peer-reviewed journal articles and conference papers	Non-peer-reviewed sources (blogs, news articles, opinion pieces)
Core Themes	Studies addressing at least two of the three: sustainability, finance, and entrepreneurship	Articles focusing only on unrelated environmental or business issues
Geographic Coverage	Studies with global or regionally diverse contexts (including developing economies)	Studies with a narrow or purely local focus without broader relevance
Research Type	Empirical, conceptual, or review-based research	Technical papers without policy, financial, or entrepreneurial context
Accessibility	Full-text available	Abstract-only or inaccessible content

Source Author's Creation

concise understanding of how the relationship between finance, sustainability, and entrepreneurship can foster climate action, as described by Sustainable Development Goal 13 (Triguero et al., 2017).

4 Findings and Discussion

The findings reveal that researchers have focused their academic interest on the intersection of sustainability, finance, and entrepreneurship, particularly after the 2015 Paris Agreement. As clearly mentioned in Fig. 3, the number of high-citation studies significantly increased between 2018 and 2023, reflecting a shift in research focus towards climate-compatible innovation and green financial instruments. Most studies in these papers focus on ESG integration, green startup ecosystems, and the role of financial products in supporting low-carbon development. This trend shows both the relevance and urgency of interdisciplinary approaches to addressing SDG 13 through entrepreneurial finance (Zhang, 2024).

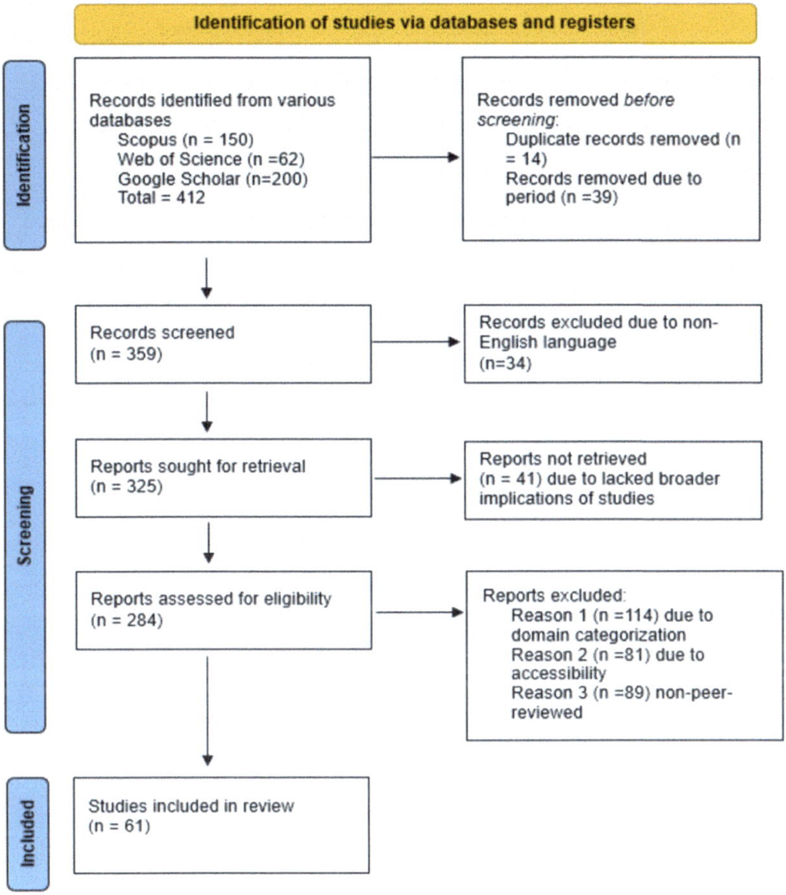

Fig. 2 PRISMA framework

4.1 Green and Impact Entrepreneurship

Green and impact entrepreneurship is rapidly becoming a cornerstone of the global shift toward sustainable development, particularly in sectors such as renewable energy, clean water access, biodiversity conservation, sustainable agriculture, and the circular economy (Sievers & Vandenberg, 2007). According to the Global Entrepreneurship Monitor (GEM) 2023, nearly 22% of new ventures globally are driven by environmental or social

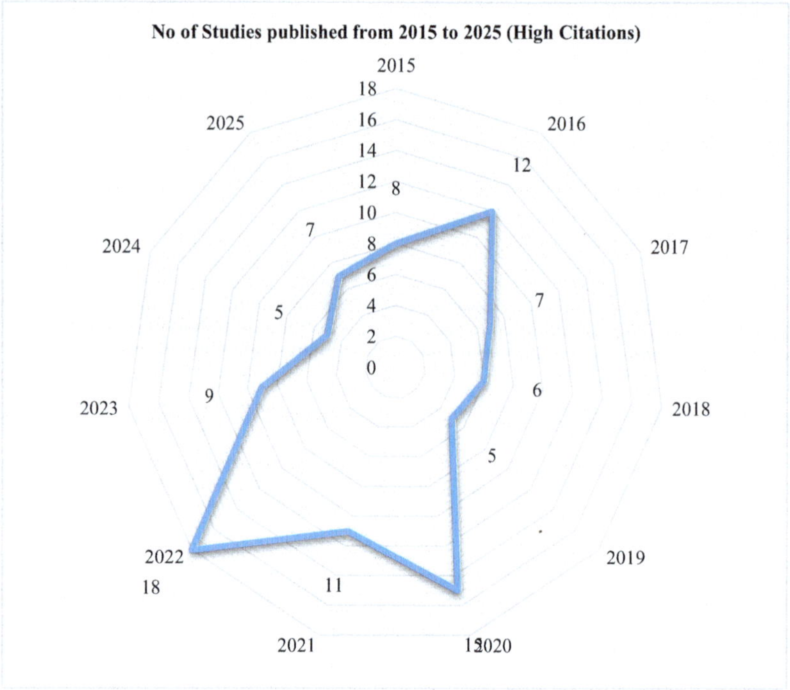

Fig. 3 Number of Studies published from 2015 to 2025 (High Citations) (*Source* Author's Creation)

missions, a sharp rise from a decade ago. In regions such as sub-Saharan Africa and Southeast Asia, green entrepreneurship has gained traction through locally driven innovations, solar-powered irrigation systems in Kenya or plastic-to-fuel conversion startups in Indonesia, for instance, catering to pressing environmental needs while generating livelihoods. These ventures often operate in resource-constrained environments and rely on frugal innovation, agile business models, and community-based approaches (Rehman et al., 2025). Recent evidence suggests that startups with a clear mission, especially those attempting to solve local environmental problems or climate risks, often receive stronger customer loyalty and community support. More recently, impact entrepreneurs use sustainability certifications such as B Corp or Fair Trade to instill trust in their enterprises and further attract investment from investors interested in social and environmental impact. This coalesces with the ever-increasing number of special programs like Clean Energy Accelerator and Climate-KIC supporting climate and sustainability-focused businesses (Woolford & Lalanne, 2024).

4.2 ESG Integration in Financial Decisions

The integration of Environmental, Social, and Governance (ESG) criteria into financial decision-making has shifted from a niche consideration to a mainstream expectation. By 2024, global assets under management (AUM) aligned with ESG principles surpassed USD 41 trillion, according to Bloomberg Intelligence, signaling strong investor demand for sustainable investment options (Das & Rangarajan, 2020).

ESG-aligned investing is no longer limited to equity markets—it now extends to private equity, venture capital, and even sovereign wealth funds. Research indicates that startups with embedded ESG practices are more resilient to market shocks and better positioned to attract long-term investors. For instance, enterprises that implement clear climate risk disclosures and inclusive governance structures often outperform their peers in capital access and stakeholder engagement (Khalid, 2023). In regions like the EU, regulatory frameworks such as the Sustainable Finance Disclosure Regulation (SFDR) are compelling fund managers to integrate ESG due diligence and reporting, creating a cascading effect on how ventures structure their governance, supply chains, and environmental strategies. The uptake of ESG is also shaping entrepreneurial ecosystems: incubators and accelerators now offer ESG mentorship, and banks are offering preferential loan terms for ventures that meet ESG benchmarks. Notably, ESG is gaining momentum in emerging economies through regional taxonomies and sustainability-linked loans, though inconsistencies in standards remain a challenge (Zhyvko & Vivchar, 2023).

4.3 Digital Platforms and Fintech for Sustainable Finance

Digital finance is revolutionizing the landscape of sustainable entrepreneurship by reducing barriers to entry, enhancing transparency, and improving capital flows to underserved segments. Fintech innovations, such as peer-to-peer (P2P) lending, tokenized green assets, and AI-driven ESG analytics, are making climate finance more inclusive and accountable (Walker et al., 2019). A 2023 World Bank report highlighted that over 70% of green fintech solutions in developing countries directly address issues of accessibility and transparency in environmental financing. Blockchain technologies are now being used to authenticate green bond use-of-proceeds, ensuring that funds are directed toward genuine climate-aligned projects. According to research, platforms like Sun Exchange and Trine gatekeep investments into solar energy projects in communities lacking electricity, thus opening climate investments to the general population. Mobile money tools are also closing the gap for complementary access to money between men and women, especially in rural areas (Xetor & Mensah, 2025). Some examples of mobile money facilitation might include M-KOPA, allowing a low-income family in East Africa to pay for a clean energy system in tiny instalments through their mobile phones. Climate fintech is also employed to track environmental impact, audit claims of carbon offset, and supply real-time scores on ESG (Environmental, Social, and Governance), thereby giving useful insights both to investors and business owners. In brief, these digital tools are coming to the rescue of financing, while facilitating fairness, inclusiveness, and efficiency for climate-conscious businesses (Schaltegger et al., 2016).

4.4 Financial Instruments Enabling Sustainable Ventures

Currently, the financial markets started to create special instruments to promote eco-financing. One of the popular instruments is green bonds (Kroll et al., 2019). The bonds are a kind of loan that raises money for specific projects which benefit the environment, such as solar power, eco-friendly transport, or green buildings. According to the Climate Bonds Initiative (2024), during the year 2023, there has been a trilling issuance amount, USD 1.2 trillion, of green bonds across the globe, with backing from both developed and developing countries. Developed countries like China, Germany, and India have now initiated government-backed green bond programs and are encouraging further investments from both the public and private sectors to combat climate change (Otanazarova, 2025).

Climate venture capital (CVC) is another fast-growing mechanism. Global climate-tech VC investment surged to USD 70.1 billion in 2022, reflecting increasing investor confidence in early-stage green startups. These funds often target scalable solutions in sectors like clean energy, sustainable agriculture, and carbon removal technologies. Notable funds include Breakthrough Energy Ventures and Low-Carbon Capital, which combine financial backing with strategic mentoring (Hussain et al., 2024).

Carbon credits provide market-based incentives for emission reductions. Verified carbon markets, especially voluntary markets, have grown rapidly, allowing entrepreneurs to monetize emissions saved through sustainable practices. However, the credibility and transparency of these markets remain areas for improvement, with new international frameworks (such as Article 6 of the Paris Agreement) aiming to standardize them (Clausen & Rudolph, 2020).

Blended finance, which combines public funds or development finance with private capital, is increasingly used to de-risk climate investments. This approach has mobilized billions for sustainable infrastructure in the Global South (Tsvetkova et al., 2020). The Global Impact Investing Network (2023) reports that blended finance deals have grown by 15% annually, particularly in sub-Saharan Africa and South Asia. Institutions like the Green Climate Fund and the IFC are actively leading such models to unlock private sector participation in climate action. Together, these instruments are not only supporting the transition to low-carbon economies but also redefining the relationship between financial markets and sustainability outcomes (Zaki et al., 2025).

4.5 *Barriers to Scaling Sustainable Entrepreneurship*

Sustainable entrepreneurial development experiences major growth obstacles that remain challenging despite financial tool advancements. The funding gap stands as the primary concern among all issues. Global South sustainable startups face severe difficulties in obtaining early investment because they lack investor connections and have minimal collateral, and have insufficient market proof. According to World Economic Forum research from 2022, only 6% of climate funds target adaptation projects for vulnerable populations, which demonstrates an incompatibility between available funding and essential requirements for these communities (Zournatzidou, 2025).

The presence of regulatory ambiguity introduces new levels of intricate operations. Business owners experience challenges due to unpredictable governmental regulations that lead to inconsistent application of green incentives or subsidies and create political debates on carbon pricing mechanisms. The Indian and United States markets face investor and consumer behavior fluctuations because of their changing electric vehicle subsidy programs. Developing countries suffer from insufficient legal structures to support green finance while also ignoring proper land use regulations and emissions trading systems that prevent investment opportunities (Tien et al., 2023).

Investors face significant difficulties in understanding climate risks as a major challenge. Traditional investment models remain focused on immediate profits and demonstrate a lack of proper valuation for environmental and social achievements. The majority of investors struggle to understand green technologies while considering them too risky to invest because of extended payback durations and regulatory standard changes (Sharma et al., 2025). When companies lack standardized ESG reporting systems, it becomes challenging for investors to evaluate sustainability claims through comparisons and validation procedures, which results in decreased confidence levels. The lack of capacity-building resources, together with technical knowledge restrictions, prevents entrepreneurs from demonstrating their ventures as both sustainable and ready for investment.

4.6 Discussion: Toward a Systemic Shift

To address these challenges and fully realise the potential of sustainable finance and entrepreneurship, a systemic change in the financial logics and institutional behaviour is needed. Old school paradigms based solely on risk and return will now be required to integrate a third dimension: impact. Forward-thinking investors and institutions are starting to embrace this "risk-return-impact" framework. As they are increasingly integrating sustainability measures in their portfolio management decisions, with 74% according to MSCI (2024), they are increasingly aware of the relative environmental risks and opportunities in the long term (Dhahri et al., 2021).

But this change entails more than investment strategy; the entire entrepreneurial ecosystem must be reconfigured. This can include policy and educational outreach, financial literacy programs, and the introduction of inclusive digital addressing to further the reach of climate ventures at all stages (Chirambo, 2018). There are many reasons that this is happening, with cross-sector collaboration being particularly important as the key enabler of this change. Collaborations among governments, multilateral organisations, private investors, academic institutions, and civil society are facilitating the construction of ecosystems promoting innovation, mitigating risk, and aligning motives (Ince, 2021).

There are successful models (like the UNDP's Climate Promise or the EU's Green Deal, and regional programs like India's Startup20 Green Energy Corridor) where the public and private sector can come together to achieve a common purpose on climate change. These collaborations improve resource mobilization as well as policy coherence, sharing of knowledge, and integrated development approaches (Hudon & Huybrechts, 2017).

In a nutshell, achieving sustainable development through entrepreneurship and finance requires a new mindset, one that values resilience, equity, and ecological balance alongside profitability. Only then can we build inclusive economic systems that are truly equipped to meet the challenges of a changing climate.

4.7 Statistical Evidence Supporting the Framework

Table 4 gives a deeper and clearer view of statistical evidence, matched with the framework. It includes global data as well as key facts from specific countries. Each data point is also explained to show how it supports your framework (Peng, 2024).

4.7.1 Sustainability and Climate Imperatives (SDG 13)

The adoption of net-zero targets by 149 countries represents a major global shift toward climate responsibility. These targets are not symbolic, they influence national policies, institutional investment mandates, and the direction of entrepreneurial innovation. In countries like the UK, Germany, and India, net-zero laws have triggered large-scale green funding programs, mandatory climate disclosures, and sectoral roadmaps aligned with SDG 13 (Glemarec et al., 2024).

4.7.2 Entrepreneurship and Green Innovation

Green entrepreneurship is growing not just in volume but in strategic importance. In many climate-vulnerable regions such as sub-Saharan Africa and Southeast Asia, these ventures are responding to local challenges with high-impact solutions. From solar-powered irrigation in Kenya to biodegradable packaging startups in Vietnam, these businesses reflect a deep integration of environmental goals within their market models. They also demonstrate strong community engagement, gender

Table 4 Statistical evidence supporting the framework

Framework component	*Indicator/metric*	*Value/statistic*	*Selected country examples*	*Source*
Sustainability (SDG 13: Climate Action)	Number of countries with net-zero targets	149 countries have net-zero pledges, covering 88% of global emissions	UK: Net-zero by 2050; India: Net-zero by 2070; Germany: Net-zero law passed with annual climate budgets	UNFCCC, Net Zero Tracker (2023) (Saqib et al., 2024)
Entrepreneurship (Green & Impact Startups)	Share of startups globally focused on environmental or social missions	22% of global entrepreneurial activity is environmentally or socially driven	Kenya: 30% of new ventures are climate-focused (Kenya Climate Innovation Center); Germany: strong focus on circular economy startups	Global Entrepreneurship Monitor (GEM) (2023)
Green Bonds	Global issuance of green bonds annually	USD 1.2 trillion issued in 2023	China: USD 131 billion (largest issuer); France: USD 42 billion; India: USD 8.5 billion in sovereign green bonds in 2023	Climate Bonds Initiative (2023)
Impact Investing	Size of global impact investing market	USD 1.2 trillion in assets under management	USA: Home to 45% of all impact funds; Netherlands: Leading in ESG-aligned pension fund investment	GIIN, Impact Investing Survey (2022)
ESG Integration in Investment	ESG-aligned global AUM	USD 41 trillion (33% of total global AUM)	EU: SFDR implementation increased ESG transparency; Japan: GPIF mandates ESG in pension fund allocation	Bloomberg Intelligence (2024)

Framework component	*Indicator/metric*	*Value/statistic*	*Selected country examples*	*Source*
Fintech for Sustainable Finance	Share of fintech platforms targeting green financing in developing economies	70% of green fintech tools address financial inclusion and sustainability in low-income regions	Nigeria: PayGo solar startups using mobile payments; India: Fintech-driven microloans for water access and clean cookstoves	World Bank, Green Fintech Report (2023)
Carbon Credit Markets	Value of the voluntary carbon market	USD 2 billion in 2023	Brazil: Voluntary forest-based offsets; Indonesia: Blue carbon credit pilots; USA: Regulated California Cap-and-Trade market	McKinsey & Company, VCM Insights (2023)
Blended Finance Mobilization	Total capital mobilized via blended finance for climate goals	USD 70 billion cumulative from 2016–2022	Bangladesh: IFC-GCF energy access program; Rwanda: Blended fund for climate-resilient agriculture	OECD & Convergence Blended Finance (2023)
Climate Policy Ecosystems	Countries with national green finance or climate investment strategies	Over 60 countries with formal frameworks	UK: Green Finance Strategy; India: Sustainable Finance Roadmap by RBI; South Africa: National Green Finance Taxonomy	UNEP FI, UNDP (2023)

(continued)

Table 4 (continued)

Framework component	*Indicator/metric*	*Value/statistic*	*Selected country examples*	*Source*
Climate-Tech Job Creation	Jobs created in the renewable energy and climate-tech sectors	13.7 million global jobs in clean energy and climate tech	China: 4.7 million jobs in renewable energy; USA: 800,000; EU: Over 1.3 million (IRENA projection to 2030: 38 million jobs)	IRENA Renewable Energy & Jobs Report (2023)
Cross-Sector Collaboration	Climate innovation projects supported by public-private-academic partnerships	44% of climate-tech projects involve at least one public-private-academic collaboration	EU: Horizon Europe Green Deal program; USA: ARPA-E public-private research; Kenya: Innovation hubs backed by universities and donors	International Energy Agency (IEA), EIC (2022)

Source Author's creation

inclusion, and circularity principles—key features that distinguish them from traditional SMEs (Jin et al., 2022).

4.7.3 *Finance and Capital Mobilization*

The financial landscape has shifted significantly to accommodate sustainability goals. Green bond issuance surpassed USD 1.2 trillion in 2023, while ESG-aligned investment accounts for one-third of total global AUM. Countries like China, France, and India are actively scaling sovereign and corporate green bonds. Meanwhile, impact investing and blended finance tools are channelling capital into underfunded regions and sectors, often backed by multilateral institutions like the IFC and GCF (Simanjuntak, 2024).

4.7.4 *Technological Enablers (Fintech, Blockchain, AI)*

Technology is no longer a support function; it is a driver of transformation in sustainable finance. Platforms such as blockchain-enabled carbon tracking and AI-driven ESG scoring tools are providing real-time, verifiable impact data to investors and regulators. In emerging economies, fintech is helping green ventures overcome legacy banking barriers by offering tailored credit, pay-as-you-go models, and decentralized investment networks (Shabbir, 2018).

4.7.5 *Policy Ecosystems and Cross-Sector Collaboration*

The strength of a climate-responsive ecosystem lies in its ability to align policy, capital, and innovation. More than 60 countries now have national green finance strategies, and many are backed by active public-private partnerships. Programs like Horizon Europe and India's GIFT City initiative highlight how academia, industry, and government can co-develop financial instruments and regulatory sandboxes that encourage climate-aligned entrepreneurship at scale.

4.7.6 *Outcomes: Scalable, Inclusive Climate Solutions*

The evidence is already visible. Clean energy alone has generated 13.7 million jobs globally, and climate tech continues to attract record levels of startup funding. Inclusive financial models are bringing green products and services to marginalized communities, especially through mobile banking and pay-as-you-go solar services (Ma et al., 2018). These outcomes not only validate the framework but reinforce the argument that sustainability, finance, and entrepreneurship must work in synergy to achieve meaningful, lasting climate action.

5 Implications

5.1 Theoretical Implications

This study offers a novel theoretical contribution by presenting an integrative framework that connects sustainable entrepreneurship with the broader climate finance ecosystem. While sustainability, entrepreneurship, and finance have been extensively studied in isolation, there remains a lack of cohesive theory that explains how these domains interact dynamically. By situating sustainable ventures as key actors in climate finance (Satiti et al., 2024), the framework bridges gaps between entrepreneurial theory and climate policy literature. It emphasizes how financial mechanisms, such as green bonds, ESG investment vehicles, and blended finance, create enabling environments for entrepreneurial innovation in response to environmental imperatives (Rahman & Hossain, 2025). Drawing from systems thinking, the framework outlines how actors (entrepreneurs, financiers, governments, and civil society) interact through feedback loops, incentives, and shared climate goals. It also introduces the concept of "finance-enabled ecological entrepreneurship" to describe ventures that are financially viable and environmentally impactful, with adaptive business models designed to align with emerging climate policies and investor expectations. This theoretical positioning supports future empirical inquiry into the co-evolution of financial tools and sustainable business practices under climate stressors (Osman & Elamin, 2023).

5.2 Practical Implications for Stakeholders

The results indeed provide a series of clear and practical guidelines for most actors in sustainable business. Policymakers should institute stable and transparent regulations to curtail investor uncertainty and to encourage long-term investments in climate-friendly businesses via measures like tax-based incentives and green grants (Morched & Jarboui, 2025). Investors, particularly socially oriented ones, should endeavor to tailor financial products to the special risk of early-stage green startups, using tools such as catalytic capital and first-loss guarantees to channel larger sums of finance into these investments (Parikh et al.,

2021). Entrepreneurs should consider using digital finance and alternative sources of funding, like green crowdfunding and tokenized assets, along with aligning operational procedures with global standards such as the Task Force on Climate-related Financial Disclosures (TCFD) for greater transparency and investor confidence. The study, in general, proposes that collaboration and concerted efforts among all stakeholders would catalyze climate finance and green businesses that are capable of scaling successfully (Kroll et al., 2019).

5.3 Policy and Ecosystem Development

Climate-responsive entrepreneurship really does require coordinated ecosystem development facilitated through multi-sectoral collaboration. Public-private-academic partnerships, combining research expertise, government support, and private capital, could become innovation incubators (Iqbal et al., 2021). For instance, Mission Innovation and Climate Launchpad demonstrate how cross-sector consortia can build a vital ecosystem to accelerate the commercialization of green technologies through funding, mentorship, and market access. The study underscores that national policies should integrate entrepreneurship within their climate agenda and therefore should support startup ecosystems that somehow quantify environmental performance in their business-building processes (Dote-Pardo et al., 2025). In fact, governments can further enable this by establishing open innovation platforms and knowledge-sharing networks interlinking universities, clean-tech startups, financial institutions, and policymakers. The policy environment should also assure global equity by laying down policies for supporting climate entrepreneurs in the Global South, especially through concessional finance, capacity-building, and infrastructure development. By infusing sustainability into the epicenter of entrepreneurial ecosystems, these partnerships can drive economies along low-carbon growth trajectories while ensuring resilient and inclusive development (Bamiro et al., 2023).

6 Conclusion

This chapter conducted a systematic literature review (SLR) by the PRISMA method to follow a transparent and structured approach in selecting and analyzing sources. Research articles published between 2015 and 2025 were extracted from the sources acknowledged internationally, including Scopus, Web of Science, and Google Scholar, by using Boolean operators to combine keywords relating to sustainable entrepreneurship, climate finance, green innovation, ESG investing, and fintech. After thorough scrutiny and thematic filtration, 61 studies were selected for having been of a high quality and being reflective of recent trends, theoretical advancements, and policy perspectives (Ali, 2021).

7 Summary of Key Findings

This chapter examined the complex intersection of sustainability, finance, and entrepreneurship within the context of global climate imperatives. The findings demonstrate that sustainable entrepreneurship is emerging as a critical pathway for achieving climate innovation, particularly through ventures that integrate environmental objectives with viable economic models. Such enterprises not only introduce green technologies and practices but also foster inclusive development, especially in vulnerable regions. The chapter further reveals how a growing array of financial instruments, such as green bonds, ESG investments, climate venture capital, and fintech solutions, are enabling these low-carbon entrepreneurial ventures by reducing funding barriers and enhancing investment flows. The strategic use of finance as a lever for sustainability is reshaping risk-return paradigms and accelerating the transition toward climate-resilient economies.

7.1 *Contributions of the Chapter*

This chapter contributes to the academic discourse by addressing critical gaps in the integration of theories from sustainability, finance, and entrepreneurship. Through a systematic literature review and the development of a conceptual framework, the study brings an interdisciplinary lens to understanding how financial innovation and entrepreneurial dynamics converge to support climate goals. It introduces a practical model that can be utilized by scholars and practitioners alike to evaluate or design interventions in climate-aligned business ecosystems. By doing so, the chapter not only advances theoretical knowledge but also offers actionable insights for policymakers, investors, and entrepreneurs working at the intersection of these domains.

7.2 Future Research Directions

Future research should aim to empirically validate the conceptual framework presented in this chapter, particularly by applying it across different socio-economic and regulatory contexts. Comparative studies between developed and developing economies would yield valuable insights into the adaptability and impact of financial tools in fostering sustainable entrepreneurship. Additionally, more region-specific investigations are needed to understand localized challenges, policy gaps, and innovation potential. Exploring how digital finance platforms and emerging technologies like blockchain are adopted in diverse entrepreneurial ecosystems would further enrich the discourse and inform global policy and investment strategies aimed at climate action.

References

Ali, M. (2021). A systematic literature review of sustainable entrepreneurship with thematic analysis. *World Journal of Entrepreneurship, Management and Sustainable Development, 17*(4), 742–764.

Ammirato, S., Felicetti, A. M., Filippelli, S., & Maran, T. (2025). Navigating paradoxical tension: The influence of big corporations on startup sustainability performance in asymmetric collaborations. *Review of Managerial Science, 19*(3), 843–870.

Anh, D. B. H., Duc, L. D. M., Yen, N. T. H., Hung, N. T., & Tien, N. H. (2022). Sustainable development of social entrepreneurship: Evidence from Vietnam. *International Journal of Entrepreneurship and Small Business, 45*(1), 62–76.

Avevor, M., Attionu, G. T., Osahor, D., Azonuche, T., & Tawo, O. (2023). *Beyond funding: rethinking small business administration strategies and public-private partnerships for minority-owned business resilience* (AI, FinTech, and Policy Synergy).

Bals, L., & Tate, W. L. (2017). What hybrid business models can teach sustainable supply chain management: The role of entrepreneurs' social identity and social capabilities. *Social and environmental dimensions of organizations and supply chains: Tradeoffs and synergies* (pp. 259–282). Springer International Publishing.

Bamiro, N. B., Zakariya, Z. B., & Nasiru, B. A. (2023). Development of halal entrepreneurship framework through business incubator service for sustainability using PRISMA. In *Contemporary discourse of halal and Islamic entrepreneurship* (pp. 79–97).

Campos, J. D. S. (2021). Analysis of entrepreneurial leadership skills and sustainable employee productivity of MSMEs. *Journal of Social Entrepreneurship Theory and Practice, 1*(1), 12.

Cezarino, L. O., Liboni, L. B., Hunter, T., Pacheco, L. M., & Martins, F. P. (2022). Corporate social responsibility in emerging markets: Opportunities and challenges for sustainability integration. *Journal of Cleaner Production, 362*, Article 132224.

Chirambo, D. (2018). Towards the achievement of SDG 7 in sub-Saharan Africa: Creating synergies between Power Africa, Sustainable Energy for All and climate finance in-order to achieve universal energy access before 2030. *Renewable and Sustainable Energy Reviews, 94*, 600–608.

Clausen, L. T., & Rudolph, D. (2020). Renewable energy for sustainable rural development: Synergies and mismatches. *Energy Policy, 138*, Article 111289.

Das, M., & Rangarajan, K. (2020). Impact of policy initiatives and collaborative synergy on sustainability and business growth of Indian SMEs. *Indian Growth and Development Review, 13*(3), 607–627.

Dhahri, S., Slimani, S., & Omri, A. (2021). Behavioral entrepreneurship for achieving the sustainable development goals. *Technological Forecasting and Social Change, 165*, Article 120561.

Ding, R., Shi, F., & Hao, S. (2022). Digital inclusive finance, environmental regulation, and regional economic growth: An empirical study based on spatial spillover effect and panel threshold effect. *Sustainability, 14*(7), 4340.

Dote-Pardo, J., Ortiz-Cea, V., Peña-Acuña, V., Severino-González, P., Contreras-Henríquez, J. M., & Ramírez-Molina, R. I. (2025). Innovative entrepreneurship and sustainability: A bibliometric analysis in emerging countries. *Sustainability, 17*(2), 658.

Ed-Dafali, S., Adardour, Z., Derj, A., Bami, A., & Hussainey, K. (2025). A PRISMA-based systematic review on economic, social, and governance practices: Insights and research agenda. *Business Strategy and the Environment, 34*(2), 1896–1916.

Frone, S., Platon, V., & Constantinescu, A. (2020). Links and synergies of sustainable development goals. Annals of 'Constantin Brancusi' University of Targu-Jiu. *Economy Series/Analele Universităţii'Constantin Brâncuşi'din Târgu-Jiu Seria Economie, 20*(5).

Glemarec, Y., Buchner, B., Gomez Echeverri, L., Fallone, M., Swaminathan, S., & Babinsky, F. (2024). *Seeking synergy solutions: A new financial system to enable both climate and SDG action.*

Grosu, V., Botez, D., Melega, A., Kicsi, R., Mihaila, S., & Macovei, A. G. (2022). Bibliometric analysis of the transformative synergies between blockchain and accounting in the uprooting of economic criminality. *Entrepreneurship and Sustainability Issues, 9*(4), 77.

Hudon, M., & Huybrechts, B. (2017). From distant neighbours to bedmates: Exploring the synergies between the social economy and sustainable development. *Annals of Public and Cooperative Economics, 88*(2), 141–154.

Hussain, Q., Qadir, G., Ali, A., & Riaz, A. (2024). Sustainable synergy: Exploring the interplay of green finance and financial technology in driving economic growth. *Library of Progress-Library Science, Information Technology & Computer, 44*(3).

Ince, F. (2021). Creating synergic entrepreneurship as support of sustainability: Opportunities and challenges. *Handbook of Research on Management Techniques and Sustainability Strategies for Handling Disruptive Situations in Corporate Settings*, 464–486.

Iqbal, Q., Ahmad, N. H., & Halim, H. A. (2021). Insights on entrepreneurial bricolage and frugal innovation for sustainable performance. *Business Strategy & Development, 4*(3), 237–245.

Jin, X., Chen, C., & Zhang, M. (2022). Research on synergy between entrepreneurial service and financial support in crowd innovation space ecosystem. *Sustainability, 14*(10), 5966.

Khalid, A. M. (2023). Creating synergies among the sustainable development goals and climate action: Insights from a developing economy. *Sustainability, 15*(17), 13137.

Kroll, C., Warchold, A., & Pradhan, P. (2019). Sustainable Development Goals (SDGs): Are we successful in turning trade-offs into synergies? *Palgrave Communications, 5*(1).

Kusnanto, E. (2022). Performance measurement based on balance scorecard perspective of sustainable leadership, corporate governance and human capital in banking industry. *International Journal of Contemporary Accounting, 4*(1), 41–58.

Ma, Y., Rong, K., Mangalagiu, D., Thornton, T. F., & Zhu, D. (2018). Co-evolution between urban sustainability and business ecosystem innovation: Evidence from the sharing mobility sector in Shanghai. *Journal of Cleaner Production, 188*, 942–953.

Morched, S., & Jarboui, A. (2025). *Synergy between Project Management and Entrepreneurship.*

Moşteanu, N. R. (2023). Navigating the intersection of sustainability and intelligent automation: Opportunities and challenges for entrepreneurs. *Human Resources Management and Services, 5*(1).

Osman, M., & Elamin, I. (2023). Advancing ethical and sustainable economy: Islamic finance solutions for environmental, social, & economic challenges in the digital age. *International Journal, 10*(5), 408–429.

Otanazarova, G. Z. (2025). Common future: Integrated solutions for global sustainability. *Journal of Analytical Synergy and Scientific Horizon, 1*(1.3 (B series)), 18–24.

Parikh, P., Diep, L., Hofmann, P., Tomei, J., Campos, L. C., Teh, T. H., Mulugetta, Y., Milligan, B., & Lakhanpaul, M. (2021). Synergies and trade-offs between sanitation and the sustainable development goals. *UCL Open Environment, 3*, e016.

Peng, B. (2024). Navigating green horizons: An empirical exploration of business practices aligned with environmental goals in the era of sustainable economy. *Managerial and Decision Economics, 45*(7), 4732–4752.

Petrariu, R., Constantin, M., Dinu, M., Pătărlăgeanu, S. R., & Deaconu, M. E. (2021). Water, energy, food, waste nexus: Between synergy and trade-offs in Romania based on entrepreneurship and economic performance. *Energies, 14*(16), 5172.

Rahman, M. M., & Hossain, M. E. (2025). Synergy of governance, finance, and technology for sustainable natural resource management. *Journal of Open Innovation: Technology, Market, and Complexity, 11*(1), Article 100468.

Raimi, L., Abdur-Rauf, I. A., & Olaide Raimi, B. (2025). Interdependence of halal entrepreneurship and Islamic finance for creating a strong halal ecosystem. *Journal of Islamic Marketing, 16*(3), 929–954.

Rehman, K., Lim, K. B., Yeo, S. F., Ameeq, M., & Asad Ullah, M. (2025). The synergy of entrepreneurial leadership and team diversity: Pathways to entrepreneurial success in Pakistan's SMEs. *Sustainability, 17*(5), 2063.

Sagar, S. (2023). Innovation and sustainability in business: Navigating the future landscape. *IOSR Journal of Business and Management (IOSR-JBM), 25*(12), 51–60.

Saqib, N., Usman, M., Ozturk, I., & Sharif, A. (2024). Harnessing the synergistic impacts of environmental innovations, financial development, green growth, and ecological footprint through the lens of SDGs policies for countries exhibiting high ecological footprints. *Energy Policy, 184*, Article 113863.

Satiti, N. R., Yin, T. S., & Pitchay, A. A. (2024). Financial and technological literacies: An integrated systematic review using PRISMA workflow, bibliometric analysis and TCCM framework for future research agenda. *International Journal of Academic Reserach in Economics and Management Sciences, 13*(2).

Schaltegger, S., Beckmann, M., & Hockerts, K. (2018). Collaborative entrepreneurship for sustainability. Creating solutions in light of the UN sustainable development goals. *International Journal of Entrepreneurial Venturing, 10*(2), 131–152.

Schaltegger, S., Lüdeke-Freund, F., & Hansen, E. G. (2016). Business models for sustainability: A co-evolutionary analysis of sustainable entrepreneurship, innovation, and transformation. *Organization & Environment, 29*(3), 264–289.

Shabbir, M. S. (2018). The combine synergies between Islamic micro finance portfolio and various structured finance solutions. *Global Review of Islamic Economics and Business, 6*(2), 117–130.

Shah, S. M. A., Qazi, A. H., & Khan, A. R. (2025). Exploring synergies: HR, finance, and sustainable supply chains. *Qualitative Research Review Letter, 3*(1), 218–254.

Sharma, M., Reddy, A. H., & Kachhi, Z. (2025). Sustainable synergy: Exploring the relationship between environmental marketing and green entrepreneurship for business. In *Agile business transformations* (pp. 147–162). Apple Academic Press.

Sievers, M., & Vandenberg, P. (2007). Synergies through linkages: Who benefits from linking micro-finance and business development services? *World Development, 35*(8), 1341–1358.

Simanjuntak, R. (2024). Navigating the dynamics of corporate financial management for sustainable growth. *Advances in Economics & Financial Studies, 2*(2), 53–66.

Sungkawati, E. (2024). Sustainable entrepreneurship: Innovative solutions for achieving SDGs in Indonesia 2030. *Revenue Journal: Management and Entrepreneurship, 2*(2), 182–198.

Tantalo, C., & Priem, R. L. (2016). Value creation through stakeholder synergy. *Strategic Management Journal, 37*(2), 314–329.

Tien, N. H., Anh, D. B. H., Ngoc, N. M., & Nhi, D. T. Y. (2019). Sustainable social entrepreneurship in Vietnam. *International Journal of Entrepreneurship, 23*(3), 1–12.

Tien, N. H., Tien, N. V., Mai, N. P., & Duc, L. D. M. (2023). Green entrepreneurship: A game changer in Vietnam business landscape. *International Journal of Entrepreneurship and Small Business, 48*(4), 408–431.

Toromade, A. S., & Chiekezie, N. R. (2024). Driving sustainable business practices in SMEs: Innovative approaches for environmental and economic synergy. *Int. J. Manag. Entrep. Res, 6*, 2637–2647.

Triguero, Á., Cuerva, M. C., & Álvarez-Aledo, C. (2017). Environmental innovation and employment: Drivers and synergies. *Sustainability, 9*(11), 2057.

Tsvetkova, A., Schmutzler, J., & Pugh, R. (Eds.). (2020). *Entrepreneurial ecosystems meet innovation systems: Synergies, policy lessons and overlooked dimensions*. Edward Elgar Publishing.

Walker, J., Pekmezovic, A., & Walker, G. (2019). *Sustainable development goals: Harnessing business to achieve the SDGs through finance, technology and law reform*. Wiley.

Watson, R., Nielsen, K. R., Wilson, H. N., Macdonald, E. K., Mera, C., & Reisch, L. (2023). Policy for sustainable entrepreneurship: A crowdsourced framework. *Journal of Cleaner Production, 383*, Article 135234.

Woolford, J., & Lalanne, M. (2024). *Funding synergies for innovation, industrial transition and entrepreneurship* (No. JRC139050). Joint Research Centre.

Xetor, L. E., & Mensah, J. (2025). *Inclusive growth and sustainable development nexus: Where is the synergy?* Sustainable Development.

Zaki, K., Alhomaid, A., Ghareb, A., Shared, H., Raslan, A., Khalifa, G. S., & Elnagar, A. K. (2025). Digital synergy and strategic vision: Unlocking sustainability-oriented innovation in Saudi SMEs. *Administrative Sciences, 15*(2), 59.

Zhang, S. (2024). Evaluation and deconstruction of the impact of digital finance on the synergy of enterprise economic development and ecological environment. *Problemy Ekorozwoju, 19*(1), 115–121.

Zhyvko, M. A., & Vivchar, S. F. (2023). Strategies for navigating in the fragmentation conditions of global finance and EC onomic digitalization: Contemporary trends in TNC management. *Problemy Ekonomiky, 3*, 15–24.

Ziolo, M., Bak, I., & Cheba, K. (2021). The role of sustainable finance in achieving sustainable development goals: Does it work? *Technological and Economic Development of Economy, 27*(1), 45–70.

Zournatzidou, G. (2025). Green finance and sustainable development: investigating the role of greentech business ecosystem through PRISMA-driven bibliometric analysis. *Administrative Sciences, 15*(4), 150.

CHAPTER 15

A Systematic Survey on Federated Learning for Sustainable Routing in Intelligent Transportation Systems: Insights into SDGs

A. Katheeja Naseeha, Manu Shukla, Purvi Pujari, and Anuj Kumar

Abstract The growing global population demands sophisticated transportation infrastructure to combat their travel needs. While the majority of people are expected to live in cities, traffic congestion is inevitable. This

A. K. Naseeha (✉)
Confab 360 Degree, New Delhi, India
e-mail: naseeha29@gmail.com

M. Shukla
Confab 360 Degree, Zurich, Switzerland

P. Pujari
VPSM, Centre of Excellence, DY Patil University, Navi Mumbai, India

A. Kumar
Faculty of Management Studies, Marwadi University Research Centre, Marwadi University, Rajkot, Gujarat, India

Rushford Business School, Luzern, Switzerland

S. Trivedi et al. (eds.), *Green Ventures*, Sustainable Development Goals Series, https://doi.org/10.1007/978-981-95-6533-7_15

also results in unavoidable environmental impacts, causing restructuring of existing transportation systems. Emerging transportation technologies can address these challenges. The intelligent transportation system (ITS), a smart transport system, includes a wide range of innovations encompassing communication networks, automation, data analytics, and real-time data collection, which work all together towards transport system optimisation, from managing traffic flow to vehicle operations. This interconnected system can overcome the problems of traffic congestion, safety concerns, and environmental impacts. Federated learning (FL) signifies a decentralised machine learning approach, which offers a promising solution for advancing smart transportation by training machine learning models on various decentralised devices while maintaining data privacy. FL applications are increasingly deployed in multiple Internet of Things (IoT) domains, including the Internet of Vehicular Things (IoVT) and smart cities. This chapter aims to comprehensively review FL for IoVT networks in ITS aimed at sustainable routing. In addition, this survey also explores how FL in ITS contributes to sustainable development goals, thus developing a sustainable transportation system. The research employs a systematic literature review mechanism called the PRISMA framework (Preferred Reporting Items for Systematic Review and Meta-Analysis (PRISMA)) to assess the studies included. A narrative approach is used to integrate the findings of the incorporated studies. The study outcomes portray recent trends, challenges, and pathways for further research. The practical implications of the study include promoting sustainable smart transport systems by adopting greener practices and encouraging inclusive industrialisation towards realising Sustainable Development Goals (SDGs).

Keywords Federated learning · Intelligent Transportation System (ITS) · Sustainable Development Goals (SDGs) · Smart transport

1 Introduction

The growing population in the world has increased vehicle ownership, contributing to severe traffic congestion, especially in cities, which is a source of stress to regular commuters. Though the optimal way is to increase the number of city roads, it will not be a suitable solution if the road network density is high. So, the effective option is to assist drivers with real-time traffic views and provide them with route guidance. This is possible with the quick advancement of traffic surveillance infrastructure, including video cameras and loop detectors, the Internet of Vehicles (IoV), and the 5G Network (Su & Li, 2023). Hence, intelligent traffic management systems are necessary to improve movement efficiency and reduce traffic congestion. A Dynamic Route Guidance System can adjust the existing routes of the vehicles based on current road status. Information about the changings cenarios of the road can be used to develop a real-time responsive Intelligent Transportation System (ITS) infrastructure, which can be realised in recent days only with the enhancement of the edge nodes' processing efficiency and IoV technology. In recent years, traffic flow prediction using artificial intelligence (AI) has been deployed to serve this purpose. However, the current approaches towards traffic flow prediction gather raw data from vehicles, subjecting them to data breaches.

Moreover, modern vehicles have increased options for interconnectivity with other vehicles, facilitating intelligent transportation. Vehicles as intelligent partners enhance the safety of passengers and neighbouring areas by exchanging real-time information that gives early alerts on live traffic flow, hazardous road conditions, lane changes, collisions with other vehicles, sudden braking possibilities, etc. This elevates vehicle coordination, promotes efficient traffic management, offers personalised route planning, and offers sophisticated driver assistance. Besides, ITS are highly desired future transportation systems due to their capability of reducing emissions from vehicles and improving connectivity between vehicles, drivers, and roads (Jia et al., 2025). However, the IoV networks are more prone to intrusion attacks as they have several communication interfaces, paving the way for invaders to take control of a remote device and access nearby vehicles, putting their safety at risk.

Cyber-attacks are taking place in smarter ways with the advancements in artificial intelligence (AI), machine learning (ML) and other sophisticated technologies. This is crucial for the operation of critical infrastructures (CIs) like the Internet of Things (IoT), the Internet of Medical Things (IoMT), Industrial IoT (IIoT), the Internet of Vehicular Things (IoVT), etc. While traditional AI algorithms are more prone to such attacks, Federated Intrusion Detection Systems (FIDS) can efficiently serve this purpose (Makris et al., 2024). Since smart transportation depends much on AI, IoT and machine learning, cyber threats are serious concerns as they could manipulate devices' operations, causing severe damage to human beings and the environment. Federated learning (FL) schemes can efficiently address safety concerns related to smart and sustainable transport.

FL is a highly secure scheme for data sharing as it does not transfer raw data between devices; instead, it engages in local training in which the model parameters are updated using the user data and shares only the local updates to the central aggregator or the central server for updating. FL's benefits can be better utilised in traffic management and the routing of ITS, improving safety in smart cities. Since a wide range of sensitive data is involved in intelligent traffic management, FL can ensure the privacy of end users while allowing them to access global model parameters with high computational power and lower latency. Importantly, it is high time to participate in the global partnership to develop a peaceful and prosperous future by caring for the people and planet. Sustainability has become a watchword in every activity of our daily lives. UN's agenda for sustainable development must be accounted for in every project to attain a more inclusive society with all prosperity, cherishing nature and human well-being. Accordingly, FL algorithms integrated with ITS also aim to provide sustainable services to achieve SDGs.

Hence, the research includes multiple objectives. The study particularly focuses on synergies between federated learning and intelligent transportation. The study also investigates the contributions of FL to sustainable routing and the realisation of sustainable development goals. Additionally, the research presents more about how federated learning can promote sustainable routing, safety and security in ITS. The subsequent sections discuss the methodology, and the key concepts involved in the research. Further, the ways FL enhances sustainable routing in ITS and their contributions to achieving SDGs are explored. Then, the trends, challenges, and directions for future research are briefly explained.

2 Literature Review

Alam et al. (2023) proposed a hybrid Federated Ensemble-Learning (FedEL) framework to determine people's transport modalities. Since the usage of smartphones and smartwatches among individuals is on the rise, it is easy to detect their live location data. Besides, these devices become a part of the IoT. In this study, the sensory inputs captured from the smartphones (edge devices) are used to detect the users' transportation modes.

This ensemble learning method includes a neural network, which is a Multi-Layer Perceptron (MLP), and two standard ML methods, random forest (RF) and XG Boost (XGB), capable of enhancing predictive performance. The FedEL technique employs a majority voting mechanism to collaborate with XGB and RF to enhance performance. Accordingly, any mistakes identified with FedMLP are rectified using RF and XGB without compromising the operational effectiveness.

Since selecting an optimal route would reduce the time required to reach the destination, time-efficient route planning is vital in the field of IoVT. In this respect, Khatua et al. (2024b) proposed a green edge framework for reducing traffic congestion using optimal route planning based on federated learning and a modified genetic algorithm (GA). The method involves roadside units (RSUs), regional servers, and the cloud. The RSUs directly connected to the vehicles process the vehicle images to estimate traffic volume on the road using a region-based CNN, forwarding local parameters to the regional server. This server identifies the optimal route using the modified Genetic Algorithm and forwards the output to the cloud and the vehicles.

Meanwhile, the regional server refines its models and shares the revised model parameters to the RSUs, enabling them to refine and ensure consistency across their local models. Since the regional server transmits the uploaded weights to the cloud-based aggregator, the cloud then refines the global models. It transmits back the model updates to the regional server, causing it to update again. This proposed approach has a 90% accuracy and reduces the time to identify the optimal route by approximately 62% and time consumption by 66% compared to the cloud-only model.

Cleaner and smarter transportation is highly sought to reduce carbon neutrality. However, citizens are unaware of how much carbon they emit and the sustainable alternative ways to travel than their regular public or private transport. Brito et al. (2024) proposed a new methodology to offer suggestions to users about sustainable mobility alternatives. The proposed approach combines Greenhouse Gas (GHG) estimation models with federated artificial intelligence (AI) to determine and compare the users' carbon footprint while using various transportation modes. This provides users with detailed information about their impact on the environment. The research has employed a simple mobile application that collects sensitive user information (like location) using sensors. Using this information, the initially trained models are iteratively retrained using

FL, and differential privacy (DP) is introduced to preserve data privacy. DP incorporates noise into the raw data, avoiding personal information leakage to any third-party entities. The output of the trained models can be given as input to the GHG models, which generate the carbon footprint estimation for each trip. Besides, this estimation is used to prepare the daily and weekly carbon digest reports, enhancing users' awareness of their carbon footprint so they can make wise choices of transport modes (e.g. foot, bicycle, motorcycle, bus, car).

2.1 Foundational Concepts

Sustainable Routing

Sustainable routing, also called green route planning, is a mechanism of planning optimal vehicle routes considering the economic, environmental, and social consequences of transporting goods from one place to another (Dukkanci et al., 2022). Reduced carbon dioxide emission is a highly sought-after environmental aspect of sustainable cities. You (2022) posited the detection of energy-efficient routes as an effective solution to reduce CO_2, enabling the establishment of smart cities. In this regard, the factors considered for sustainable routing include distance travelled, travel time, traffic flow, street segments, traffic congestion, vehicle type, and velocity variations. Therefore, sustainable routing can offer several suggestions to all stakeholders, including transportation companies, drivers, and customers.

Intelligent Transportation as a Sustainable Solution

ITS integrates devices and communication technologies into vehicles and transportation infrastructure. The ITS structures are networks between the Internet of Vehicles and the roadside units (RSUs); these networks are referred to as Vehicular Edge Network (VEN) (Alam et al., 2023). VENs, the modern ITS architectures, perform real-time operations by combining both the internal and external sensors, such as traffic, speed, and density sensors. They also installed cloud servers to access and process real-time data. ITS development in the present period targets three main domains: traffic management through the wide deployment of cameras and wireless sensors, prioritisation of public transportation and shared mobility, and autonomous driving (Jia et al., 2025).

Traffic Management

It can provide proactive re-routing guidance to individual drivers by incorporating a wide range of sensor information (Su & Li, 2023). While the ITS system emphasises vehicle-light coordination and traffic light control, the fast-paced progress of AI and big data analyses has widened the scope of ITS towards predicting future traffic flow. Due to increased intelligence, a vast amount of raw data is collected, leading to security issues.

Emission Reduction

ITS is highly capable of contributing towards achieving sustainable benefits. Jia et al. (2025) found ITS as a sustainable solution for reducing emissions in future transportation. The authors analysed how the Intelligent Transportation Speed Guidance System (ITSGS) could lower emissions and attain environmental gains depending on a spatio-temporal data analysis. The scheme integrates a wide range of real-world trajectory data and ML algorithms-based emission models to quantify emissions. The results indicated a reduction in emissions of pollutants like carbon monoxide (CO), carbon dioxide (CO_2), hydrocarbons (HC), and nitrogen oxides (NOx) between 3.84% and 18.17%.

Federated Learning

Federated learning enables multiple IoT edge devices to collaboratively train a machine learning model while keeping the raw data local (Khatua et al., 2024a). FL facilitates decentralised training of complex models stored across isolated islands from remote data sources while ensuring the data is local and private (Xianjia et al., 2021). Thus, FL improves the efficiency of wireless systems since parameter sets of the updated mode are exchanged alone among the local clients and central servers during the training process (Alam et al., 2023). This has immense benefits in terms of bandwidth and latency savings because a large amount of data is processed locally, and only the corresponding model is shared. Hence, FL invokes faster responses and is most suitable for real-time applications. The key to data privacy is preserving personal data processing to limited devices closer to the data source, thus eliminating the travel of raw personal data over long distances, posing a threat of being interrupted on the way.

Federated Learning in Sustainable Routing

Nowadays, traffic congestion is a serious problem in urban areas, necessitating traffic flow prediction for safe and smoother vehicle travel. In this regard, Su and Li (2023) studied the possibilities that federated learning holds to enhance the efficiency of regional transportation. They proposed an approach that includes a vehicle scheduling system capable of controlling the dispatch of vehicles and their route planning. Vehicle travel routes are optimised to reduce average travel time by combining a road weight monitoring system with real-time traffic updates. Besides, the scheduling of vehicles is optimised using departure strategies, which in turn improve the overall traffic efficiency in the region. A convolutional neural network (CNN) model has been used for short-term dynamic road weight tracking and measurement. FL technology has been employed to support the training of real-world models aimed at developing an ITS responsive framework. This chapter's proposed traffic flow prediction model has reduced the scheduling completion time.

3 Methodology

A systematic literature review of different types of studies, including quantitative, qualitative, and mixed methods, was employed to thoroughly explore the core concepts: sustainable routing, intelligent transportation, and federated learning (FL). Furthermore, the PRISMA 2020 guidelines (PRISMA - Preferred Reporting Items for Systematic Review and Meta-Analysis and the flow diagram were adopted to summarise the studies from the predefined databases. All papers were retrieved only from databases. The authors did the initial screening based on the criteria for exclusion and inclusion of articles. Figure 1 shows the flow diagram of the Systematic Review Through Databases.

3.1 Criteria for Exclusion and Inclusion of articles

The paper's criteria of inclusion consist of primary studies from 2019 to 2025. The authors chose 2019 as the starting point for understanding

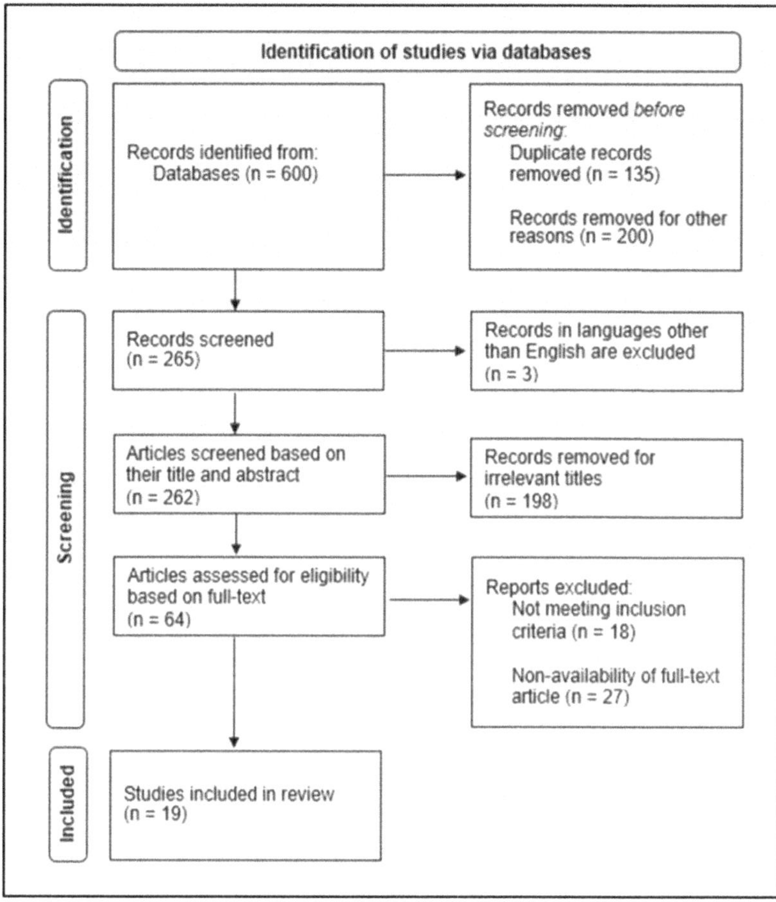

Fig. 1 PRISMA flow diagram for the systematic review through databases (*Source* Author)

the impact of IoT and FL on the environment. The year 2025 was selected as the endpoint to guarantee that the latest and highest-impact studies are included for analysis. The preliminary search focused on the keywords "Federated Learning", "Internet of Things", "Sustainable Routing", "Intelligent Transportation System", "Smart transport", and

"Sustainable Development Goals". The study did not include unpublished research studies such as conference proceedings, opinion surveys, theses, dissertations, and other grey literature, as they did not provide in-depth insights and analysis.

3.2 Information Sources

The research papers have been retrieved from scholarly databases such as IEEE Xplore, Google Scholar, ScienceDirect, SpringerLink, and ResearchGate.

3.3 Search Strategies

The preliminary search in ScienceDirect retrieved 70 papers, ResearchGate retrieved 100 articles, IEEE Xplore retrieved 5 articles, Springer retrieved 12 articles, and Google Scholar retrieved 413 papers. Among 600 Articles, only 19 papers were included in the final study. Among the 19 papers, 11 papers were chosen from ScienceDirect, 3 papers from IEEE Xplore, 2 papers from ResearchGate and Google Scholar, and 1 from SpringerLink. 4 Papers (21%) focussed on ITS and IoT from 2019 to 2021 generated interest in SDG. From 2022 onwards, FL, ITS, Sustainable Routing and SDG gained significance with the remaining 15 papers (79%). Hence, with evolving technological advancements and increased emphasis on inclusive, sustainable development, it became inevitable to incorporate the relevant studies.

4 Discussion

4.1 Synergising Sustainability and Technology: Contributions to SDGs

Sustainable Development Goals (SDGs) have been built by the United Nations (UN) for decades with the aim to improve peace and prosperity for the people and the planet for now and in the future (United Nations, 2024). In this regard, "The 2030 Agenda for Sustainable Development" incorporates 17 important goals, namely, *No Poverty (1), Zero Hunger (2), Good Health and Well-being (3), Quality Education (4), Gender Equality (5), Clean Water and Sanitation (6), Affordable and Clean Energy (7), Decent Work and Economic Growth (8),*

Industry, Innovation, and Infrastructure (9), Reduced Inequalities (10), Sustainable Cities and Communities (11), Responsible Consumption and Production (12), Climate Action (13), Life Below Water (14), Life on Land (15), Peace, Justice, and Strong Institutions (16), and Partnerships for the Goals (17) (Komatsu, 2023). These goals call for urgent action by all developed and developing countries for a global partnership to eradicate poverty while promoting equality, supporting societal progress, promoting environmental sustainability, ensuring ecological balance, advancing climate-conscious conservation, and driving inclusive growth. The current research contributes to achieving different SDGs.

Since smart traffic management can reduce commuting hours, it would reduce the stress of regular commuters, complementing SDG-3 and emphasising good health and well-being. The lower emission objective of the functioning of the smart transport system is also synonymous with the goals of SDG-7, which highlights affordable and clean energy, and SDG-13, which emphasises climate action. Cleaner transportation facilitates the reduction of carbon footprint. IoT-based applications such as smart traffic, bridges, lights and smart homes reduce fuel consumption and transportation-related emissions, optimise energy utilisation, reduce energy waste (Varjovi & Babaie, 2020), monitor air and water pollution, conserve natural resources (Awotunde et al., 2023), detect forest fires, enhance the lifespan of crops through optimal utilization of water, predict radiation patterns and erosion from the heat data, keep track of farm animals and farm soil conditions, and equipping fields with advanced weather monitoring systems (Ayaz et al., 2019). Hence, reducing the need for centralised AI processing, federated learning (FL), and an IoT-driven intelligent traffic management system, provide the environment's flexibility and contribute to a an eco-friendly future rooted in sustainability.

The amalgamation of digital technology with transportation networks gives rise to smart transports that enhance safety, sustainability, and efficiency. The distributive aspect of FL includes a range of vehicles and other devices in ITS to modulate the global model, thus allowing all of them to participate in training the machine learning models, promoting collaboration and inclusiveness (Singh, 2023). Besides, this harmonises with the fundamental methods of SDG-9, stating Industry, Innovation, and Infrastructure because a wide number of edge nodes are involved in infrastructure development, reflecting the possibility of equitable access to technological advancements. In addition, integrating FL with various smart city applications such as AIoT, Big Data, and Edge Computing strengthens data security and fosters innovation in industries (Pandya et al., 2023). By minimising the dependency on cloud computing and optimising the transportation networks, FL and sustainable routing reduce operational costs, infrastructural costs, transportation costs, fuel and power consumption, wastage and carbon emissions while enhancing business efficiency and economic productivity.

Moreover, FL preserves sensitive data, ensuring the privacy of individual information. The data privacy aspect of FL in ITS supports SDG-16, denoting Peace, Justice, and Strong Institutions and SDG-17, indicating Partnerships for the goals. FL's data privacy facilitates the fundamental human right of having control over their personal information, which echoes SDG-16. Since maintaining data security requires global cooperation adhering to data privacy rulings about FL algorithms, the concept also contributes to SDG-17. Moreover, sustainable routing exactly reflects SDG-11, which signifies sustainable cities and communities since the research concept facilitates the promotion of sustainable cities through low-carbon urban planning. Thus, sustainable development goals (SDGs) can be achieved in many ways when FL works with IoT to optimise routes and enhance traffic management.

4.2 *Emerging Trends in Sustainable and Intelligent Transportation*

The modes of transport and the way people commute between places can be monitored by sensing their location and monitoring them. This can help authorities offer them suitable transportation plans, contributing to reducing traffic congestion (Alam et al., 2023). Moreover, FL-based IoVT in traffic management enables the fastest detection of safest paths for vehicles, especially emergency vehicles, facilitating the quick reach of lives in danger to healthcare centres, which can be seen as a boon for saving lives (Khatua et al., 2024a).

The trend of encouraging greener choices by engaging commuters through gamification mechanisms powered by simple mobile applications is on the rise. Projects like the one proposed by Brito et al. (2024) enable policymakers to provide incentive programs to encourage citizens to opt for sustainable mobility alternatives so that they leave a minimum carbon footprint. Furthermore, responses from multiple devices enable maintenance crews to repair pathways on time, avoiding accidents, thereby improving the safety of the travellers.

4.3 *Challenges of Federated Learning Enabled Sustainable Transportation*

FL consumes a significant number of communication resources, and the issue is bigger when there are many fragmented local clients, mostly wirelessly connected devices, same as that of IoT applications (Su & Li, 2023). However, this problem is often overcome by deploying optimal strategies for data compression and communication resources management. In addition, another challenge denoted by Su and Li (2023) is the lower accuracy of the edge devices due to their lower computational power, uneven data distribution, and smaller datasets. This could be overcome by advanced FL schemes and ensemble learning approaches. Another important fact is the quality of connectivity between different devices in the IoVT. Since FL functions are based on data sharing across devices, areas with limited connectivity are a severe challenge in this regard, compromising model efficiency and accuracy.

Though FL is known for its privacy by design aspect, it can be easily exploited by adversarial inputs. Utomo et al. (2023) proposed federated adversarial training (FAT) approaches to overcome this complication. The FAT strategies employed by these authors could withstand even the projected gradient descent (PGD) attacks, which can effectively impact the global models. However, they found a difference in accuracy of about 10% between FAT-PGD and baseline FL models, which is expected to be mitigated using a larger and more complex model with more clients. As the number of clients increases, the precision of the final aggregated model will be enhanced due to the involvement of more data.

Moreover, the decentralised feature of FL itself is highly susceptible to data manipulation threats like targeted and untargeted poisoning. Clients can be easily manipulated to send malicious model updates that collapse the functioning of the global model. In targeted poisoning, attackers will manipulate chosen inputs, thus degrading the performance of the global model. Untargeted poisoning reduces the overall accuracy by compromising the global model. Though the current defence methods addressing these challenges are capable of handling small clients, they have many limitations. Zhu et al. (2024) introduced a powerful poisoning scheme known as the PMM (Perturbation coefficient Multiplied by Maximum value), which could withstand some strong defence schemes. The authors also proposed an innovative countermeasure called Cluster Layer By Layer

(CLBL). They demonstrated the potential of these methods, particularly CLBL in successfully resisting poisoning attacks and outperforming existing defense methods such as Krum, Trimmed_mean, and FedAVG. Hence, amidst the presence of these many challenges, there are also possibilities of overcoming them.

5 Future Research Directions

Since autonomous driving is a highly researched area in the current scenario, FL-based IoVT can complement the functioning of autonomous driving by making accurate decisions by integrating information from multiple devices like cameras and sensors and enhancing road safety. Hence, FL in autonomous vehicles is a prospective research area. Several real-time studies can be made in this regard to improve existing datasets and offer more valuable content for the modelling of automatic vehicles. Moreover, research in the future could incorporate both empirical and non-empirical studies exploring how sustainable routing in ITS using FL could overcome the challenges associated with climate change. Further, to build on the above findings, future studies can examine ways to mitigate connectivity issues while enhancing precision and operational efficiency. In addition, more nuanced techniques to overcome adversarial attacks must be explored to substantiate the reliability of FL-integrated vehicular networks.

6 Conclusion

Intelligent transportation systems, an emerging transportation technology, can cater to the needs of future transportation requirements owing to an increase in population leading to more traffic congestion. ITS incorporating a network of devices incurs communications at different levels. The existing ML schemes involve sharing raw data, making it an easy target for cyberattacks. Federated learning could overcome the leakage of private data from vehicles as it shares only model updates, fostering privacy protection. Besides, the decentralised approach of FL reduces data propagation delay. Moreover, a sustainable environment is associated with all global systems and every aspect of our lives. Sustainable routing can provide dynamic routing paths for vehicles with less travel time, minimum travel cost, less congestion, low emission, and high safety. FL's potential utilised in ITS offers a range of benefits facilitating the accomplishment of the UN's SDGs. This review has identified trends associated with sustainable routing facilitated by FL in ITS, such as detecting transportation modes of people to provide relevant transportation plans, fastly detecting the safest paths for vehicles, encouraging greener transportation choices through gamification mechanisms and incentive programs, and facilitating timely maintenance through responses from multiple devices. The review also identified a few challenges and stated future research directions. Importantly, various smart transport system objectives are synonymous with different SDGs. In this regard, the research findings harmonise with SDGs 7, 9, 11, 13, 16, and 17.

References

Alam, Md. M., Ahmed, T., Hossain, M., Emo, M. H., Kausar, M., Reza, Md. T., Alam, R., Hassan, M. M., Pupo, F., & Fortino, G. (2023). Federated ensemble-learning for transport mode detection in vehicular edge network. *Future Generation Computer Systems, 149*, 89–104. https://doi.org/10.1016/j.future.2023.07.022

Awotunde, J. B., Sur, S. N., Jimoh, R. G., Aremu, D. R., Do, D.-T., & Lee, B. M. (2023). A federated learning enabled edge-based green internet of things system: A short survey. *IEEE Access, 11*, 136150–136165. https://doi.org/10.1109/access.2023.3335245

Ayaz, M., Ammad-uddin, M., Sharif, Z., Mansour, A., & Aggoune, el-Hadi M. (2019). Internet-of-Things (IoT) based smart agriculture: Towards making the fields talk. *IEEE Access, 7*, 1–1. https://doi.org/10.1109/access.2019.2932609

Brito, C., Pina, N., Esteves, T., Vitorino, R., Cunha, I., & Paulo, J. (2024). Promoting sustainable and personalized travel behaviors while preserving data privacy. *Transportation Engineering, 19*(100237), 1–8. https://doi.org/10.1016/j.treng.2024.100237

Dukkanci, O., Karsu, Ö., & Kara, B. Y. (2022). Planning sustainable routes: Economic, environmental and welfare concerns. *European Journal of Operational Research, [online] 301*(1), 110–123. https://doi.org/10.1016/j.ejor.2021.09.036

Jia, Z., Yin, J., Cao, Z., Wei, N., Jiang, Z., Zhang, Y., Wu, L., Zhang, Q., & Mao, H. (2025). Sustainable transportation emission reduction through intelligent transportation systems: Mitigation drivers, and temporal trends. *Environmental Impact Assessment Review, [online] 112*, 107767. https://doi.org/10.1016/j.eiar.2024.107767

Khatua, S., De, D., Maji, S., Maity, S., & Nielsen, I.E. (2024a). A federated learning model for integrating sustainable routing with the Internet of Vehicular Things using genetic algorithm. *Decision Analytics Journal, [online] 11*, 100486. https://doi.org/10.1016/j.dajour.2024.100486

Khatua, S., Mukherjee, A., & De, D. (2024b). FedGen: Federated learning-based green edge computing for optimal route selection using genetic algorithm in Internet of Vehicular Things. *Vehicular Communications, [online] 49*, 100812. https://doi.org/10.1016/j.vehcom.2024.100812

Komatsu, Y. (2023). Polypharmacy and sustainable developmental goals: Linking evidence-based medicine, patient engagement, and shared decision-making. *Komatsu Renal Replacement Therapy, [online] 9*(1). https://doi.org/10.1186/s41100-023-00474-3

Makris, I., Karampasi, A., Radoglou-Grammatikis, P., Episkopos, N., Iturbe, E., Rios, E., Piperigkos, N., Lalos, A., Xenakis, C., Lagkas, T., Argyriou, V., & Sarigiannidis, P. (2024). A comprehensive survey of Federated Intrusion Detection Systems: Techniques, challenges and solutions. *Computer Science Review, [online] 56*, 100717, 1–35. https://doi.org/10.1016/j.cosrev.2024.100717

Pandya, S., Srivastava, G., Jhaveri, R., Babu, M. R., Bhattacharya, S., Maddikunta, P. K. R., Mastorakis, S., Piran, Md. J., & Gadekallu, T. R. (2023). Federated learning for smart cities: A comprehensive survey. *Sustainable Energy Technologies and Assessments, [online] 55*, 102987. https://doi.org/10.1016/j.seta.2022.102987

PRISMA. (2020). *Preferred Reporting Items for Systematic reviews and Meta-Analyses (PRISMA).* [online] www.prisma-statement.org. https://www.prisma-statement.org/. Accessed 18 February 2025.

Singh, B. (2023). Federated learning for envision future trajectory smart transport system for climate preservation and smart green planet: Insights into global governance and SDG-9 (industry, innovation and infrastructure). *National Journal of Environmental Law, 6*(2), 6–17.

Su, Z., & Li, C. (2023). On improving the regional transportation efficiency based on federated learning. *Journal of the Franklin Institute, [online] 360*(7), 4973–5000. https://doi.org/10.1016/j.jfranklin.2023.03.035

United Nations. (2024). *The 17 Sustainable Development Goals*. [online] United Nations. https://sdgs.un.org/goals. Accessed 15 February 2025.

Utomo, S., Rouniyar, A., Hsu, H.-C., & Hsiung, P.-A. (2023). Federated adversarial training strategies for achieving privacy and security in sustainable smart city applications. *Future Internet, [online] 15*(11), 371. https://doi.org/10.3390/fi15110371

Varjovi, A. E., & Babaie, S. (2020). Green Internet of Things (GIoT): Vision, applications and research challenges. *Sustainable Computing: Informatics and Systems, 28*, Article 100448. https://doi.org/10.1016/j.suscom.2020.100448

Xianjia, Y., Queralta, J. P., Heikkonen, J., & Westerlund, T. (2021). Federated learning in robotic and autonomous systems. *Procedia Computer Science, 191*, 135–142. https://doi.org/10.1016/j.procs.2021.07.041

You, G. (2022). Sustainable vehicle routing problem on real-time roads: The restrictive inheritance-based heuristic algorithm. *Sustainable Cities and Society, [online] 79*, 103682. https://doi.org/10.1016/j.scs.2022.103682

Zhu, Y., Liu, C., Chen, C., Lyu, X., Chen, Z., Wang, B., Hu, F., Li, H., Dai, J., Cai, B., & Wang, W. (2024). Privacy-preserving large-scale AI models for intelligent railway transportation systems: Hierarchical poisoning attacks and defenses in federated learning. *Computer Modeling in Engineering & Sciences, [online] 141*(2), 1305–1325. https://doi.org/10.32604/cmes.2024.054820

Index

S. Trivedi et al. (eds.), *Green Ventures*, Sustainable Development Goals Series, https://doi.org/10.1007/978-981-95-6533-7

S

The manufacturer's authorised representative in the EU is Springer Nature Customer Service Centre GmbH, Europaplatz 3, 69115 Heidelberg, Germany. If you have any concerns regarding our products, please contact ProductSafety@springernature.com

Printed and bound by CPI Group (UK) Ltd, Croydon, CR0 4YY
21/09/2026
02219964-0001